American Vampire

AMERICAN

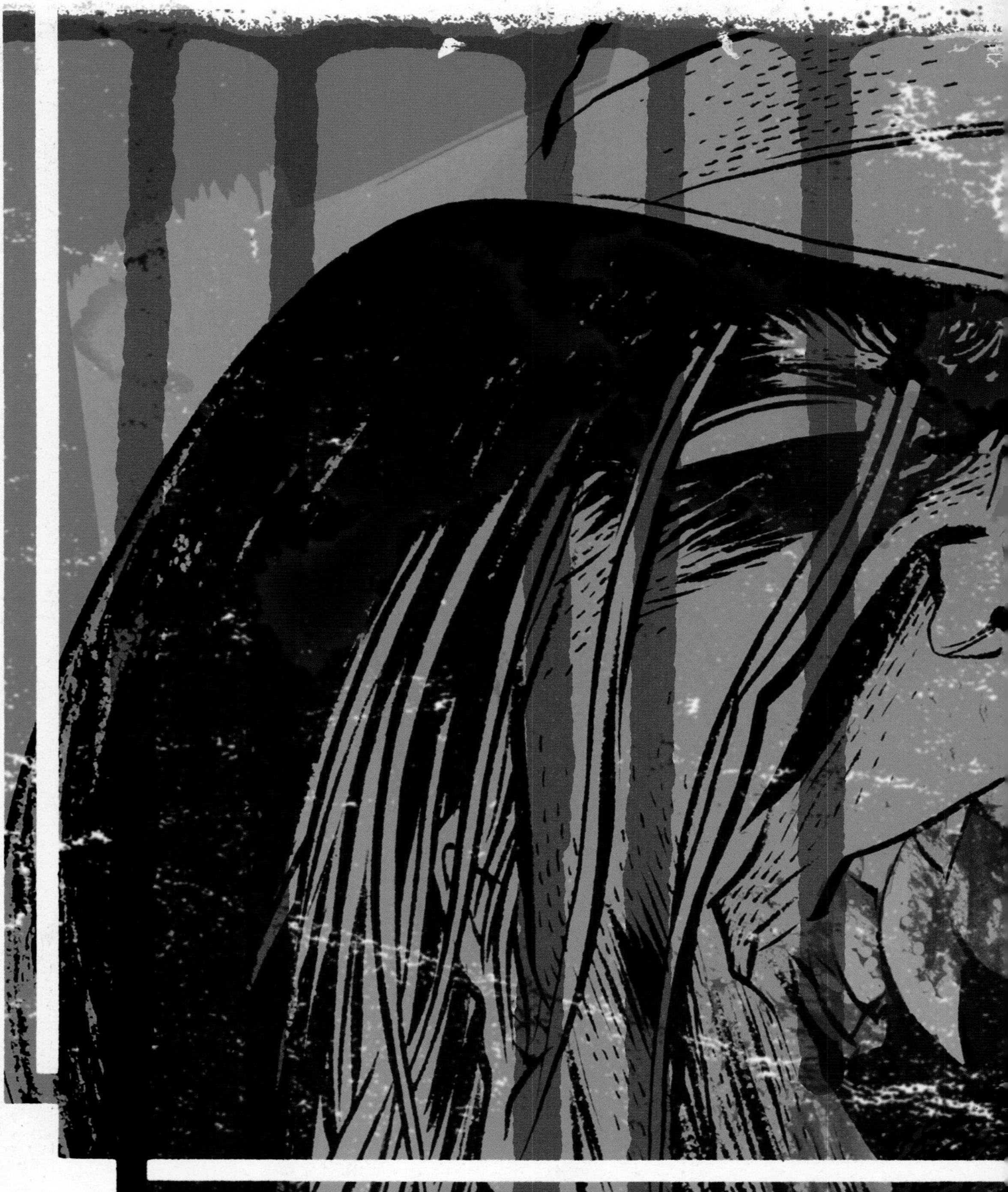

VAMPIRE

VOLUME TWO

Scott Snyder Writer

Rafael Albuquerque Mateus Santolouco Artists

Dave McCaig Colorist

Steve Wands Letterer

Rafael Albuquerque Cover Artist

American Vampire created by Scott Snyder

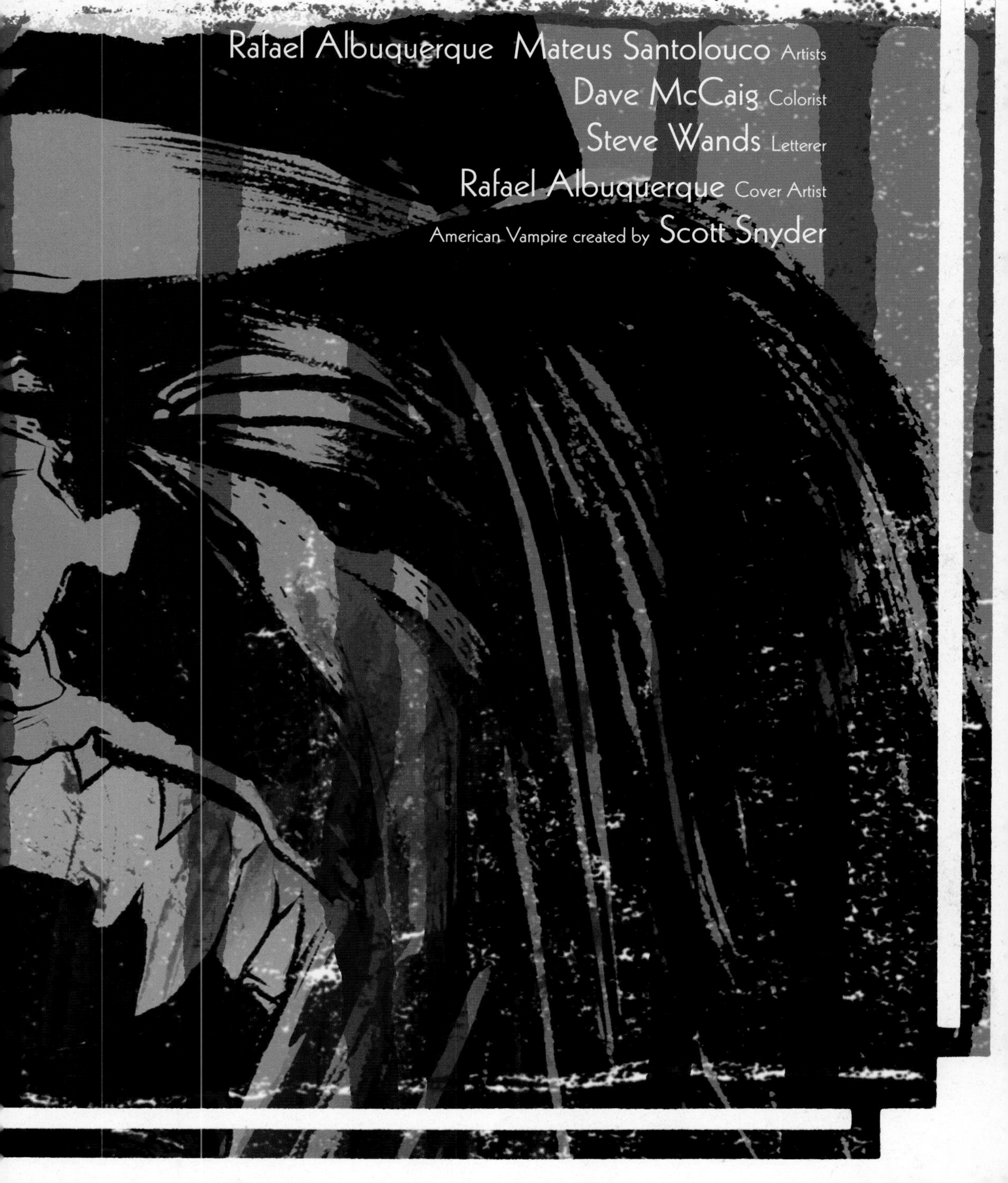

AMERICAN VAMPIRE Volume Two
Published by DC Comics. Cover, text and compilation Copyright ©
2011 Scott Snyder and DC Comics. All Rights Reserved.

Originally published in single magazine form as AMERICAN
VAMPIRE 6-11 Copyright © 2010, 2011 Scott Snyder and DC Comics.
All Rights Reserved. VERTIGO and all characters, their distinctive
likenesses and related elements featured in this publication are trademarks
of DC Comics. The stories, characters and incidents featured in this
publication are entirely fictional. DC Comics does not read or accept
unsolicited submissions of ideas, stories or artwork.

DC Comics, 1700 Broadway, New York, NY 10019
A Warner Bros. Entertainment Company.
Printed in the U.S.A. First Printing.
ISBN: 978-1-4012-3069-2

SUSTAINABLE
FORESTRY
INITIATIVE
Certified Chain of Custody
Promoting Sustainable
Forest Management
www.sfiprogram.org
Fiber used in this product line meets the
sourcing requirements of the SFI program.
www.sfiprogram.org SGS-SFI/COC-US10/81072

Library of Congress Cataloging-in-Publication Data

Snyder, Scott.
   American vampire vol. 2 / writer, Scott Snyder ; pencils, Rafael
Albuquerque.
      p. cm.
   "Originally published in single magazine form as American Vampire
#6-11."
   ISBN 978-1-4012-3069-2 (hardcover)
   1. Graphic novels. I. Albuquerque, Rafael, 1981- II. Title.
PN6727.S555A44 2011
741.5'973--dc22
                    2011008934

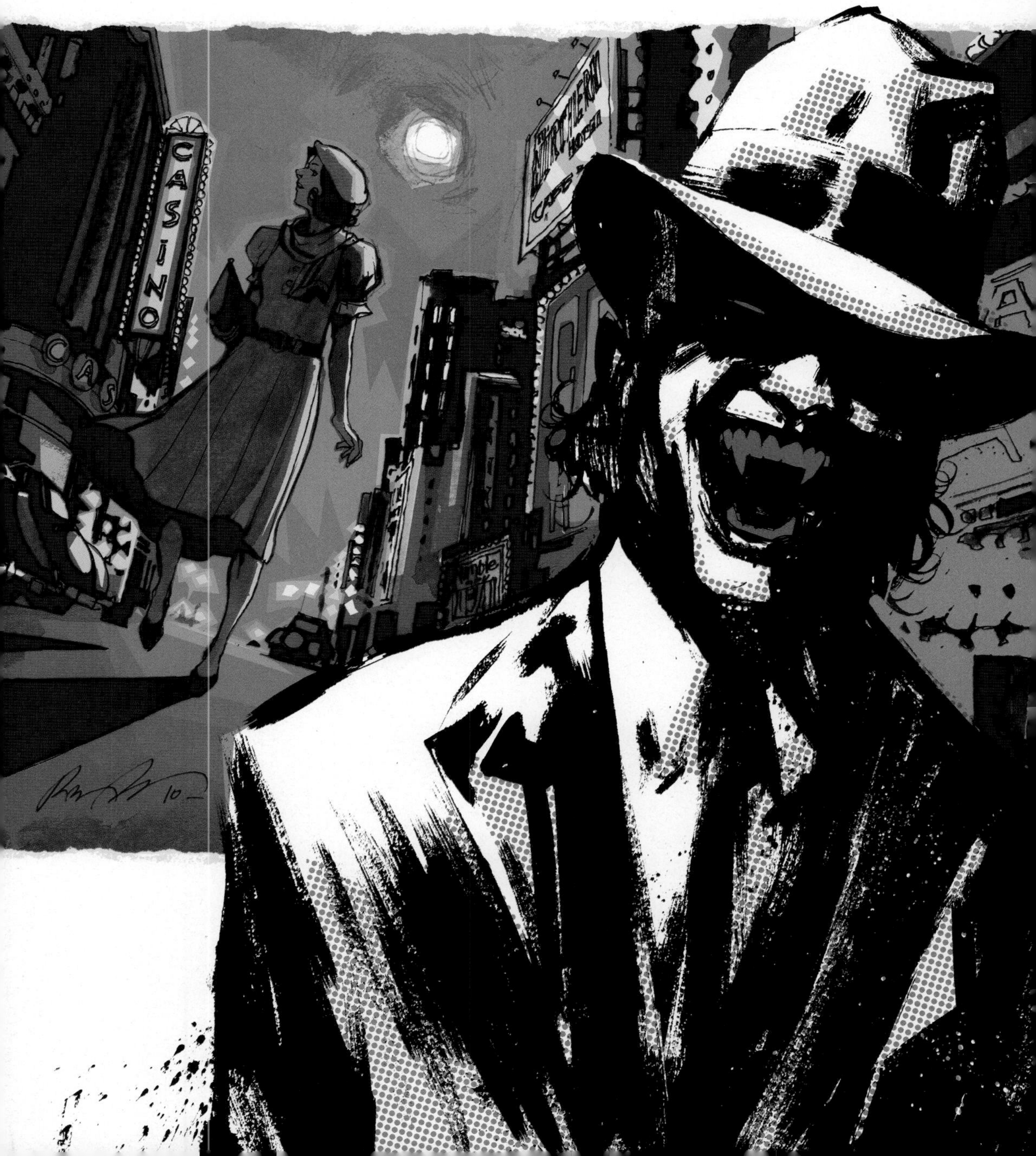
CASINO
CAS

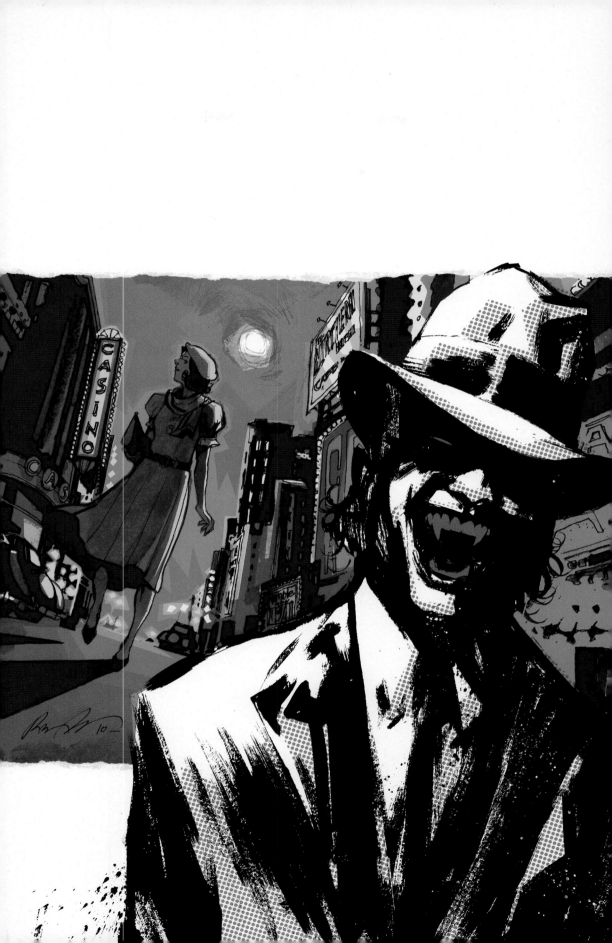

Devil in the Sand

Part One

Rafael Albuquerque

Artist

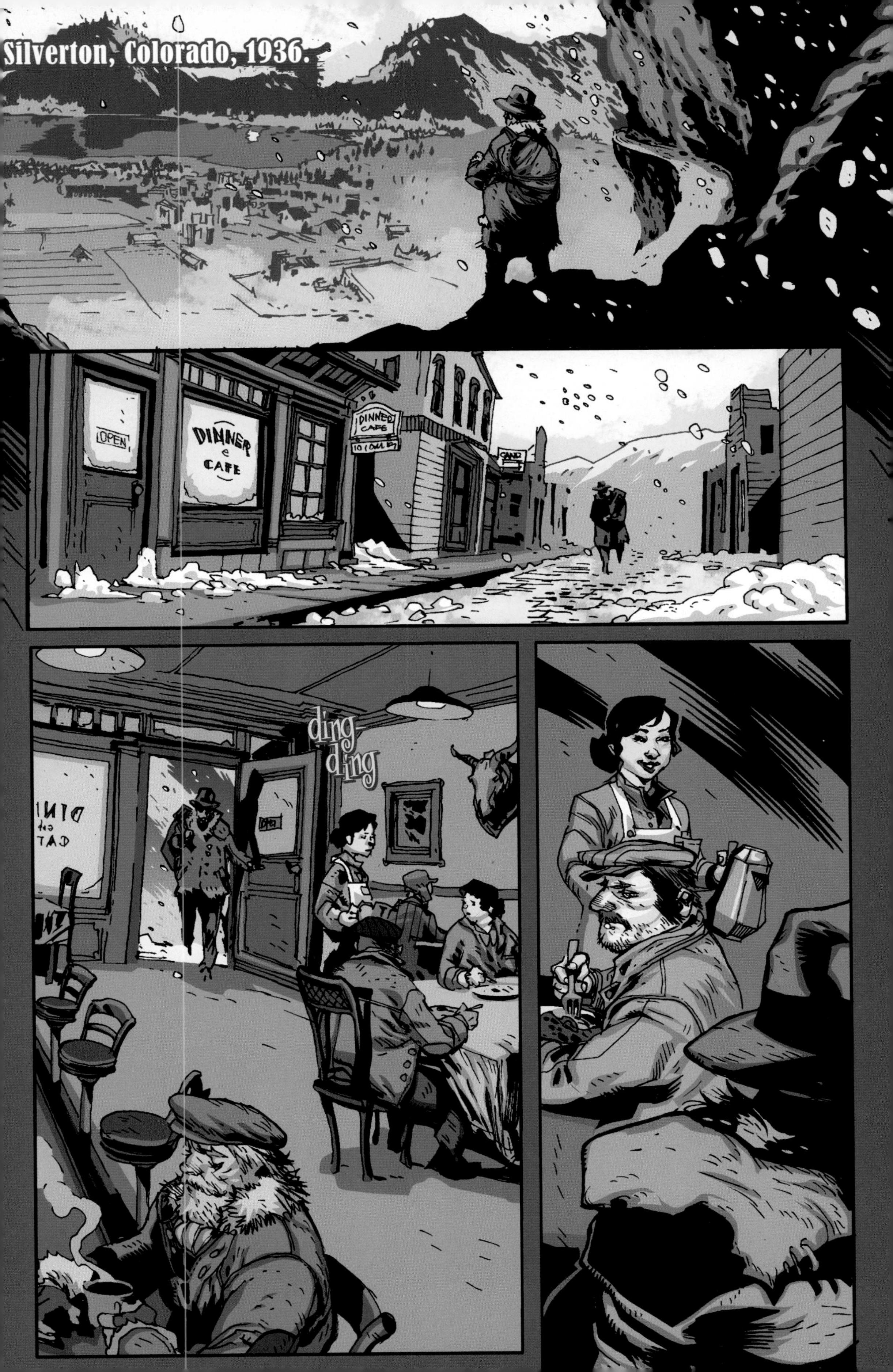
Silverton, Colorado, 1936.
OPEN
DINNER & CAFE
DINNER CAFE
ding-ding

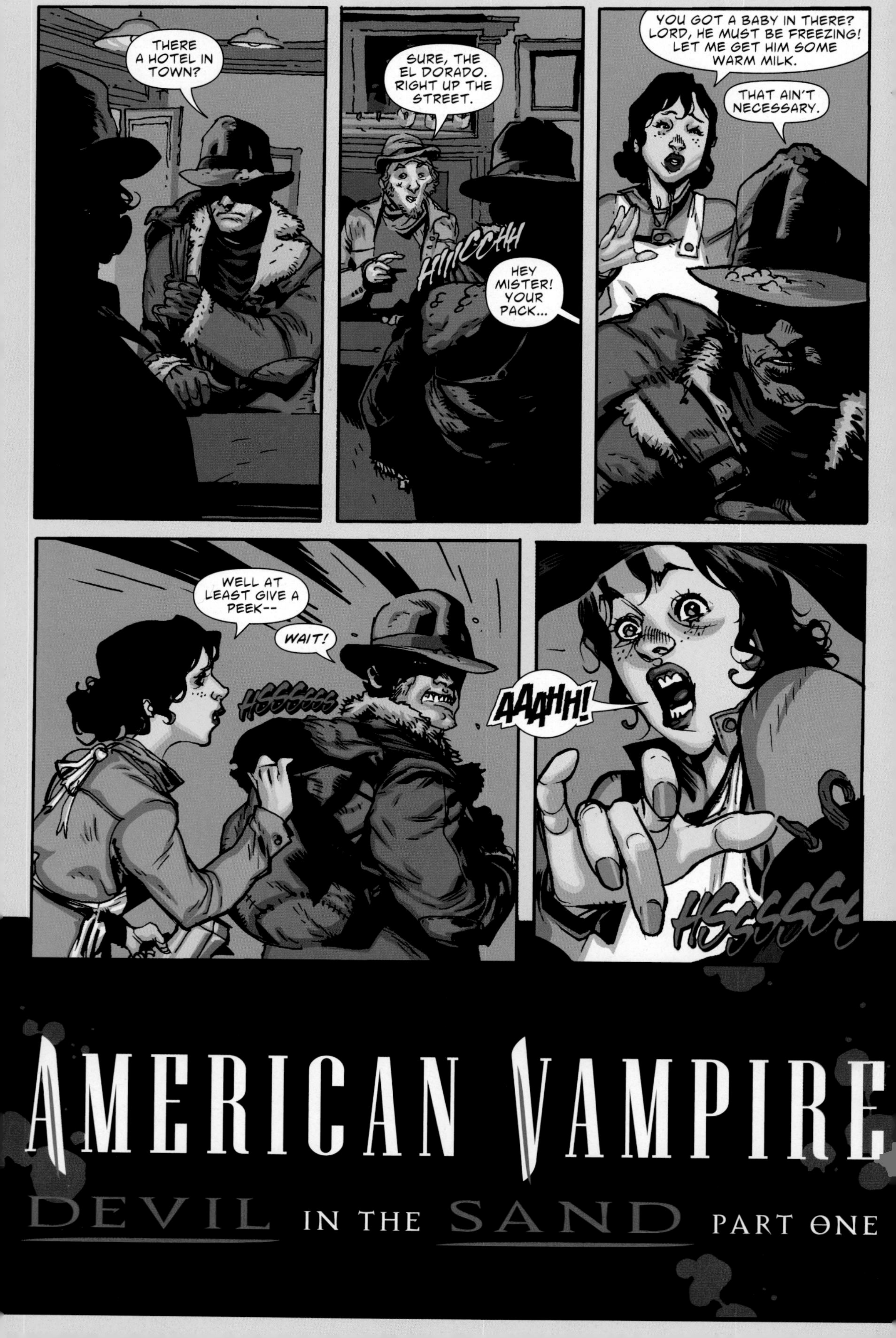
THERE A HOTEL IN TOWN?
SURE, THE EL DORADO. RIGHT UP THE STREET.
HEY MISTER! YOUR PACK...
YOU GOT A BABY IN THERE? LORD, HE MUST BE FREEZING! LET ME GET HIM SOME WARM MILK.
THAT AIN'T NECESSARY.
WELL AT LEAST GIVE A PEEK--
WAIT!
AAAHH!

AMERICAN VAMPIRE

DEVIL IN THE SAND PART ONE

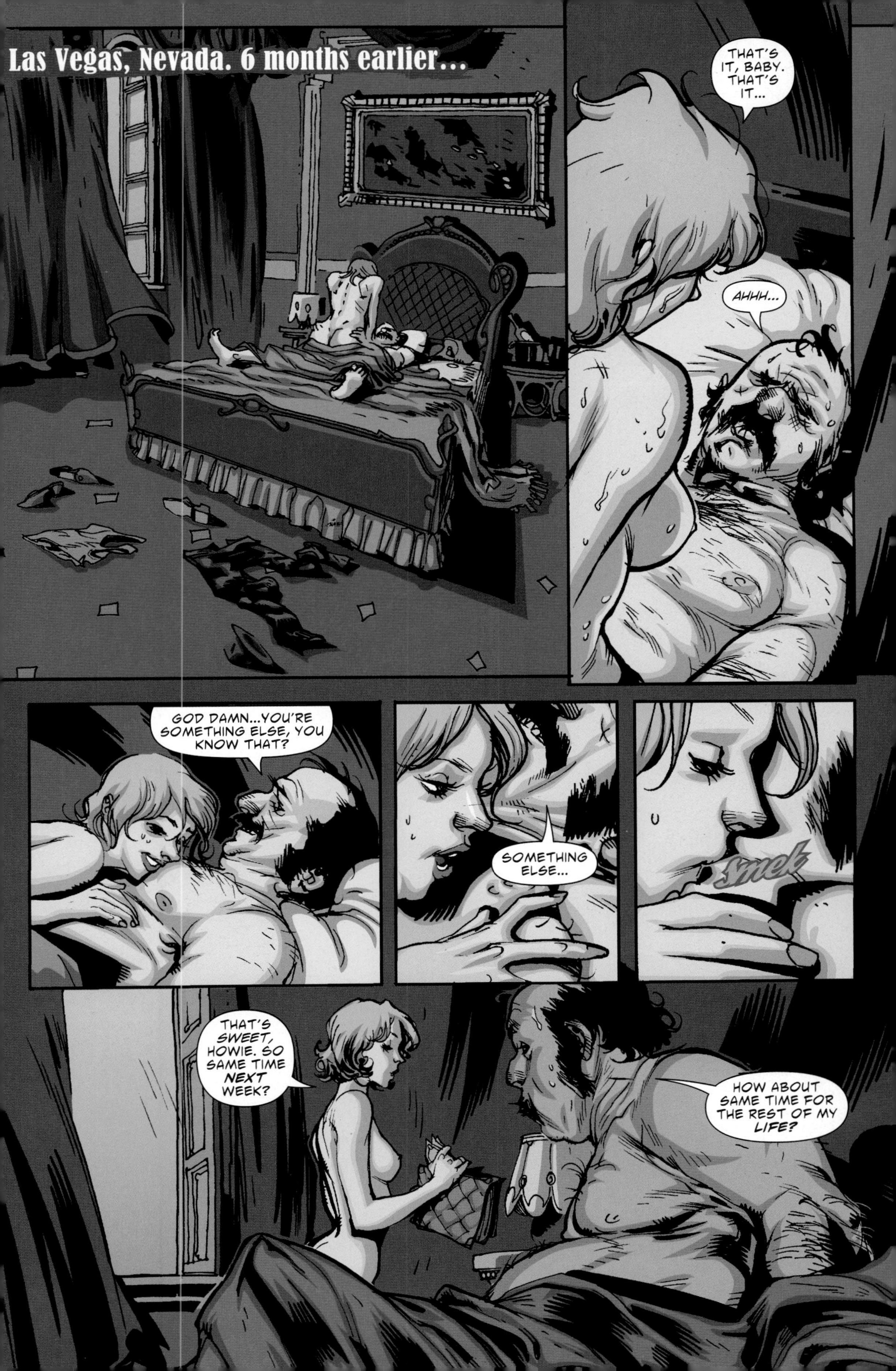
Las Vegas, Nevada. 6 months earlier...
THAT'S IT, BABY. THAT'S IT...
AHHH...
GOD DAMN...YOU'RE SOMETHING ELSE, YOU KNOW THAT?
SOMETHING ELSE...
SMEK
THAT'S SWEET, HOWIE. SO SAME TIME NEXT WEEK?
HOW ABOUT SAME TIME FOR THE REST OF MY LIFE?

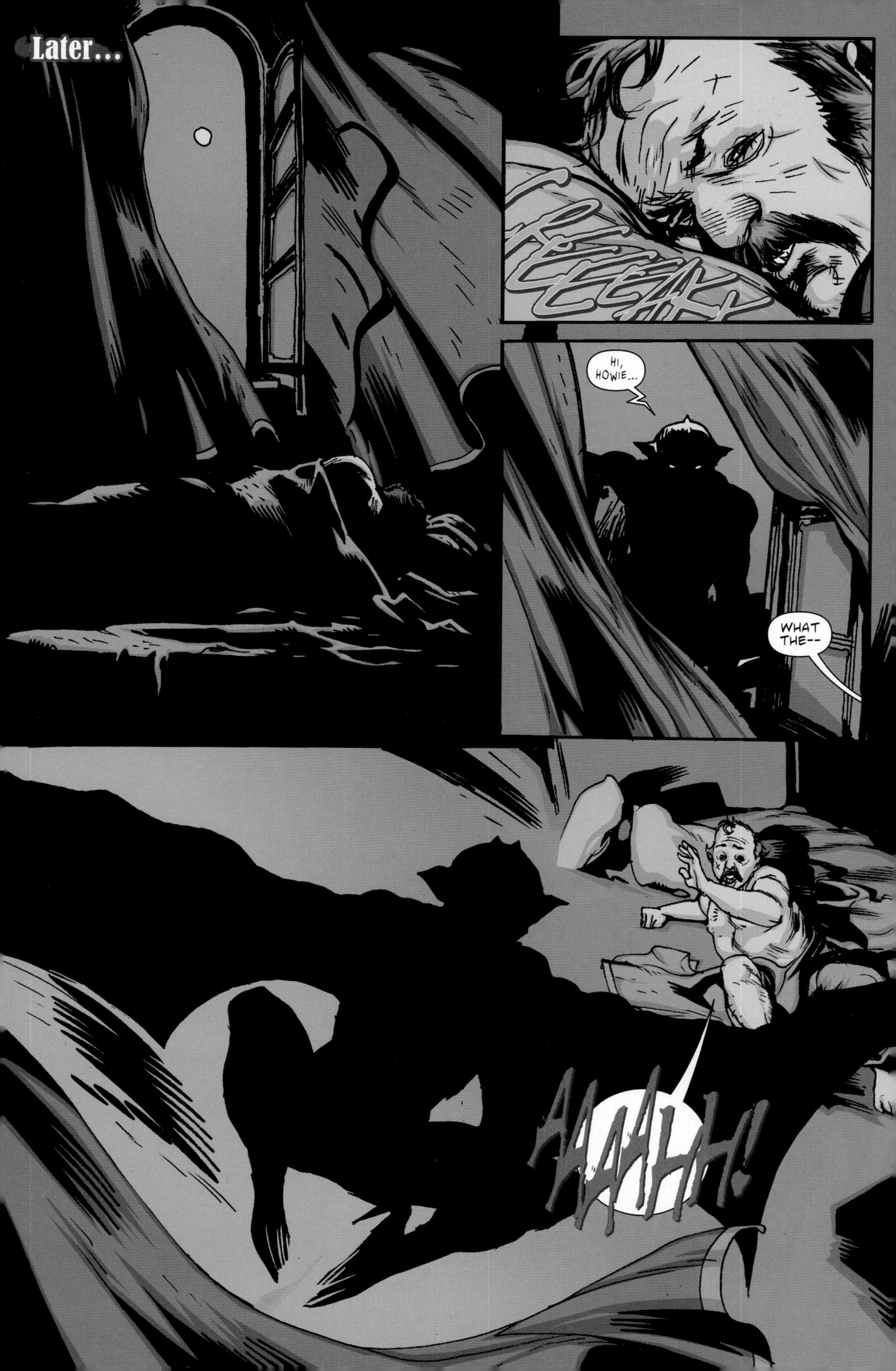
Later...
CREEEAAKK
HI, HOWIE...
WHAT THE--
AAAAHH!

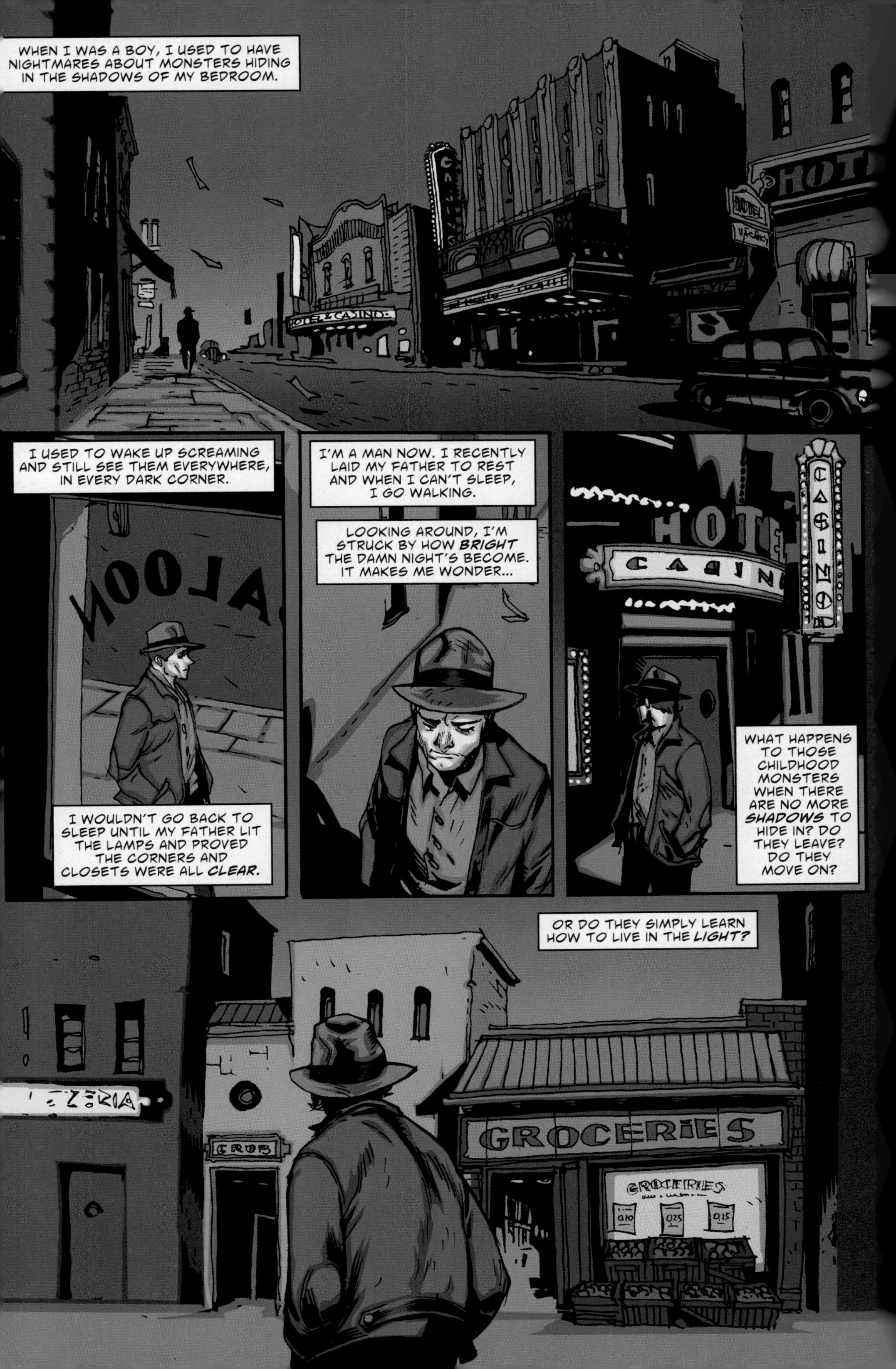
WHEN I WAS A BOY, I USED TO HAVE NIGHTMARES ABOUT MONSTERS HIDING IN THE SHADOWS OF MY BEDROOM.
HOTEL
I USED TO WAKE UP SCREAMING AND STILL SEE THEM EVERYWHERE, IN EVERY DARK CORNER.
I WOULDN'T GO BACK TO SLEEP UNTIL MY FATHER LIT THE LAMPS AND PROVED THE CORNERS AND CLOSETS WERE ALL *CLEAR.*
I'M A MAN NOW. I RECENTLY LAID MY FATHER TO REST AND WHEN I CAN'T SLEEP, I GO WALKING.
LOOKING AROUND, I'M STRUCK BY HOW *BRIGHT* THE DAMN NIGHT'S BECOME. IT MAKES ME WONDER...
CASINO
WHAT HAPPENS TO THOSE CHILDHOOD MONSTERS WHEN THERE ARE NO MORE *SHADOWS* TO HIDE IN? DO THEY LEAVE? DO THEY MOVE ON?
OR DO THEY SIMPLY LEARN HOW TO LIVE IN THE *LIGHT?*
GROCERIES
GROCERIES
0.10
0.25
0.15

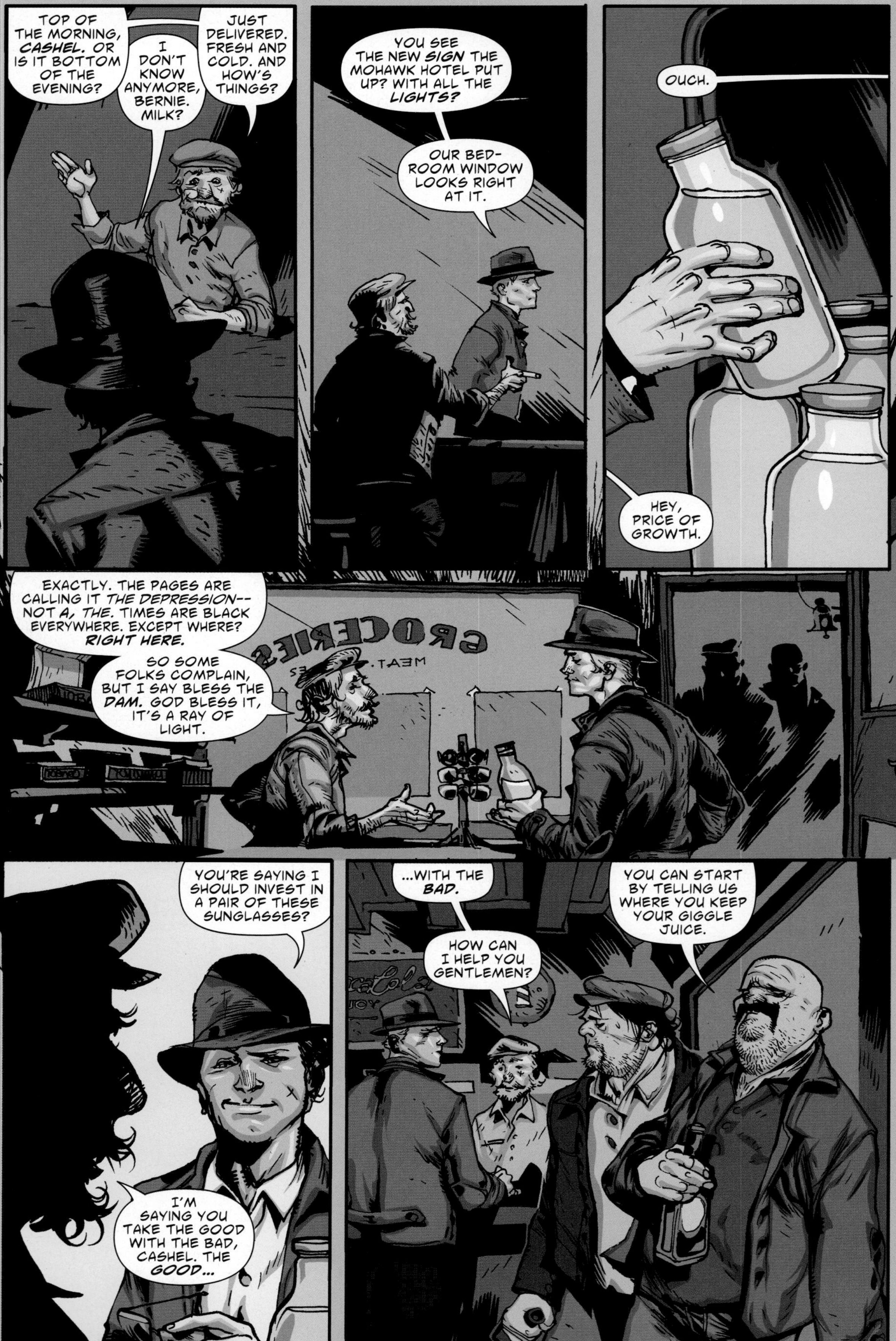
TOP OF THE MORNING, *CASHEL.* OR IS IT BOTTOM OF THE EVENING?
I DON'T KNOW ANYMORE, BERNIE. MILK?
JUST DELIVERED. FRESH AND COLD. AND HOW'S THINGS?
YOU SEE THE NEW *SIGN* THE MOHAWK HOTEL PUT UP? WITH ALL THE *LIGHTS?*
OUR BED-ROOM WINDOW LOOKS RIGHT AT IT.
OUCH.
HEY, PRICE OF GROWTH.
EXACTLY. THE PAGES ARE CALLING IT *THE DEPRESSION*-- NOT *A, THE.* TIMES ARE BLACK EVERYWHERE. EXCEPT WHERE? ***RIGHT HERE.***
GROCERIES
MEAT
SO SOME FOLKS COMPLAIN, BUT I SAY BLESS THE *DAM.* GOD BLESS IT, IT'S A RAY OF LIGHT.
YOU'RE SAYING I SHOULD INVEST IN A PAIR OF THESE SUNGLASSES?
I'M SAYING YOU TAKE THE GOOD WITH THE BAD, CASHEL. THE *GOOD...*
...WITH THE *BAD.*
HOW CAN I HELP YOU GENTLEMEN?
YOU CAN START BY TELLING US WHERE YOU KEEP YOUR GIGGLE JUICE.

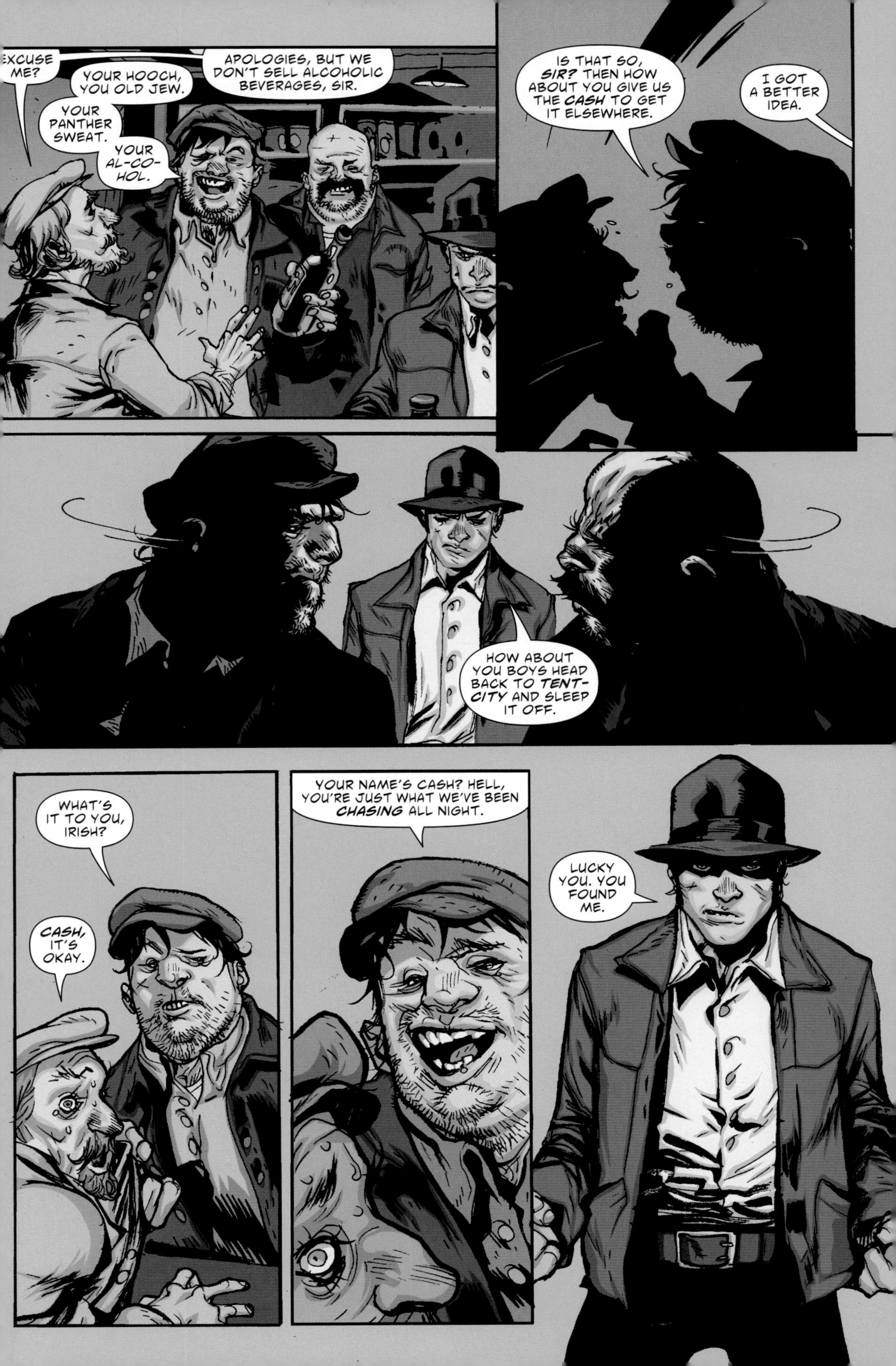

APOLOGIES, BUT WE DON'T SELL ALCOHOLIC BEVERAGES, SIR.
EXCUSE ME?
YOUR HOOCH, YOU OLD JEW.
YOUR PANTHER SWEAT.
YOUR AL-CO-HOL.
IS THAT SO, SIR? THEN HOW ABOUT YOU GIVE US THE CASH TO GET IT ELSEWHERE.
I GOT A BETTER IDEA.
HOW ABOUT YOU BOYS HEAD BACK TO TENT-CITY AND SLEEP IT OFF.
WHAT'S IT TO YOU, IRISH?
CASH, IT'S OKAY.
YOUR NAME'S CASH? HELL, YOU'RE JUST WHAT WE'VE BEEN CHASING ALL NIGHT.
LUCKY YOU. YOU FOUND ME.

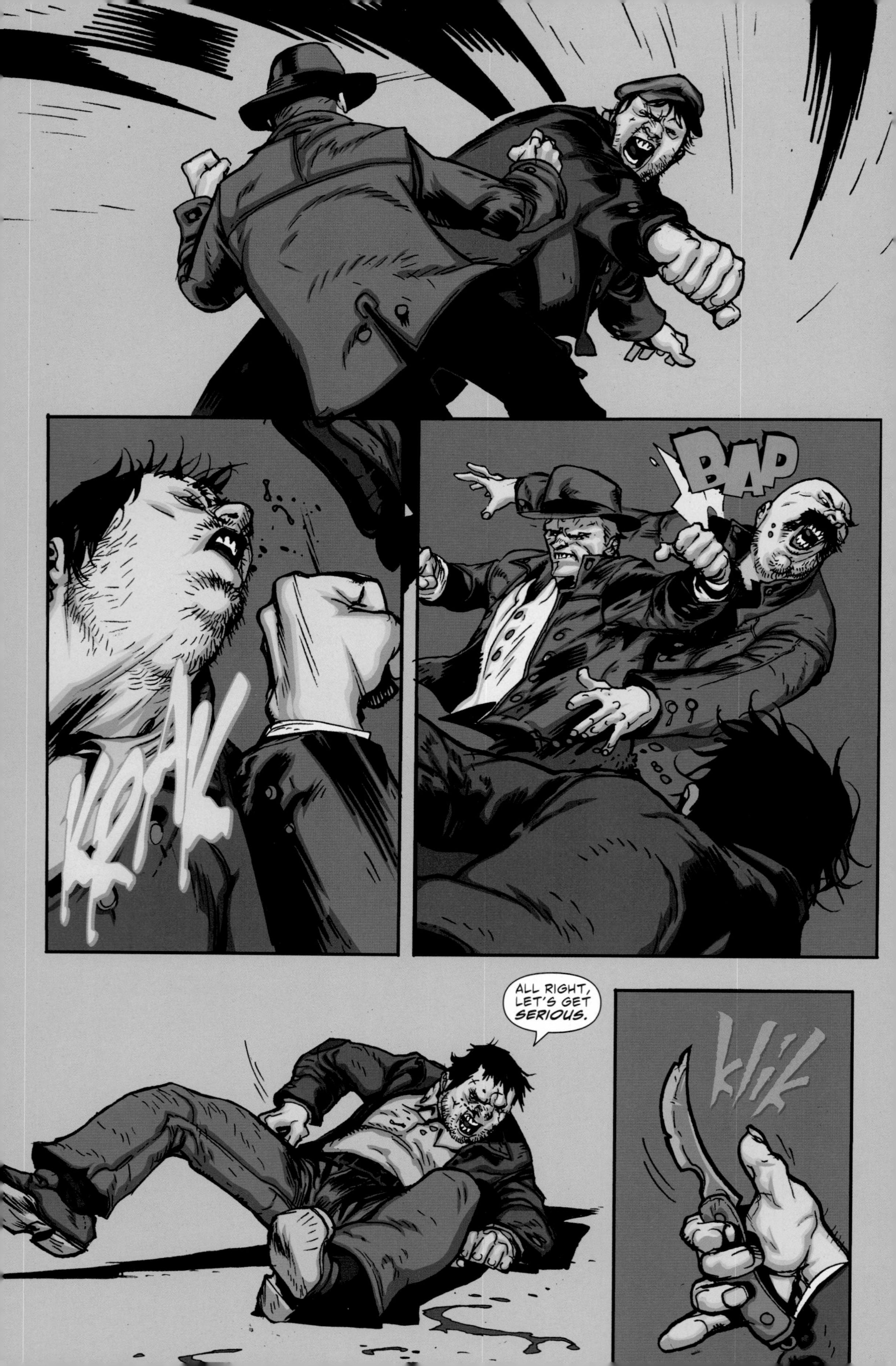
KRAK
BAP
ALL RIGHT, LET'S GET SERIOUS.
klik

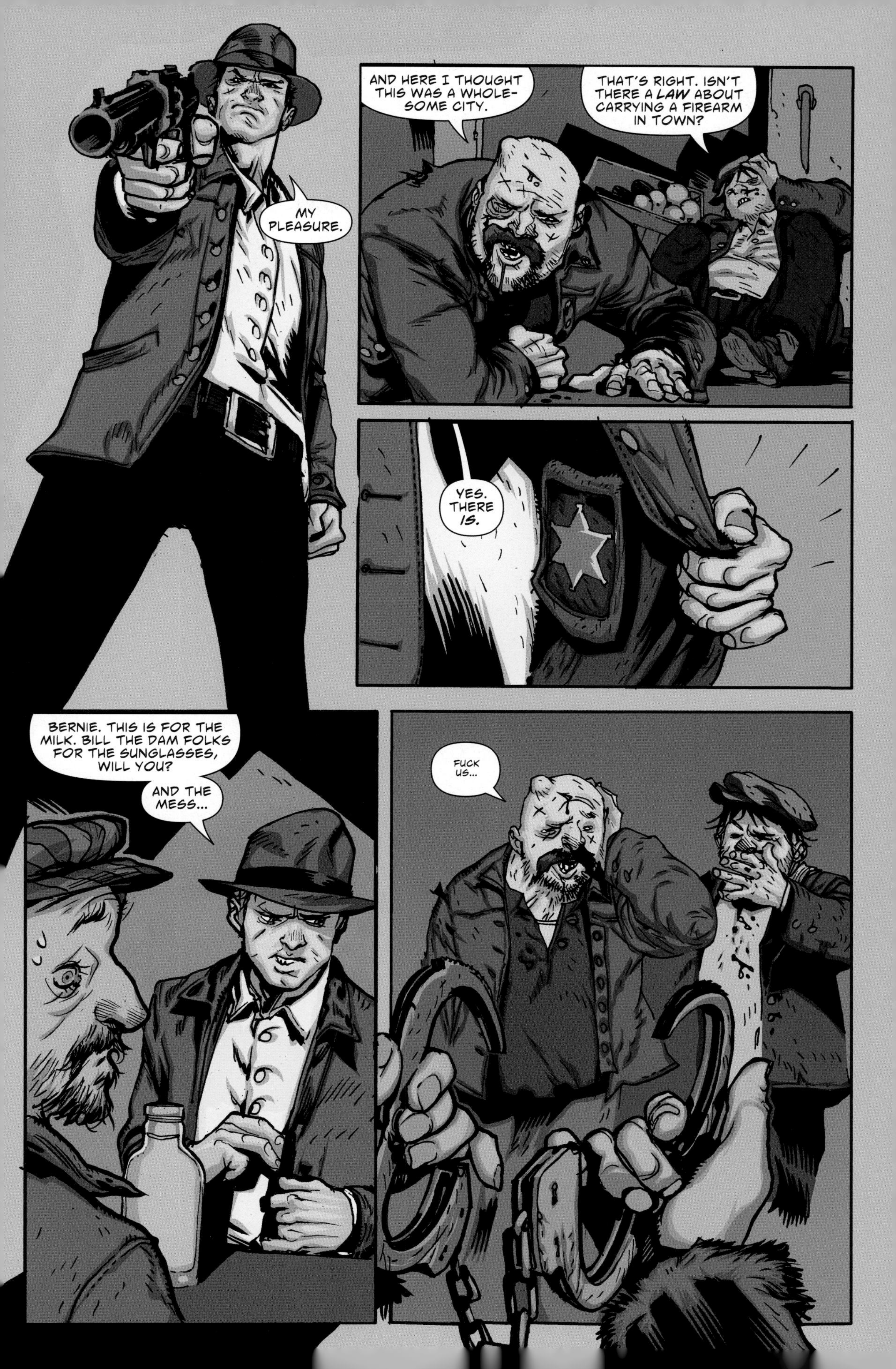
MY PLEASURE.
AND HERE I THOUGHT THIS WAS A WHOLESOME CITY.
THAT'S RIGHT. ISN'T THERE A LAW ABOUT CARRYING A FIREARM IN TOWN?
YES. THERE IS.
BERNIE. THIS IS FOR THE MILK. BILL THE DAM FOLKS FOR THE SUNGLASSES, WILL YOU?
AND THE MESS...
FUCK US...

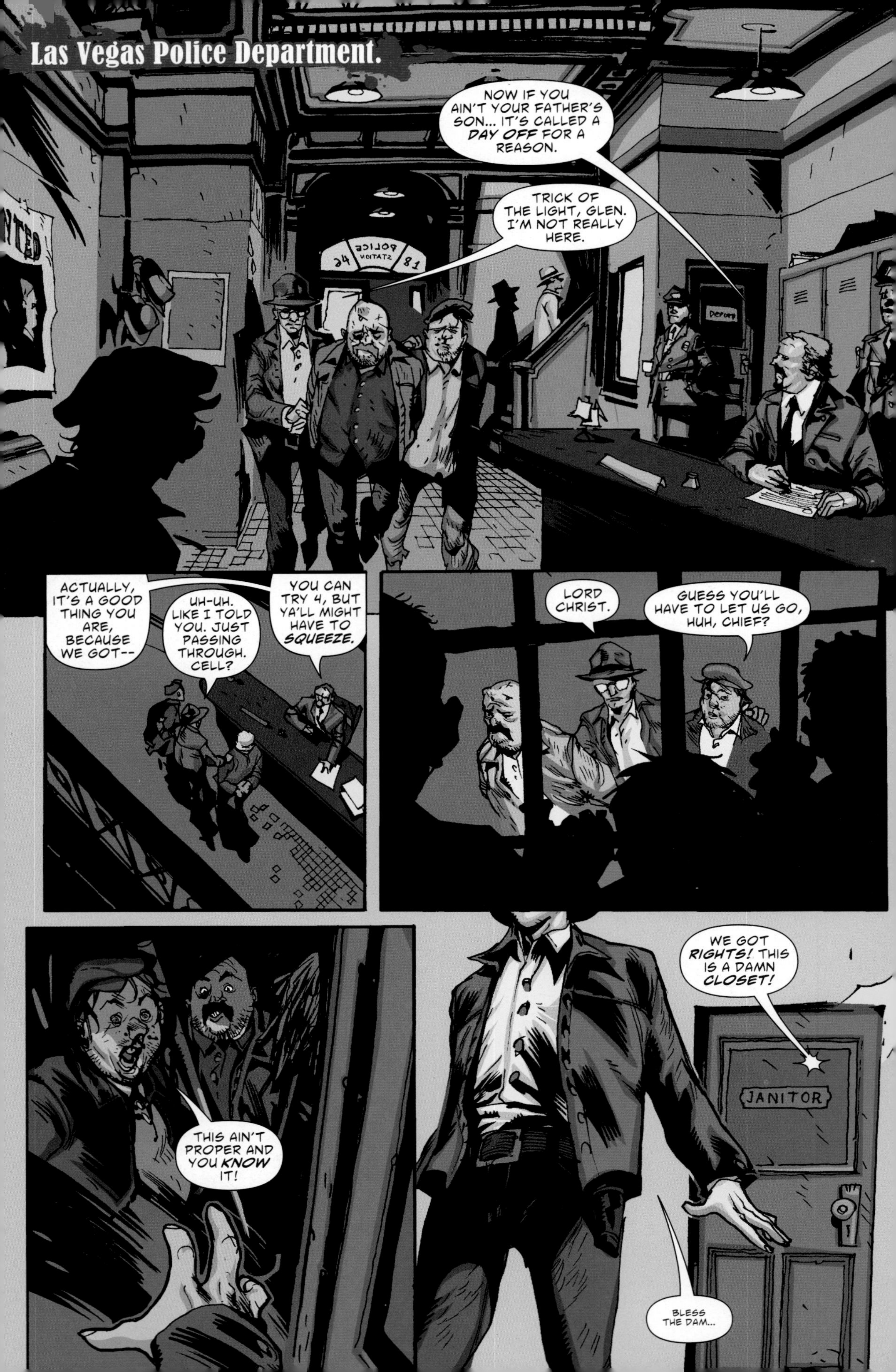
Las Vegas Police Department.
NOW IF YOU AIN'T YOUR FATHER'S SON... IT'S CALLED A DAY OFF FOR A REASON.
TRICK OF THE LIGHT, GLEN. I'M NOT REALLY HERE.
ACTUALLY, IT'S A GOOD THING YOU ARE, BECAUSE WE GOT--
UH-UH. LIKE I TOLD YOU. JUST PASSING THROUGH. CELL?
YOU CAN TRY 4, BUT YA'LL MIGHT HAVE TO SQUEEZE.
LORD CHRIST.
GUESS YOU'LL HAVE TO LET US GO, HUH, CHIEF?
THIS AIN'T PROPER AND YOU KNOW IT!
WE GOT RIGHTS! THIS IS A DAMN CLOSET!
JANITOR
BLESS THE DAM...

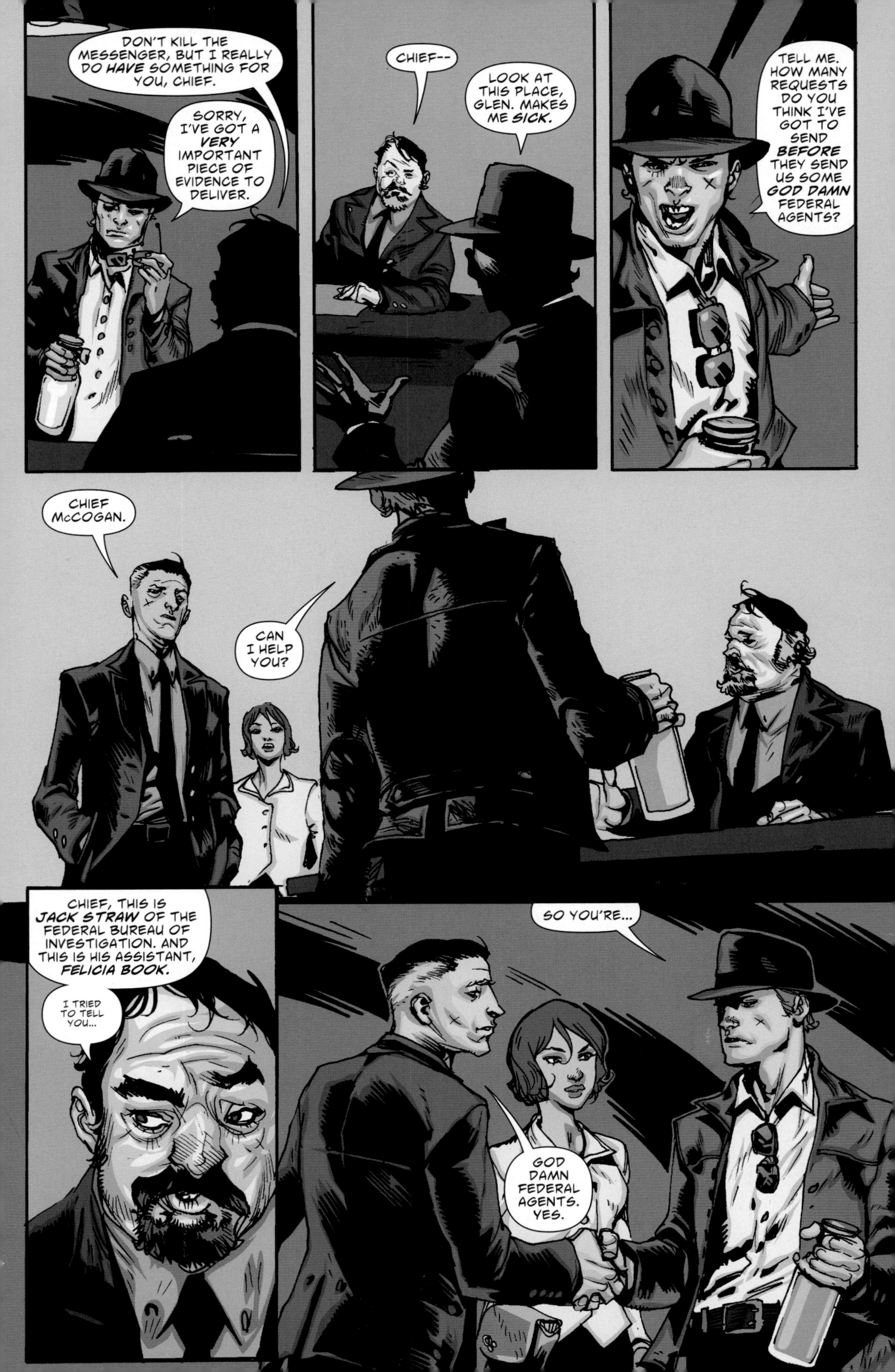
DON'T KILL THE MESSENGER, BUT I REALLY DO HAVE SOMETHING FOR YOU, CHIEF.
SORRY, I'VE GOT A VERY IMPORTANT PIECE OF EVIDENCE TO DELIVER.
CHIEF--
LOOK AT THIS PLACE, GLEN. MAKES ME SICK.
TELL ME. HOW MANY REQUESTS DO YOU THINK I'VE GOT TO SEND BEFORE THEY SEND US SOME GOD DAMN FEDERAL AGENTS?
CHIEF McCOGAN.
CAN I HELP YOU?
CHIEF, THIS IS JACK STRAW OF THE FEDERAL BUREAU OF INVESTIGATION. AND THIS IS HIS ASSISTANT, FELICIA BOOK.
I TRIED TO TELL YOU...
SO YOU'RE...
GOD DAMN FEDERAL AGENTS. YES.

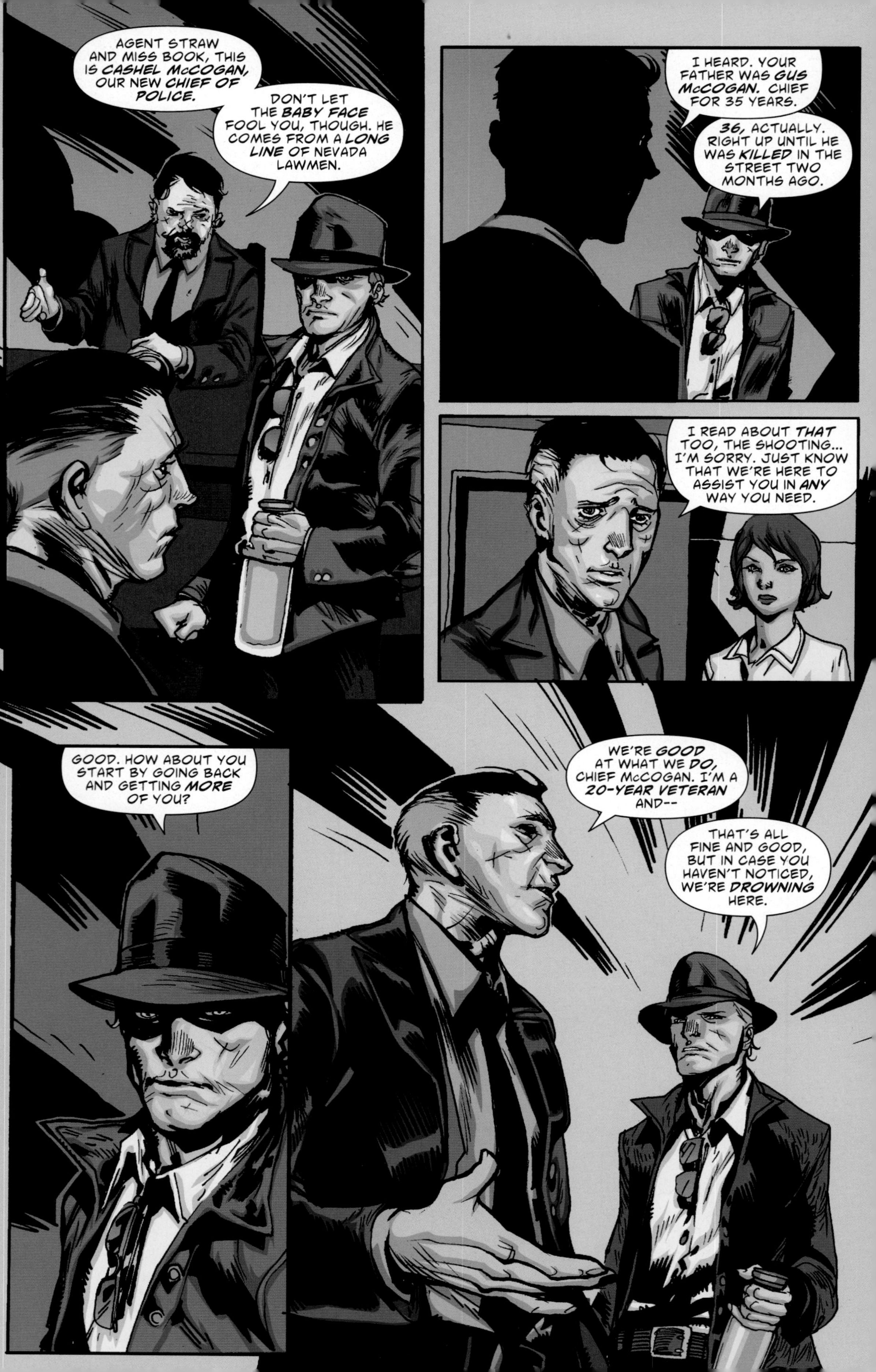

AGENT STRAW AND MISS BOOK, THIS IS CASHEL McCOGAN, OUR NEW CHIEF OF POLICE.
DON'T LET THE BABY FACE FOOL YOU, THOUGH. HE COMES FROM A LONG LINE OF NEVADA LAWMEN.
I HEARD. YOUR FATHER WAS GUS McCOGAN. CHIEF FOR 35 YEARS.
36, ACTUALLY. RIGHT UP UNTIL HE WAS KILLED IN THE STREET TWO MONTHS AGO.
I READ ABOUT THAT TOO, THE SHOOTING... I'M SORRY. JUST KNOW THAT WE'RE HERE TO ASSIST YOU IN ANY WAY YOU NEED.
GOOD. HOW ABOUT YOU START BY GOING BACK AND GETTING MORE OF YOU?
WE'RE GOOD AT WHAT WE DO, CHIEF McCOGAN. I'M A 20-YEAR VETERAN AND--
THAT'S ALL FINE AND GOOD, BUT IN CASE YOU HAVEN'T NOTICED, WE'RE DROWNING HERE.

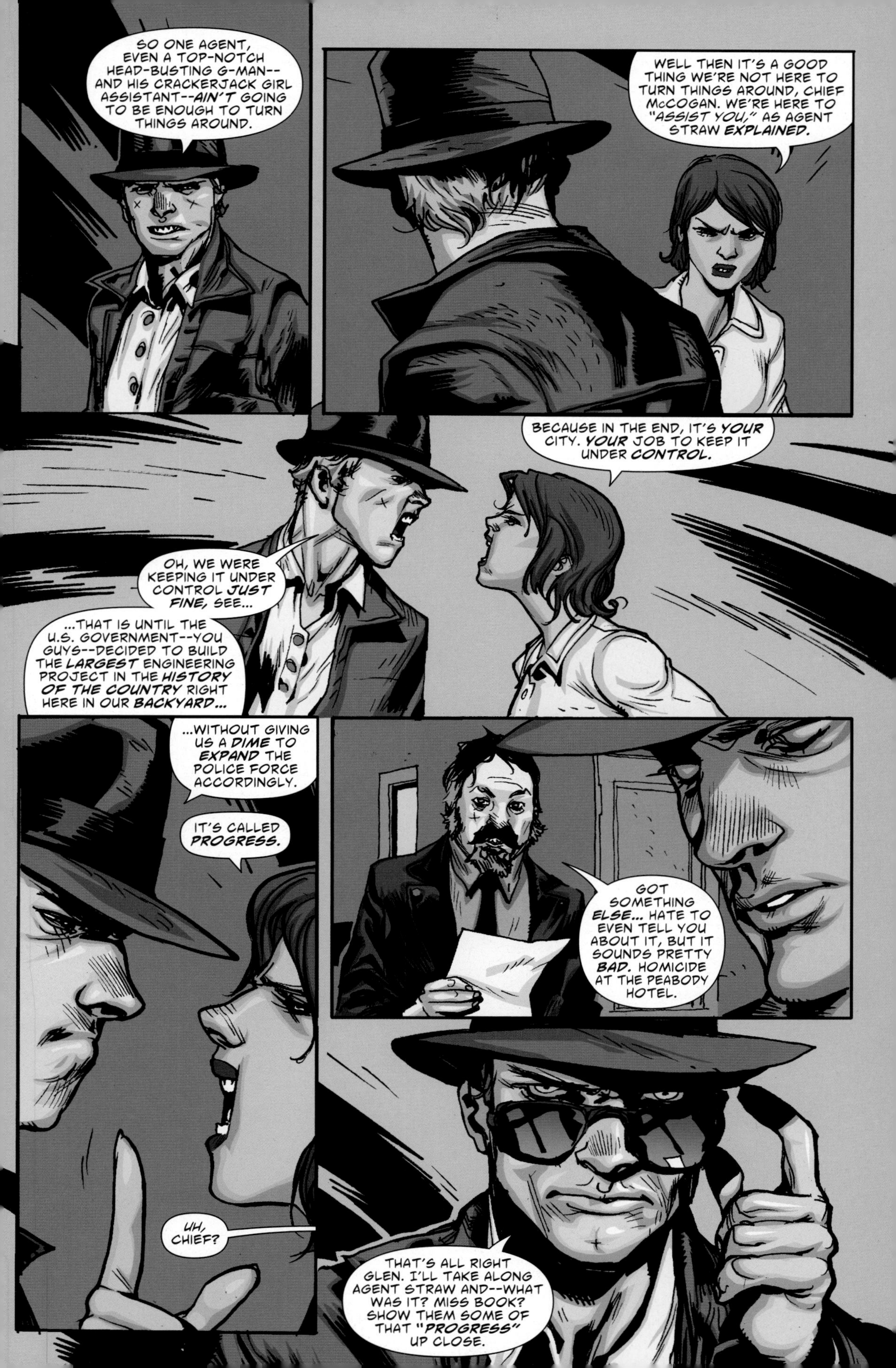
SO ONE AGENT, EVEN A TOP-NOTCH HEAD-BUSTING G-MAN-- AND HIS CRACKERJACK GIRL ASSISTANT--AIN'T GOING TO BE ENOUGH TO TURN THINGS AROUND.
WELL THEN IT'S A GOOD THING WE'RE NOT HERE TO TURN THINGS AROUND, CHIEF McCOGAN. WE'RE HERE TO "ASSIST YOU," AS AGENT STRAW EXPLAINED.
BECAUSE IN THE END, IT'S YOUR CITY. YOUR JOB TO KEEP IT UNDER CONTROL.
OH, WE WERE KEEPING IT UNDER CONTROL JUST FINE, SEE...
...THAT IS UNTIL THE U.S. GOVERNMENT--YOU GUYS--DECIDED TO BUILD THE LARGEST ENGINEERING PROJECT IN THE HISTORY OF THE COUNTRY RIGHT HERE IN OUR BACKYARD...
...WITHOUT GIVING US A DIME TO EXPAND THE POLICE FORCE ACCORDINGLY.
IT'S CALLED PROGRESS.
UH, CHIEF?
GOT SOMETHING ELSE... HATE TO EVEN TELL YOU ABOUT IT, BUT IT SOUNDS PRETTY BAD. HOMICIDE AT THE PEABODY HOTEL.
THAT'S ALL RIGHT GLEN. I'LL TAKE ALONG AGENT STRAW AND--WHAT WAS IT? MISS BOOK? SHOW THEM SOME OF THAT "PROGRESS" UP CLOSE.

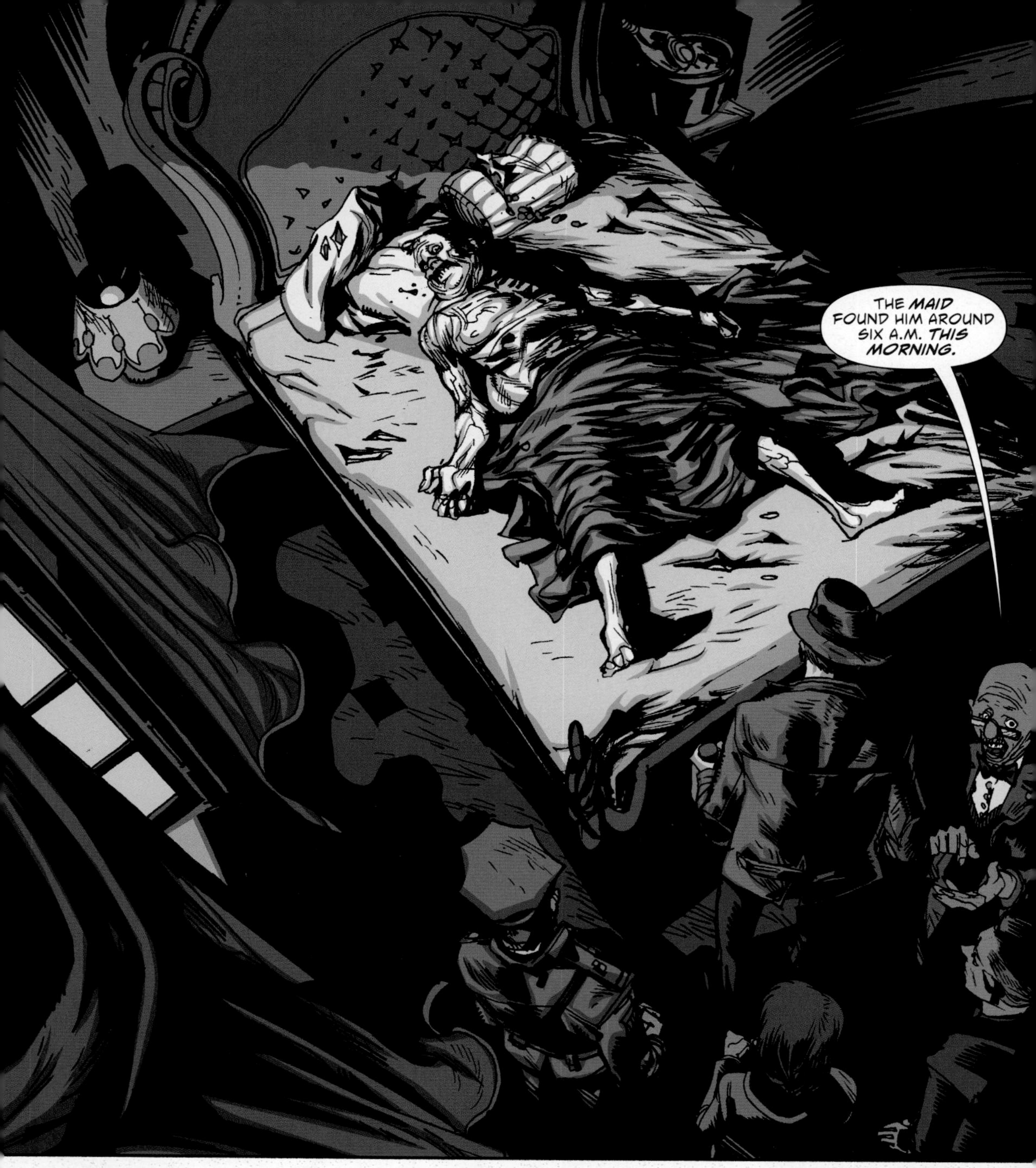
THE MAID FOUND HIM AROUND SIX A.M. THIS MORNING.

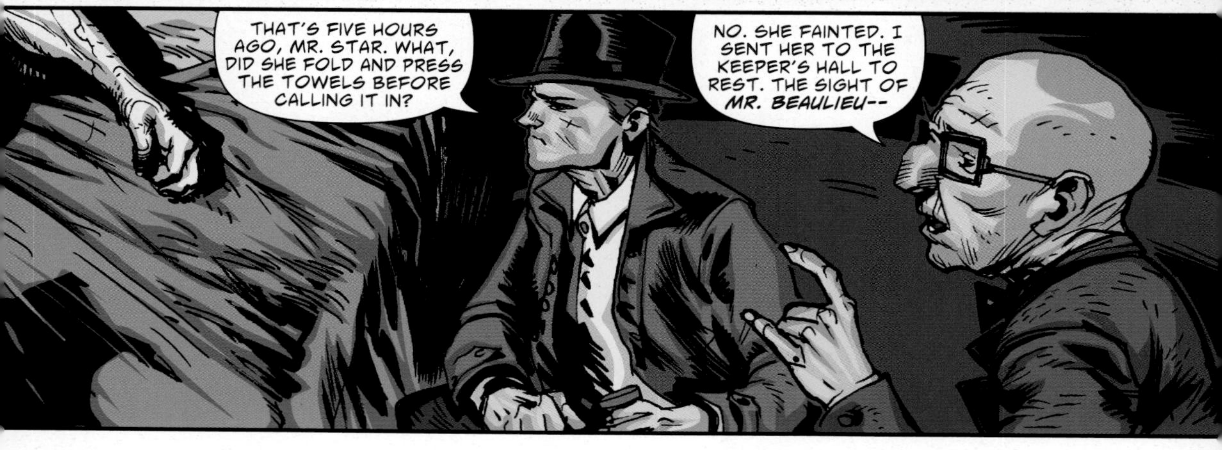
THAT'S FIVE HOURS AGO, MR. STAR. WHAT, DID SHE FOLD AND PRESS THE TOWELS BEFORE CALLING IT IN?
NO. SHE FAINTED. I SENT HER TO THE KEEPER'S HALL TO REST. THE SIGHT OF MR. BEAULIEU--

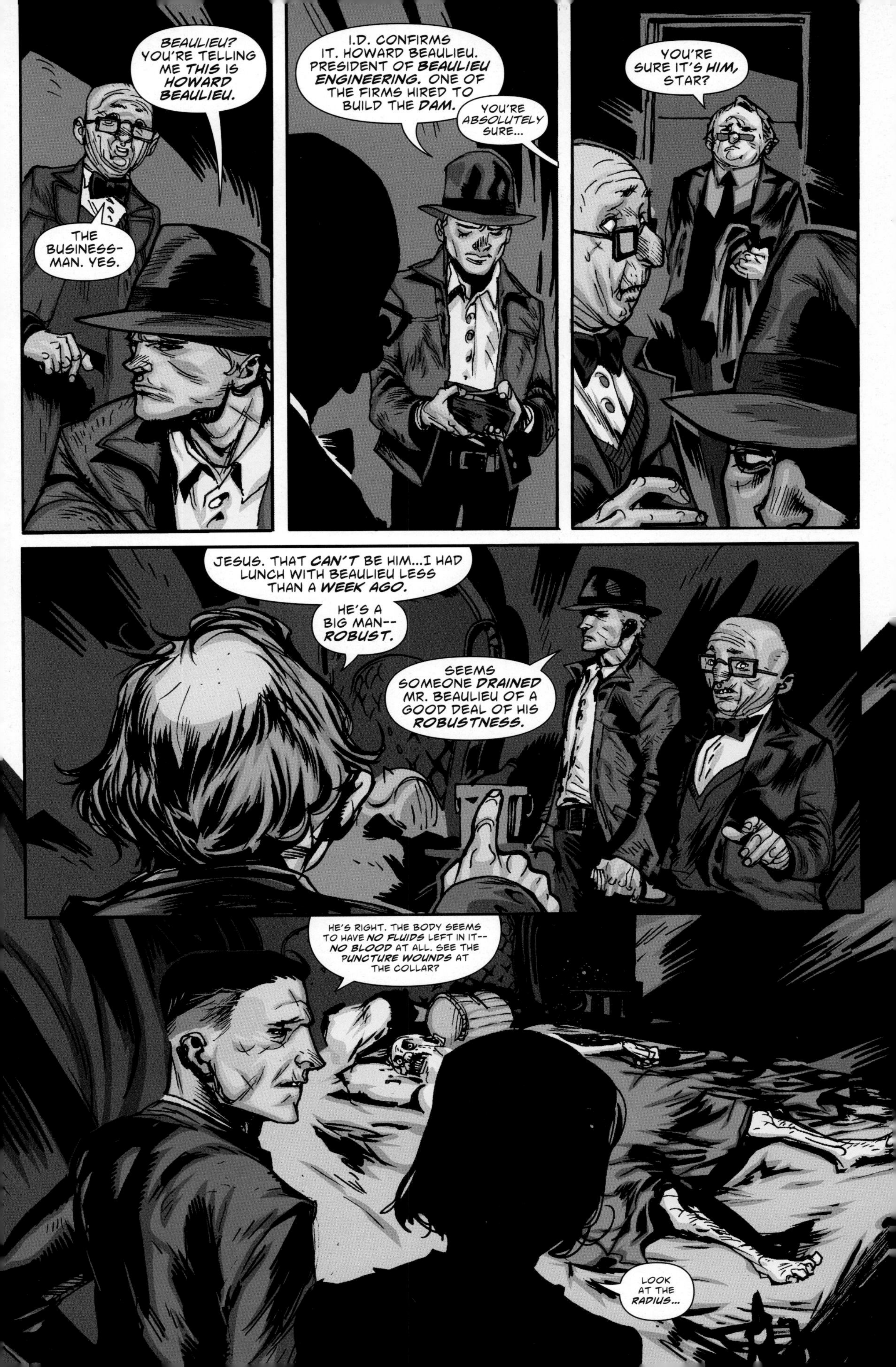
BEAULIEU? YOU'RE TELLING ME THIS IS HOWARD BEAULIEU.
THE BUSINESS-MAN. YES.
I.D. CONFIRMS IT. HOWARD BEAULIEU. PRESIDENT OF BEAULIEU ENGINEERING. ONE OF THE FIRMS HIRED TO BUILD THE DAM.
YOU'RE ABSOLUTELY SURE...
YOU'RE SURE IT'S HIM, STAR?
JESUS. THAT CAN'T BE HIM...I HAD LUNCH WITH BEAULIEU LESS THAN A WEEK AGO.
HE'S A BIG MAN-- ROBUST.
SEEMS SOMEONE DRAINED MR. BEAULIEU OF A GOOD DEAL OF HIS ROBUSTNESS.
HE'S RIGHT. THE BODY SEEMS TO HAVE NO FLUIDS LEFT IN IT-- NO BLOOD AT ALL. SEE THE PUNCTURE WOUNDS AT THE COLLAR?
LOOK AT THE RADIUS...

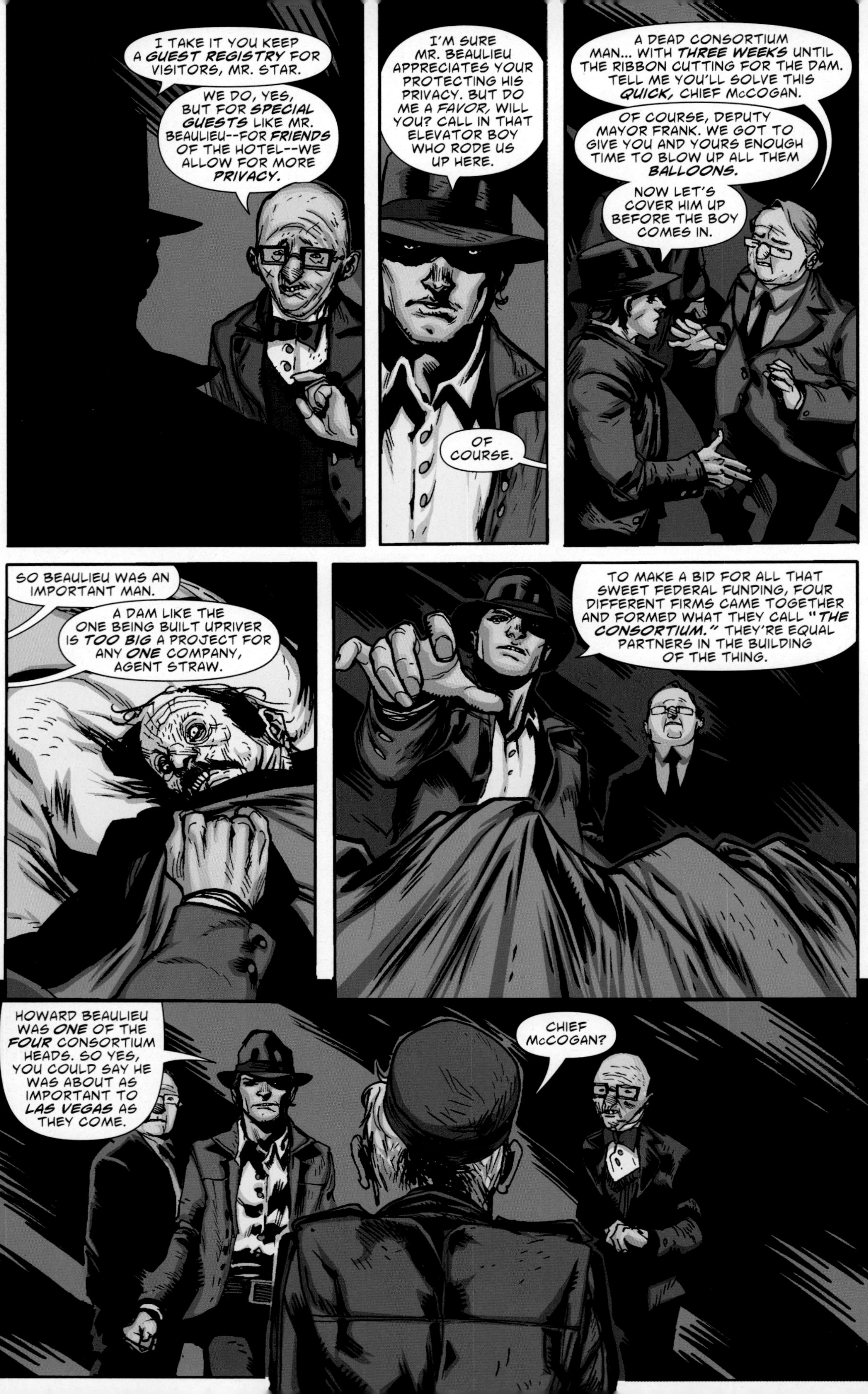
I TAKE IT YOU KEEP A GUEST REGISTRY FOR VISITORS, MR. STAR.
WE DO, YES, BUT FOR SPECIAL GUESTS LIKE MR. BEAULIEU--FOR FRIENDS OF THE HOTEL--WE ALLOW FOR MORE PRIVACY.
I'M SURE MR. BEAULIEU APPRECIATES YOUR PROTECTING HIS PRIVACY. BUT DO ME A FAVOR, WILL YOU? CALL IN THAT ELEVATOR BOY WHO RODE US UP HERE.
OF COURSE.
A DEAD CONSORTIUM MAN... WITH THREE WEEKS UNTIL THE RIBBON CUTTING FOR THE DAM. TELL ME YOU'LL SOLVE THIS QUICK, CHIEF McCOGAN.
OF COURSE, DEPUTY MAYOR FRANK. WE GOT TO GIVE YOU AND YOURS ENOUGH TIME TO BLOW UP ALL THEM BALLOONS.
NOW LET'S COVER HIM UP BEFORE THE BOY COMES IN.
SO BEAULIEU WAS AN IMPORTANT MAN.
A DAM LIKE THE ONE BEING BUILT UPRIVER IS TOO BIG A PROJECT FOR ANY ONE COMPANY, AGENT STRAW.
TO MAKE A BID FOR ALL THAT SWEET FEDERAL FUNDING, FOUR DIFFERENT FIRMS CAME TOGETHER AND FORMED WHAT THEY CALL "THE CONSORTIUM." THEY'RE EQUAL PARTNERS IN THE BUILDING OF THE THING.
HOWARD BEAULIEU WAS ONE OF THE FOUR CONSORTIUM HEADS. SO YES, YOU COULD SAY HE WAS ABOUT AS IMPORTANT TO LAS VEGAS AS THEY COME.
CHIEF McCOGAN?

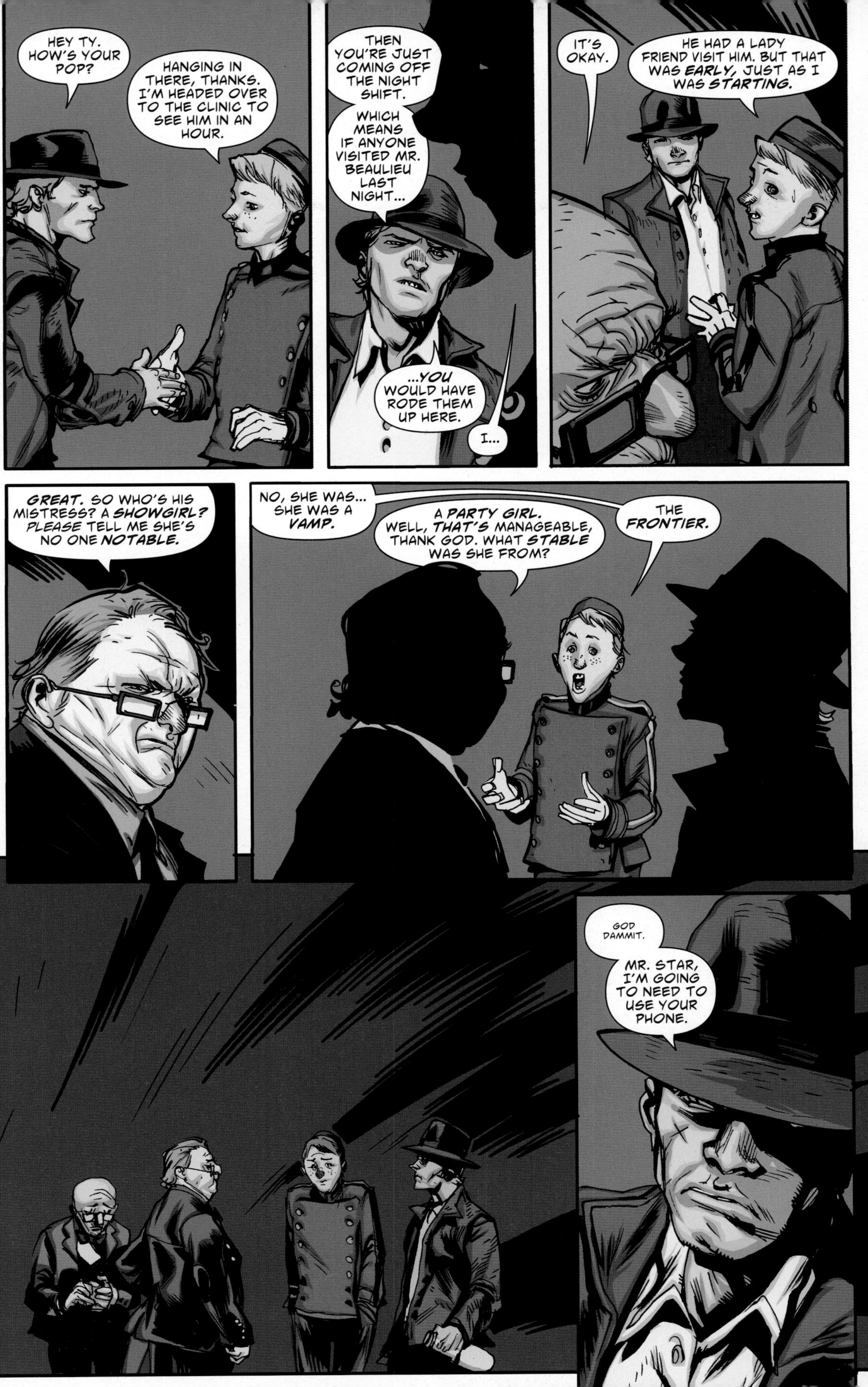
HEY TY. HOW'S YOUR POP?
HANGING IN THERE, THANKS. I'M HEADED OVER TO THE CLINIC TO SEE HIM IN AN HOUR.
THEN YOU'RE JUST COMING OFF THE NIGHT SHIFT.
WHICH MEANS IF ANYONE VISITED MR. BEAULIEU LAST NIGHT...
...YOU WOULD HAVE RODE THEM UP HERE.
I...
IT'S OKAY.
HE HAD A LADY FRIEND VISIT HIM. BUT THAT WAS EARLY, JUST AS I WAS STARTING.
GREAT. SO WHO'S HIS MISTRESS? A SHOWGIRL? PLEASE TELL ME SHE'S NO ONE NOTABLE.
NO, SHE WAS... SHE WAS A VAMP.
A PARTY GIRL. WELL, THAT'S MANAGEABLE, THANK GOD. WHAT STABLE WAS SHE FROM?
THE FRONTIER.
GOD DAMMIT.
MR. STAR, I'M GOING TO NEED TO USE YOUR PHONE.

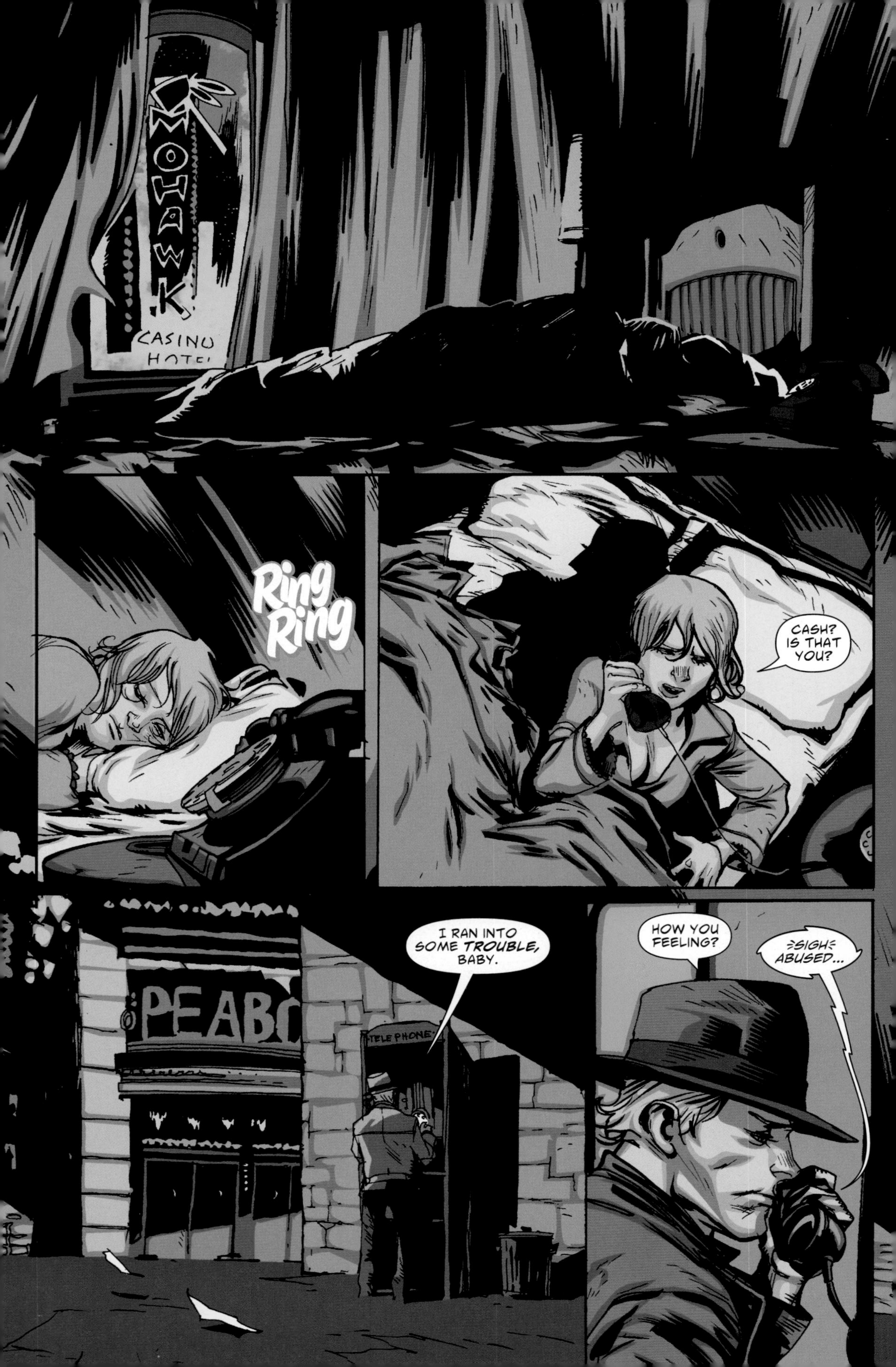
MOHAWK
CASINO
HOTEL
Ring Ring
CASH? IS THAT YOU?
PEABO
TELEPHONE
I RAN INTO SOME TROUBLE, BABY.
HOW YOU FEELING?
SIGH ABUSED...

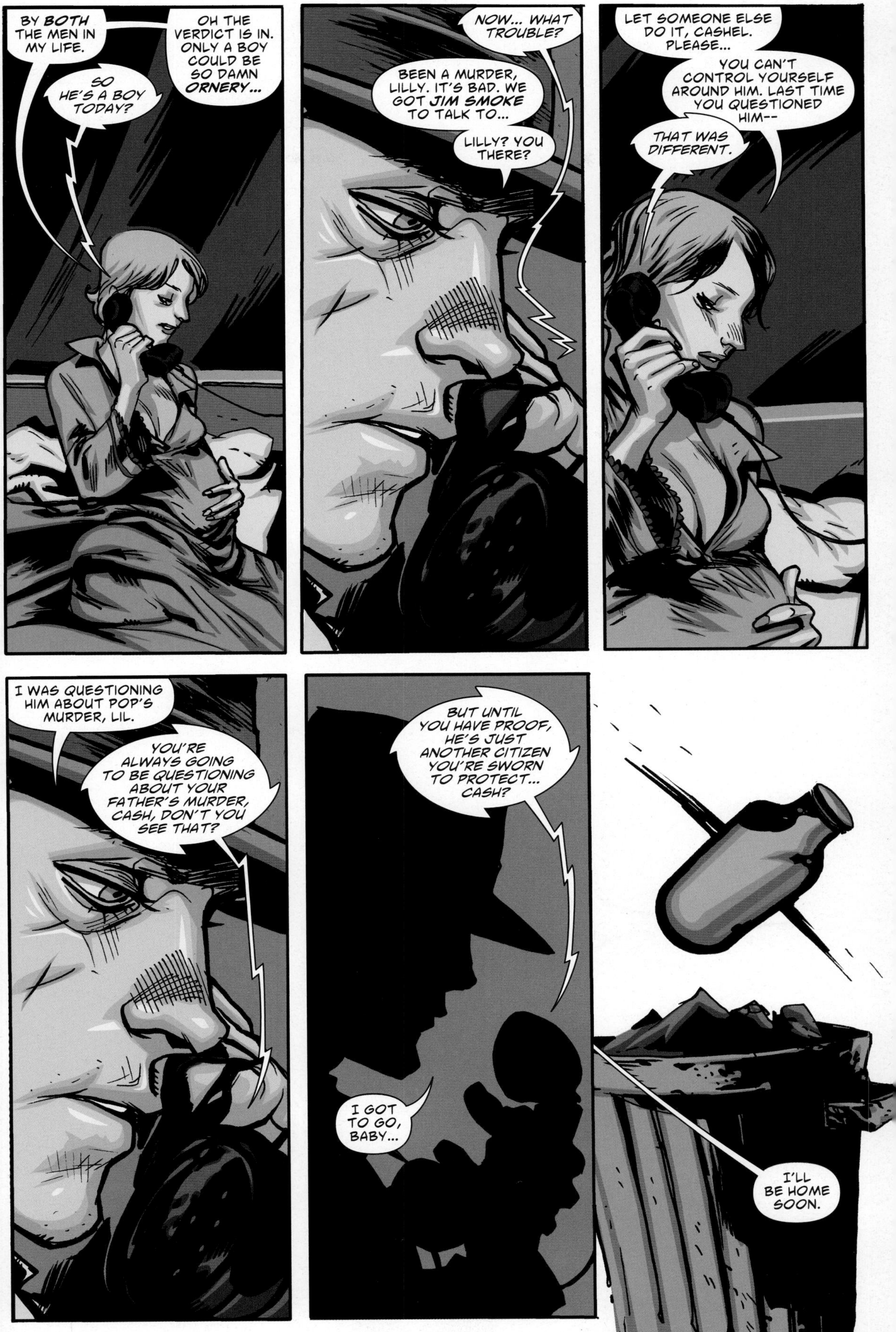
BY BOTH THE MEN IN MY LIFE.
OH THE VERDICT IS IN. ONLY A BOY COULD BE SO DAMN ORNERY...
SO HE'S A BOY TODAY?
NOW... WHAT TROUBLE?
BEEN A MURDER, LILLY. IT'S BAD. WE GOT JIM SMOKE TO TALK TO...
LILLY? YOU THERE?
LET SOMEONE ELSE DO IT, CASHEL. PLEASE...
YOU CAN'T CONTROL YOURSELF AROUND HIM. LAST TIME YOU QUESTIONED HIM--
THAT WAS DIFFERENT.
I WAS QUESTIONING HIM ABOUT POP'S MURDER, LIL.
YOU'RE ALWAYS GOING TO BE QUESTIONING ABOUT YOUR FATHER'S MURDER, CASH, DON'T YOU SEE THAT?
BUT UNTIL YOU HAVE PROOF, HE'S JUST ANOTHER CITIZEN YOU'RE SWORN TO PROTECT... CASH?
I GOT TO GO, BABY...
I'LL BE HOME SOON.

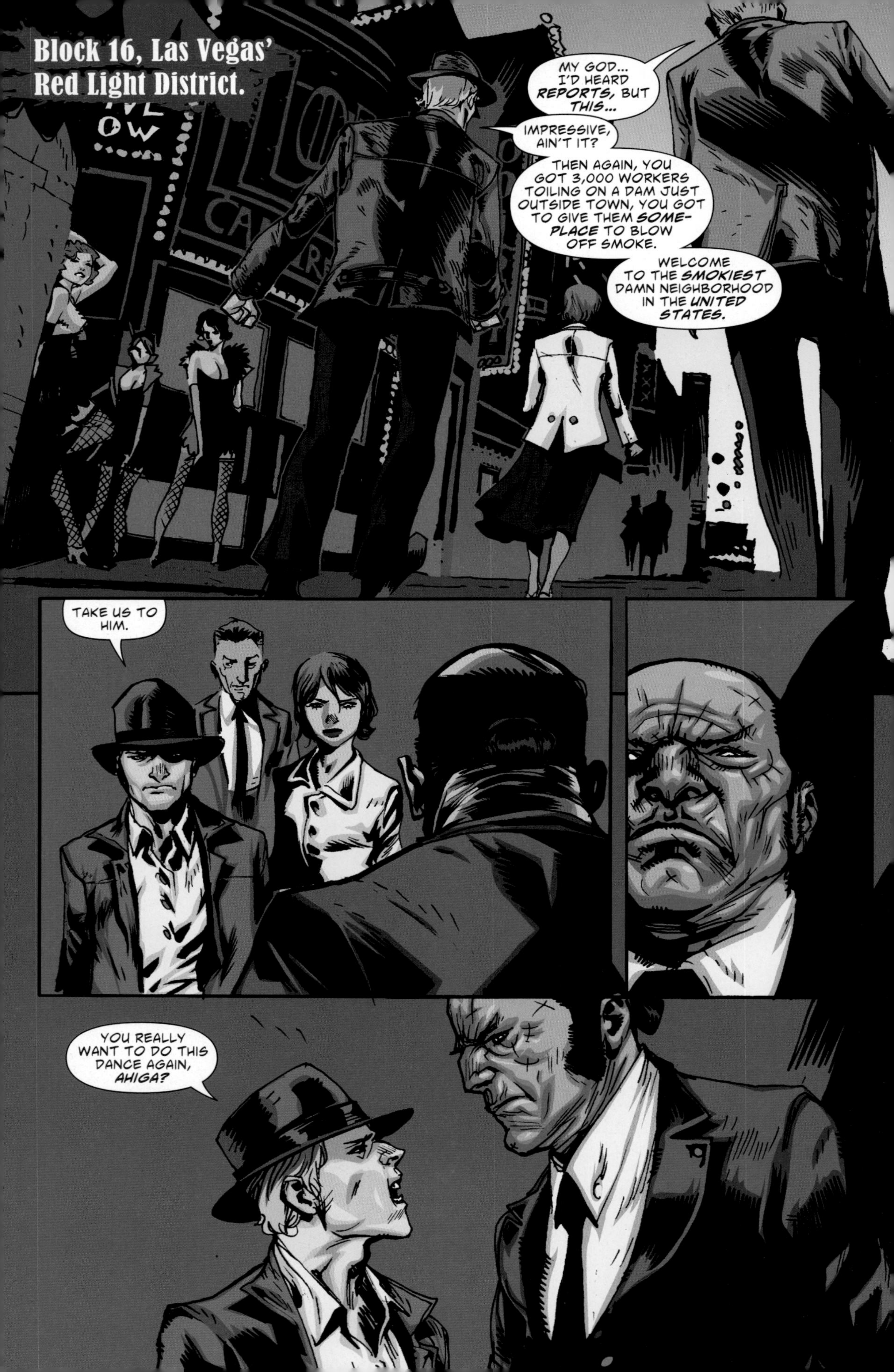
Block 16, Las Vegas' Red Light District.
MY GOD... I'D HEARD REPORTS, BUT THIS...
IMPRESSIVE, AIN'T IT?
THEN AGAIN, YOU GOT 3,000 WORKERS TOILING ON A DAM JUST OUTSIDE TOWN, YOU GOT TO GIVE THEM SOME-PLACE TO BLOW OFF SMOKE.
WELCOME TO THE SMOKIEST DAMN NEIGHBORHOOD IN THE UNITED STATES.
TAKE US TO HIM.
YOU REALLY WANT TO DO THIS DANCE AGAIN, AHIGA?

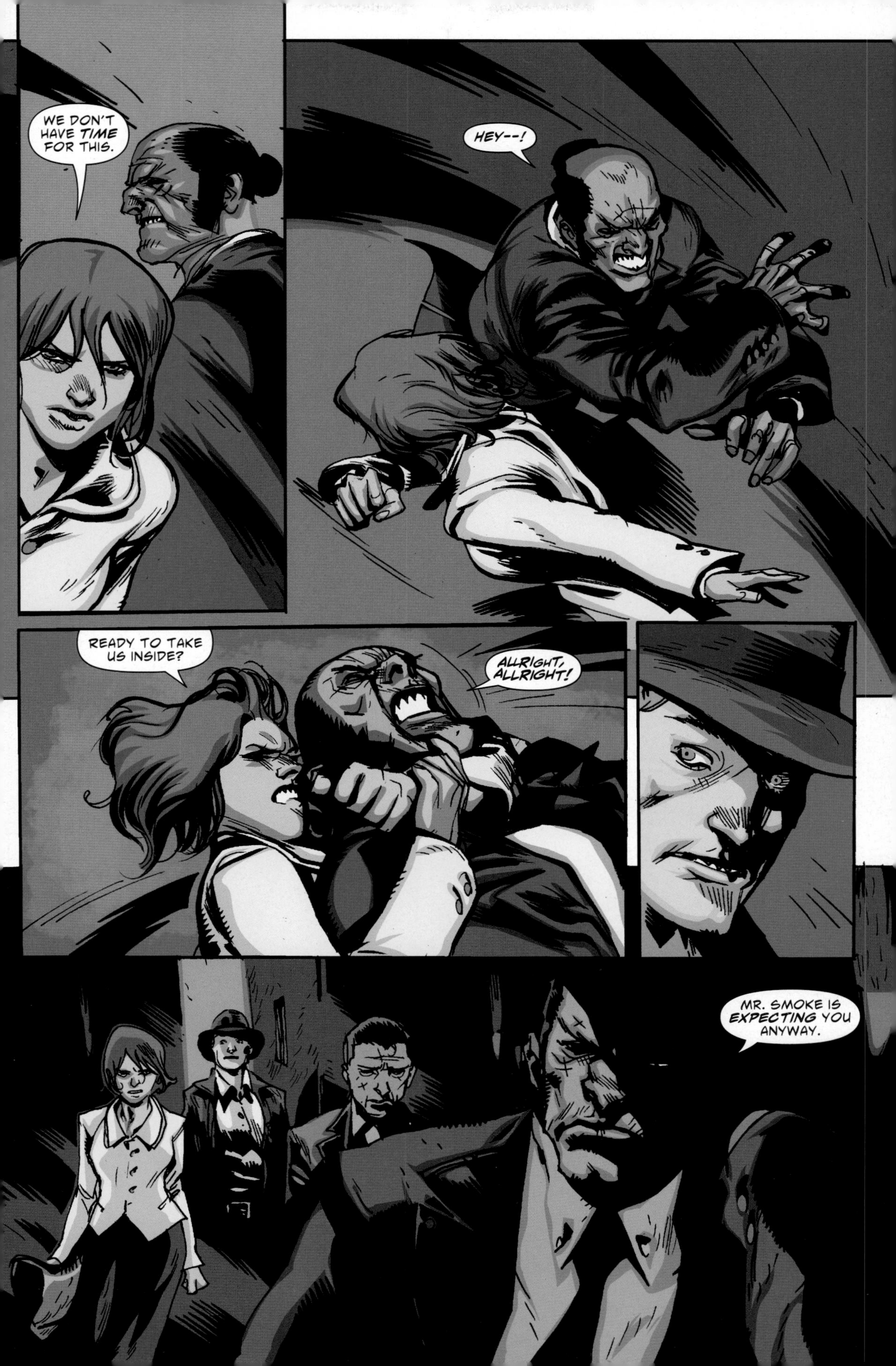

WE DON'T HAVE TIME FOR THIS.
HEY--!
READY TO TAKE US INSIDE?
ALLRIGHT, ALLRIGHT!
MR. SMOKE IS EXPECTING YOU ANYWAY.

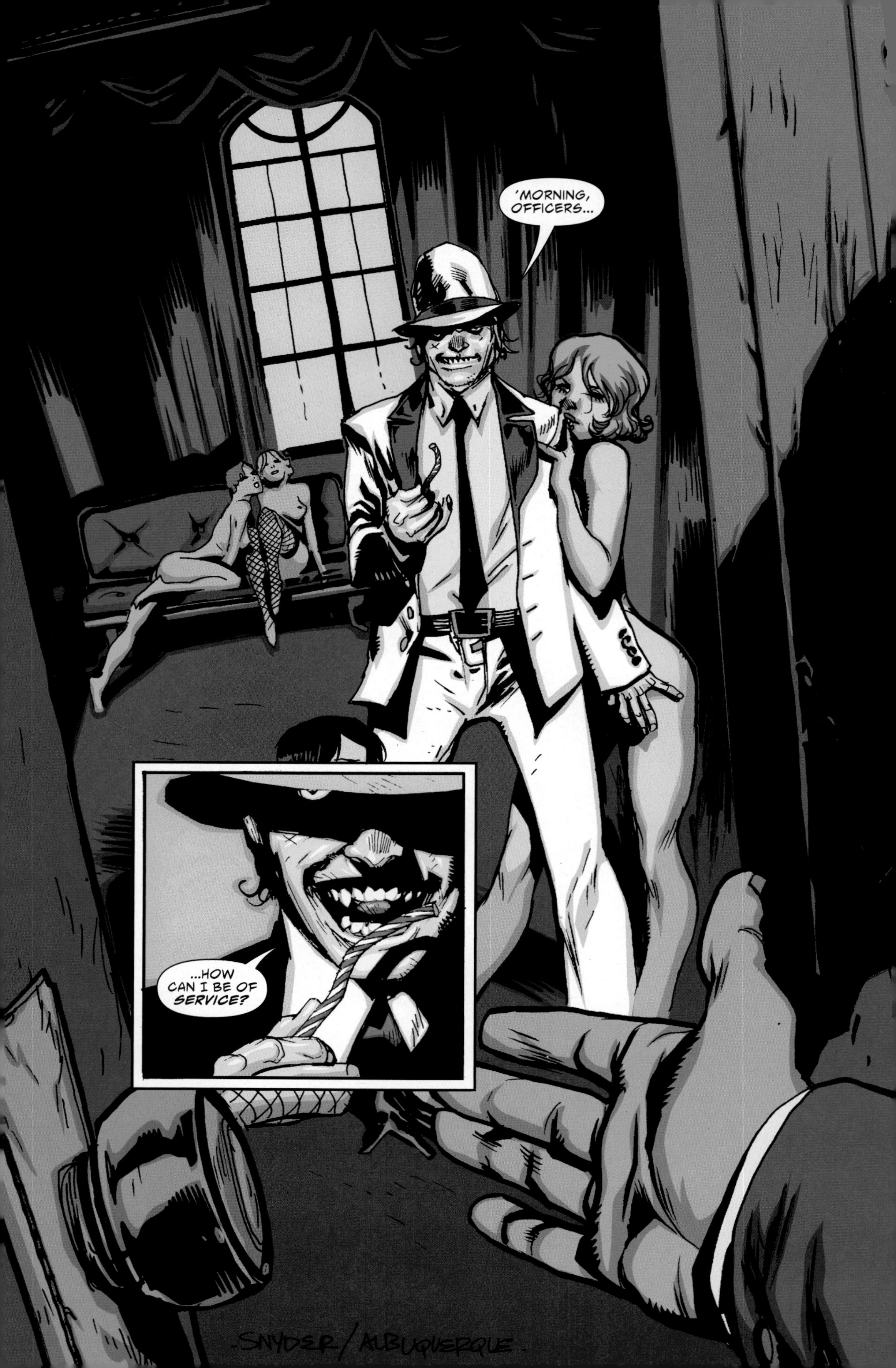
'MORNING, OFFICERS...
...HOW CAN I BE OF *SERVICE?*
-SNYDER/ALBUQUERQUE-

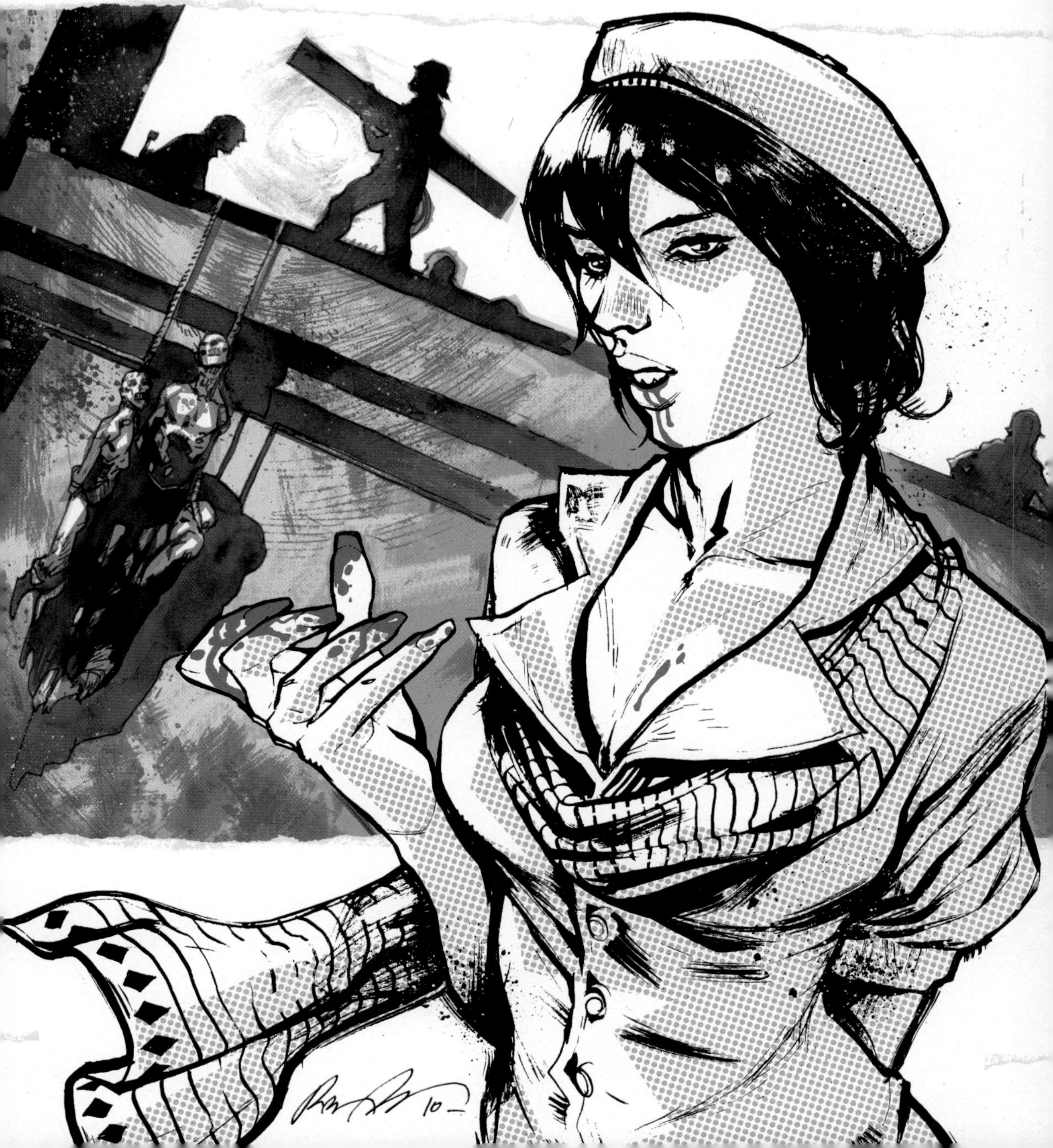

Devil in the Sand

Part Two

Rafael Albuquerque
Mateus Santolouco
(pages 37-39)
Artists

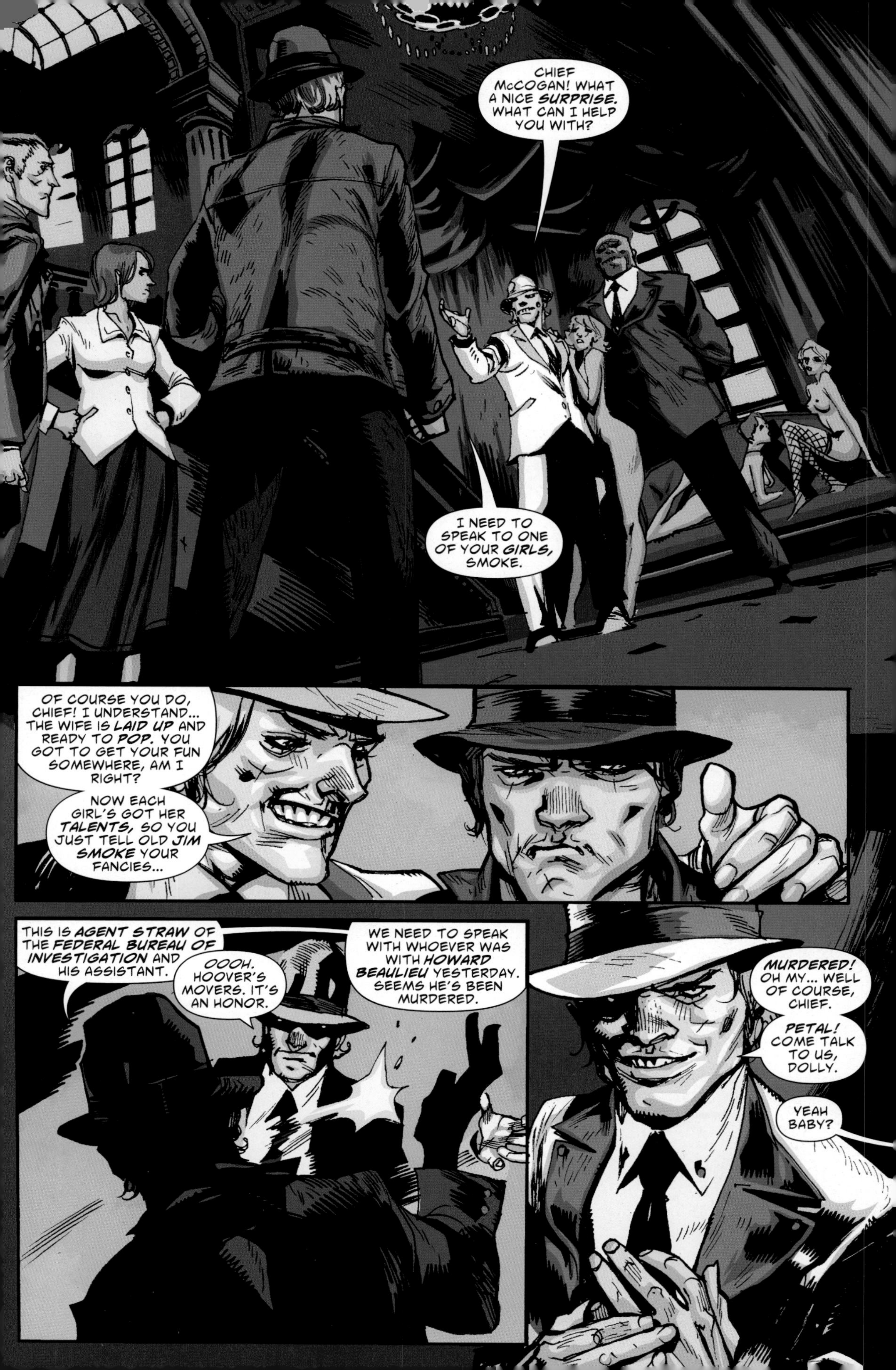
CHIEF McCOGAN! WHAT A NICE SURPRISE. WHAT CAN I HELP YOU WITH?
I NEED TO SPEAK TO ONE OF YOUR GIRLS, SMOKE.
OF COURSE YOU DO, CHIEF! I UNDERSTAND... THE WIFE IS LAID UP AND READY TO POP. YOU GOT TO GET YOUR FUN SOMEWHERE, AM I RIGHT?
NOW EACH GIRL'S GOT HER TALENTS, SO YOU JUST TELL OLD JIM SMOKE YOUR FANCIES...
THIS IS AGENT STRAW OF THE FEDERAL BUREAU OF INVESTIGATION AND HIS ASSISTANT.
OOOH. HOOVER'S MOVERS. IT'S AN HONOR.
WE NEED TO SPEAK WITH WHOEVER WAS WITH HOWARD BEAULIEU YESTERDAY. SEEMS HE'S BEEN MURDERED.
MURDERED! OH MY... WELL OF COURSE, CHIEF.
PETAL! COME TALK TO US, DOLLY.
YEAH BABY?

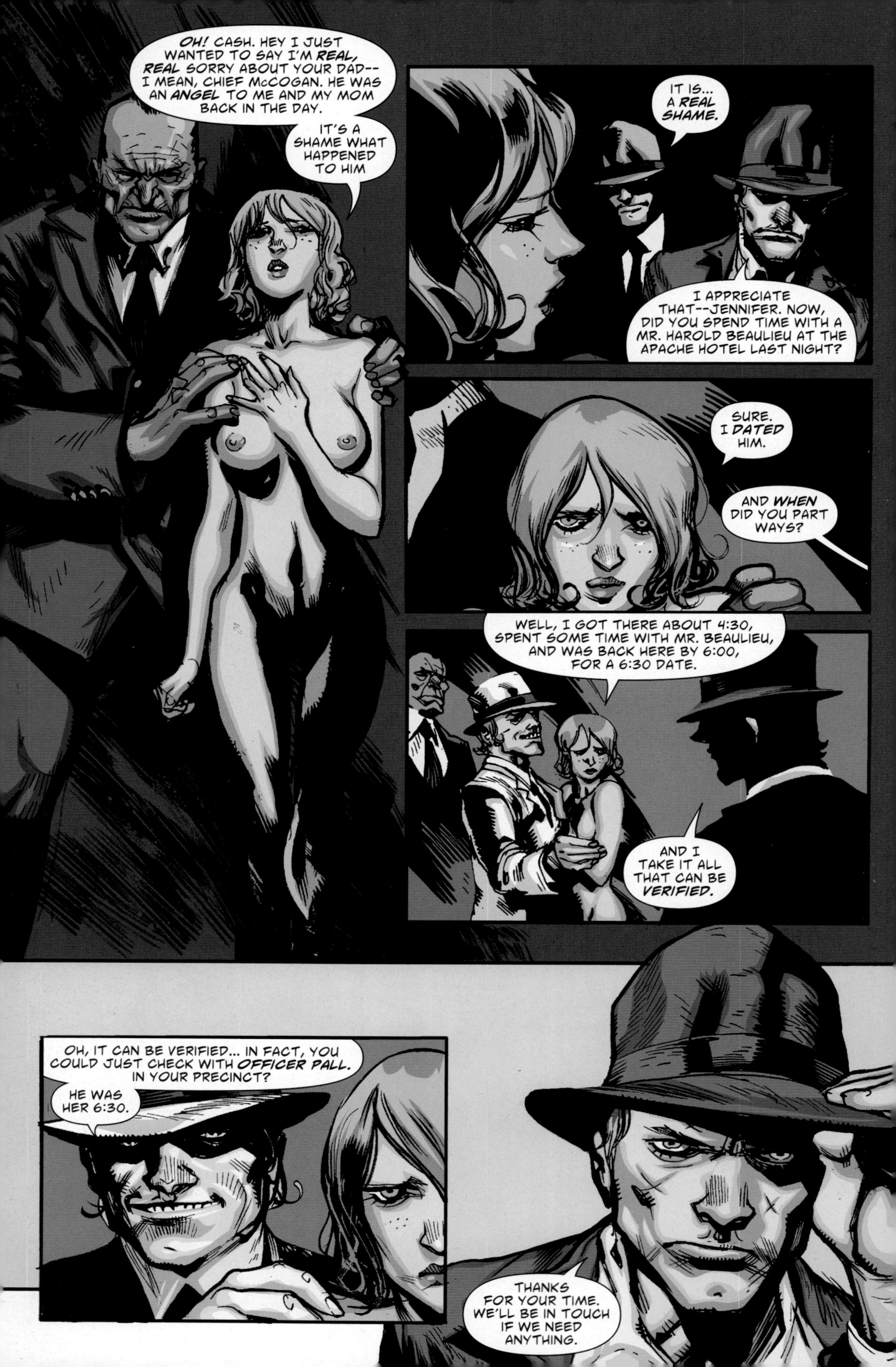

OH! CASH. HEY I JUST WANTED TO SAY I'M REAL, REAL SORRY ABOUT YOUR DAD-- I MEAN, CHIEF McCOGAN. HE WAS AN ANGEL TO ME AND MY MOM BACK IN THE DAY.
IT'S A SHAME WHAT HAPPENED TO HIM
IT IS... A REAL SHAME.
I APPRECIATE THAT--JENNIFER. NOW, DID YOU SPEND TIME WITH A MR. HAROLD BEAULIEU AT THE APACHE HOTEL LAST NIGHT?
SURE. I DATED HIM.
AND WHEN DID YOU PART WAYS?
WELL, I GOT THERE ABOUT 4:30, SPENT SOME TIME WITH MR. BEAULIEU, AND WAS BACK HERE BY 6:00, FOR A 6:30 DATE.
AND I TAKE IT ALL THAT CAN BE VERIFIED.
OH, IT CAN BE VERIFIED... IN FACT, YOU COULD JUST CHECK WITH OFFICER PALL. IN YOUR PRECINCT?
HE WAS HER 6:30.
THANKS FOR YOUR TIME. WE'LL BE IN TOUCH IF WE NEED ANYTHING.

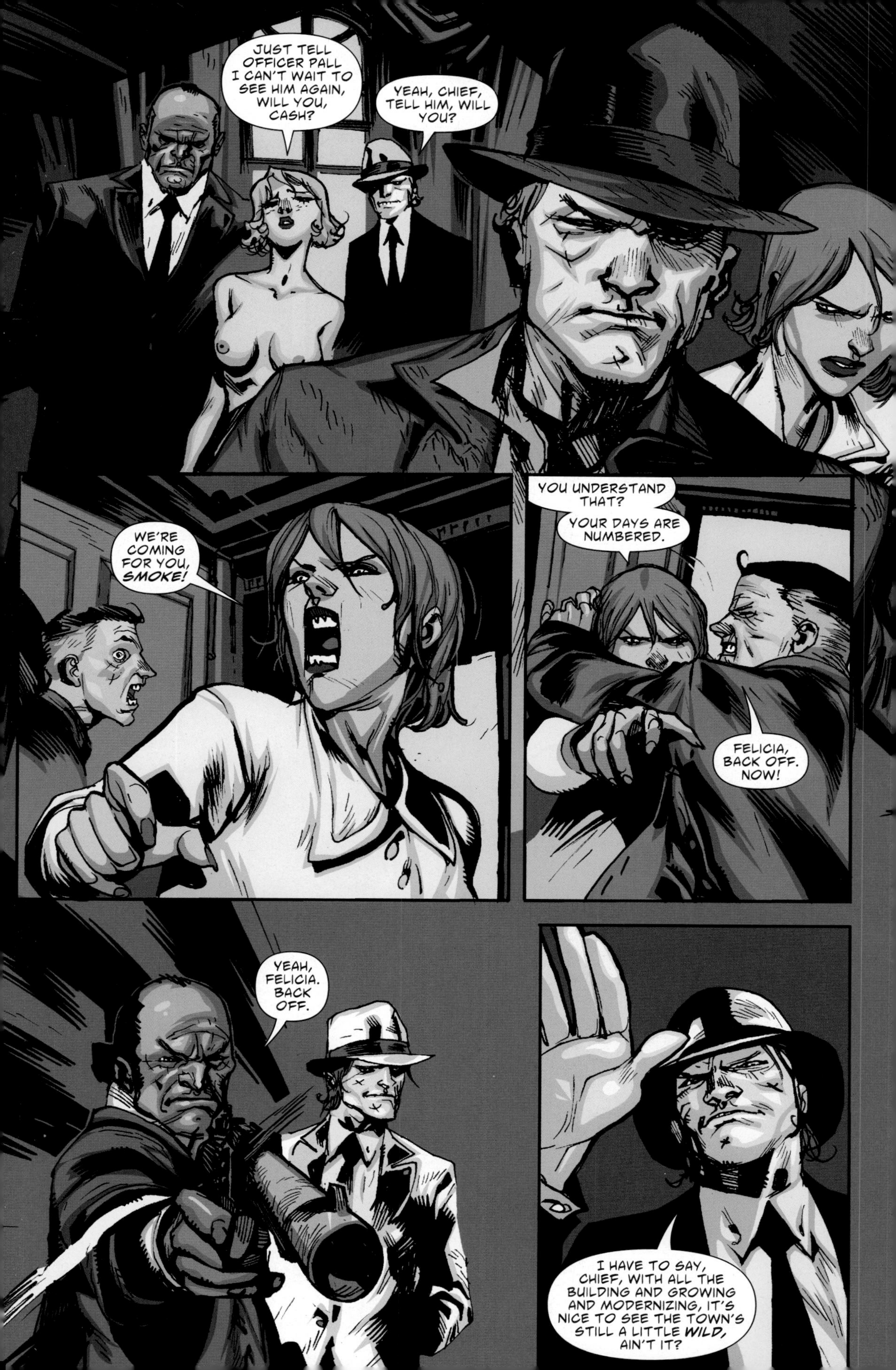
JUST TELL OFFICER PALL I CAN'T WAIT TO SEE HIM AGAIN, WILL YOU, CASH?
YEAH, CHIEF, TELL HIM, WILL YOU?
WE'RE COMING FOR YOU, *SMOKE!*
YOU UNDERSTAND THAT?
YOUR DAYS ARE NUMBERED.
FELICIA, BACK OFF. NOW!
YEAH, FELICIA. BACK OFF.
I HAVE TO SAY, CHIEF, WITH ALL THE BUILDING AND GROWING AND MODERNIZING, IT'S NICE TO SEE THE TOWN'S STILL A LITTLE *WILD,* AIN'T IT?

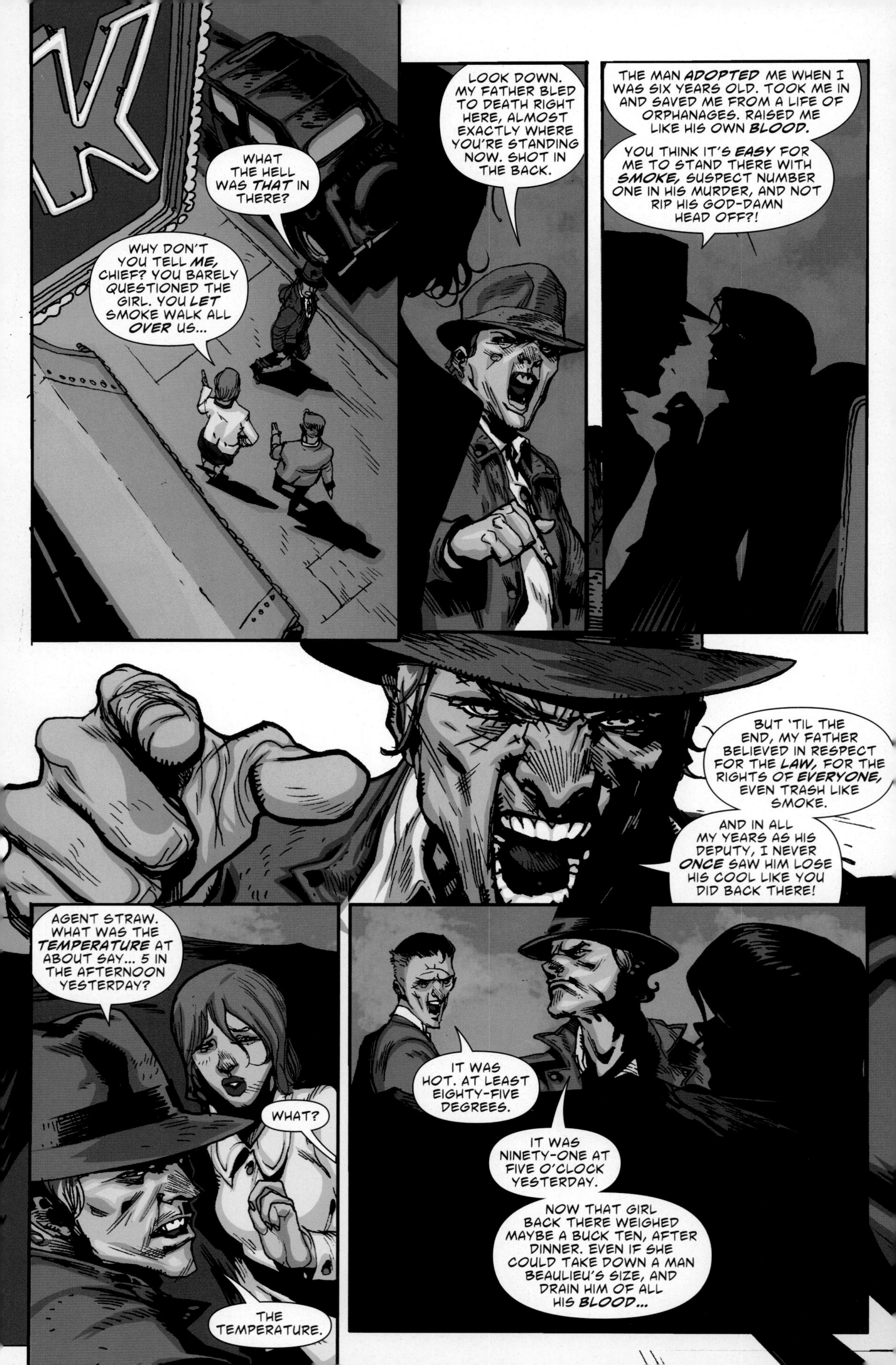

WHAT THE HELL WAS THAT IN THERE?
WHY DON'T YOU TELL ME, CHIEF? YOU BARELY QUESTIONED THE GIRL. YOU LET SMOKE WALK ALL OVER US...
LOOK DOWN. MY FATHER BLED TO DEATH RIGHT HERE, ALMOST EXACTLY WHERE YOU'RE STANDING NOW. SHOT IN THE BACK.
THE MAN ADOPTED ME WHEN I WAS SIX YEARS OLD. TOOK ME IN AND SAVED ME FROM A LIFE OF ORPHANAGES. RAISED ME LIKE HIS OWN BLOOD.
YOU THINK IT'S EASY FOR ME TO STAND THERE WITH SMOKE, SUSPECT NUMBER ONE IN HIS MURDER, AND NOT RIP HIS GOD-DAMN HEAD OFF?!
BUT 'TIL THE END, MY FATHER BELIEVED IN RESPECT FOR THE LAW, FOR THE RIGHTS OF EVERYONE, EVEN TRASH LIKE SMOKE.
AND IN ALL MY YEARS AS HIS DEPUTY, I NEVER ONCE SAW HIM LOSE HIS COOL LIKE YOU DID BACK THERE!
AGENT STRAW. WHAT WAS THE TEMPERATURE AT ABOUT SAY... 5 IN THE AFTERNOON YESTERDAY?
WHAT?
THE TEMPERATURE.
IT WAS HOT. AT LEAST EIGHTY-FIVE DEGREES.
IT WAS NINETY-ONE AT FIVE O'CLOCK YESTERDAY.
NOW THAT GIRL BACK THERE WEIGHED MAYBE A BUCK TEN, AFTER DINNER. EVEN IF SHE COULD TAKE DOWN A MAN BEAULIEU'S SIZE, AND DRAIN HIM OF ALL HIS BLOOD...

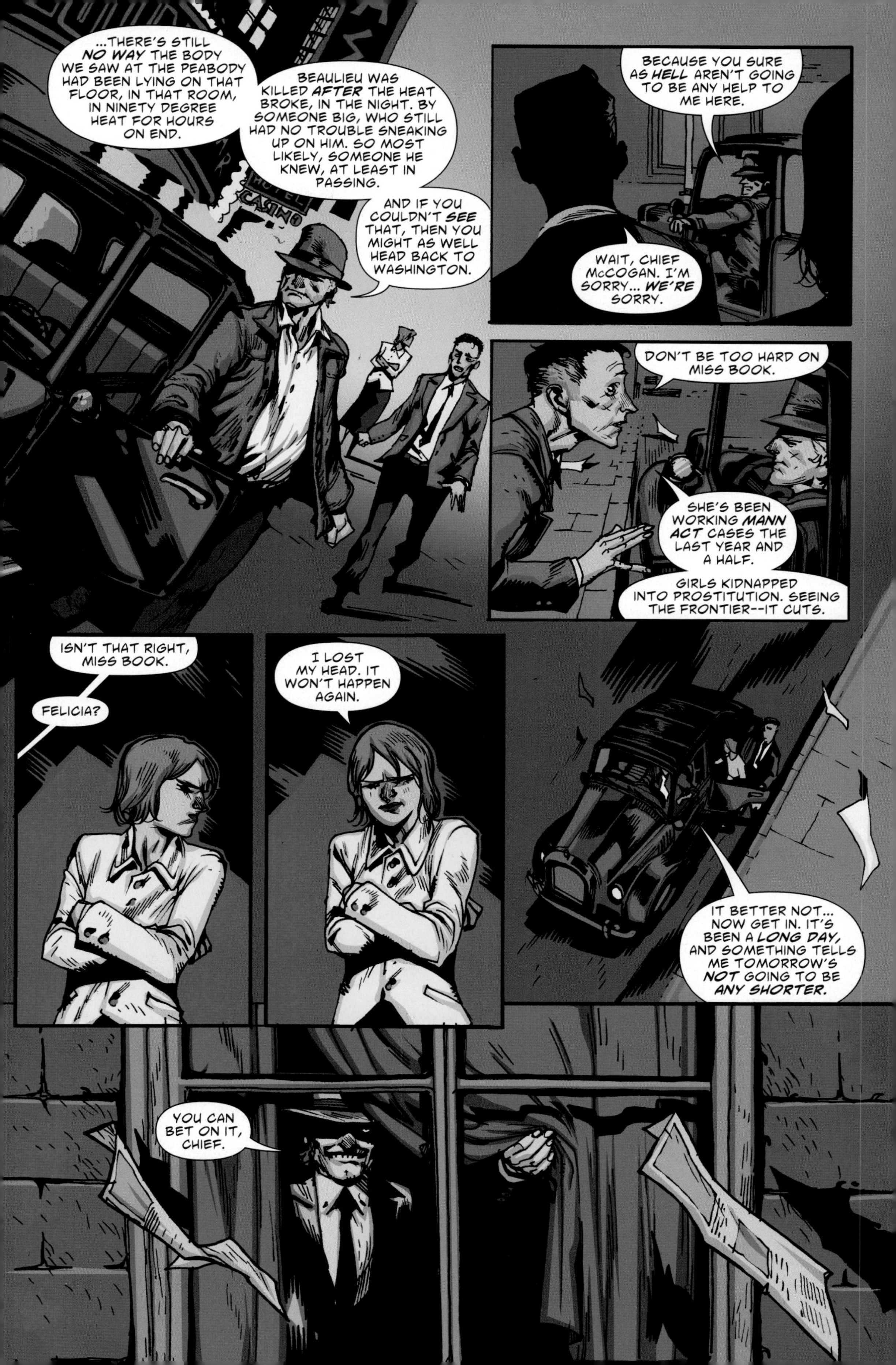
...THERE'S STILL NO WAY THE BODY WE SAW AT THE PEABODY HAD BEEN LYING ON THAT FLOOR, IN THAT ROOM, IN NINETY DEGREE HEAT FOR HOURS ON END.
BEAULIEU WAS KILLED AFTER THE HEAT BROKE, IN THE NIGHT. BY SOMEONE BIG, WHO STILL HAD NO TROUBLE SNEAKING UP ON HIM. SO MOST LIKELY, SOMEONE HE KNEW, AT LEAST IN PASSING.
AND IF YOU COULDN'T SEE THAT, THEN YOU MIGHT AS WELL HEAD BACK TO WASHINGTON.
HOTEL
CASINO
BECAUSE YOU SURE AS HELL AREN'T GOING TO BE ANY HELP TO ME HERE.
WAIT, CHIEF McCOGAN. I'M SORRY... WE'RE SORRY.
DON'T BE TOO HARD ON MISS BOOK.
SHE'S BEEN WORKING MANN ACT CASES THE LAST YEAR AND A HALF.
GIRLS KIDNAPPED INTO PROSTITUTION. SEEING THE FRONTIER--IT CUTS.
ISN'T THAT RIGHT, MISS BOOK.
FELICIA?
I LOST MY HEAD. IT WON'T HAPPEN AGAIN.
IT BETTER NOT... NOW GET IN. IT'S BEEN A LONG DAY, AND SOMETHING TELLS ME TOMORROW'S NOT GOING TO BE ANY SHORTER.
YOU CAN BET ON IT, CHIEF.

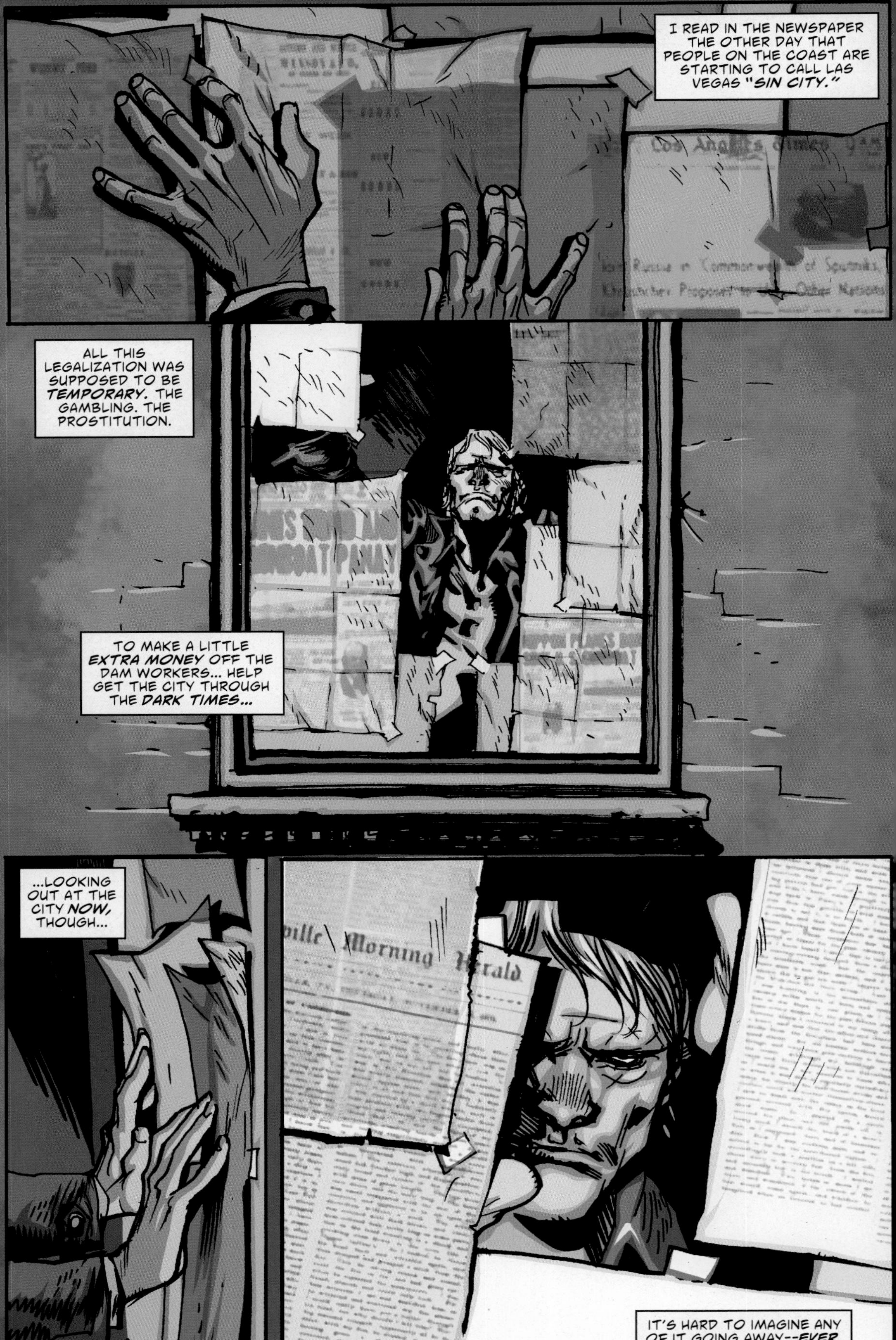

I READ IN THE NEWSPAPER THE OTHER DAY THAT PEOPLE ON THE COAST ARE STARTING TO CALL LAS VEGAS "SIN CITY."
ALL THIS LEGALIZATION WAS SUPPOSED TO BE TEMPORARY. THE GAMBLING. THE PROSTITUTION.
TO MAKE A LITTLE EXTRA MONEY OFF THE DAM WORKERS... HELP GET THE CITY THROUGH THE DARK TIMES...
...LOOKING OUT AT THE CITY NOW, THOUGH...
IT'S HARD TO IMAGINE ANY OF IT GOING AWAY--EVER.

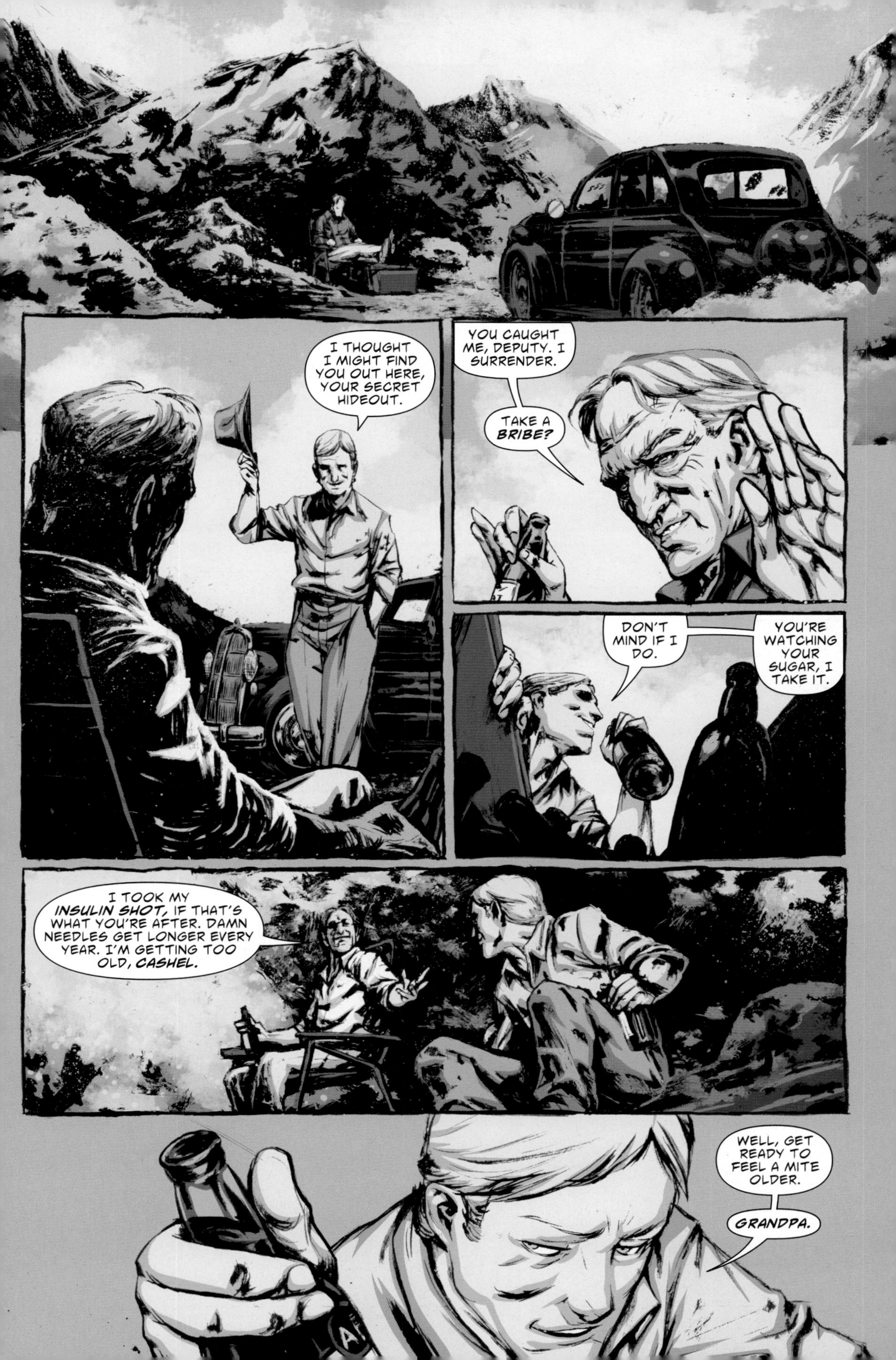
I THOUGHT I MIGHT FIND YOU OUT HERE, YOUR SECRET HIDEOUT.
YOU CAUGHT ME, DEPUTY. I SURRENDER.
TAKE A *BRIBE?*
DON'T MIND IF I DO.
YOU'RE WATCHING YOUR SUGAR, I TAKE IT.
I TOOK MY *INSULIN SHOT,* IF THAT'S WHAT YOU'RE AFTER. DAMN NEEDLES GET LONGER EVERY YEAR. I'M GETTING TOO OLD, *CASHEL.*
WELL, GET READY TO FEEL A MITE OLDER.
GRANDPA.

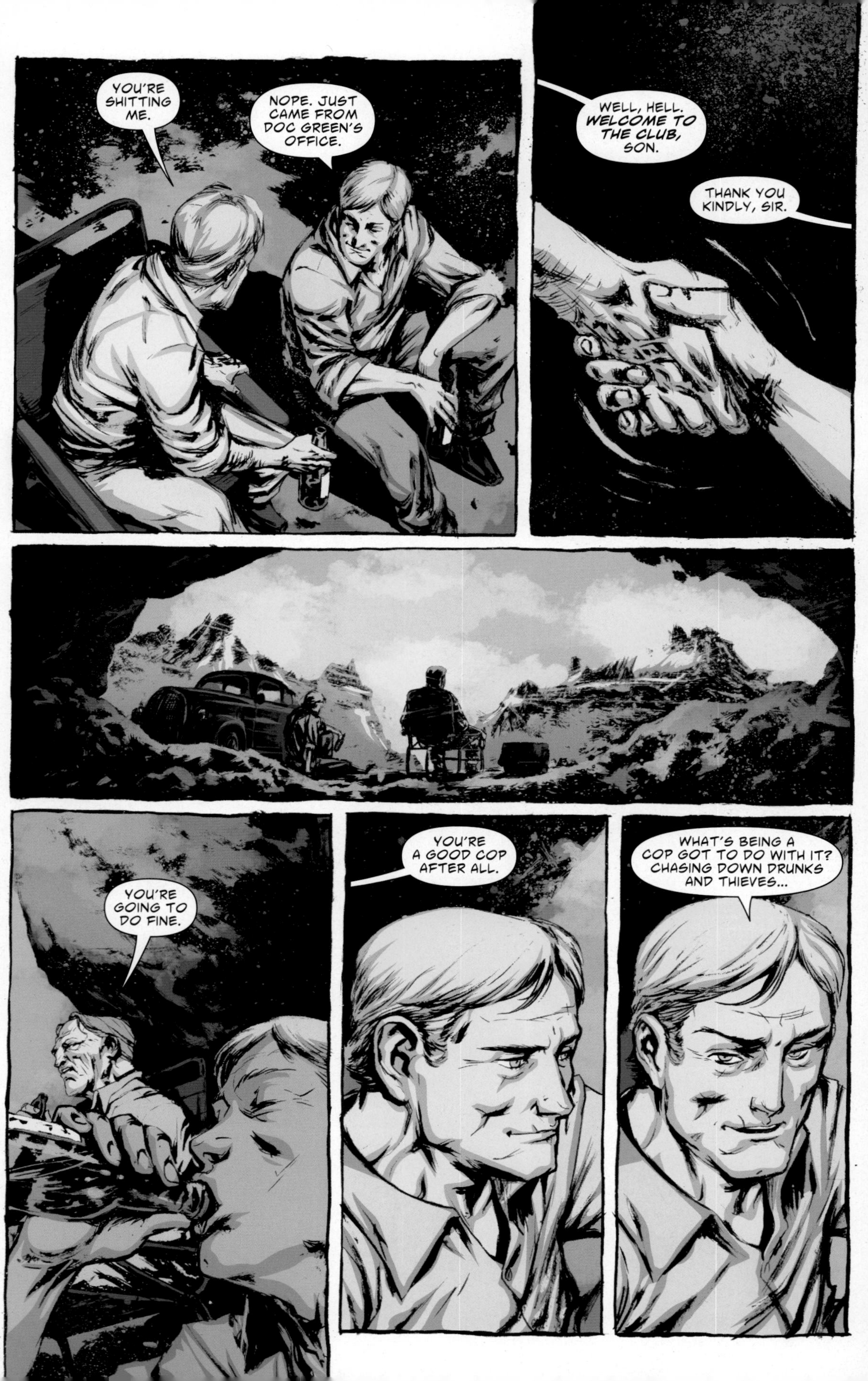
YOU'RE SHITTING ME.
NOPE. JUST CAME FROM DOC GREEN'S OFFICE.
WELL, HELL. *WELCOME TO THE CLUB,* SON.
THANK YOU KINDLY, SIR.
YOU'RE GOING TO DO FINE.
YOU'RE A GOOD COP AFTER ALL.
WHAT'S BEING A COP GOT TO DO WITH IT? CHASING DOWN DRUNKS AND THIEVES...

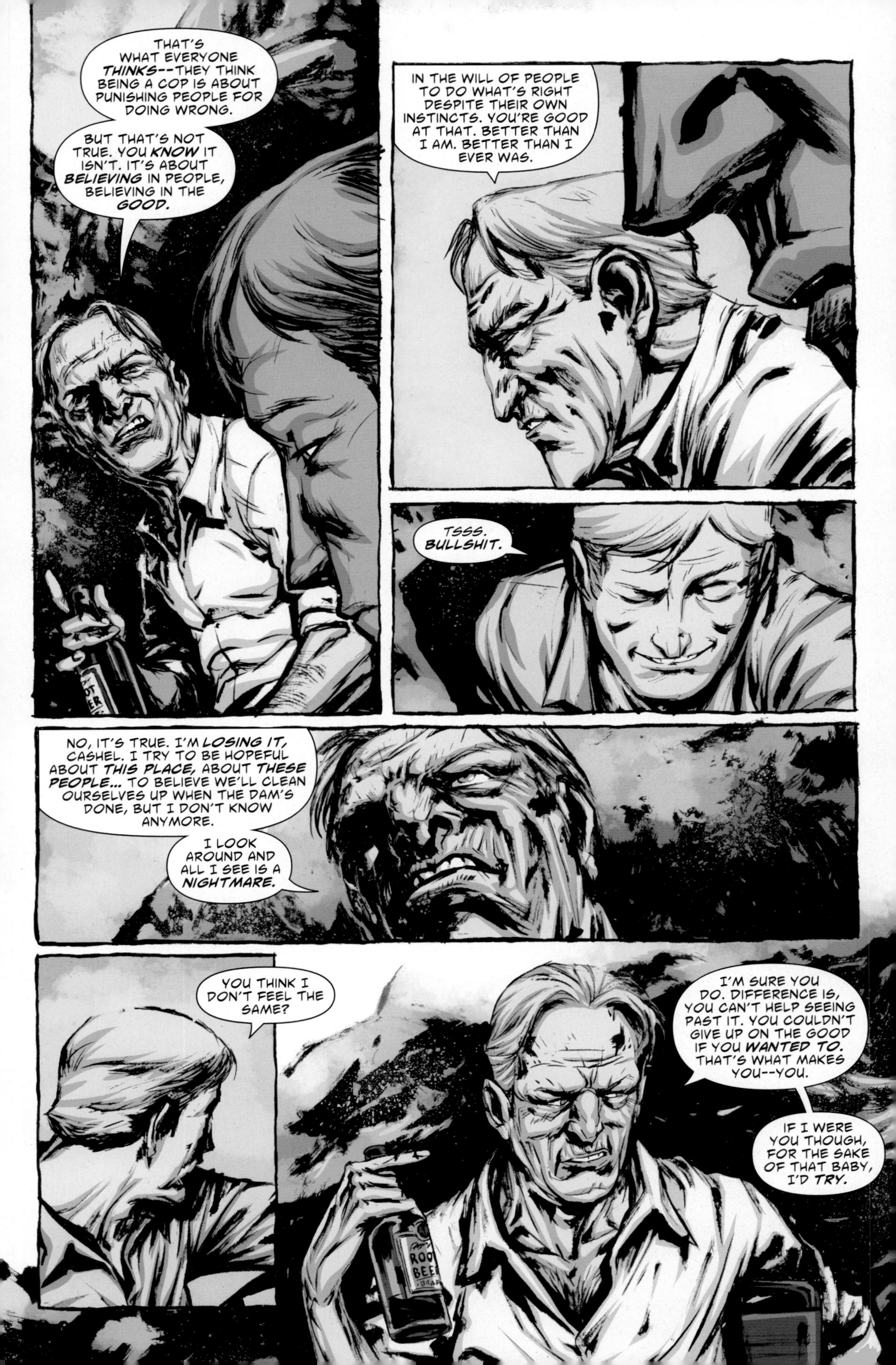
THAT'S WHAT EVERYONE THINKS--THEY THINK BEING A COP IS ABOUT PUNISHING PEOPLE FOR DOING WRONG.
BUT THAT'S NOT TRUE. YOU KNOW IT ISN'T. IT'S ABOUT BELIEVING IN PEOPLE, BELIEVING IN THE GOOD.
IN THE WILL OF PEOPLE TO DO WHAT'S RIGHT DESPITE THEIR OWN INSTINCTS. YOU'RE GOOD AT THAT. BETTER THAN I AM. BETTER THAN I EVER WAS.
TSSS. BULLSHIT.
NO, IT'S TRUE. I'M LOSING IT, CASHEL. I TRY TO BE HOPEFUL ABOUT THIS PLACE, ABOUT THESE PEOPLE... TO BELIEVE WE'LL CLEAN OURSELVES UP WHEN THE DAM'S DONE, BUT I DON'T KNOW ANYMORE.
I LOOK AROUND AND ALL I SEE IS A NIGHTMARE.
YOU THINK I DON'T FEEL THE SAME?
I'M SURE YOU DO. DIFFERENCE IS, YOU CAN'T HELP SEEING PAST IT. YOU COULDN'T GIVE UP ON THE GOOD IF YOU WANTED TO. THAT'S WHAT MAKES YOU--YOU.
IF I WERE YOU THOUGH, FOR THE SAKE OF THAT BABY, I'D TRY.

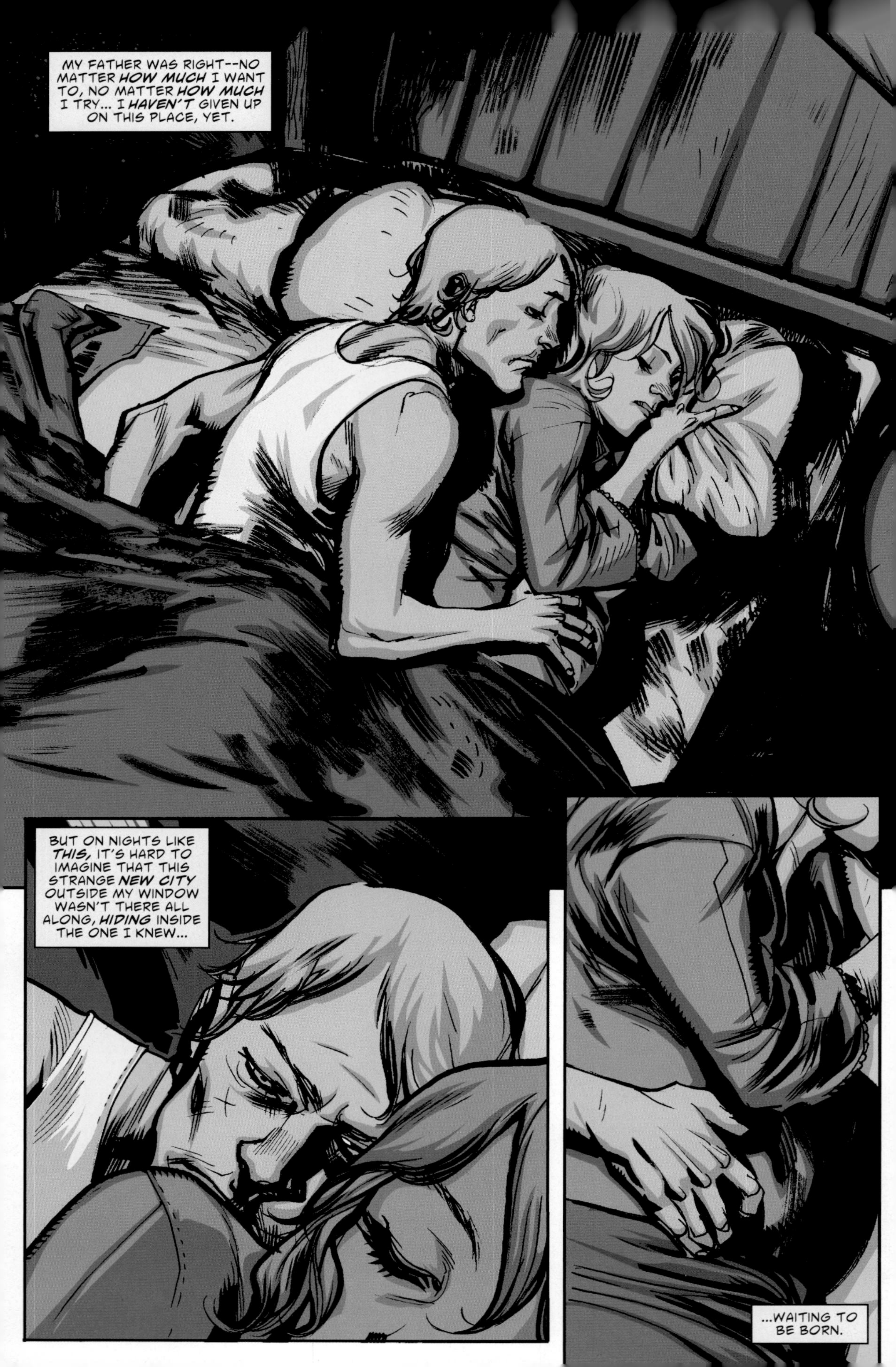
MY FATHER WAS RIGHT--NO MATTER HOW MUCH I WANT TO, NO MATTER HOW MUCH I TRY... I HAVEN'T GIVEN UP ON THIS PLACE, YET.
BUT ON NIGHTS LIKE THIS, IT'S HARD TO IMAGINE THAT THIS STRANGE NEW CITY OUTSIDE MY WINDOW WASN'T THERE ALL ALONG, HIDING INSIDE THE ONE I KNEW...
...WAITING TO BE BORN.

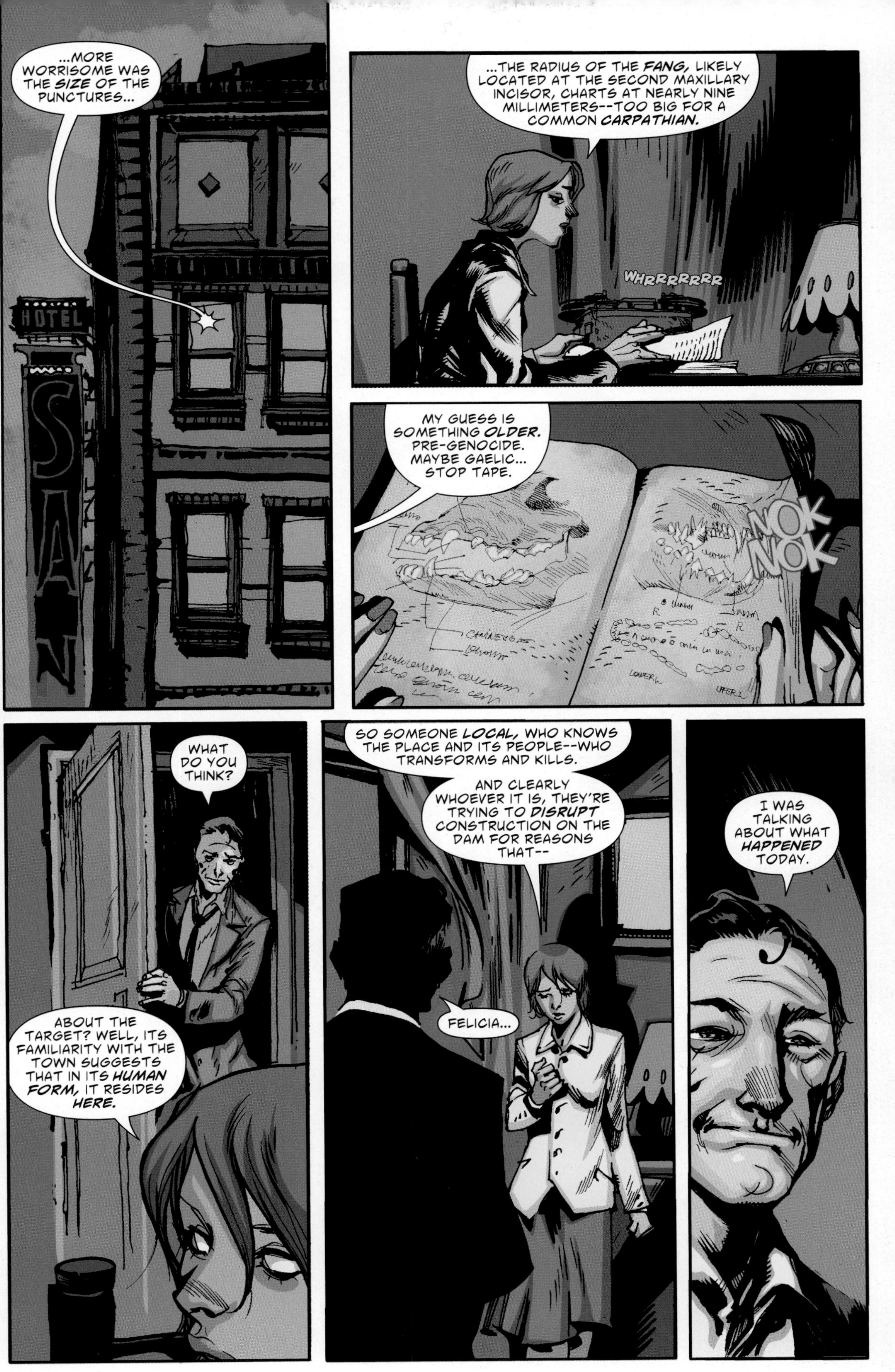
...MORE WORRISOME WAS THE SIZE OF THE PUNCTURES...
HOTEL
...THE RADIUS OF THE FANG, LIKELY LOCATED AT THE SECOND MAXILLARY INCISOR, CHARTS AT NEARLY NINE MILLIMETERS--TOO BIG FOR A COMMON CARPATHIAN.
WHRRRRRRR
MY GUESS IS SOMETHING OLDER. PRE-GENOCIDE. MAYBE GAELIC... STOP TAPE.
NOK NOK
WHAT DO YOU THINK?
ABOUT THE TARGET? WELL, ITS FAMILIARITY WITH THE TOWN SUGGESTS THAT IN ITS HUMAN FORM, IT RESIDES HERE.
SO SOMEONE LOCAL, WHO KNOWS THE PLACE AND ITS PEOPLE--WHO TRANSFORMS AND KILLS.
AND CLEARLY WHOEVER IT IS, THEY'RE TRYING TO DISRUPT CONSTRUCTION ON THE DAM FOR REASONS THAT--
FELICIA...
I WAS TALKING ABOUT WHAT HAPPENED TODAY.

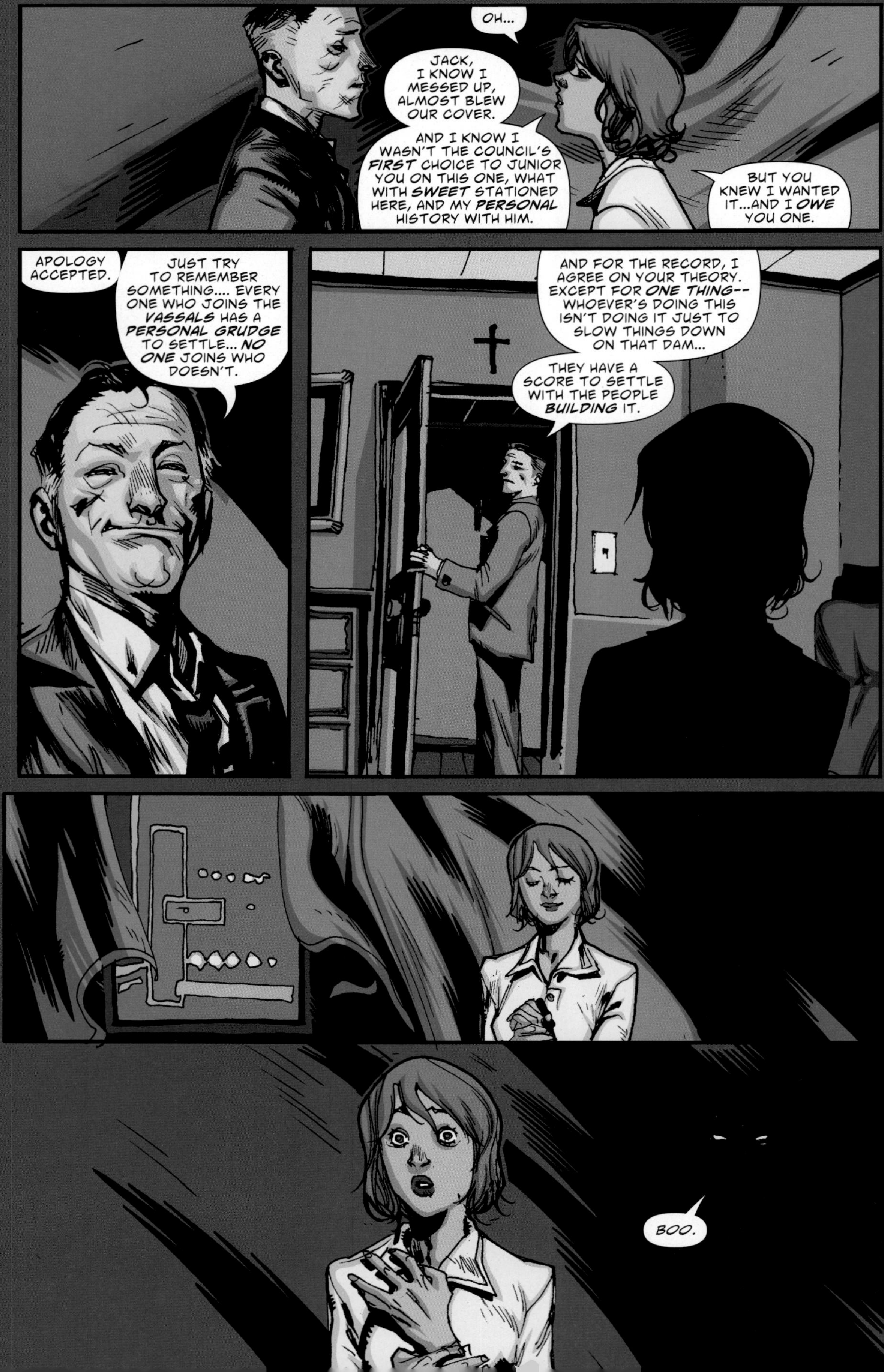
OH...
JACK, I KNOW I MESSED UP, ALMOST BLEW OUR COVER.
AND I KNOW I WASN'T THE COUNCIL'S FIRST CHOICE TO JUNIOR YOU ON THIS ONE, WHAT WITH SWEET STATIONED HERE, AND MY PERSONAL HISTORY WITH HIM.
BUT YOU KNEW I WANTED IT...AND I OWE YOU ONE.
APOLOGY ACCEPTED.
JUST TRY TO REMEMBER SOMETHING.... EVERY ONE WHO JOINS THE VASSALS HAS A PERSONAL GRUDGE TO SETTLE... NO ONE JOINS WHO DOESN'T.
AND FOR THE RECORD, I AGREE ON YOUR THEORY. EXCEPT FOR ONE THING-- WHOEVER'S DOING THIS ISN'T DOING IT JUST TO SLOW THINGS DOWN ON THAT DAM...
THEY HAVE A SCORE TO SETTLE WITH THE PEOPLE BUILDING IT.
BOO.

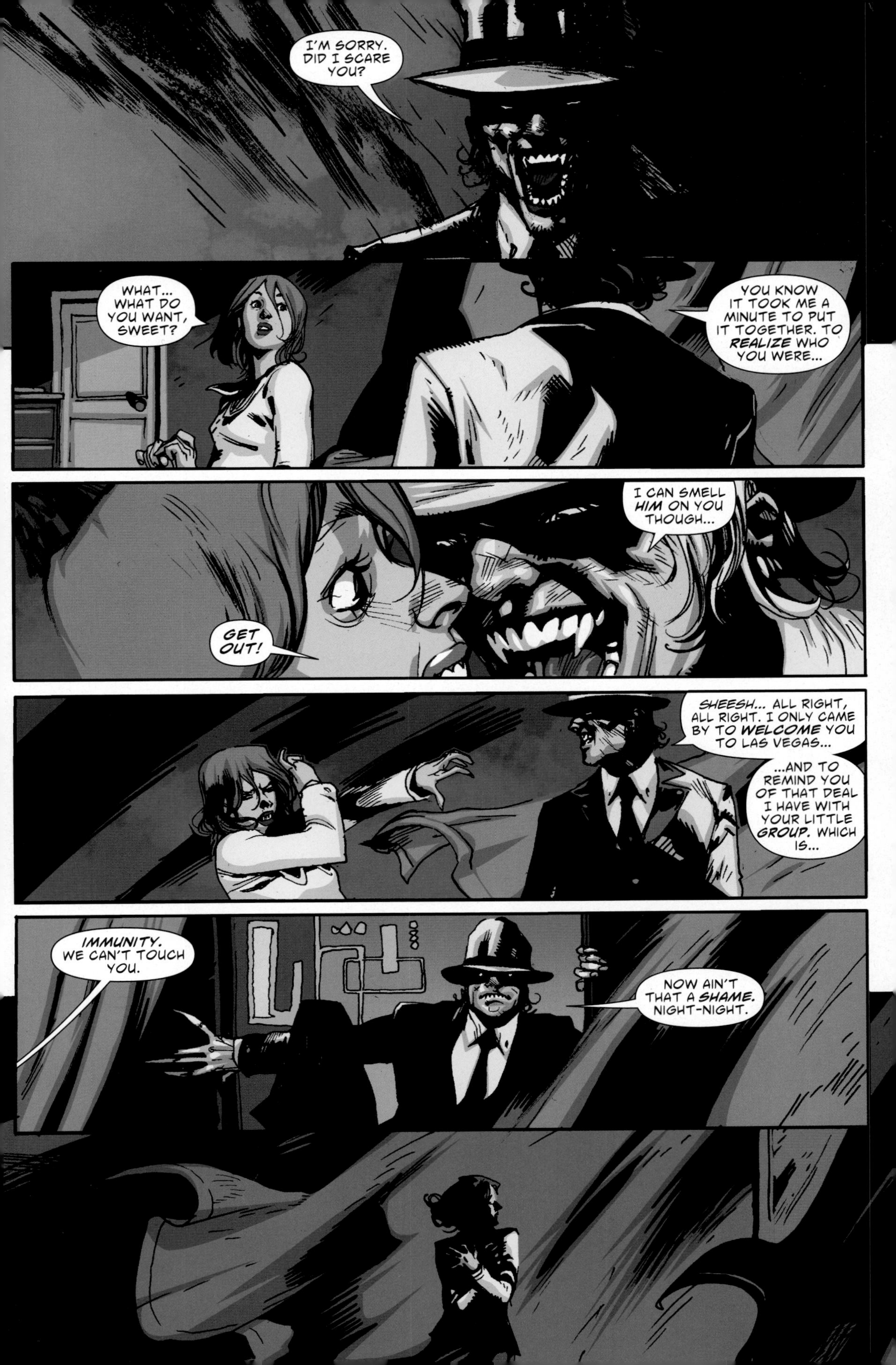
I'M SORRY. DID I SCARE YOU?
WHAT... WHAT DO YOU WANT, SWEET?
YOU KNOW IT TOOK ME A MINUTE TO PUT IT TOGETHER. TO REALIZE WHO YOU WERE...
I CAN SMELL HIM ON YOU THOUGH...
GET OUT!
SHEESH... ALL RIGHT, ALL RIGHT. I ONLY CAME BY TO WELCOME YOU TO LAS VEGAS...
...AND TO REMIND YOU OF THAT DEAL I HAVE WITH YOUR LITTLE GROUP. WHICH IS...
IMMUNITY. WE CAN'T TOUCH YOU.
NOW AIN'T THAT A SHAME. NIGHT-NIGHT.

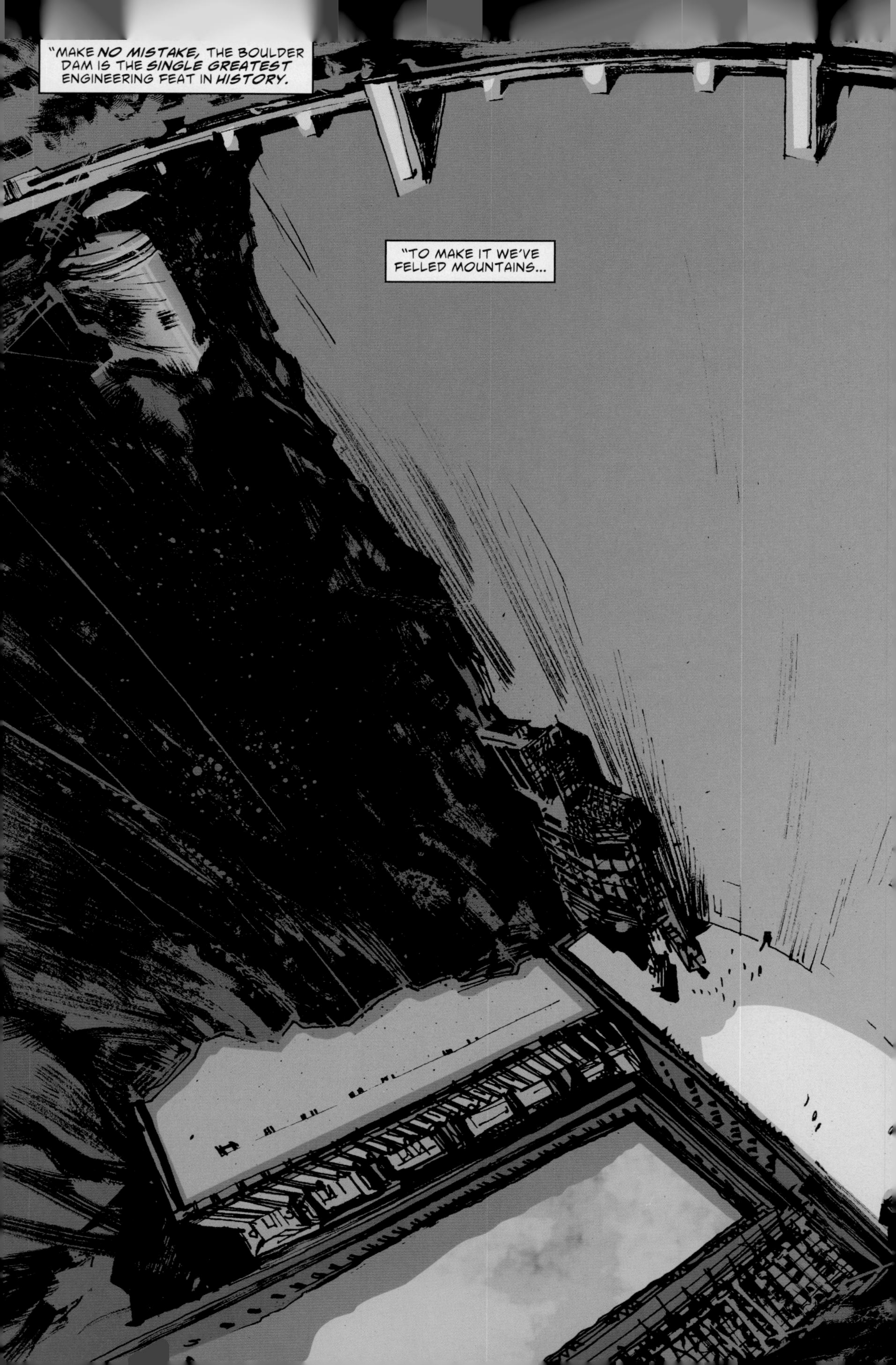
"MAKE NO MISTAKE, THE BOULDER DAM IS THE SINGLE GREATEST ENGINEERING FEAT IN HISTORY.
"TO MAKE IT WE'VE FELLED MOUNTAINS...

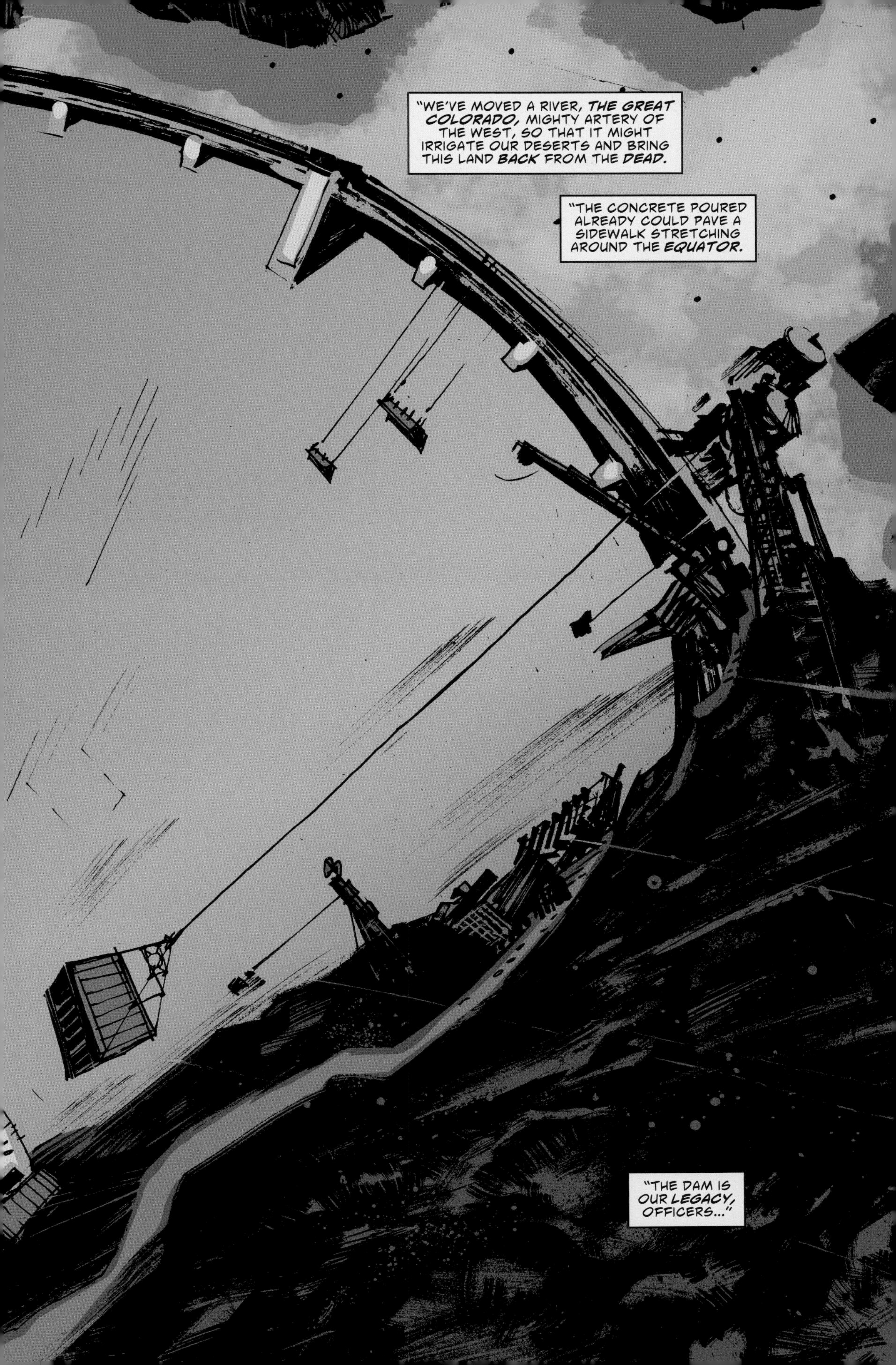
"WE'VE MOVED A RIVER, *THE GREAT COLORADO,* MIGHTY ARTERY OF THE WEST, SO THAT IT MIGHT IRRIGATE OUR DESERTS AND BRING THIS LAND *BACK* FROM THE *DEAD.*
"THE CONCRETE POURED ALREADY COULD PAVE A SIDEWALK STRETCHING AROUND THE *EQUATOR.*
"THE DAM IS OUR *LEGACY,* OFFICERS..."

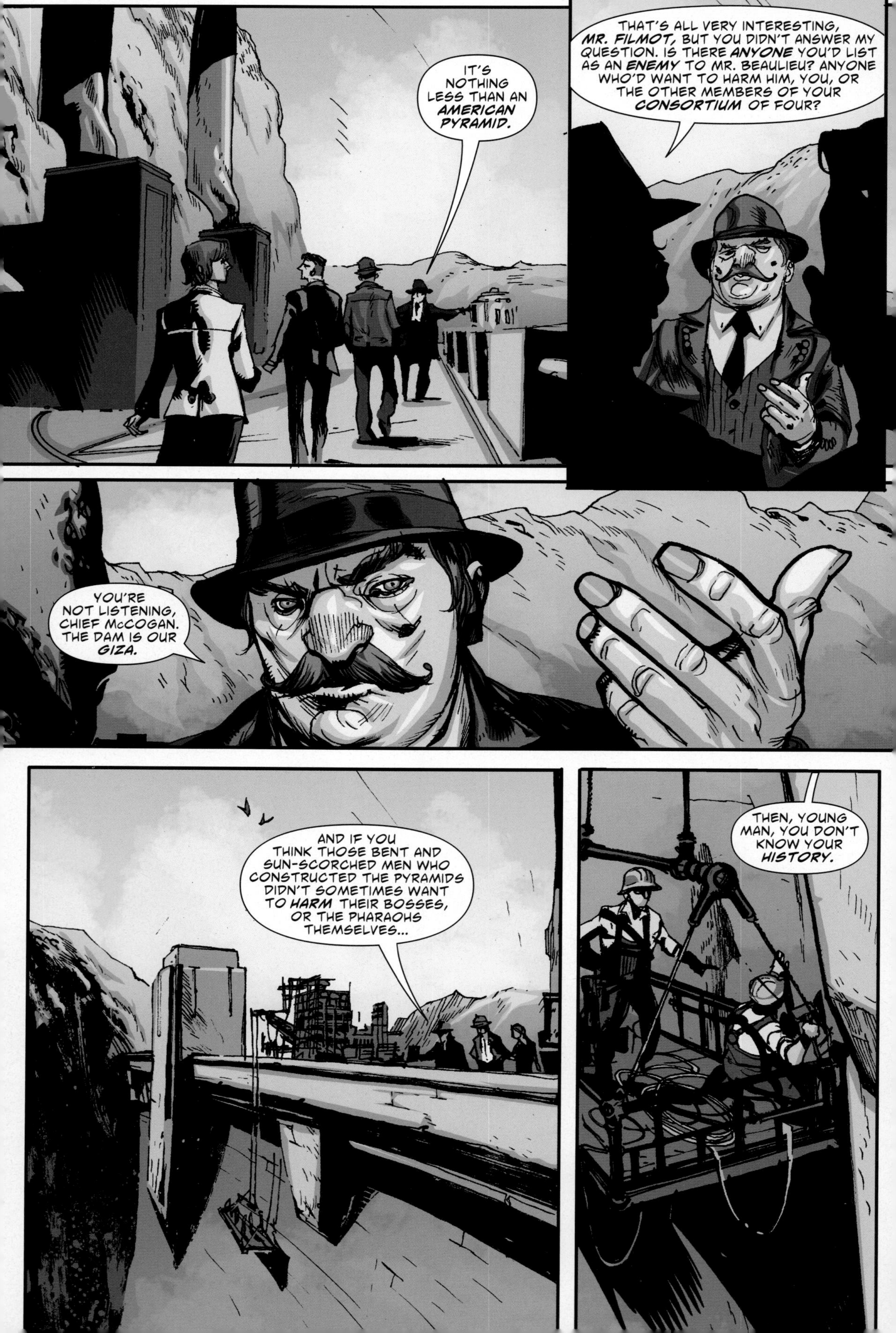
IT'S NOTHING LESS THAN AN AMERICAN PYRAMID.
THAT'S ALL VERY INTERESTING, MR. FILMOT, BUT YOU DIDN'T ANSWER MY QUESTION. IS THERE ANYONE YOU'D LIST AS AN ENEMY TO MR. BEAULIEU? ANYONE WHO'D WANT TO HARM HIM, YOU, OR THE OTHER MEMBERS OF YOUR CONSORTIUM OF FOUR?
YOU'RE NOT LISTENING, CHIEF McCOGAN. THE DAM IS OUR GIZA.
AND IF YOU THINK THOSE BENT AND SUN-SCORCHED MEN WHO CONSTRUCTED THE PYRAMIDS DIDN'T SOMETIMES WANT TO HARM THEIR BOSSES, OR THE PHARAOHS THEMSELVES...
THEN, YOUNG MAN, YOU DON'T KNOW YOUR HISTORY.

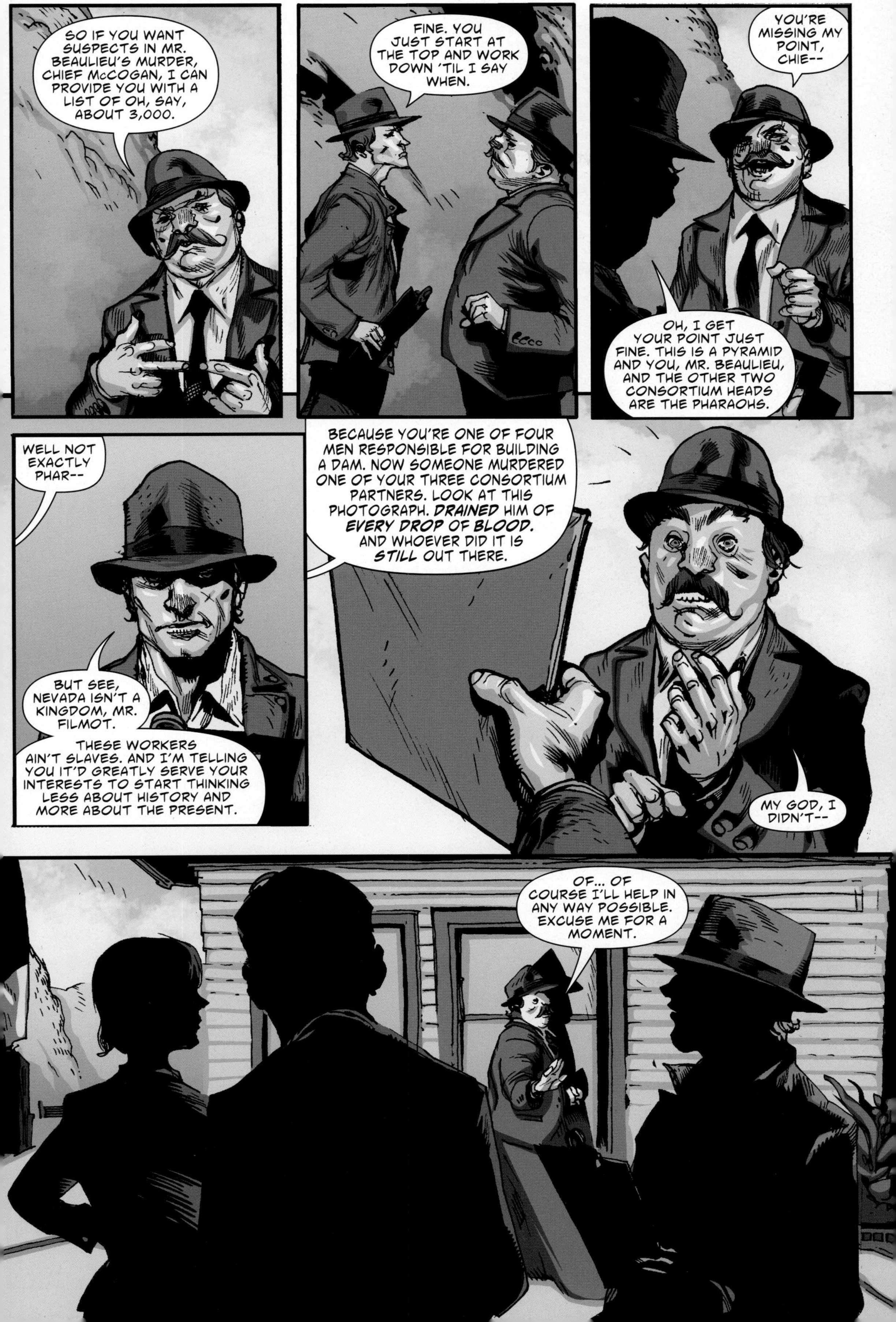
SO IF YOU WANT SUSPECTS IN MR. BEAULIEU'S MURDER, CHIEF McCOGAN, I CAN PROVIDE YOU WITH A LIST OF OH, SAY, ABOUT 3,000.
FINE. YOU JUST START AT THE TOP AND WORK DOWN 'TIL I SAY WHEN.
YOU'RE MISSING MY POINT, CHIE--
OH, I GET YOUR POINT JUST FINE. THIS IS A PYRAMID AND YOU, MR. BEAULIEU, AND THE OTHER TWO CONSORTIUM HEADS ARE THE PHARAOHS.
WELL NOT EXACTLY PHAR--
BUT SEE, NEVADA ISN'T A KINGDOM, MR. FILMOT.
THESE WORKERS AIN'T SLAVES. AND I'M TELLING YOU IT'D GREATLY SERVE YOUR INTERESTS TO START THINKING LESS ABOUT HISTORY AND MORE ABOUT THE PRESENT.
BECAUSE YOU'RE ONE OF FOUR MEN RESPONSIBLE FOR BUILDING A DAM. NOW SOMEONE MURDERED ONE OF YOUR THREE CONSORTIUM PARTNERS. LOOK AT THIS PHOTOGRAPH. DRAINED HIM OF EVERY DROP OF BLOOD. AND WHOEVER DID IT IS STILL OUT THERE.
MY GOD, I DIDN'T--
OF... OF COURSE I'LL HELP IN ANY WAY POSSIBLE. EXCUSE ME FOR A MOMENT.

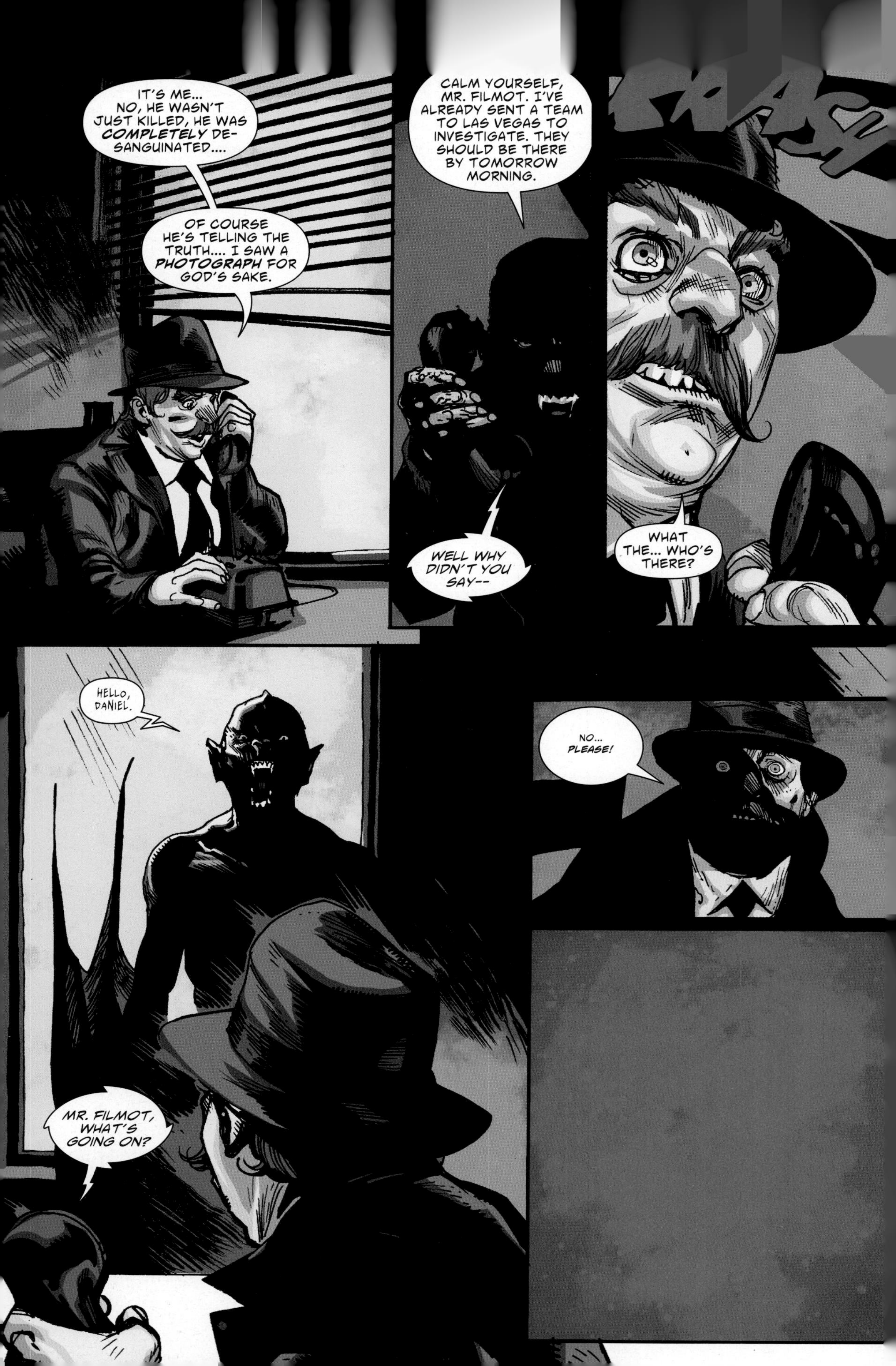
IT'S ME... NO, HE WASN'T JUST KILLED, HE WAS *COMPLETELY* DE-SANGUINATED....
OF COURSE HE'S TELLING THE TRUTH.... I SAW A *PHOTOGRAPH* FOR GOD'S SAKE.
CALM YOURSELF, MR. FILMOT. I'VE ALREADY SENT A TEAM TO LAS VEGAS TO INVESTIGATE. THEY SHOULD BE THERE BY TOMORROW MORNING.
WELL WHY DIDN'T YOU SAY--
WHAT THE... WHO'S THERE?
HELLO, DANIEL.
MR. FILMOT, WHAT'S GOING ON?
NO... PLEASE!

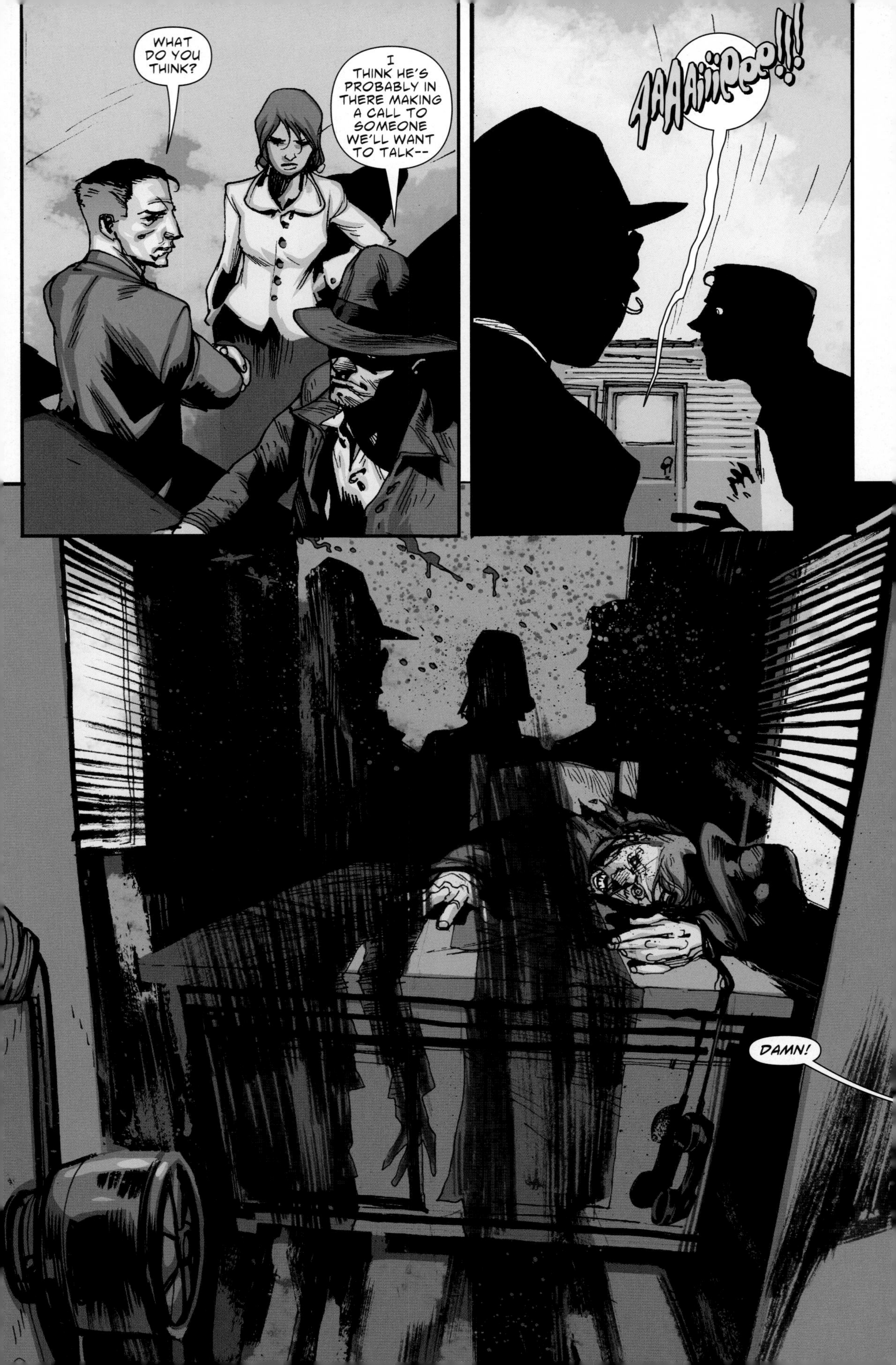
WHAT DO YOU THINK?
I THINK HE'S PROBABLY IN THERE MAKING A CALL TO SOMEONE WE'LL WANT TO TALK--
AAAAiiiEEE!!!
DAMN!

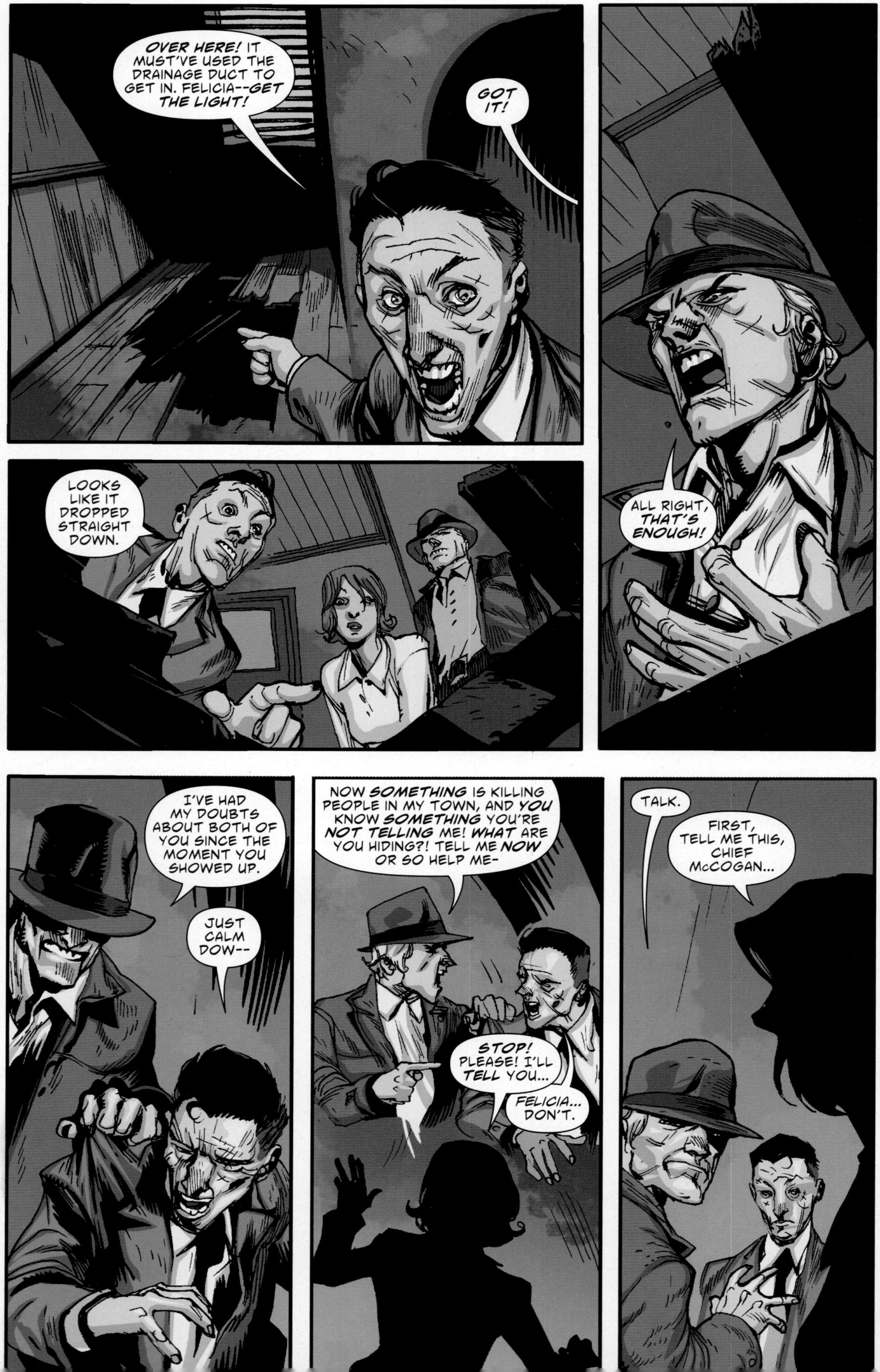
OVER HERE! IT MUST'VE USED THE DRAINAGE DUCT TO GET IN. FELICIA--GET THE LIGHT!
GOT IT!
ALL RIGHT, THAT'S ENOUGH!
LOOKS LIKE IT DROPPED STRAIGHT DOWN.
I'VE HAD MY DOUBTS ABOUT BOTH OF YOU SINCE THE MOMENT YOU SHOWED UP.
JUST CALM DOW--
NOW SOMETHING IS KILLING PEOPLE IN MY TOWN, AND YOU KNOW SOMETHING YOU'RE NOT TELLING ME! WHAT ARE YOU HIDING?! TELL ME NOW OR SO HELP ME-
STOP! PLEASE! I'LL TELL YOU...
FELICIA... DON'T.
TALK.
FIRST, TELL ME THIS, CHIEF McCOGAN...

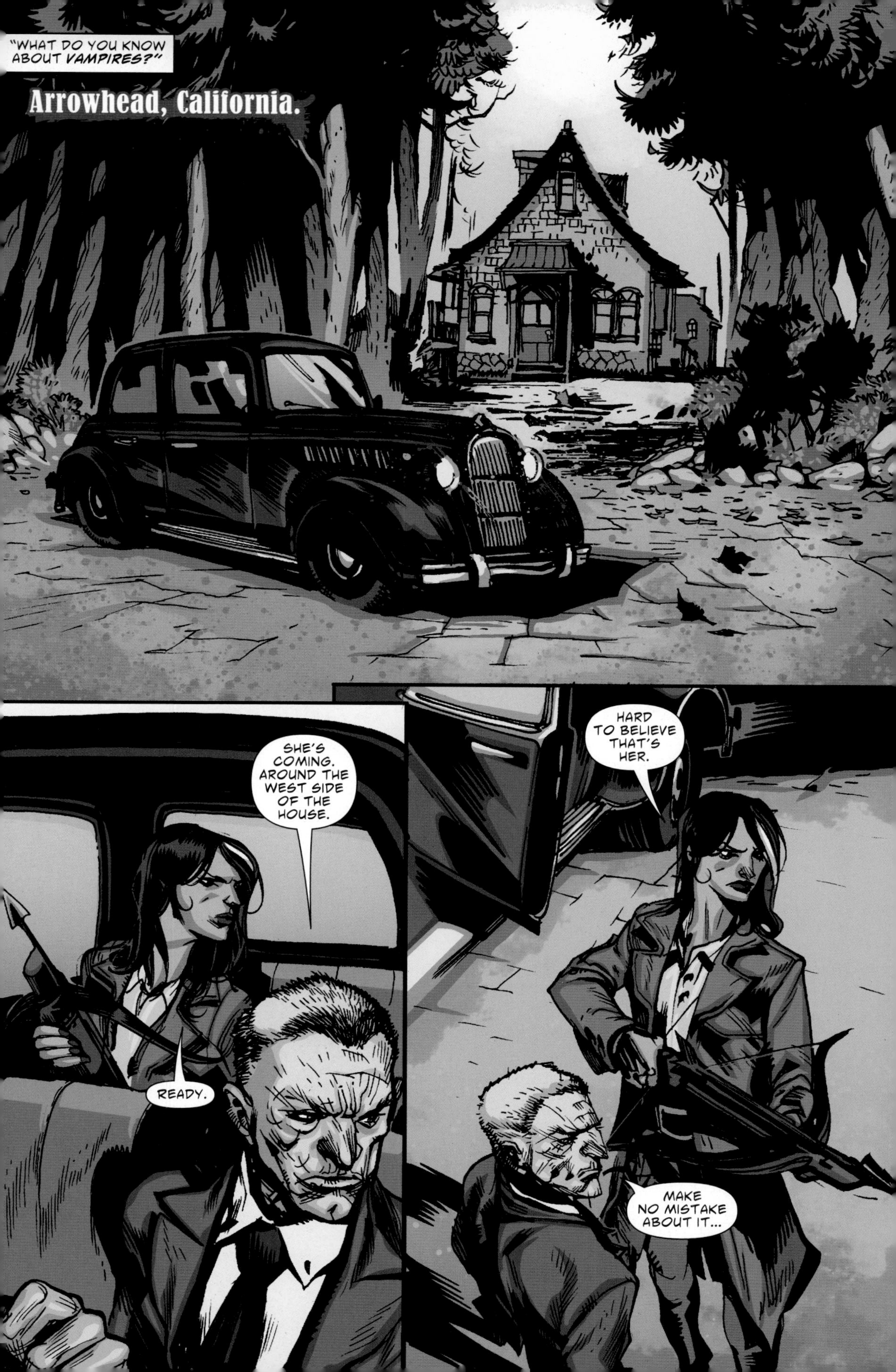

"WHAT DO YOU KNOW ABOUT VAMPIRES?"
Arrowhead, California.
SHE'S COMING. AROUND THE WEST SIDE OF THE HOUSE.
READY.
HARD TO BELIEVE THAT'S HER.
MAKE NO MISTAKE ABOUT IT...

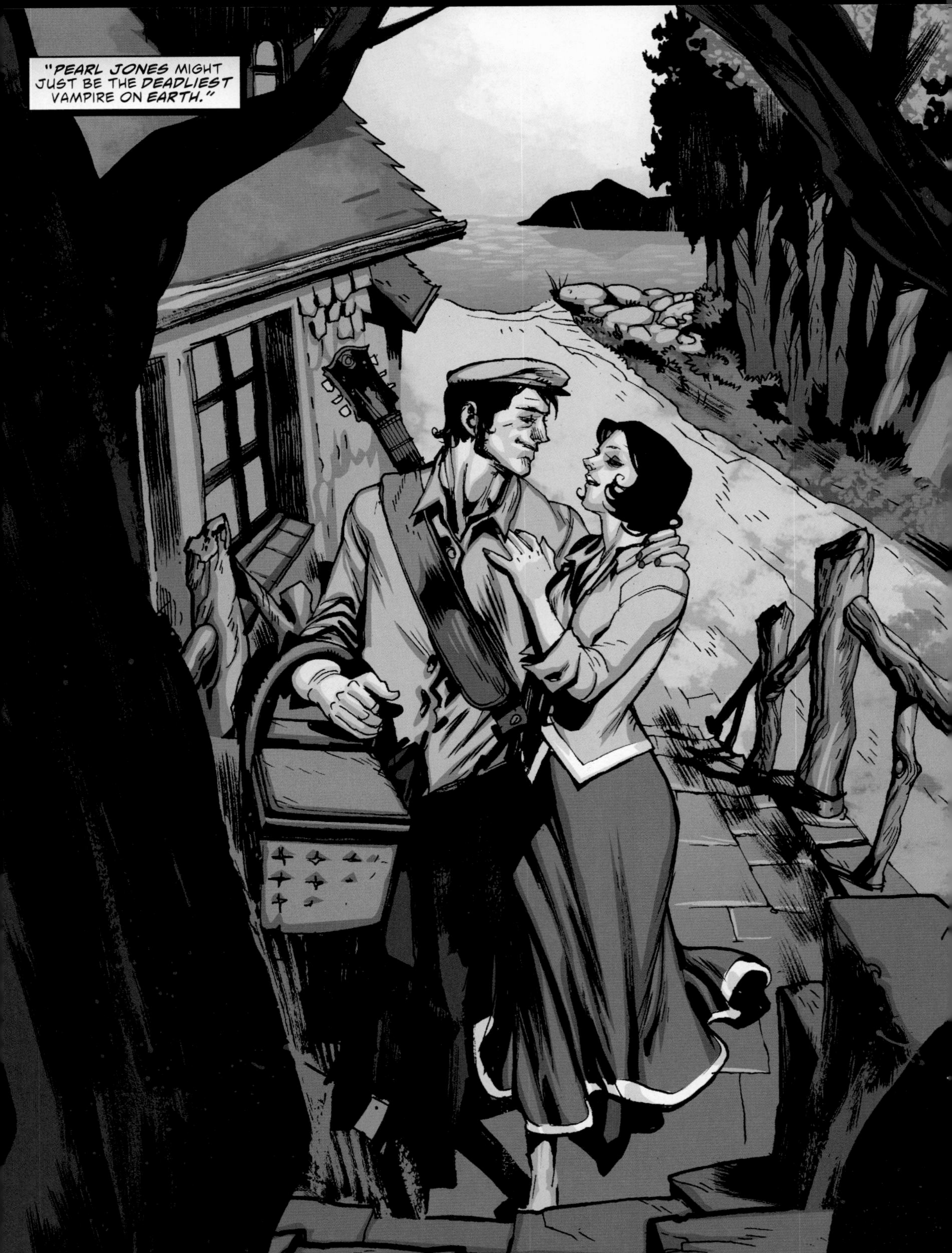
"PEARL JONES MIGHT JUST BE THE DEADLIEST VAMPIRE ON EARTH."

DEVIL IN THE SAND PART TWO

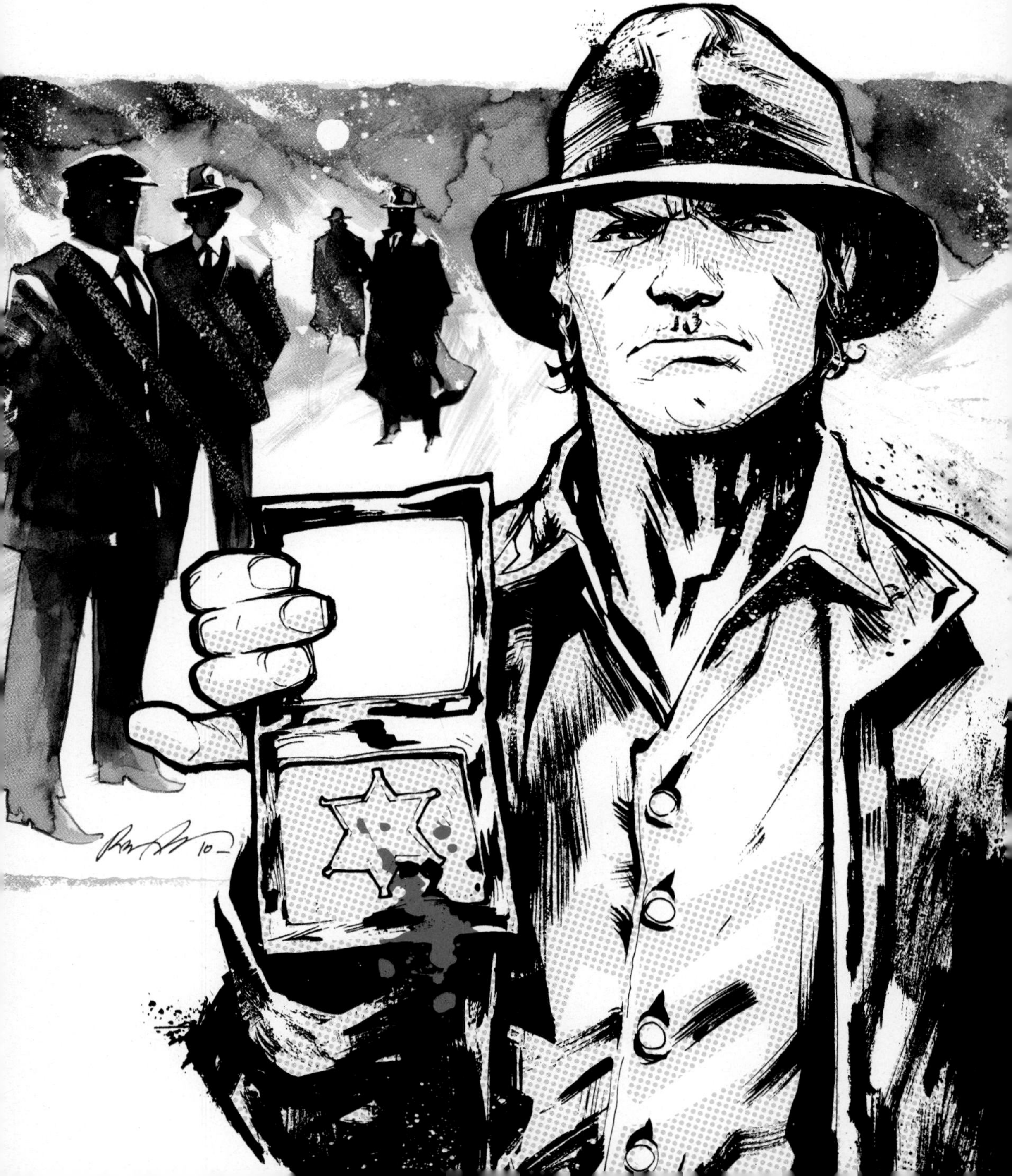

Devil in the Sand

Part Three

Rafael Albuquerque

Artist

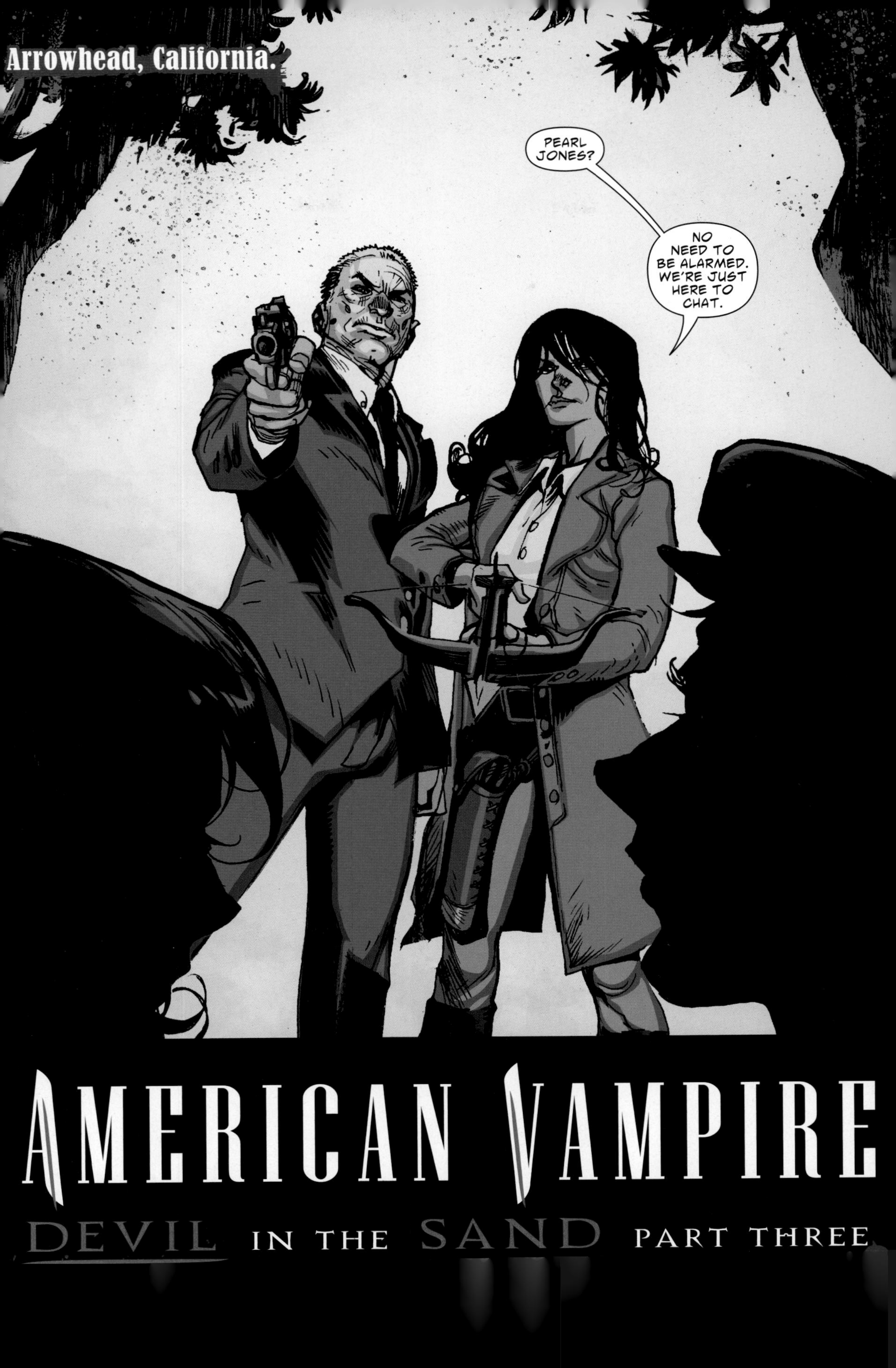
Arrowhead, California.
PEARL JONES?
NO NEED TO BE ALARMED. WE'RE JUST HERE TO CHAT.
AMERICAN VAMPIRE
DEVIL IN THE SAND PART THREE

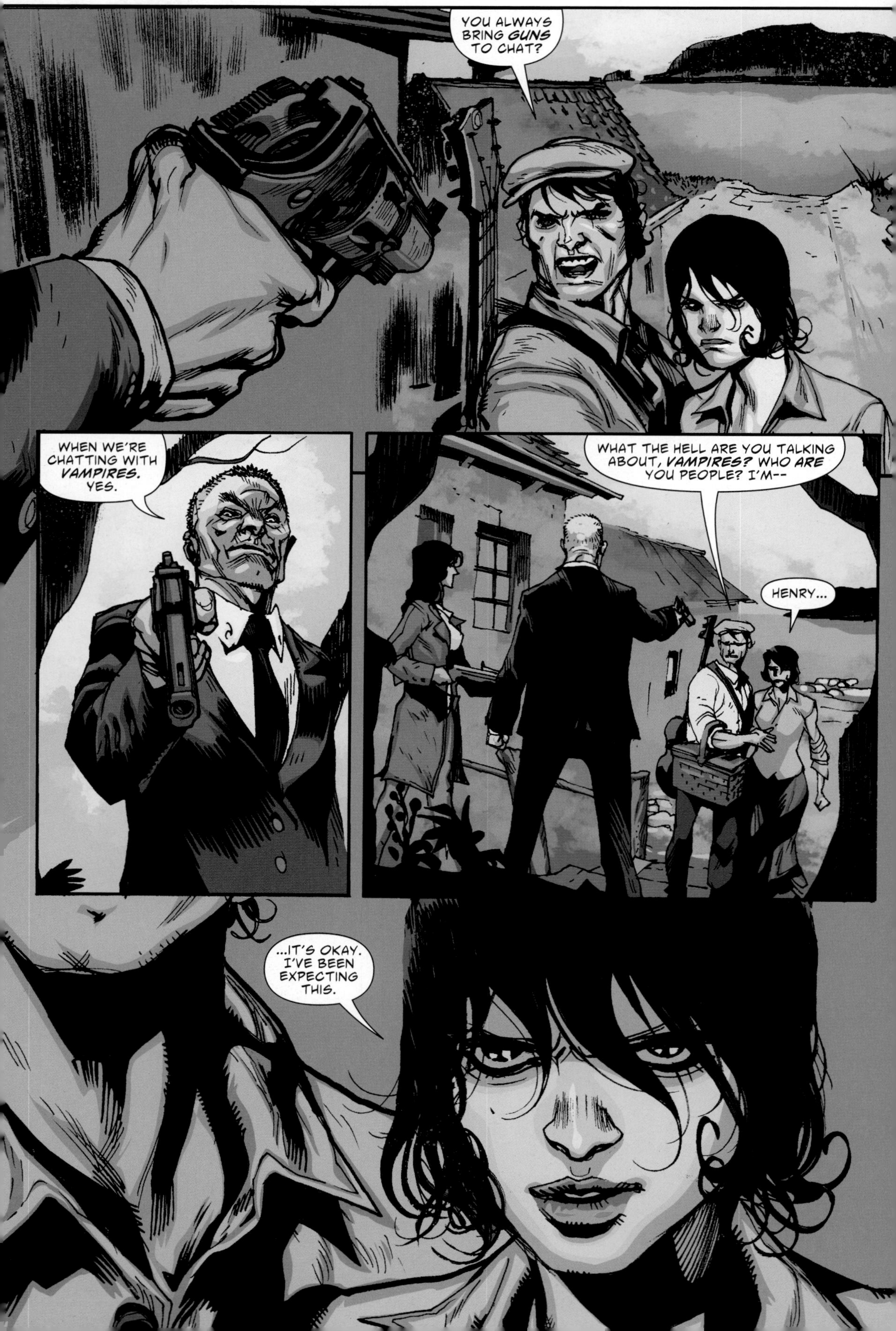
YOU ALWAYS BRING GUNS TO CHAT?
WHEN WE'RE CHATTING WITH VAMPIRES. YES.
WHAT THE HELL ARE YOU TALKING ABOUT, VAMPIRES? WHO ARE YOU PEOPLE? I'M--
HENRY...
...IT'S OKAY. I'VE BEEN EXPECTING THIS.

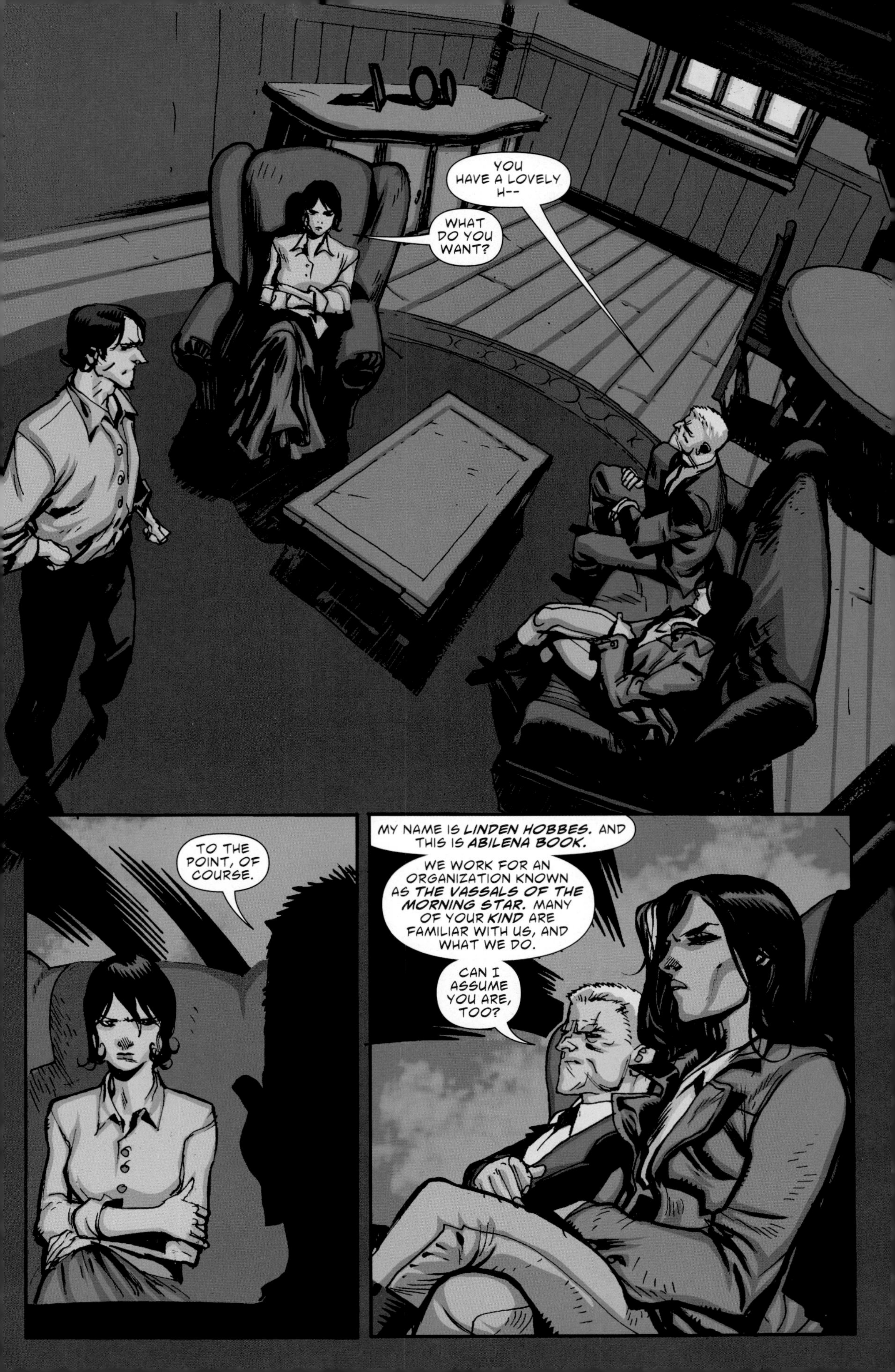
YOU HAVE A LOVELY H--
WHAT DO YOU WANT?
TO THE POINT, OF COURSE.
MY NAME IS *LINDEN HOBBES.* AND THIS IS *ABILENA BOOK.*
WE WORK FOR AN ORGANIZATION KNOWN AS *THE VASSALS OF THE MORNING STAR.* MANY OF YOUR *KIND* ARE FAMILIAR WITH US, AND WHAT WE DO.
CAN I ASSUME YOU ARE, TOO?

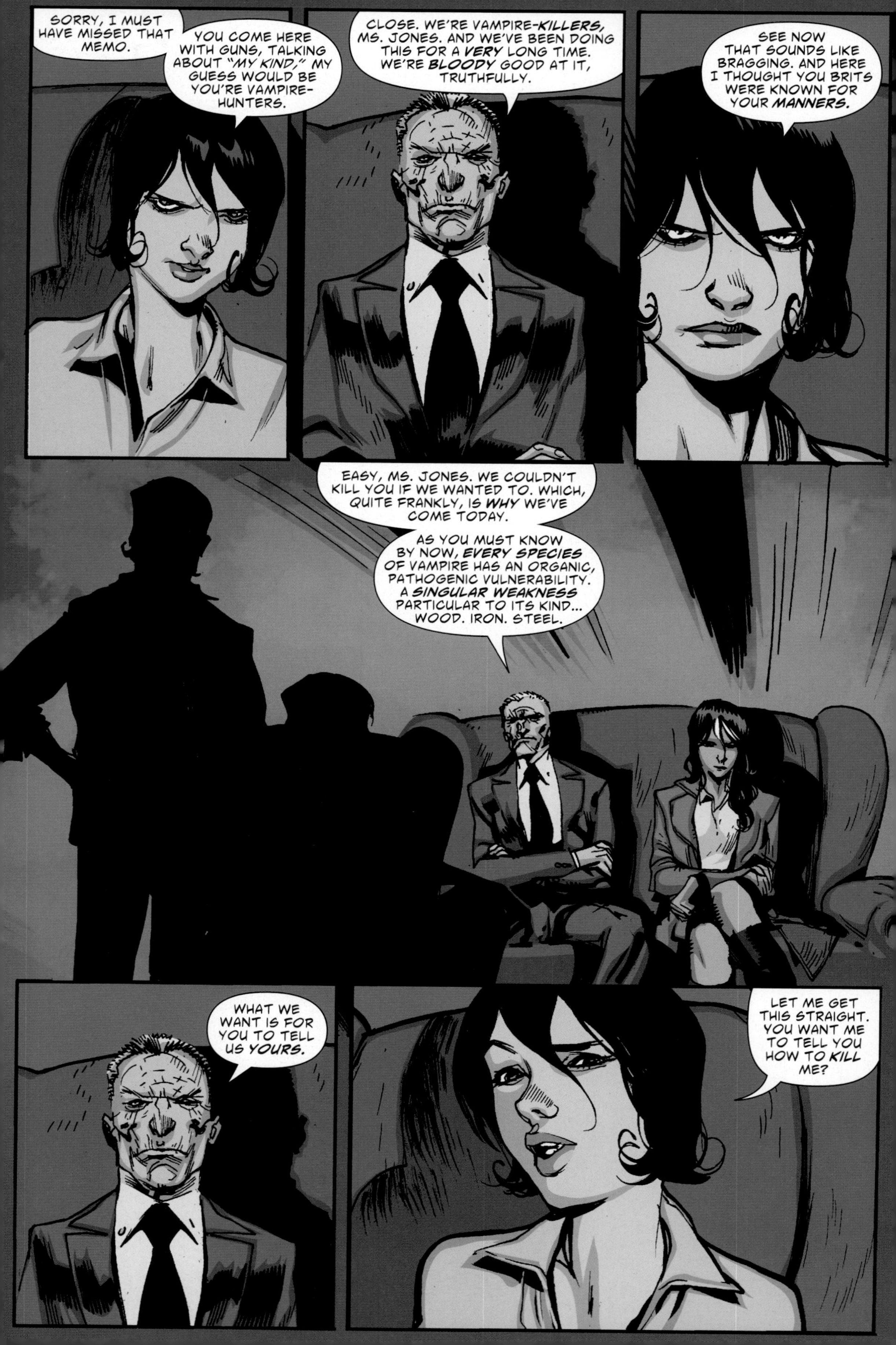
SORRY, I MUST HAVE MISSED THAT MEMO.
YOU COME HERE WITH GUNS, TALKING ABOUT "MY KIND," MY GUESS WOULD BE YOU'RE VAMPIRE-HUNTERS.
CLOSE. WE'RE VAMPIRE-KILLERS, MS. JONES. AND WE'VE BEEN DOING THIS FOR A VERY LONG TIME. WE'RE BLOODY GOOD AT IT, TRUTHFULLY.
SEE NOW THAT SOUNDS LIKE BRAGGING. AND HERE I THOUGHT YOU BRITS WERE KNOWN FOR YOUR MANNERS.
EASY, MS. JONES. WE COULDN'T KILL YOU IF WE WANTED TO. WHICH, QUITE FRANKLY, IS WHY WE'VE COME TODAY.
AS YOU MUST KNOW BY NOW, EVERY SPECIES OF VAMPIRE HAS AN ORGANIC, PATHOGENIC VULNERABILITY. A SINGULAR WEAKNESS PARTICULAR TO ITS KIND... WOOD. IRON. STEEL.
WHAT WE WANT IS FOR YOU TO TELL US YOURS.
LET ME GET THIS STRAIGHT. YOU WANT ME TO TELL YOU HOW TO KILL ME?

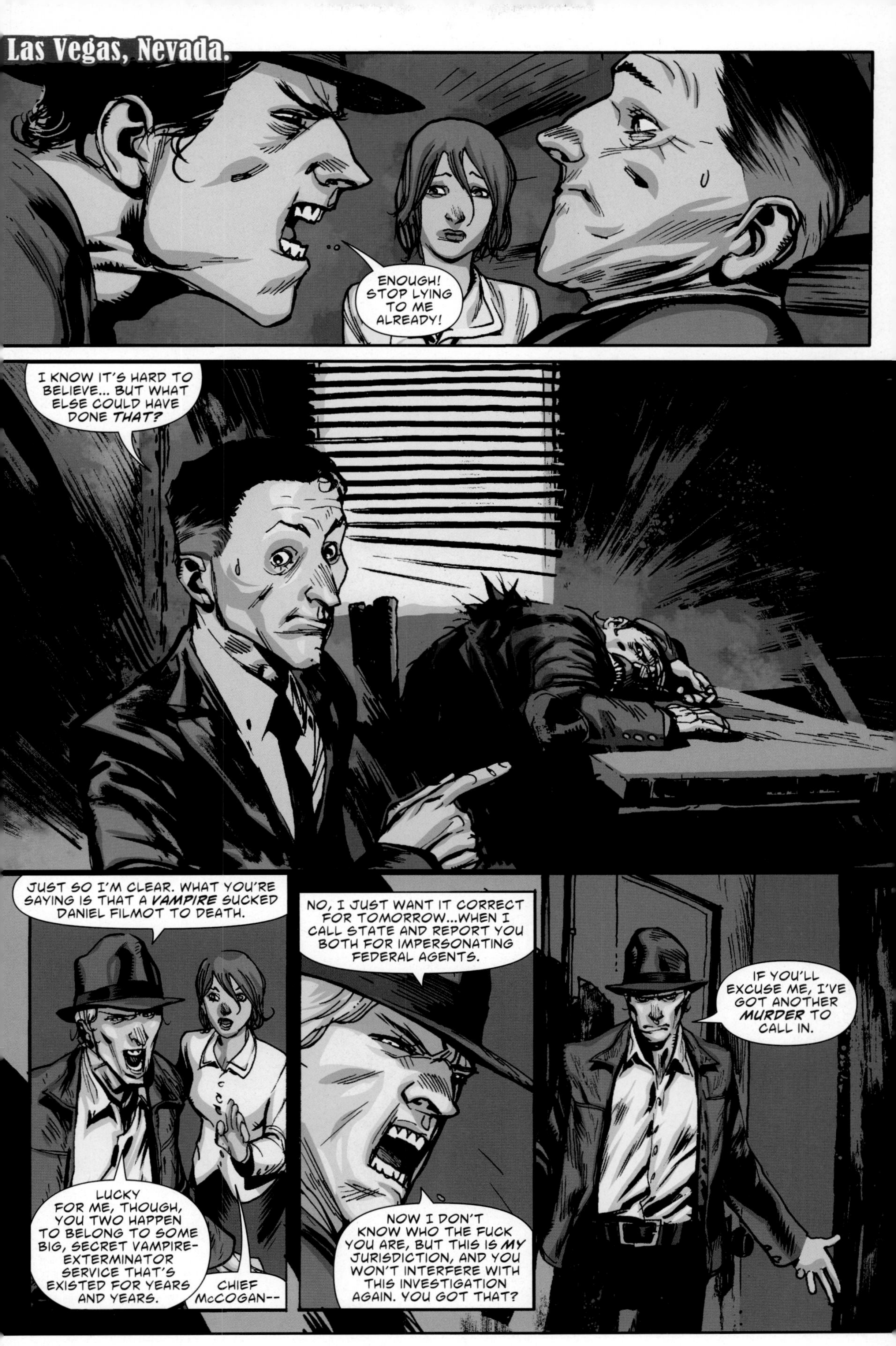
Las Vegas, Nevada.
ENOUGH! STOP LYING TO ME ALREADY!
I KNOW IT'S HARD TO BELIEVE... BUT WHAT ELSE COULD HAVE DONE *THAT?*
JUST SO I'M CLEAR. WHAT YOU'RE SAYING IS THAT A *VAMPIRE* SUCKED DANIEL FILMOT TO DEATH.
LUCKY FOR ME, THOUGH, YOU TWO HAPPEN TO BELONG TO SOME BIG, SECRET VAMPIRE-EXTERMINATOR SERVICE THAT'S EXISTED FOR YEARS AND YEARS.
CHIEF McCOGAN--
NO, I JUST WANT IT CORRECT FOR TOMORROW...WHEN I CALL STATE AND REPORT YOU BOTH FOR IMPERSONATING FEDERAL AGENTS.
NOW I DON'T KNOW WHO THE FUCK YOU ARE, BUT THIS IS *MY* JURISDICTION, AND YOU WON'T INTERFERE WITH THIS INVESTIGATION AGAIN. YOU GOT THAT?
IF YOU'LL EXCUSE ME, I'VE GOT ANOTHER *MURDER* TO CALL IN.

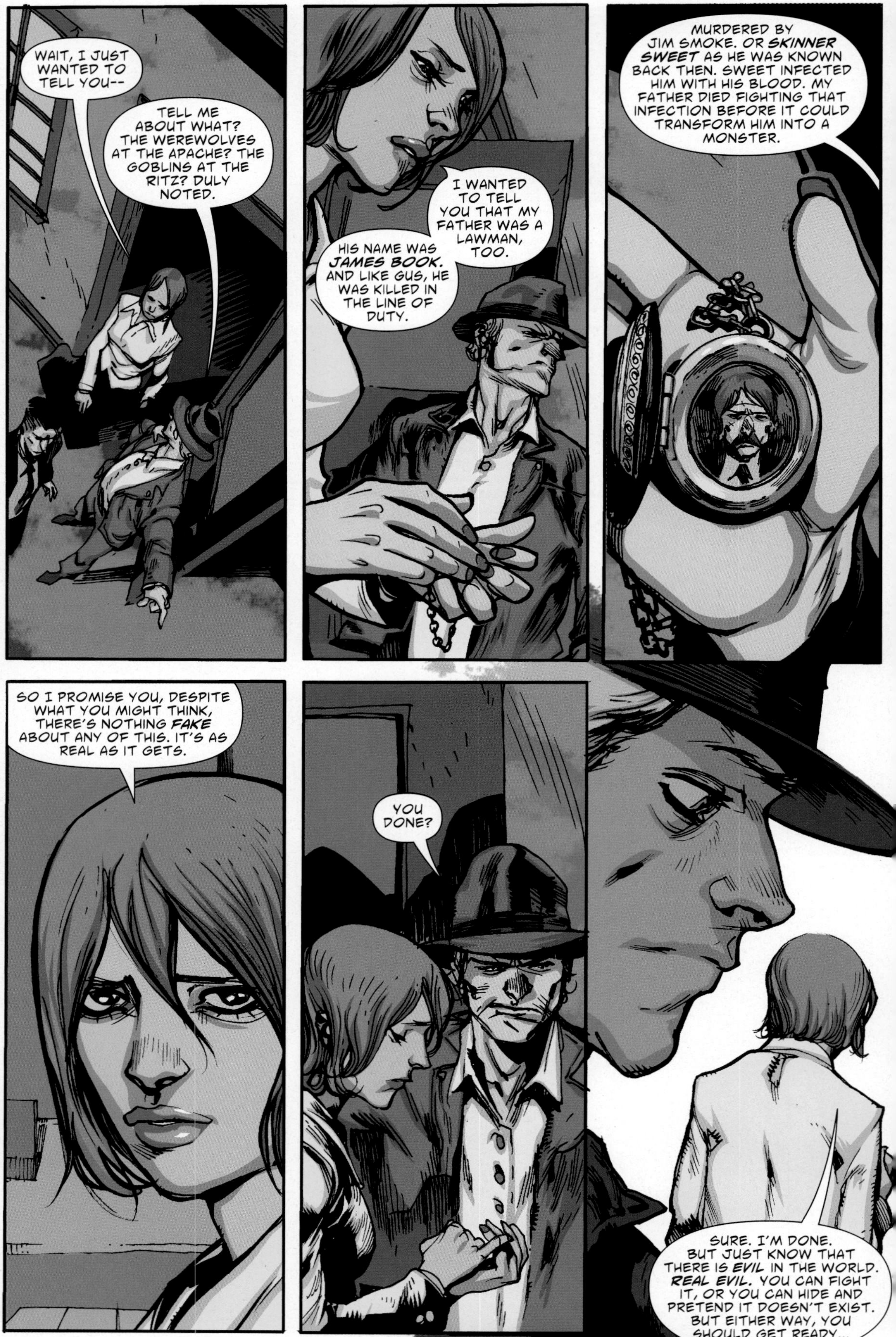
WAIT, I JUST WANTED TO TELL YOU--
TELL ME ABOUT WHAT? THE WEREWOLVES AT THE APACHE? THE GOBLINS AT THE RITZ? DULY NOTED.
I WANTED TO TELL YOU THAT MY FATHER WAS A LAWMAN, TOO.
HIS NAME WAS JAMES BOOK. AND LIKE GUS, HE WAS KILLED IN THE LINE OF DUTY.
MURDERED BY JIM SMOKE. OR SKINNER SWEET AS HE WAS KNOWN BACK THEN. SWEET INFECTED HIM WITH HIS BLOOD. MY FATHER DIED FIGHTING THAT INFECTION BEFORE IT COULD TRANSFORM HIM INTO A MONSTER.
SO I PROMISE YOU, DESPITE WHAT YOU MIGHT THINK, THERE'S NOTHING FAKE ABOUT ANY OF THIS. IT'S AS REAL AS IT GETS.
YOU DONE?
SURE. I'M DONE. BUT JUST KNOW THAT THERE IS EVIL IN THE WORLD. REAL EVIL. YOU CAN FIGHT IT, OR YOU CAN HIDE AND PRETEND IT DOESN'T EXIST. BUT EITHER WAY, YOU SHOULD GET READY...

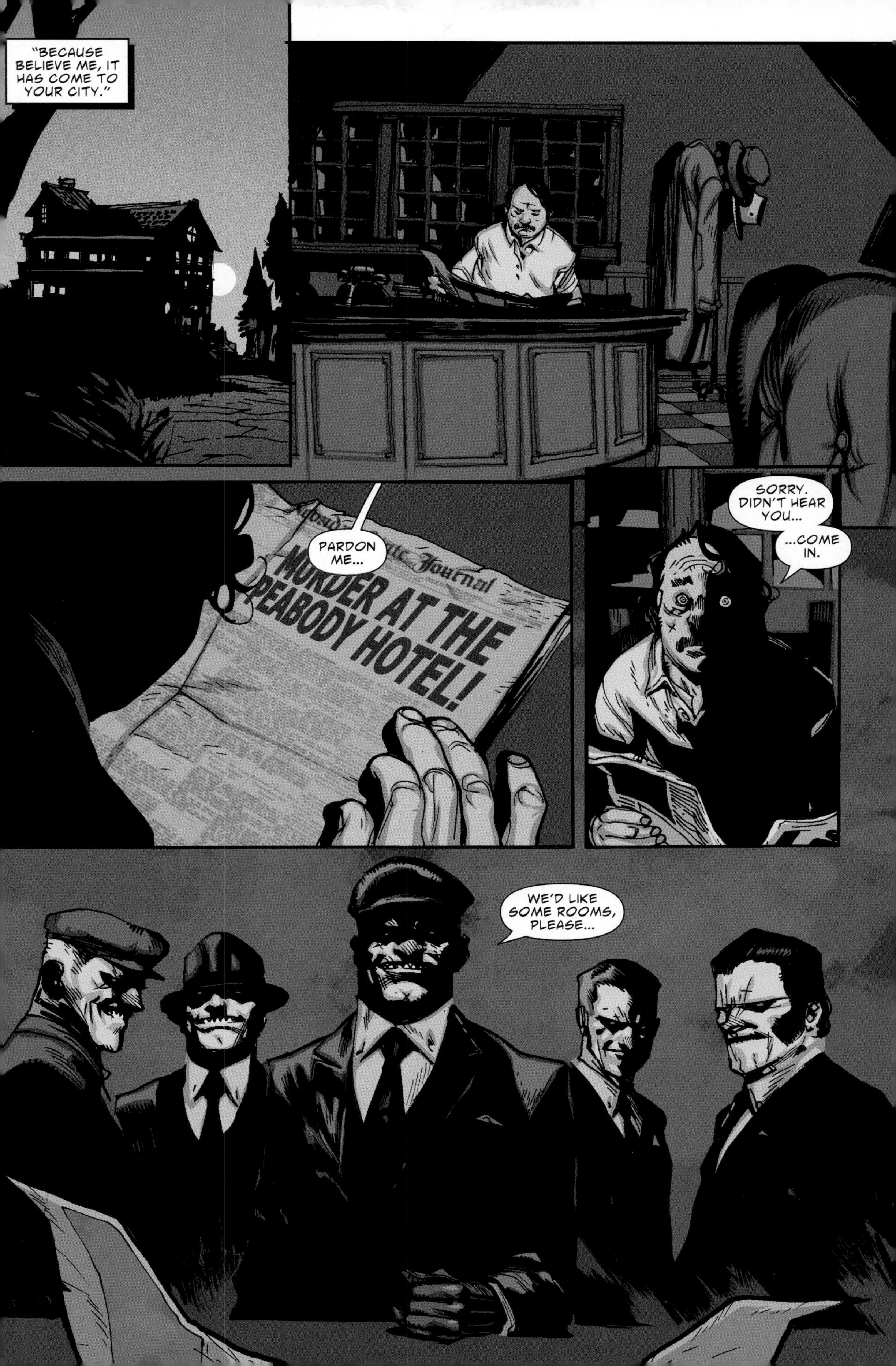
"BECAUSE BELIEVE ME, IT HAS COME TO YOUR CITY."
PARDON ME...
MURDER AT THE PEABODY HOTEL!
SORRY. DIDN'T HEAR YOU...
...COME IN.
WE'D LIKE SOME ROOMS, PLEASE...

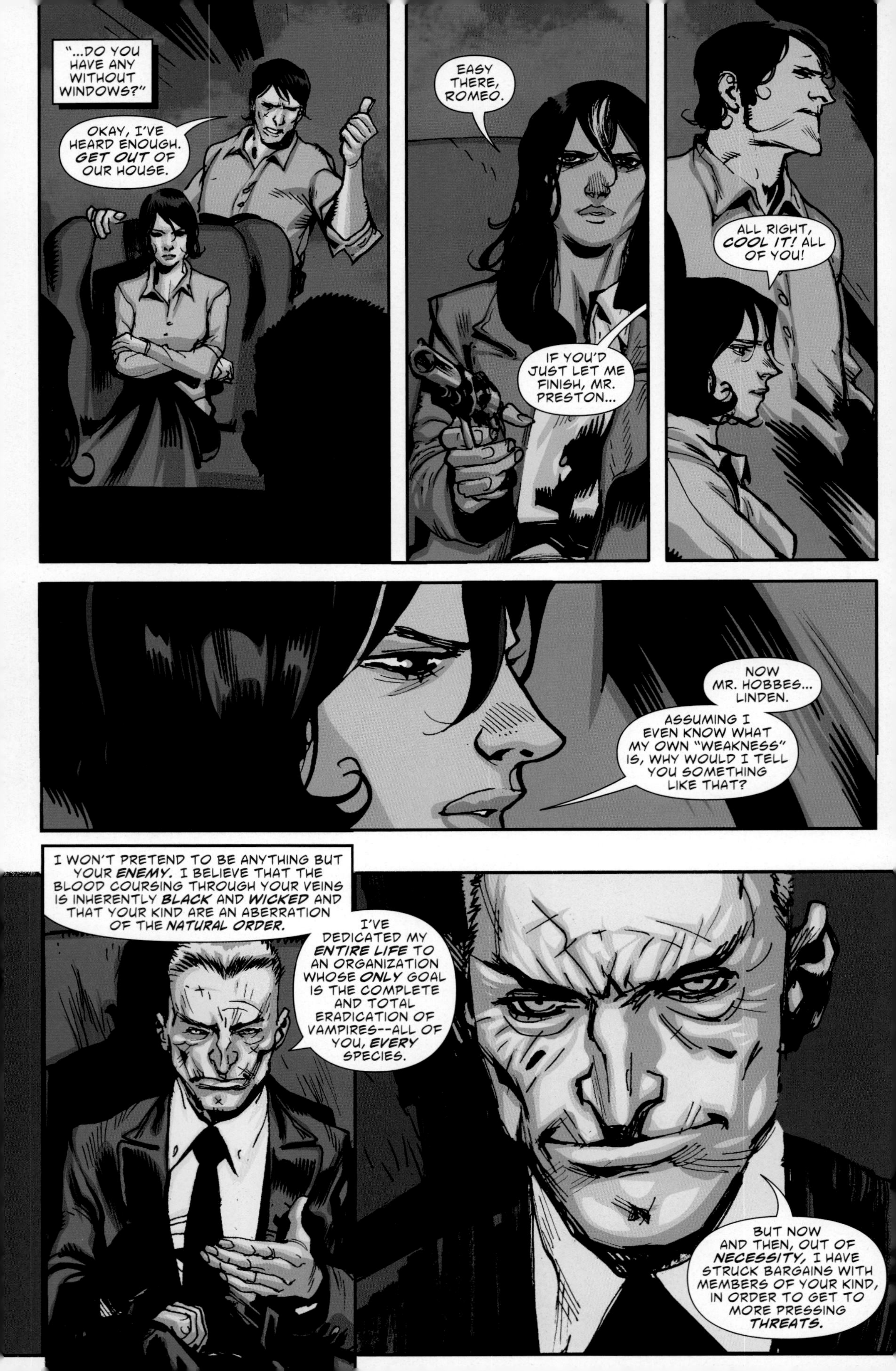
"...DO YOU HAVE ANY WITHOUT WINDOWS?"
OKAY, I'VE HEARD ENOUGH. GET OUT OF OUR HOUSE.
EASY THERE, ROMEO.
IF YOU'D JUST LET ME FINISH, MR. PRESTON...
ALL RIGHT, COOL IT! ALL OF YOU!
NOW MR. HOBBES... LINDEN.
ASSUMING I EVEN KNOW WHAT MY OWN "WEAKNESS" IS, WHY WOULD I TELL YOU SOMETHING LIKE THAT?
I WON'T PRETEND TO BE ANYTHING BUT YOUR ENEMY. I BELIEVE THAT THE BLOOD COURSING THROUGH YOUR VEINS IS INHERENTLY BLACK AND WICKED AND THAT YOUR KIND ARE AN ABERRATION OF THE NATURAL ORDER.
I'VE DEDICATED MY ENTIRE LIFE TO AN ORGANIZATION WHOSE ONLY GOAL IS THE COMPLETE AND TOTAL ERADICATION OF VAMPIRES--ALL OF YOU, EVERY SPECIES.
BUT NOW AND THEN, OUT OF NECESSITY, I HAVE STRUCK BARGAINS WITH MEMBERS OF YOUR KIND, IN ORDER TO GET TO MORE PRESSING THREATS.

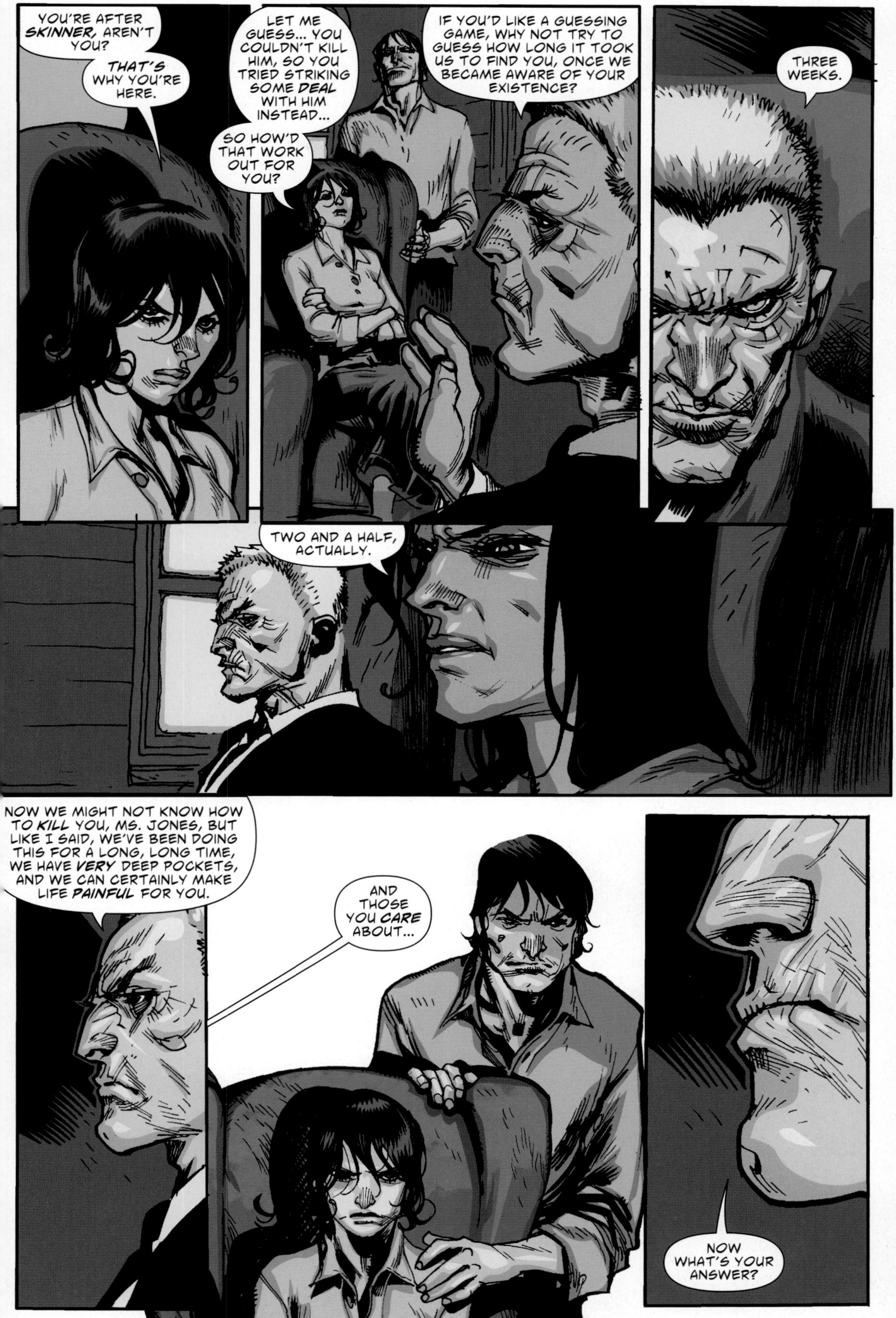
YOU'RE AFTER SKINNER, AREN'T YOU?
THAT'S WHY YOU'RE HERE.
LET ME GUESS... YOU COULDN'T KILL HIM, SO YOU TRIED STRIKING SOME DEAL WITH HIM INSTEAD...
SO HOW'D THAT WORK OUT FOR YOU?
IF YOU'D LIKE A GUESSING GAME, WHY NOT TRY TO GUESS HOW LONG IT TOOK US TO FIND YOU, ONCE WE BECAME AWARE OF YOUR EXISTENCE?
THREE WEEKS.
TWO AND A HALF, ACTUALLY.
NOW WE MIGHT NOT KNOW HOW TO KILL YOU, MS. JONES, BUT LIKE I SAID, WE'VE BEEN DOING THIS FOR A LONG, LONG TIME, WE HAVE VERY DEEP POCKETS, AND WE CAN CERTAINLY MAKE LIFE PAINFUL FOR YOU.
AND THOSE YOU CARE ABOUT...
NOW WHAT'S YOUR ANSWER?

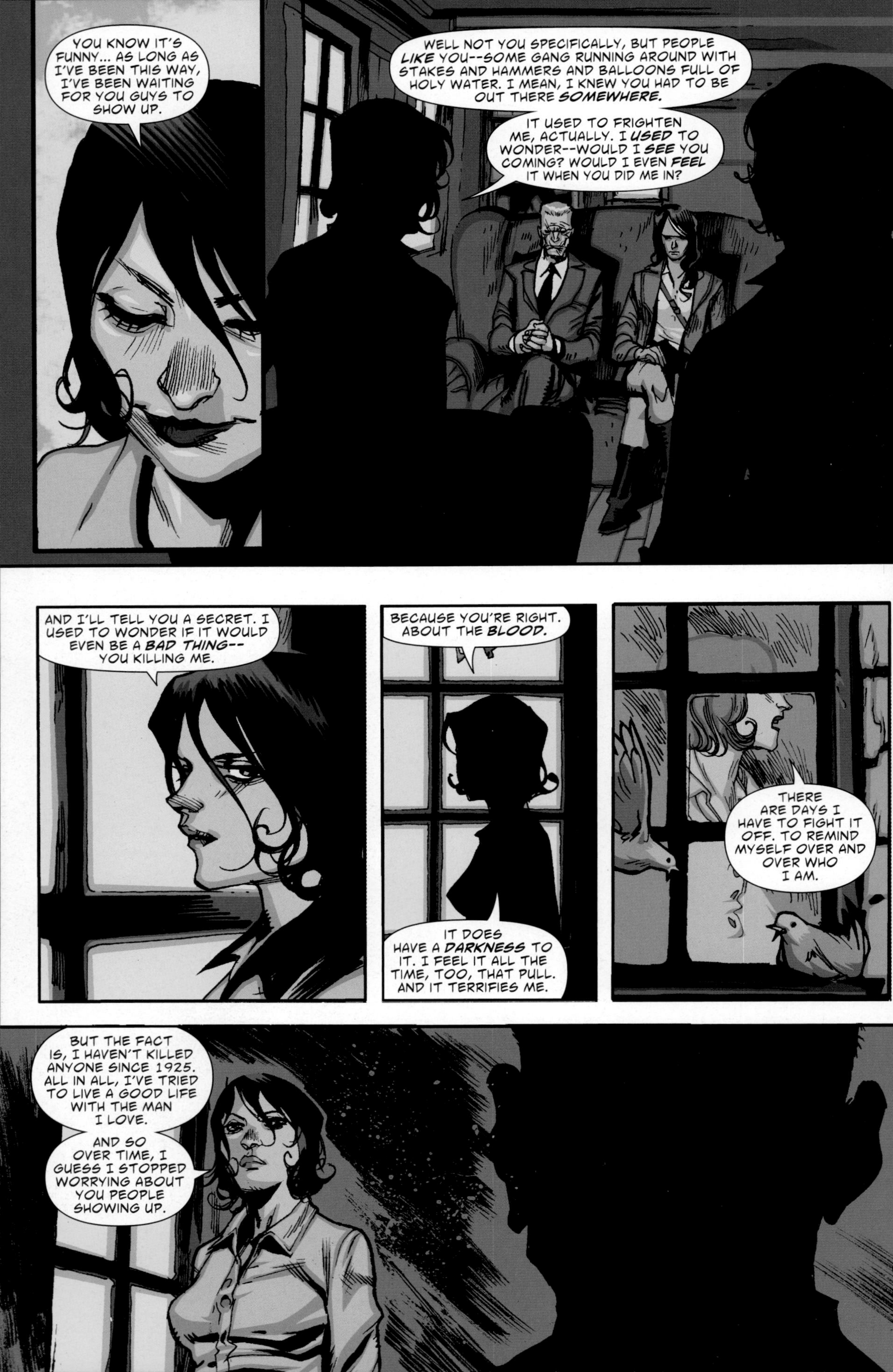
YOU KNOW IT'S FUNNY... AS LONG AS I'VE BEEN THIS WAY, I'VE BEEN WAITING FOR YOU GUYS TO SHOW UP.
WELL NOT YOU SPECIFICALLY, BUT PEOPLE LIKE YOU--SOME GANG RUNNING AROUND WITH STAKES AND HAMMERS AND BALLOONS FULL OF HOLY WATER. I MEAN, I KNEW YOU HAD TO BE OUT THERE SOMEWHERE.
IT USED TO FRIGHTEN ME, ACTUALLY. I USED TO WONDER--WOULD I SEE YOU COMING? WOULD I EVEN FEEL IT WHEN YOU DID ME IN?
AND I'LL TELL YOU A SECRET. I USED TO WONDER IF IT WOULD EVEN BE A BAD THING-- YOU KILLING ME.
BECAUSE YOU'RE RIGHT. ABOUT THE BLOOD.
IT DOES HAVE A DARKNESS TO IT. I FEEL IT ALL THE TIME, TOO, THAT PULL. AND IT TERRIFIES ME.
THERE ARE DAYS I HAVE TO FIGHT IT OFF. TO REMIND MYSELF OVER AND OVER WHO I AM.
BUT THE FACT IS, I HAVEN'T KILLED ANYONE SINCE 1925. ALL IN ALL, I'VE TRIED TO LIVE A GOOD LIFE WITH THE MAN I LOVE.
AND SO OVER TIME, I GUESS I STOPPED WORRYING ABOUT YOU PEOPLE SHOWING UP.

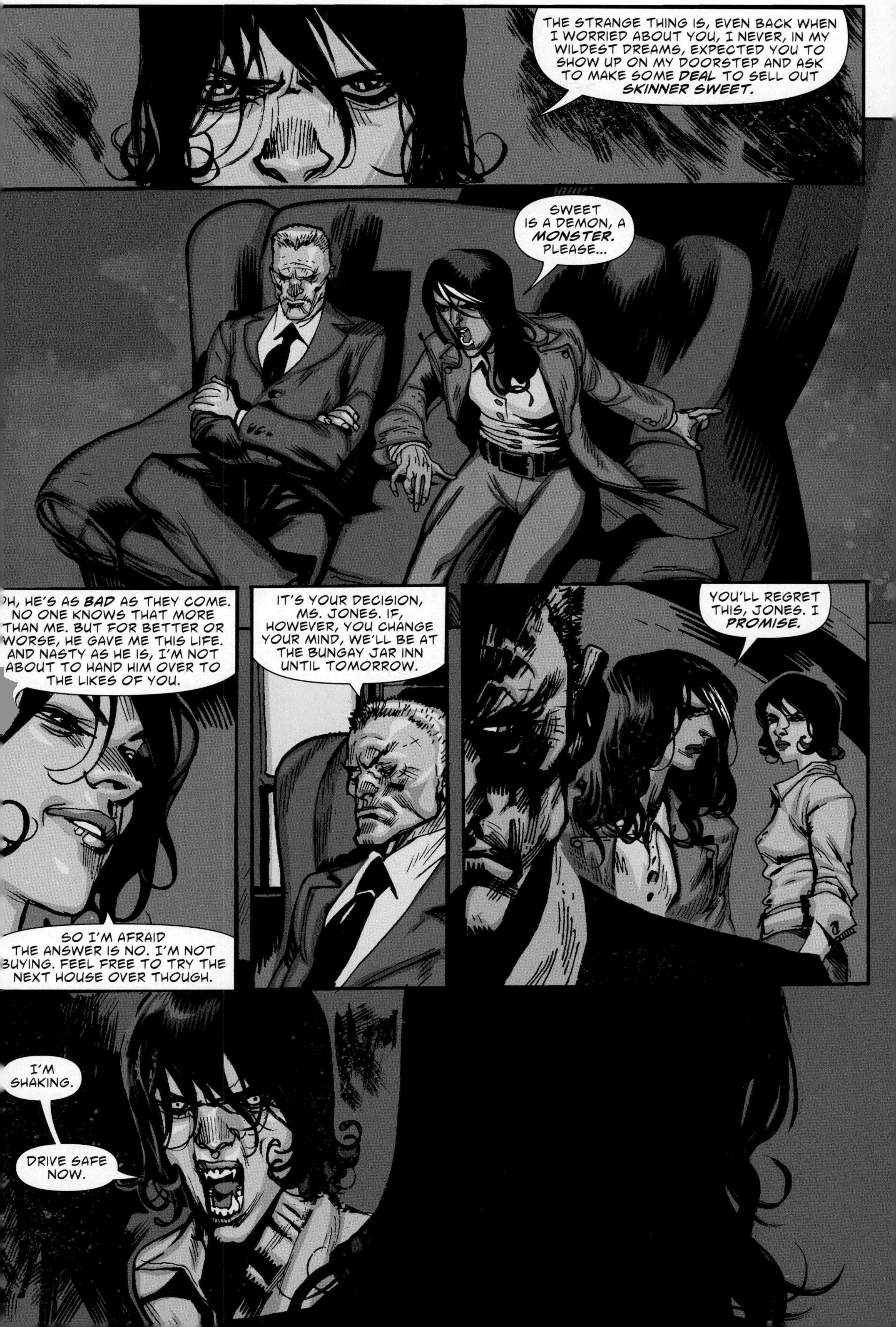
THE STRANGE THING IS, EVEN BACK WHEN I WORRIED ABOUT YOU, I NEVER, IN MY WILDEST DREAMS, EXPECTED YOU TO SHOW UP ON MY DOORSTEP AND ASK TO MAKE SOME DEAL TO SELL OUT SKINNER SWEET.
SWEET IS A DEMON, A MONSTER. PLEASE...
OH, HE'S AS BAD AS THEY COME. NO ONE KNOWS THAT MORE THAN ME. BUT FOR BETTER OR WORSE, HE GAVE ME THIS LIFE. AND NASTY AS HE IS, I'M NOT ABOUT TO HAND HIM OVER TO THE LIKES OF YOU.
SO I'M AFRAID THE ANSWER IS NO. I'M NOT BUYING. FEEL FREE TO TRY THE NEXT HOUSE OVER THOUGH.
IT'S YOUR DECISION, MS. JONES. IF, HOWEVER, YOU CHANGE YOUR MIND, WE'LL BE AT THE BUNGAY JAR INN UNTIL TOMORROW.
YOU'LL REGRET THIS, JONES. I PROMISE.
I'M SHAKING.
DRIVE SAFE NOW.

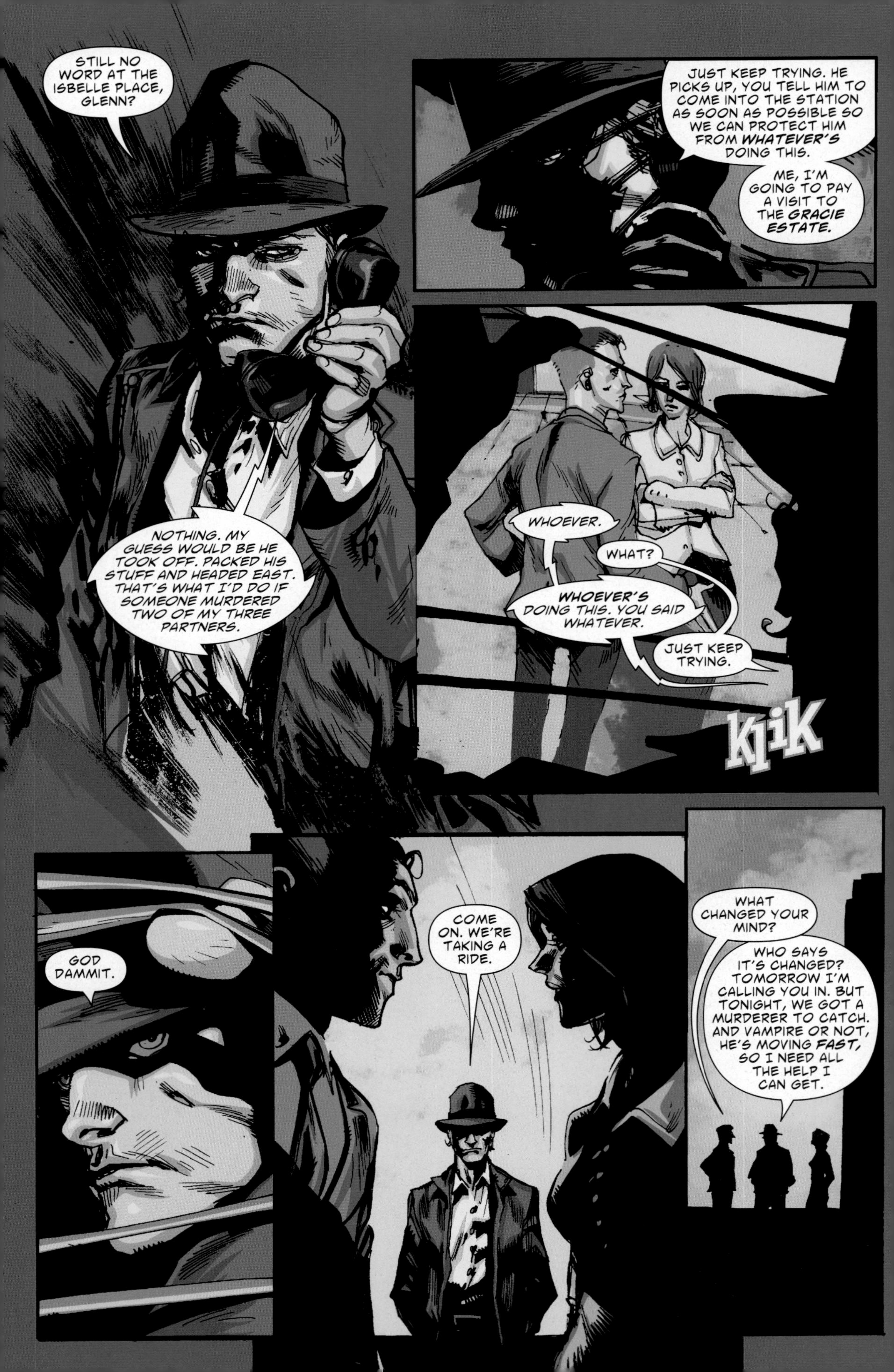
STILL NO WORD AT THE ISBELLE PLACE, GLENN?
JUST KEEP TRYING. HE PICKS UP, YOU TELL HIM TO COME INTO THE STATION AS SOON AS POSSIBLE SO WE CAN PROTECT HIM FROM WHATEVER'S DOING THIS.
ME, I'M GOING TO PAY A VISIT TO THE GRACIE ESTATE.
NOTHING. MY GUESS WOULD BE HE TOOK OFF. PACKED HIS STUFF AND HEADED EAST. THAT'S WHAT I'D DO IF SOMEONE MURDERED TWO OF MY THREE PARTNERS.
WHOEVER.
WHAT?
WHOEVER'S DOING THIS. YOU SAID WHATEVER.
JUST KEEP TRYING.
KLIK
GOD DAMMIT.
COME ON. WE'RE TAKING A RIDE.
WHAT CHANGED YOUR MIND?
WHO SAYS IT'S CHANGED? TOMORROW I'M CALLING YOU IN. BUT TONIGHT, WE GOT A MURDERER TO CATCH. AND VAMPIRE OR NOT, HE'S MOVING FAST, SO I NEED ALL THE HELP I CAN GET.

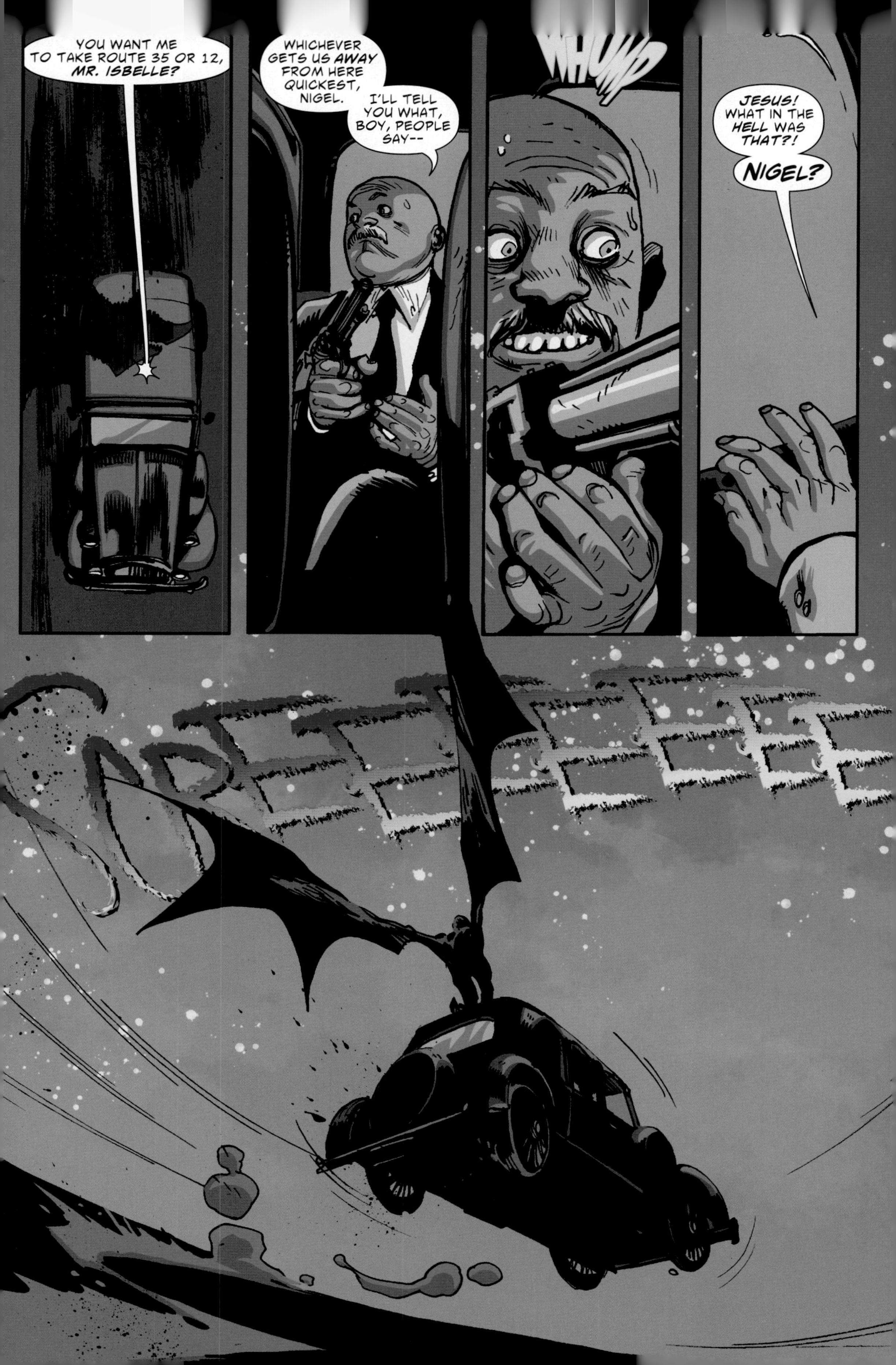

YOU WANT ME TO TAKE ROUTE 35 OR 12, MR. ISBELLE?
WHICHEVER GETS US AWAY FROM HERE QUICKEST, NIGEL.
I'LL TELL YOU WHAT, BOY, PEOPLE SAY--
WHUMP
JESUS! WHAT IN THE HELL WAS THAT?!
NIGEL?

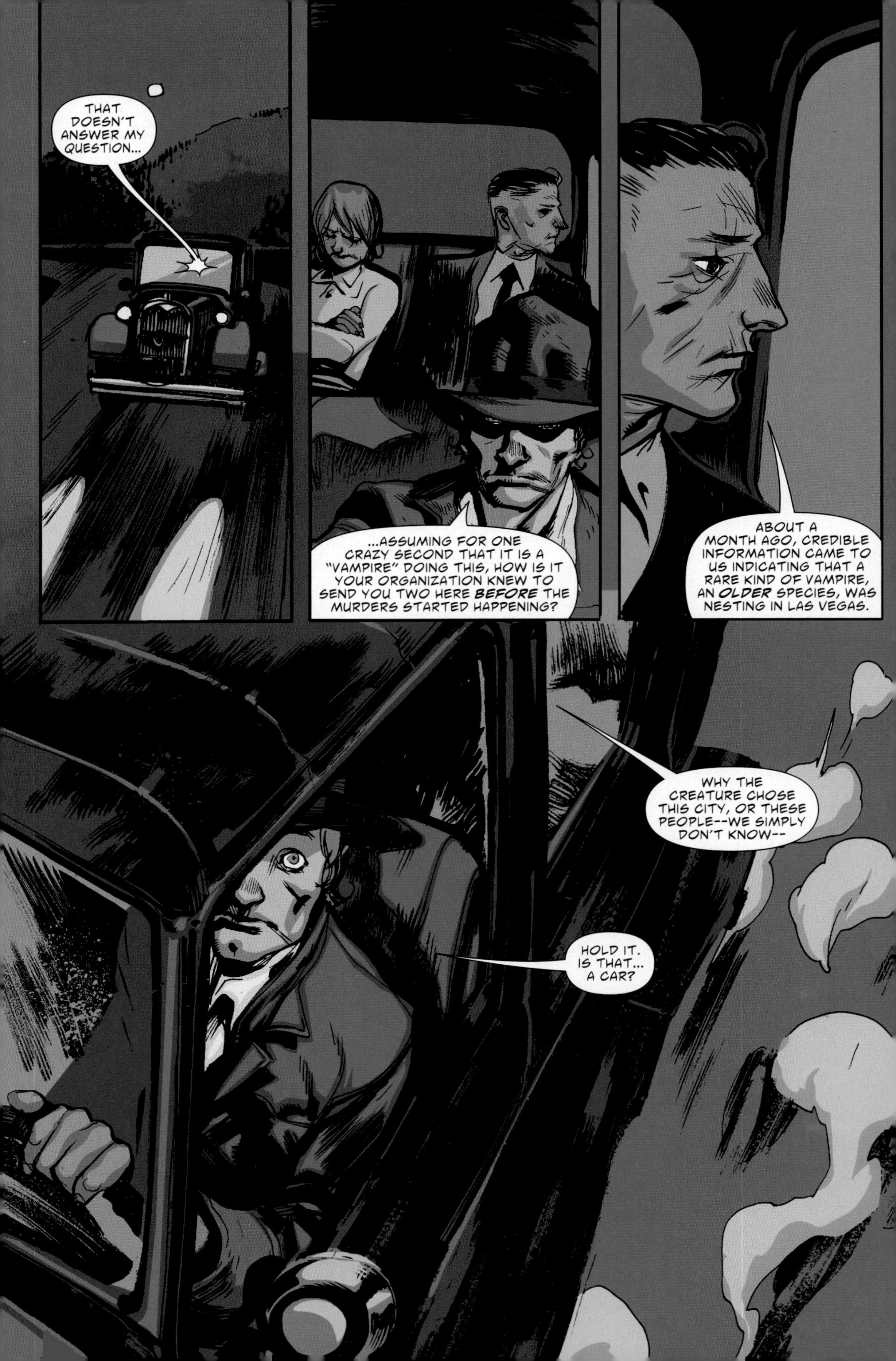
THAT DOESN'T ANSWER MY QUESTION...
...ASSUMING FOR ONE CRAZY SECOND THAT IT IS A "VAMPIRE" DOING THIS, HOW IS IT YOUR ORGANIZATION KNEW TO SEND YOU TWO HERE *BEFORE* THE MURDERS STARTED HAPPENING?
ABOUT A MONTH AGO, CREDIBLE INFORMATION CAME TO US INDICATING THAT A RARE KIND OF VAMPIRE, AN *OLDER* SPECIES, WAS NESTING IN LAS VEGAS.
WHY THE CREATURE CHOSE THIS CITY, OR THESE PEOPLE--WE SIMPLY DON'T KNOW--
HOLD IT. IS THAT... A CAR?

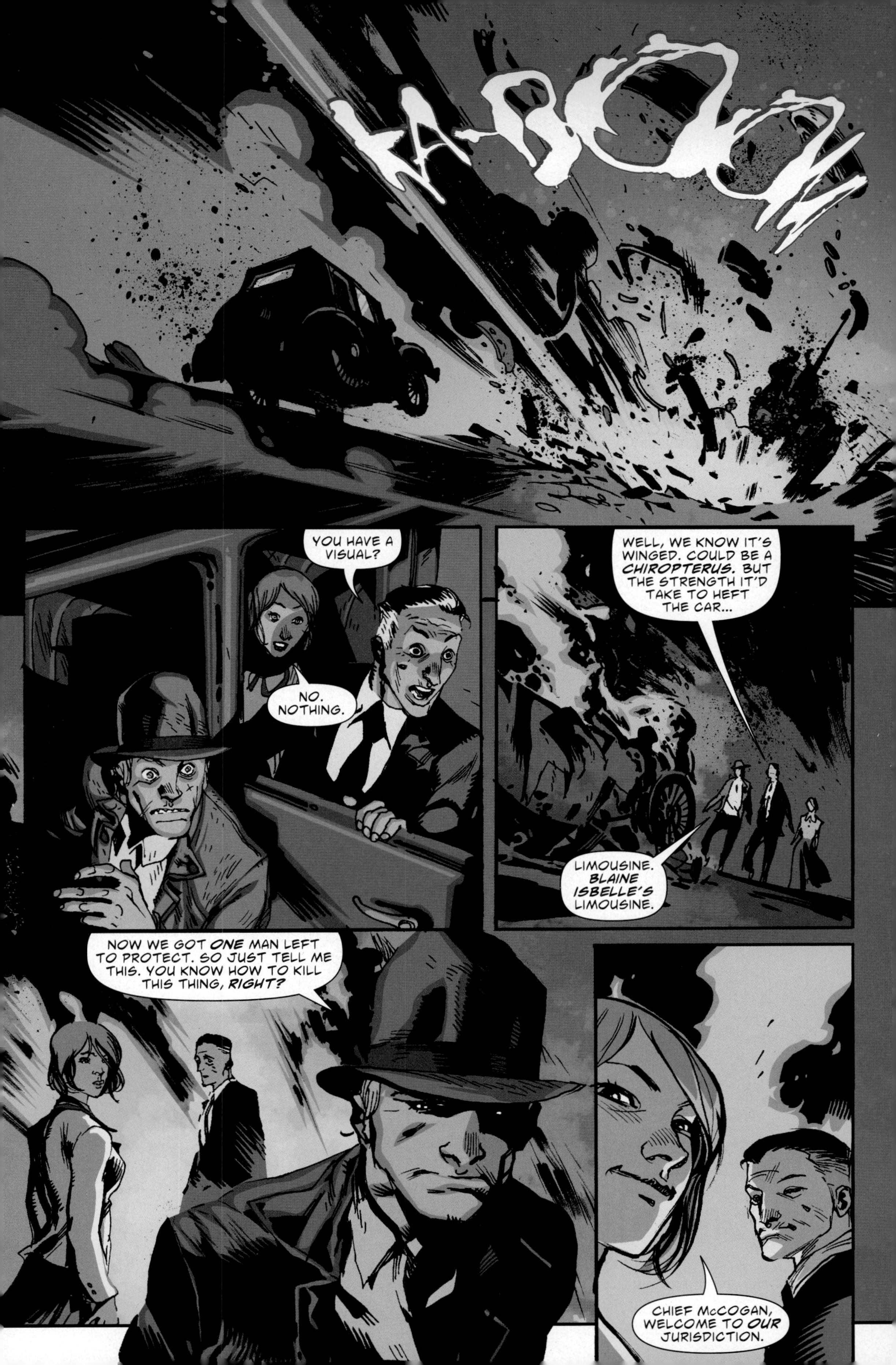
KA-BOOM
YOU HAVE A VISUAL?
NO. NOTHING.
WELL, WE KNOW IT'S WINGED. COULD BE A *CHIROPTERUS.* BUT THE STRENGTH IT'D TAKE TO HEFT THE CAR...
LIMOUSINE. *BLAINE ISBELLE'S* LIMOUSINE.
NOW WE GOT *ONE* MAN LEFT TO PROTECT. SO JUST TELL ME THIS. YOU KNOW HOW TO KILL THIS THING, *RIGHT?*
CHIEF McCOGAN, WELCOME TO *OUR* JURISDICTION.

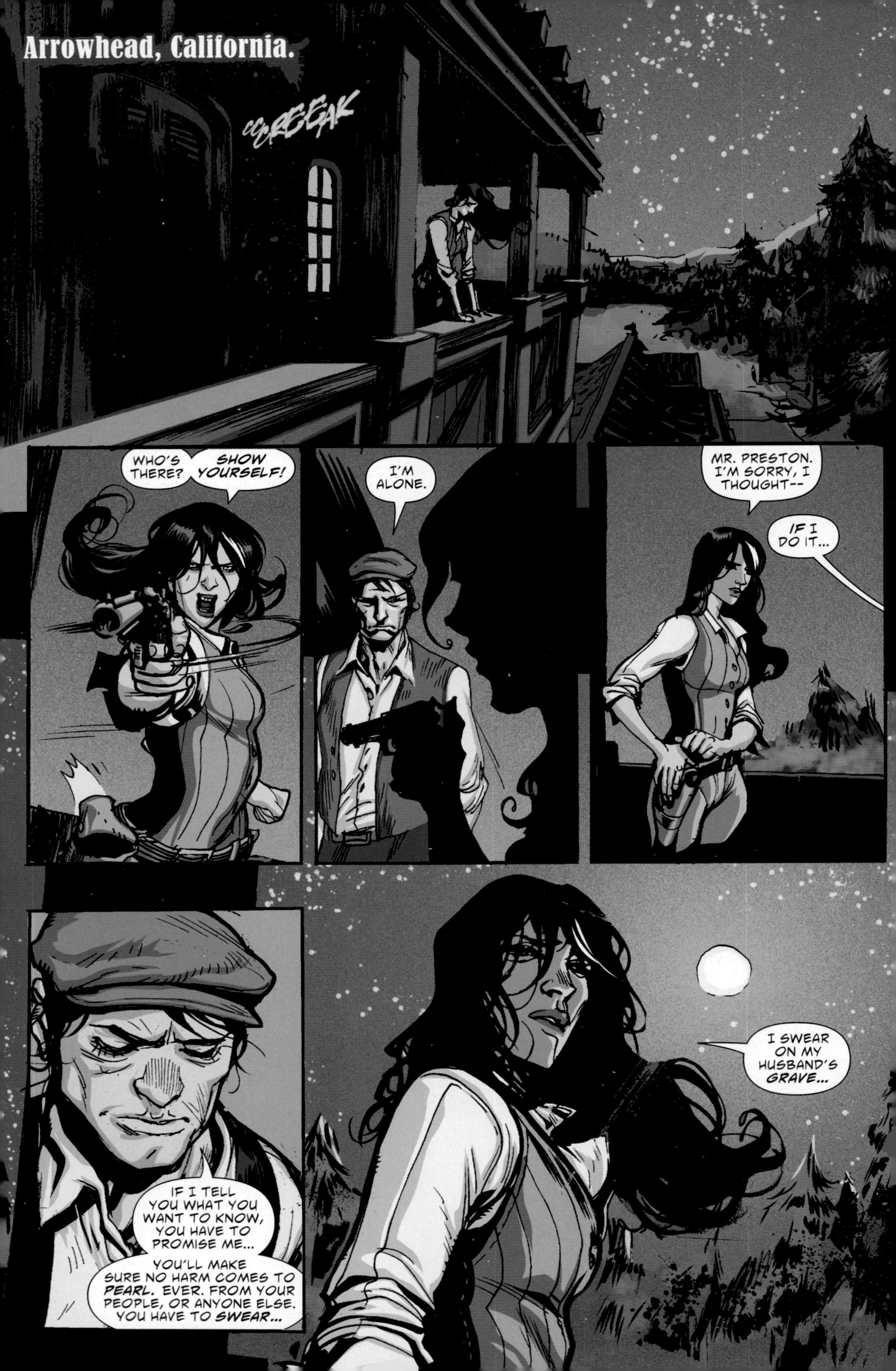

Arrowhead, California.
CCCREEAK
WHO'S THERE?
SHOW YOURSELF!
I'M ALONE.
MR. PRESTON. I'M SORRY, I THOUGHT--
IF I DO IT...
IF I TELL YOU WHAT YOU WANT TO KNOW, YOU HAVE TO PROMISE ME...
YOU'LL MAKE SURE NO HARM COMES TO PEARL. EVER. FROM YOUR PEOPLE, OR ANYONE ELSE. YOU HAVE TO SWEAR...
I SWEAR ON MY HUSBAND'S GRAVE...

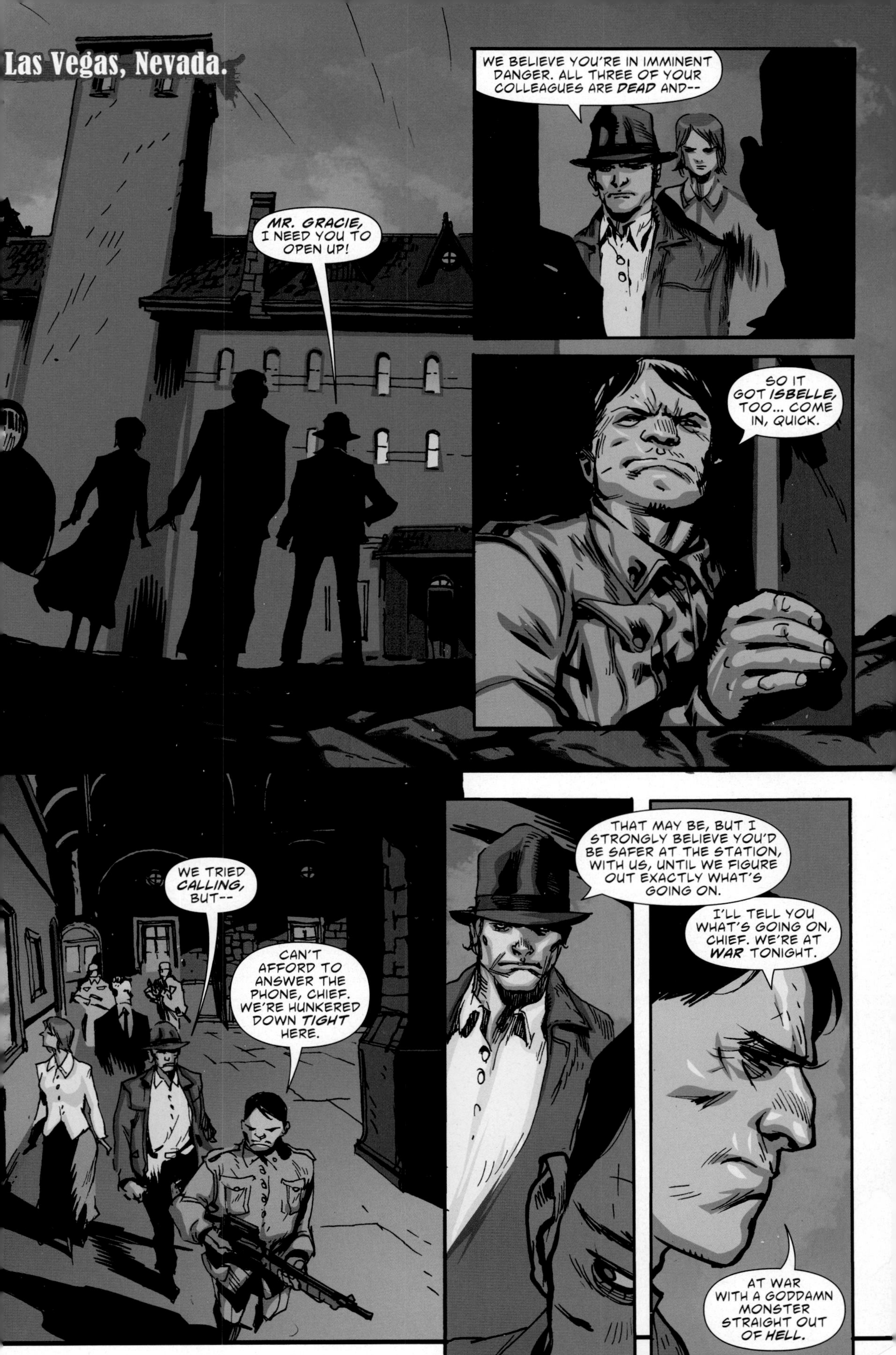
Las Vegas, Nevada.
MR. GRACIE, I NEED YOU TO OPEN UP!
WE BELIEVE YOU'RE IN IMMINENT DANGER. ALL THREE OF YOUR COLLEAGUES ARE DEAD AND--
SO IT GOT ISBELLE, TOO... COME IN, QUICK.
WE TRIED CALLING, BUT--
CAN'T AFFORD TO ANSWER THE PHONE, CHIEF. WE'RE HUNKERED DOWN TIGHT HERE.
THAT MAY BE, BUT I STRONGLY BELIEVE YOU'D BE SAFER AT THE STATION, WITH US, UNTIL WE FIGURE OUT EXACTLY WHAT'S GOING ON.
I'LL TELL YOU WHAT'S GOING ON, CHIEF. WE'RE AT WAR TONIGHT.
AT WAR WITH A GODDAMN MONSTER STRAIGHT OUT OF HELL.

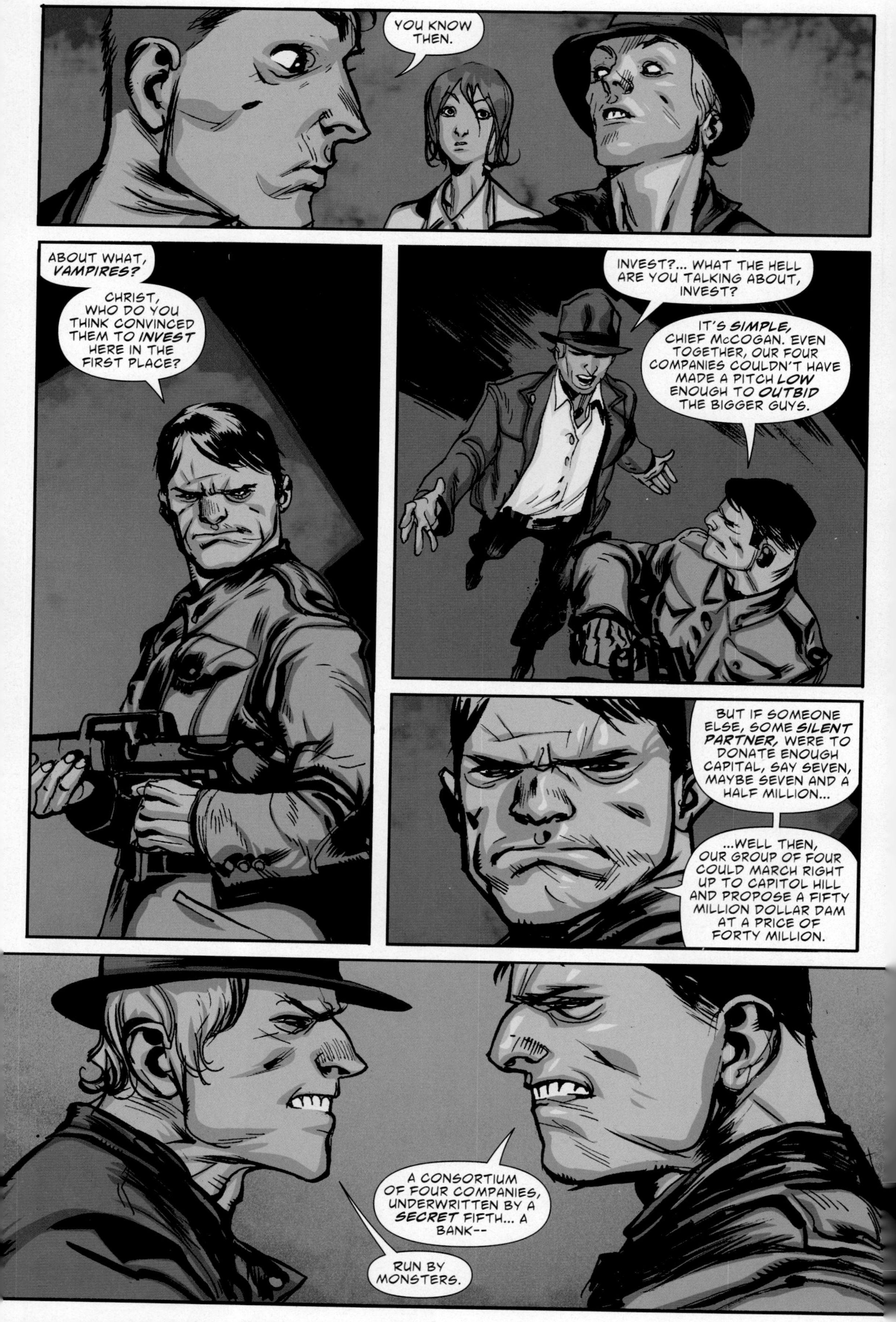

YOU KNOW THEN.
ABOUT WHAT, *VAMPIRES?*
CHRIST, WHO DO YOU THINK CONVINCED THEM TO *INVEST* HERE IN THE FIRST PLACE?
INVEST?... WHAT THE HELL ARE YOU TALKING ABOUT, INVEST?
IT'S *SIMPLE,* CHIEF McCOGAN. EVEN TOGETHER, OUR FOUR COMPANIES COULDN'T HAVE MADE A PITCH *LOW* ENOUGH TO *OUTBID* THE BIGGER GUYS.
BUT IF SOMEONE ELSE, SOME *SILENT PARTNER,* WERE TO DONATE ENOUGH CAPITAL, SAY SEVEN, MAYBE SEVEN AND A HALF MILLION...
...WELL THEN, OUR GROUP OF FOUR COULD MARCH RIGHT UP TO CAPITOL HILL AND PROPOSE A FIFTY MILLION DOLLAR DAM AT A PRICE OF FORTY MILLION.
A CONSORTIUM OF FOUR COMPANIES, UNDERWRITTEN BY A *SECRET* FIFTH... A BANK--
RUN BY MONSTERS.

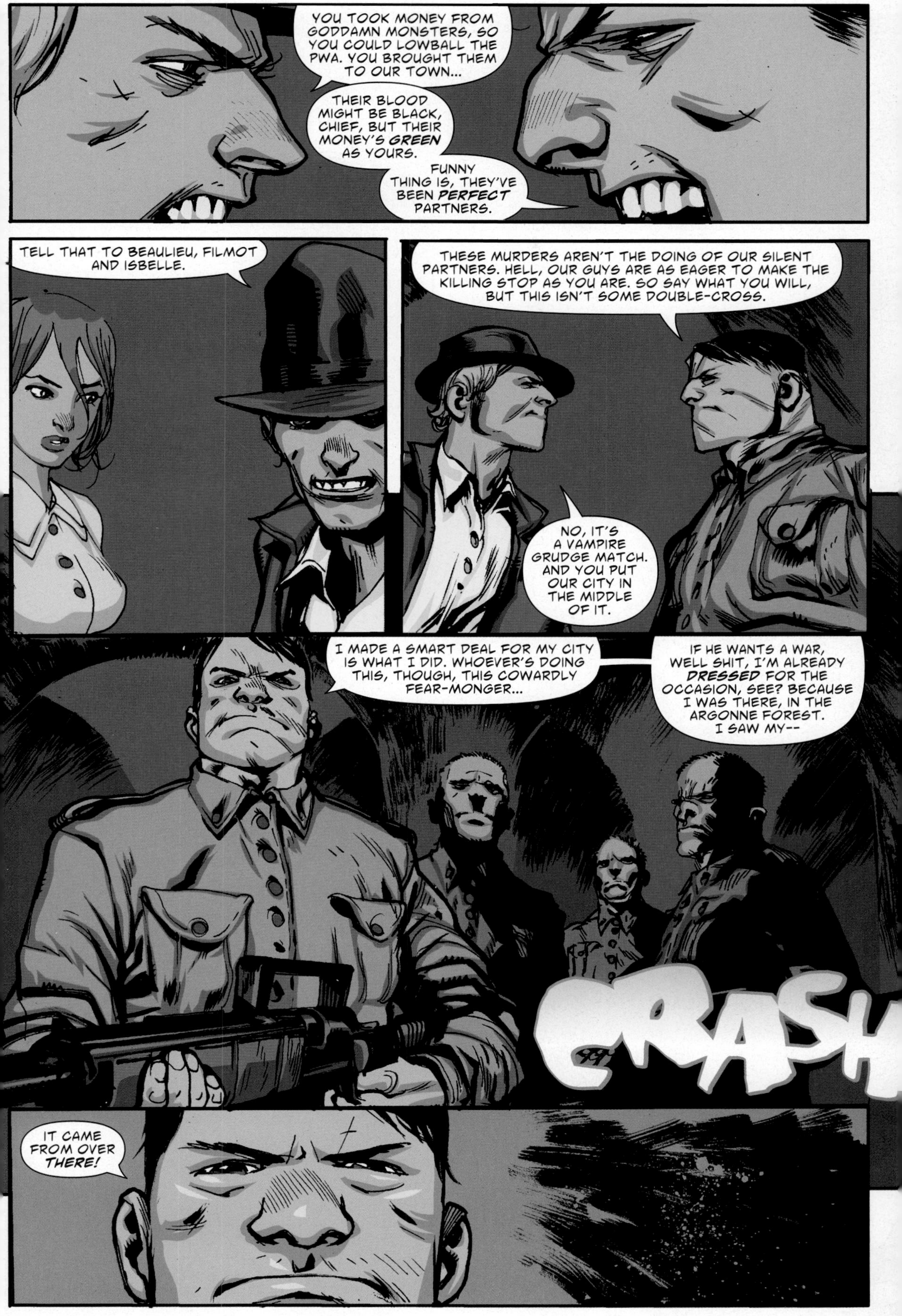
YOU TOOK MONEY FROM GODDAMN MONSTERS, SO YOU COULD LOWBALL THE PWA. YOU BROUGHT THEM TO OUR TOWN...
THEIR BLOOD MIGHT BE BLACK, CHIEF, BUT THEIR MONEY'S GREEN AS YOURS.
FUNNY THING IS, THEY'VE BEEN PERFECT PARTNERS.
TELL THAT TO BEAULIEU, FILMOT AND ISBELLE.
THESE MURDERS AREN'T THE DOING OF OUR SILENT PARTNERS. HELL, OUR GUYS ARE AS EAGER TO MAKE THE KILLING STOP AS YOU ARE. SO SAY WHAT YOU WILL, BUT THIS ISN'T SOME DOUBLE-CROSS.
NO, IT'S A VAMPIRE GRUDGE MATCH. AND YOU PUT OUR CITY IN THE MIDDLE OF IT.
I MADE A SMART DEAL FOR MY CITY IS WHAT I DID. WHOEVER'S DOING THIS, THOUGH, THIS COWARDLY FEAR-MONGER...
IF HE WANTS A WAR, WELL SHIT, I'M ALREADY DRESSED FOR THE OCCASION, SEE? BECAUSE I WAS THERE, IN THE ARGONNE FOREST. I SAW MY--
CRASH
IT CAME FROM OVER THERE!

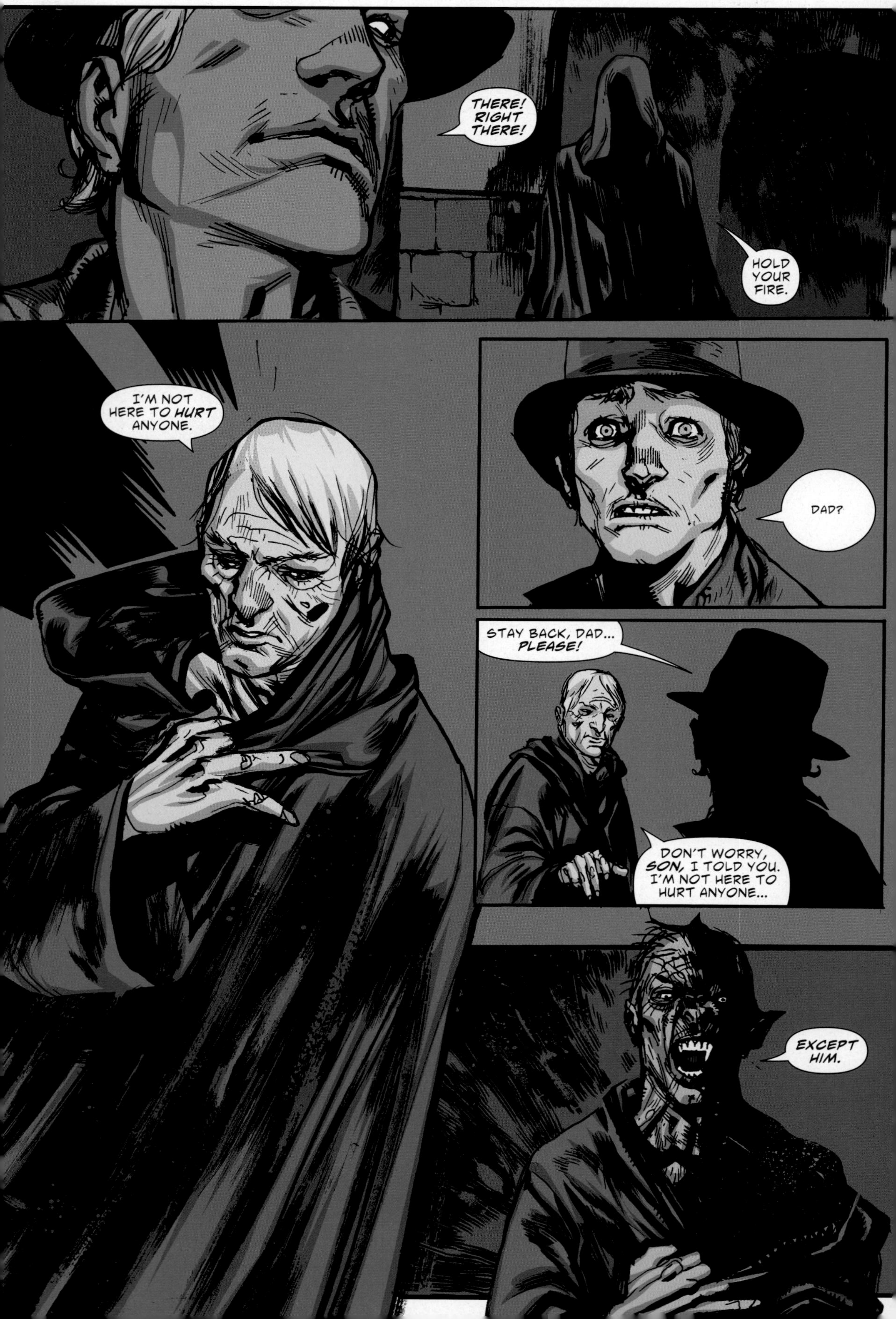
THERE! RIGHT THERE!
HOLD YOUR FIRE.
I'M NOT HERE TO *HURT* ANYONE.
DAD?
STAY BACK, DAD... *PLEASE!*
DON'T WORRY, *SON,* I TOLD YOU. I'M NOT HERE TO HURT ANYONE...
EXCEPT HIM.

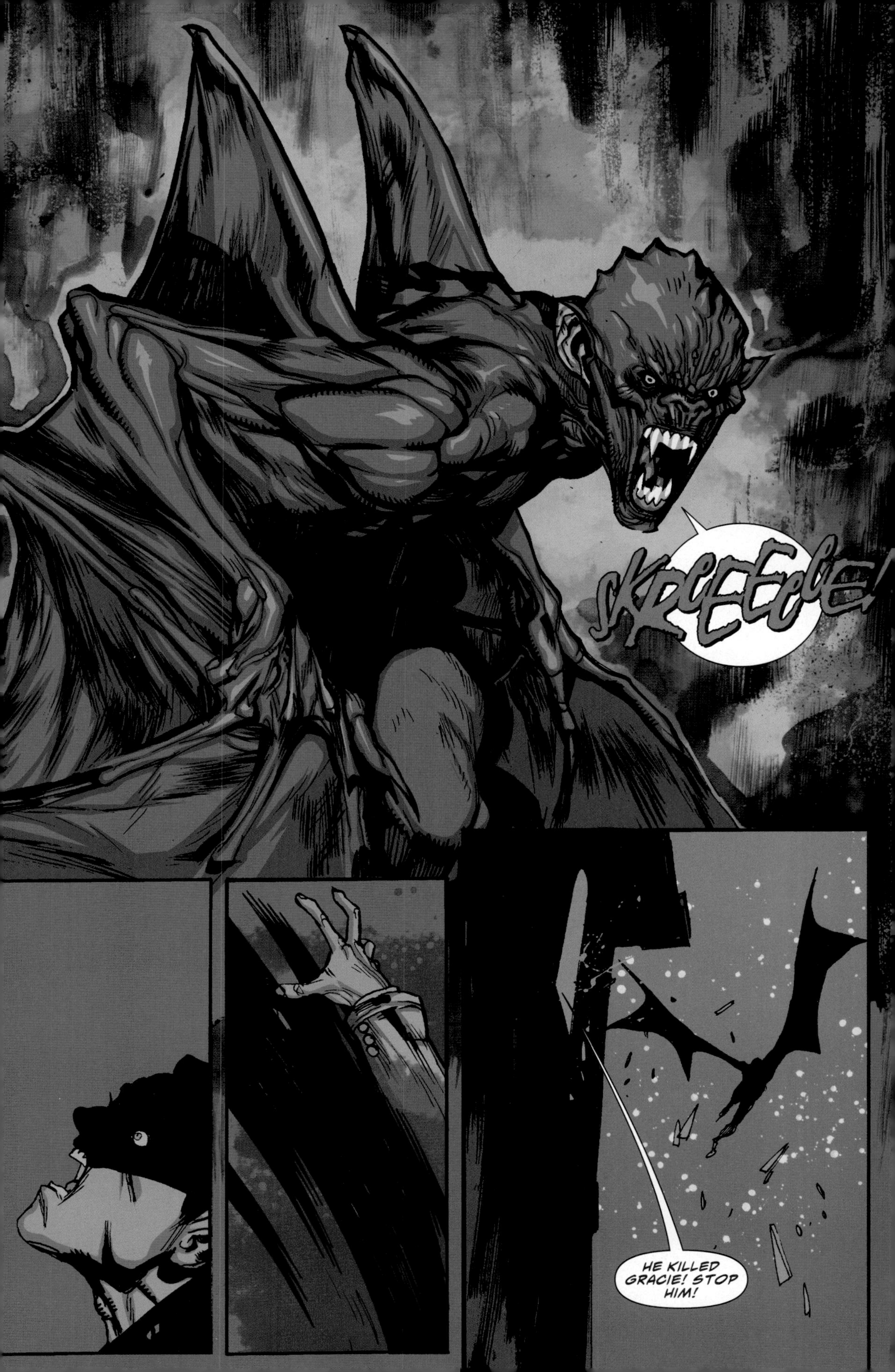
SKREEEEEE!
HE KILLED GRACIE! STOP HIM!

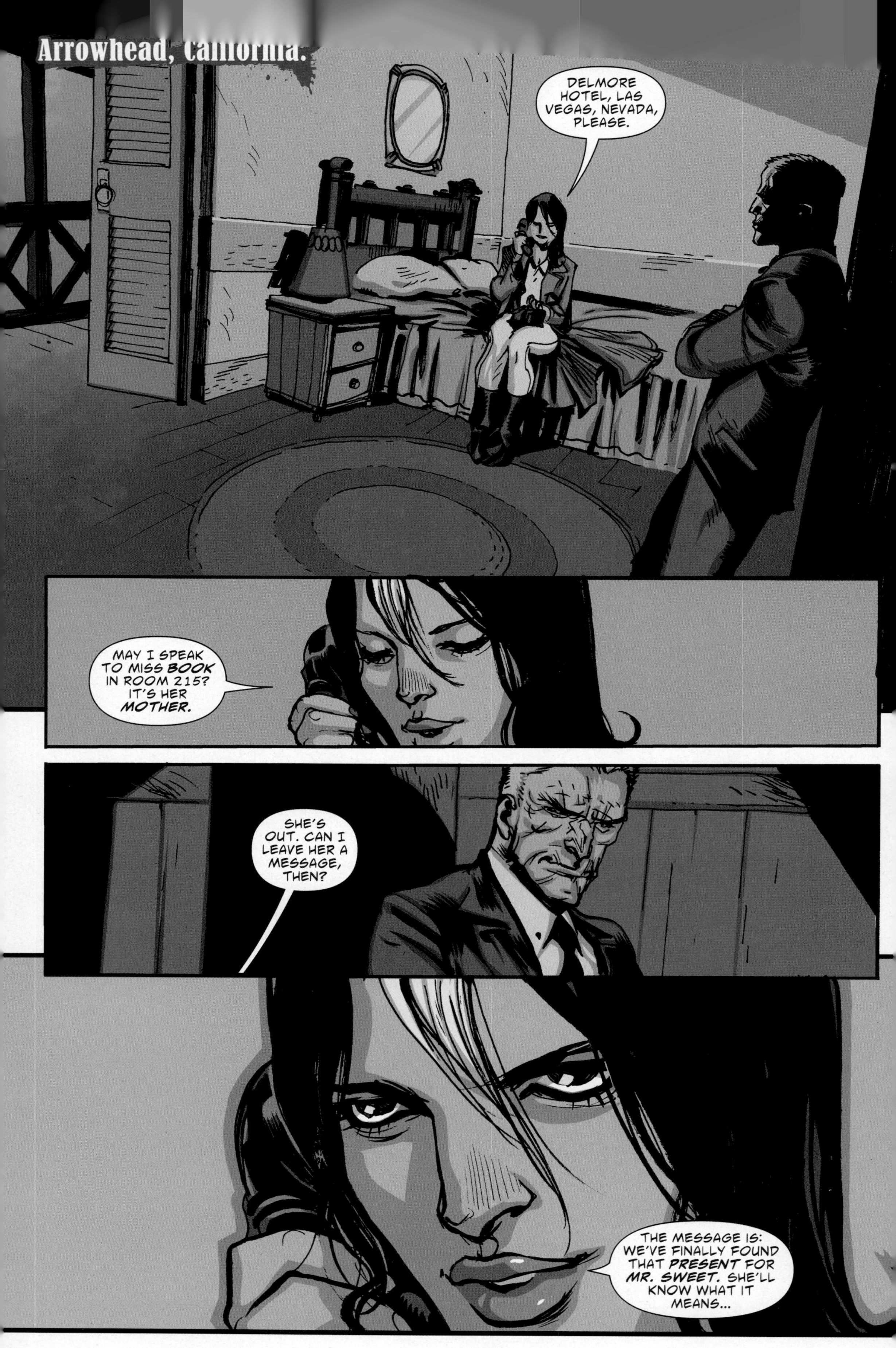
Arrowhead, California.
DELMORE HOTEL, LAS VEGAS, NEVADA, PLEASE.
MAY I SPEAK TO MISS BOOK IN ROOM 215? IT'S HER MOTHER.
SHE'S OUT. CAN I LEAVE HER A MESSAGE, THEN?
THE MESSAGE IS: WE'VE FINALLY FOUND THAT PRESENT FOR MR. SWEET. SHE'LL KNOW WHAT IT MEANS...

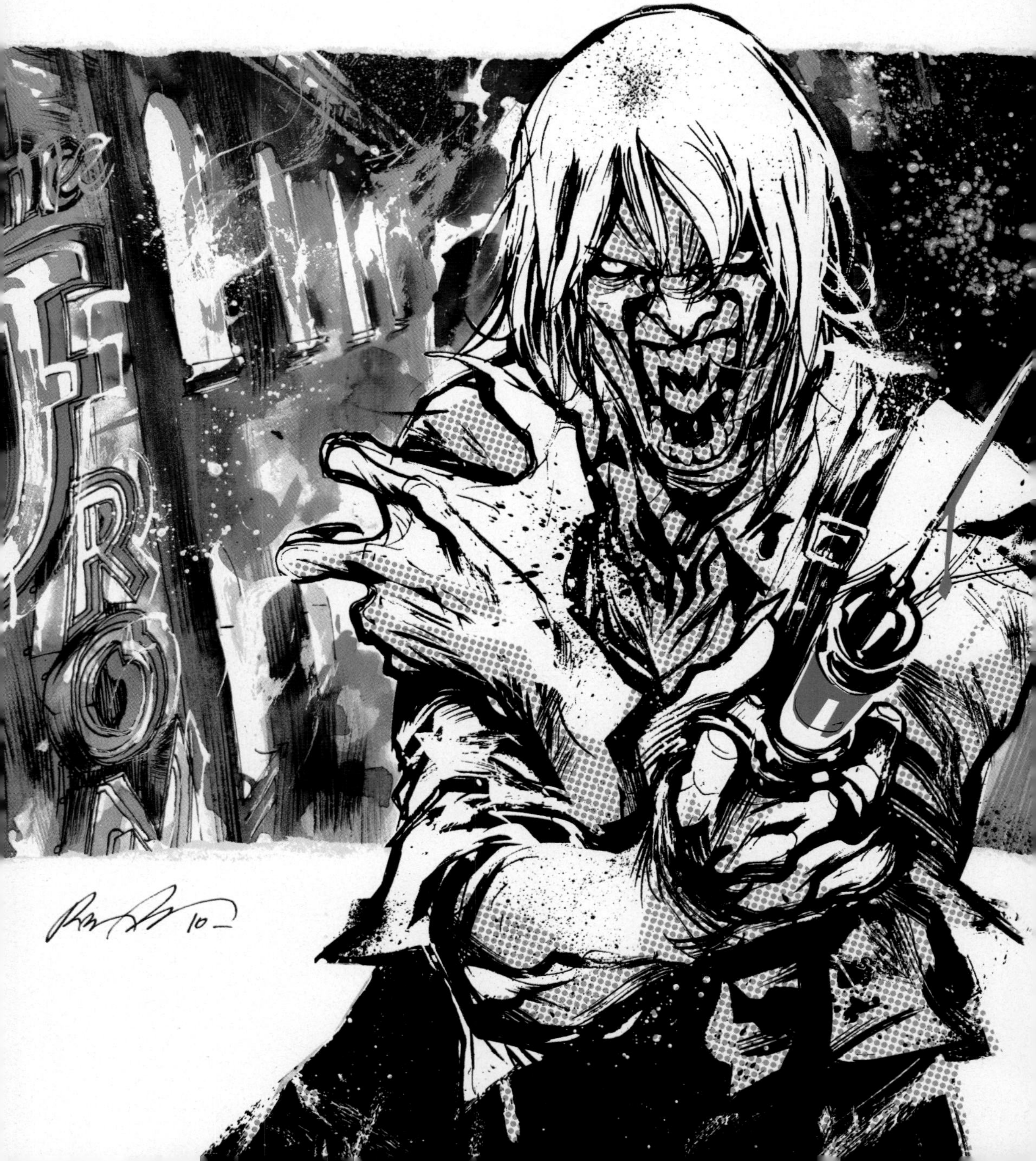

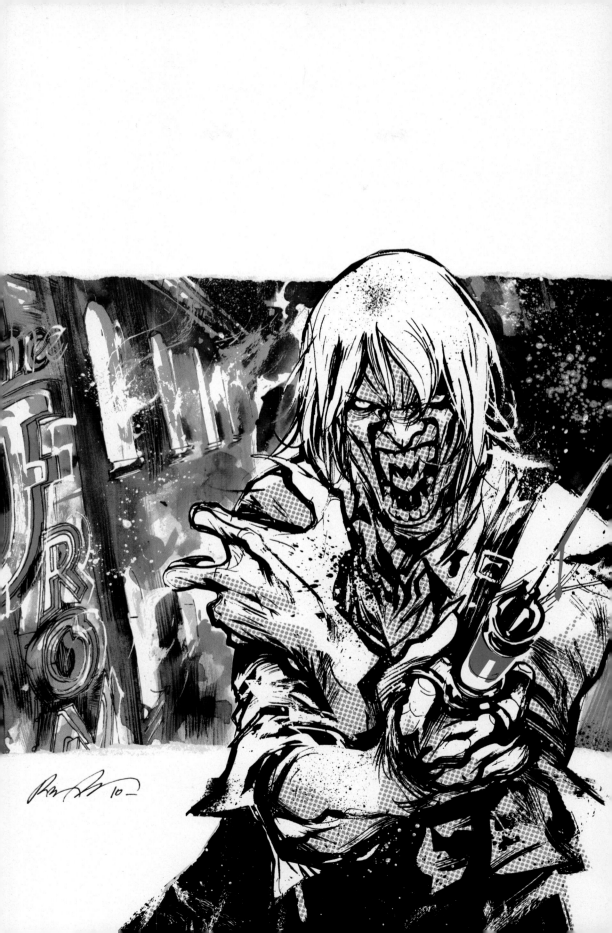

Devil in the Sand

Conclusion

Rafael Albuquerque
Mateus Santolouco
(pages 79-81)
Artists

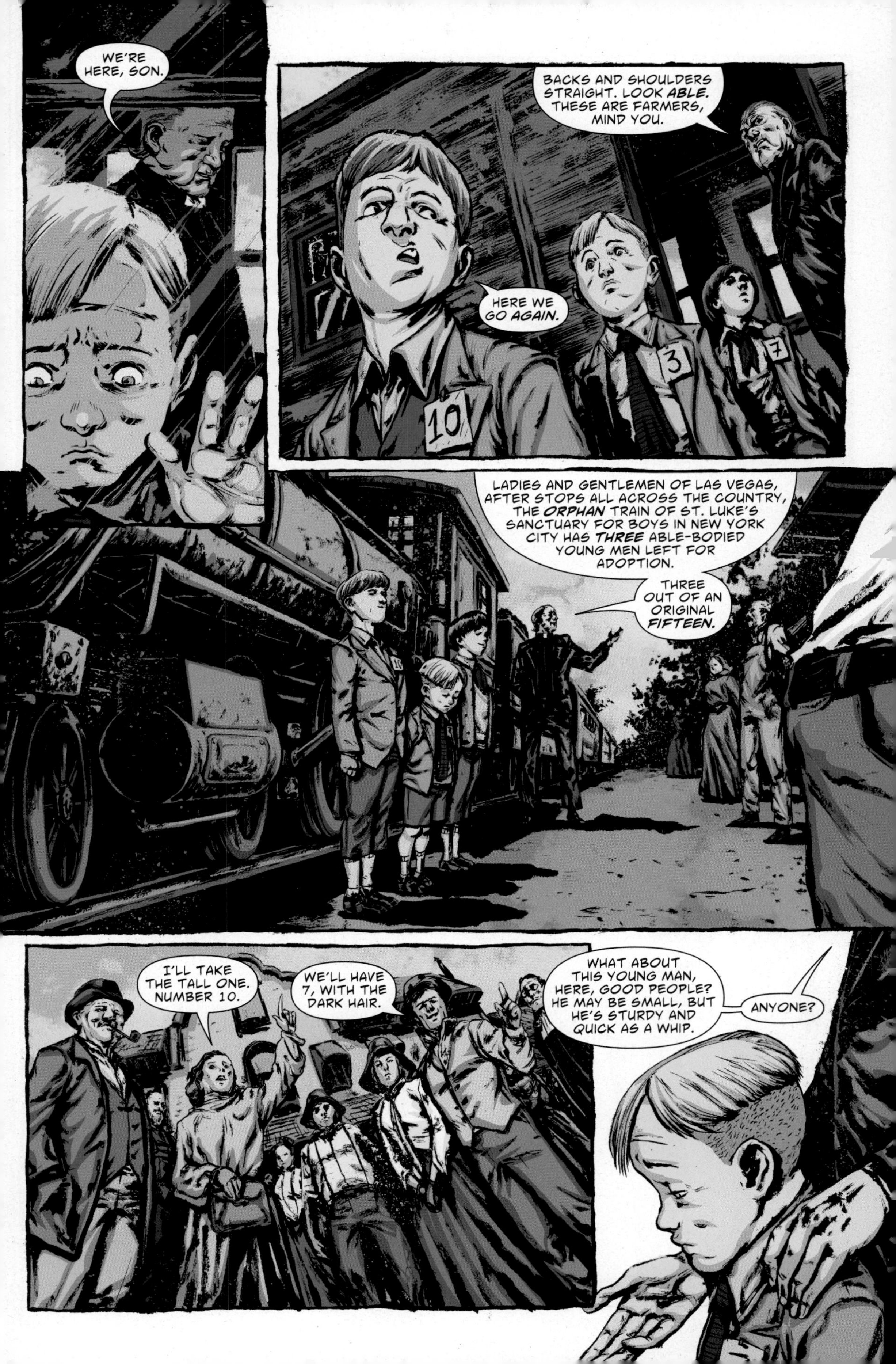
WE'RE HERE, SON.
BACKS AND SHOULDERS STRAIGHT. LOOK *ABLE.* THESE ARE FARMERS, MIND YOU.
HERE WE GO *AGAIN.*
10
3
7
LADIES AND GENTLEMEN OF LAS VEGAS, AFTER STOPS ALL ACROSS THE COUNTRY, THE *ORPHAN* TRAIN OF ST. LUKE'S SANCTUARY FOR BOYS IN NEW YORK CITY HAS *THREE* ABLE-BODIED YOUNG MEN LEFT FOR ADOPTION.
THREE OUT OF AN ORIGINAL *FIFTEEN.*
I'LL TAKE THE TALL ONE. NUMBER 10.
WE'LL HAVE 7, WITH THE DARK HAIR.
WHAT ABOUT THIS YOUNG MAN, HERE, GOOD PEOPLE? HE MAY BE SMALL, BUT HE'S STURDY AND QUICK AS A WHIP.
ANYONE?

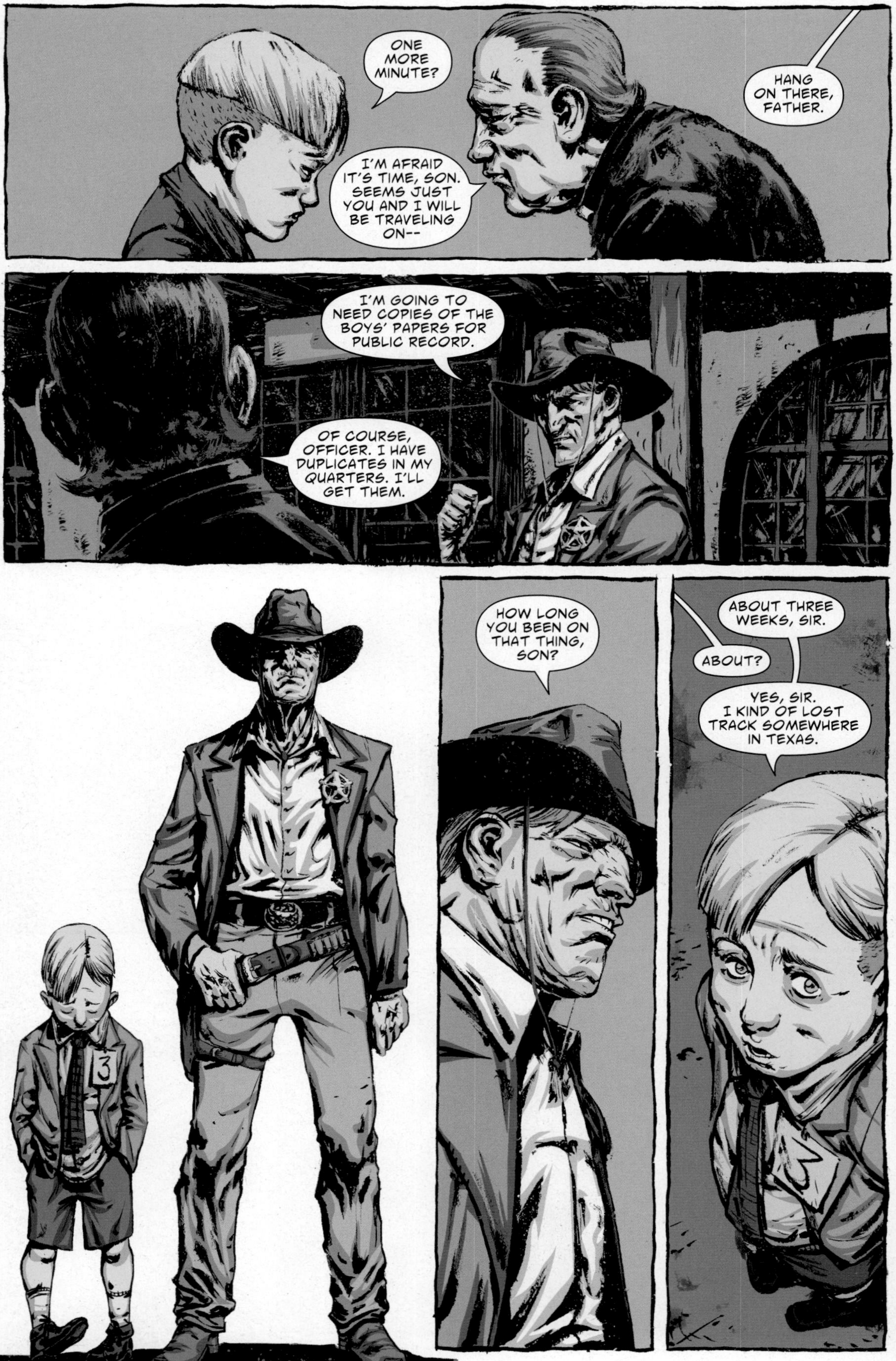
ONE MORE MINUTE?
I'M AFRAID IT'S TIME, SON. SEEMS JUST YOU AND I WILL BE TRAVELING ON--
HANG ON THERE, FATHER.
I'M GOING TO NEED COPIES OF THE BOYS' PAPERS FOR PUBLIC RECORD.
OF COURSE, OFFICER. I HAVE DUPLICATES IN MY QUARTERS. I'LL GET THEM.
3
HOW LONG YOU BEEN ON THAT THING, SON?
ABOUT THREE WEEKS, SIR.
ABOUT?
YES, SIR. I KIND OF LOST TRACK SOMEWHERE IN TEXAS.

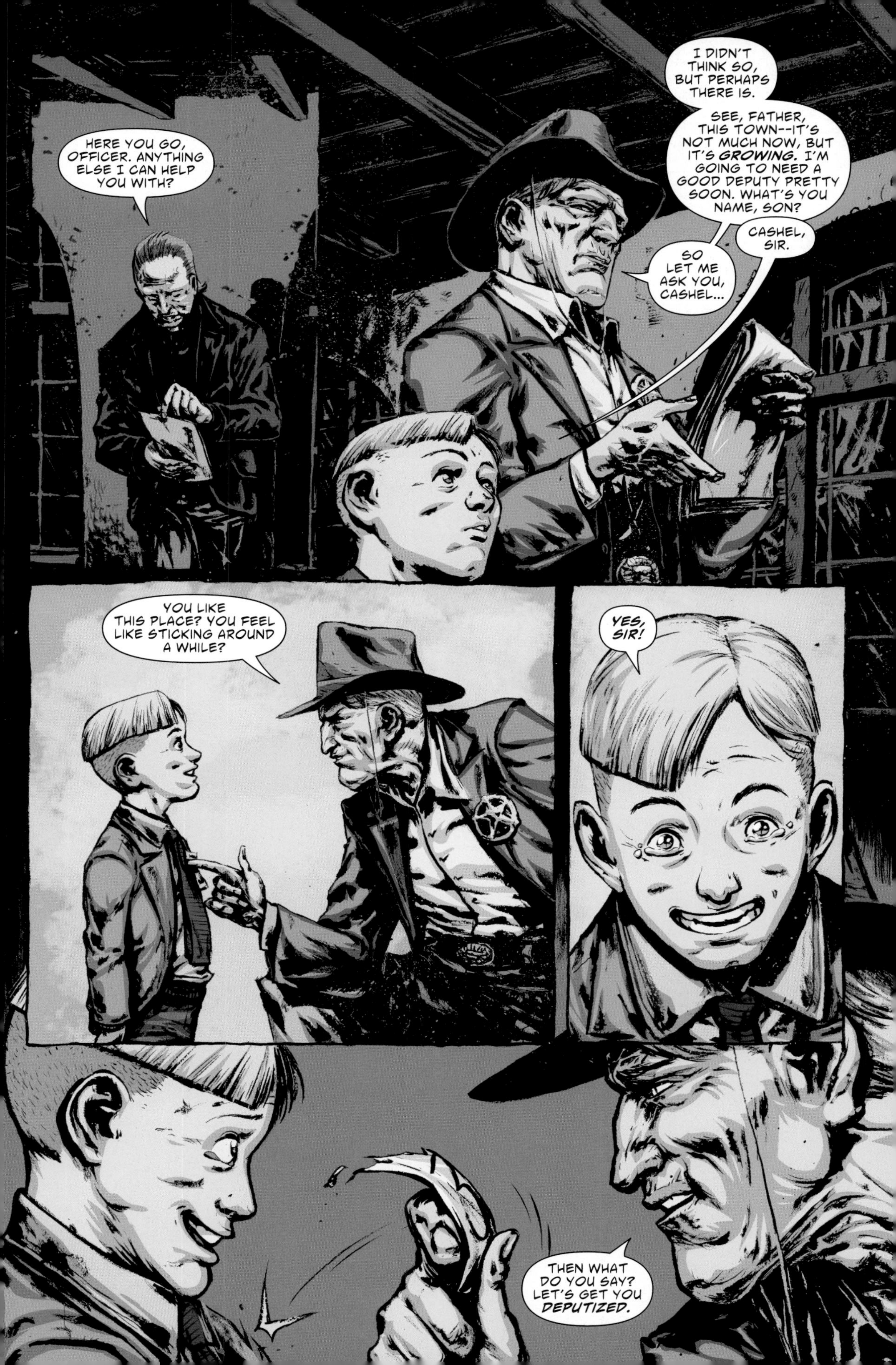
HERE YOU GO, OFFICER. ANYTHING ELSE I CAN HELP YOU WITH?
I DIDN'T THINK SO, BUT PERHAPS THERE IS.
SEE, FATHER, THIS TOWN--IT'S NOT MUCH NOW, BUT IT'S GROWING. I'M GOING TO NEED A GOOD DEPUTY PRETTY SOON. WHAT'S YOU NAME, SON?
CASHEL, SIR.
SO LET ME ASK YOU, CASHEL...
YOU LIKE THIS PLACE? YOU FEEL LIKE STICKING AROUND A WHILE?
YES, SIR!
THEN WHAT DO YOU SAY? LET'S GET YOU DEPUTIZED.

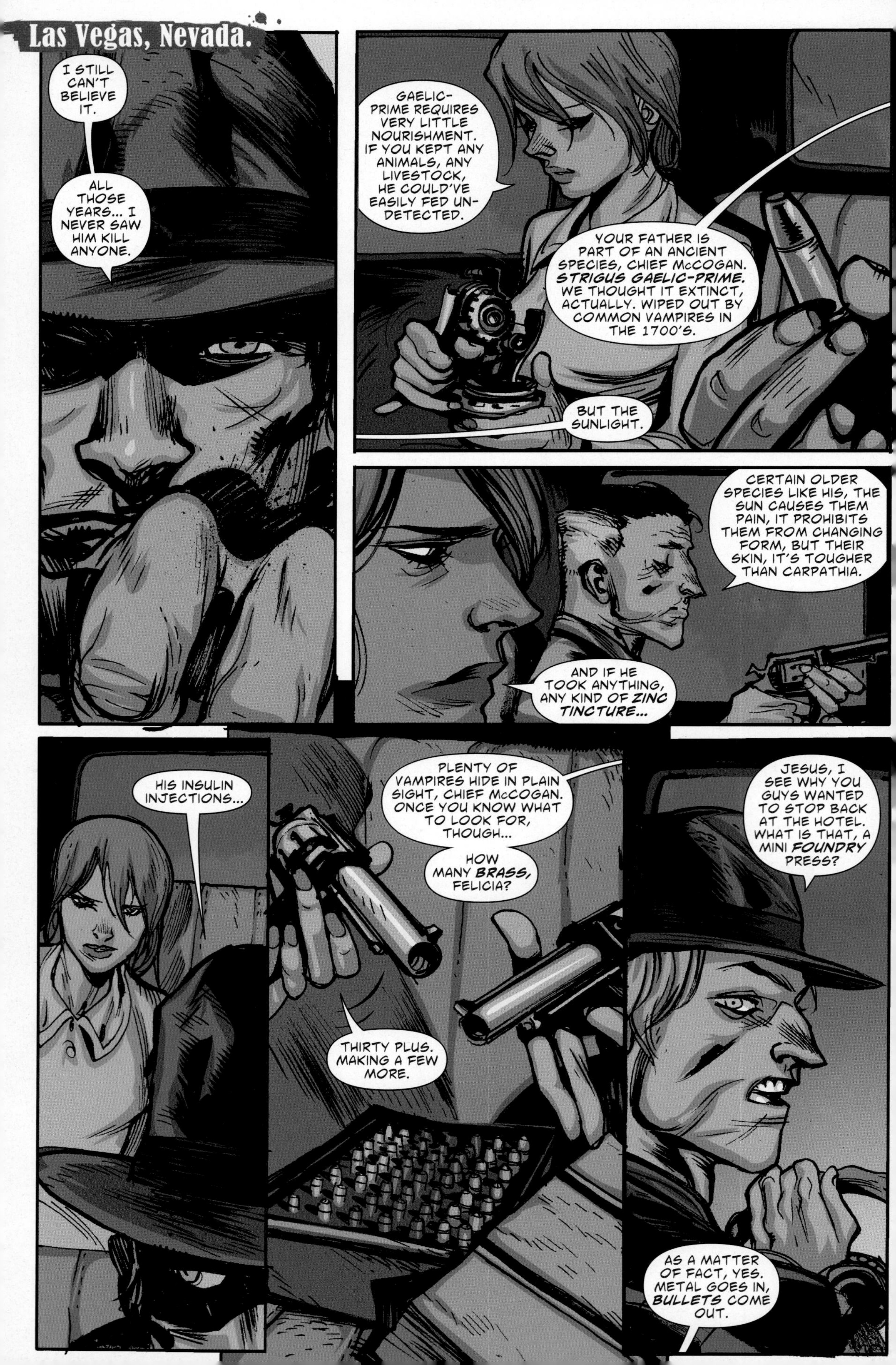
Las Vegas, Nevada.
I STILL CAN'T BELIEVE IT.
ALL THOSE YEARS... I NEVER SAW HIM KILL ANYONE.
GAELIC-PRIME REQUIRES VERY LITTLE NOURISHMENT. IF YOU KEPT ANY ANIMALS, ANY LIVESTOCK, HE COULD'VE EASILY FED UN-DETECTED.
YOUR FATHER IS PART OF AN ANCIENT SPECIES, CHIEF McCOGAN. STRIGUS GAELIC-PRIME. WE THOUGHT IT EXTINCT, ACTUALLY. WIPED OUT BY COMMON VAMPIRES IN THE 1700'S.
BUT THE SUNLIGHT.
CERTAIN OLDER SPECIES LIKE HIS, THE SUN CAUSES THEM PAIN, IT PROHIBITS THEM FROM CHANGING FORM, BUT THEIR SKIN, IT'S TOUGHER THAN CARPATHIA.
AND IF HE TOOK ANYTHING, ANY KIND OF ZINC TINCTURE...
HIS INSULIN INJECTIONS...
PLENTY OF VAMPIRES HIDE IN PLAIN SIGHT, CHIEF McCOGAN. ONCE YOU KNOW WHAT TO LOOK FOR, THOUGH...
HOW MANY BRASS, FELICIA?
THIRTY PLUS. MAKING A FEW MORE.
JESUS, I SEE WHY YOU GUYS WANTED TO STOP BACK AT THE HOTEL. WHAT IS THAT, A MINI FOUNDRY PRESS?
AS A MATTER OF FACT, YES. METAL GOES IN, BULLETS COME OUT.

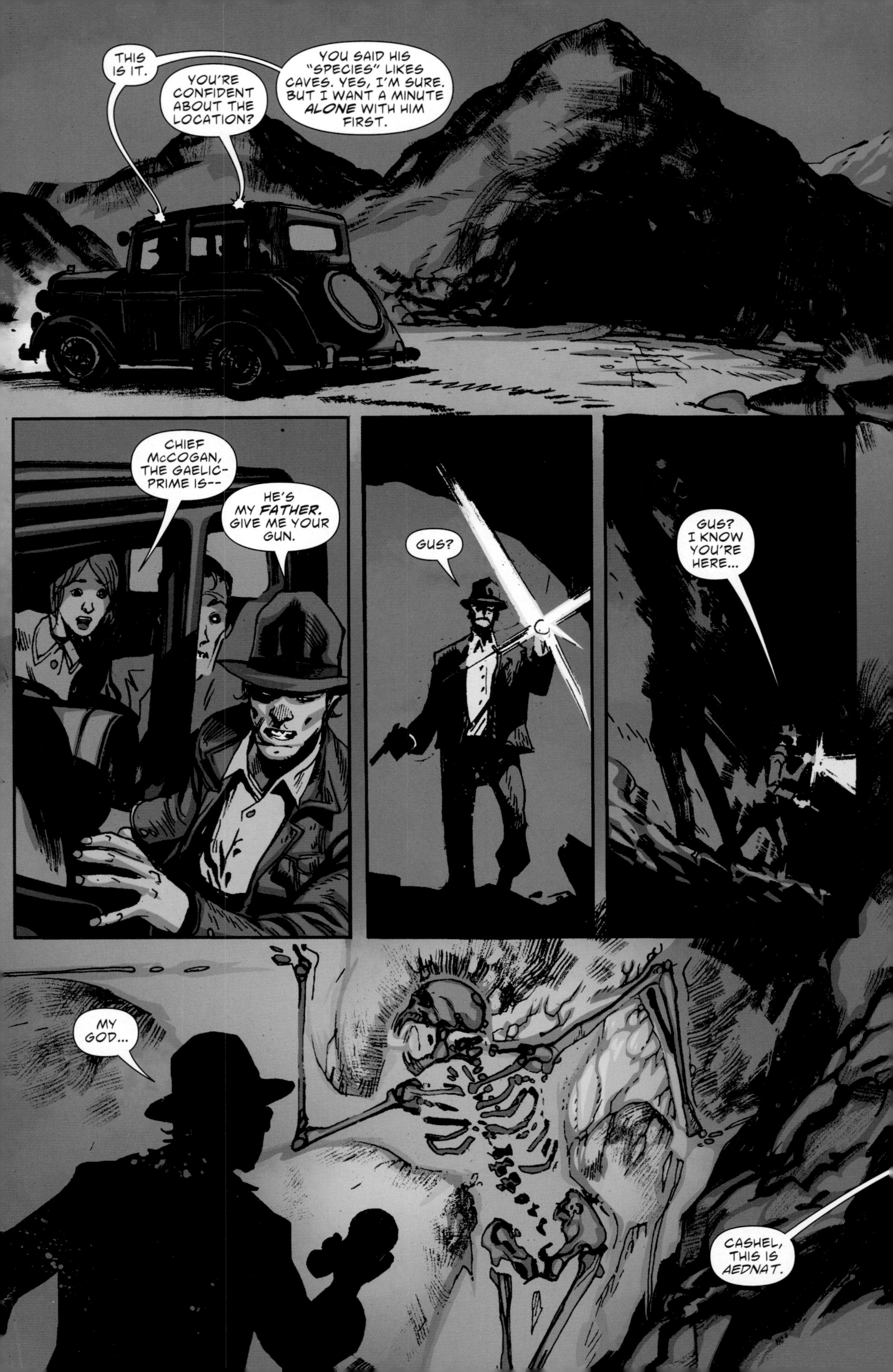
THIS IS IT.
YOU'RE CONFIDENT ABOUT THE LOCATION?
YOU SAID HIS "SPECIES" LIKES CAVES. YES, I'M SURE. BUT I WANT A MINUTE *ALONE* WITH HIM FIRST.
CHIEF McCOGAN, THE GAELIC-PRIME IS--
HE'S MY *FATHER.* GIVE ME YOUR GUN.
GUS?
GUS? I KNOW YOU'RE HERE...
MY GOD...
CASHEL, THIS IS AEDNAT.

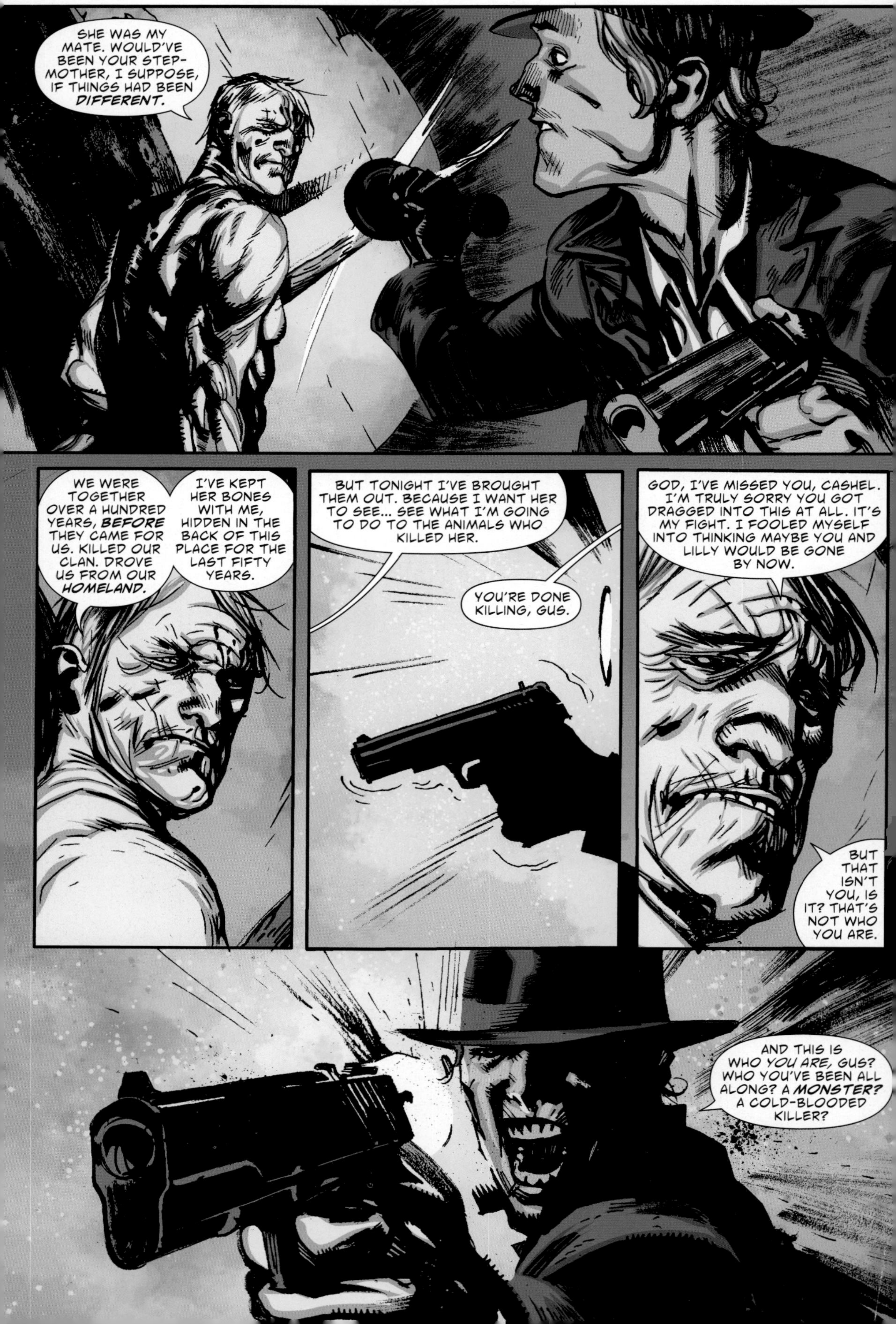
SHE WAS MY MATE. WOULD'VE BEEN YOUR STEP-MOTHER, I SUPPOSE, IF THINGS HAD BEEN *DIFFERENT*.
WE WERE TOGETHER OVER A HUNDRED YEARS, *BEFORE* THEY CAME FOR US. KILLED OUR CLAN. DROVE US FROM OUR *HOMELAND*.
I'VE KEPT HER BONES WITH ME, HIDDEN IN THE BACK OF THIS PLACE FOR THE LAST FIFTY YEARS.
BUT TONIGHT I'VE BROUGHT THEM OUT. BECAUSE I WANT HER TO SEE... SEE WHAT I'M GOING TO DO TO THE ANIMALS WHO KILLED HER.
YOU'RE DONE KILLING, GUS.
GOD, I'VE MISSED YOU, CASHEL. I'M TRULY SORRY YOU GOT DRAGGED INTO THIS AT ALL. IT'S MY FIGHT. I FOOLED MYSELF INTO THINKING MAYBE YOU AND LILLY WOULD BE GONE BY NOW.
BUT THAT ISN'T YOU, IS IT? THAT'S NOT WHO YOU ARE.
AND THIS IS WHO *YOU ARE*, GUS? WHO YOU'VE BEEN ALL ALONG? A *MONSTER?* A COLD-BLOODED KILLER?

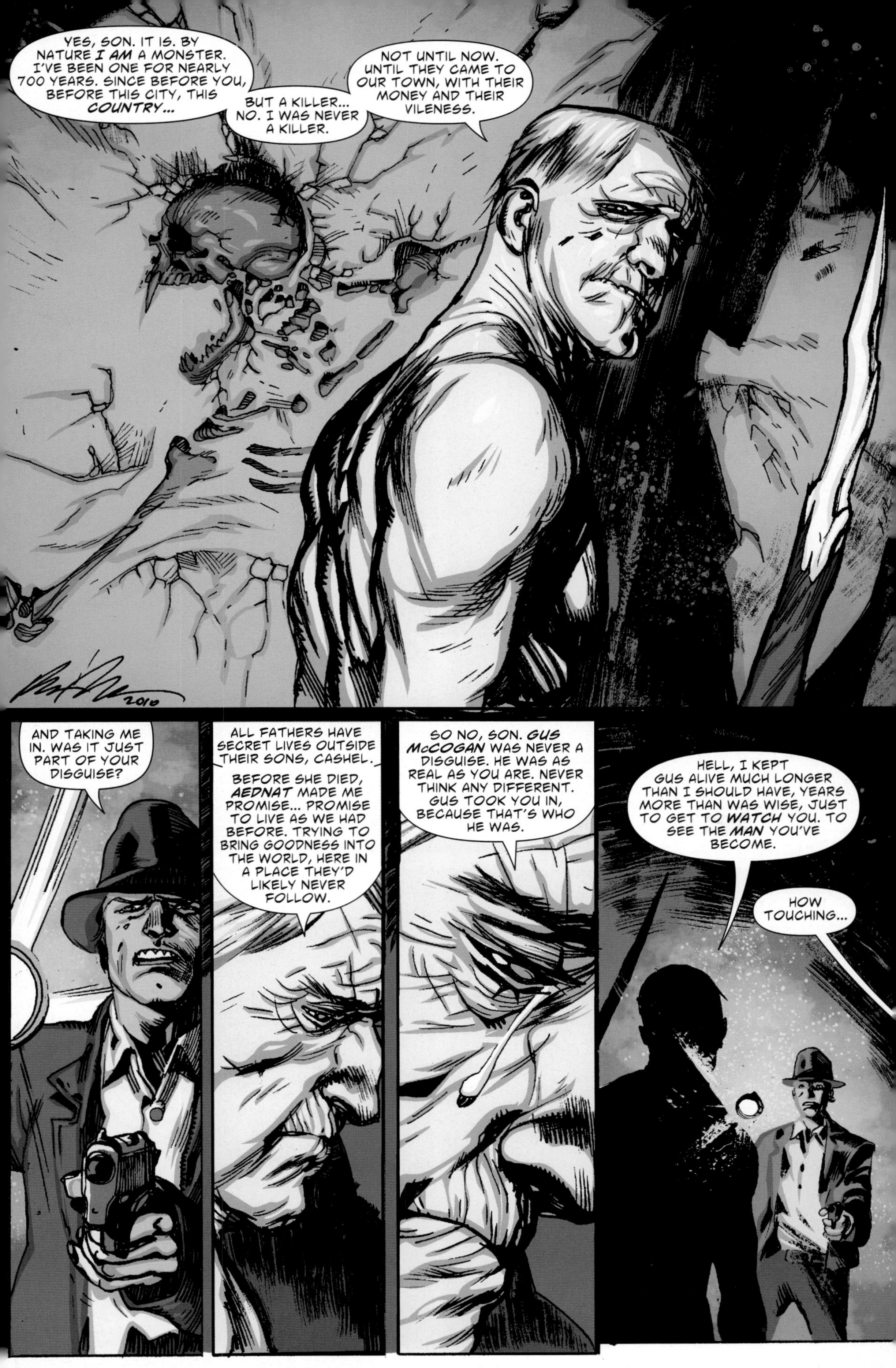
YES, SON. IT IS. BY NATURE I AM A MONSTER. I'VE BEEN ONE FOR NEARLY 700 YEARS. SINCE BEFORE YOU, BEFORE THIS CITY, THIS COUNTRY...
BUT A KILLER... NO. I WAS NEVER A KILLER.
NOT UNTIL NOW. UNTIL THEY CAME TO OUR TOWN, WITH THEIR MONEY AND THEIR VILENESS.
AND TAKING ME IN. WAS IT JUST PART OF YOUR DISGUISE?
ALL FATHERS HAVE SECRET LIVES OUTSIDE THEIR SONS, CASHEL.
BEFORE SHE DIED, AEDNAT MADE ME PROMISE... PROMISE TO LIVE AS WE HAD BEFORE. TRYING TO BRING GOODNESS INTO THE WORLD, HERE IN A PLACE THEY'D LIKELY NEVER FOLLOW.
SO NO, SON. GUS McCOGAN WAS NEVER A DISGUISE. HE WAS AS REAL AS YOU ARE. NEVER THINK ANY DIFFERENT. GUS TOOK YOU IN, BECAUSE THAT'S WHO HE WAS.
HELL, I KEPT GUS ALIVE MUCH LONGER THAN I SHOULD HAVE, YEARS MORE THAN WAS WISE, JUST TO GET TO WATCH YOU. TO SEE THE MAN YOU'VE BECOME.
HOW TOUCHING...

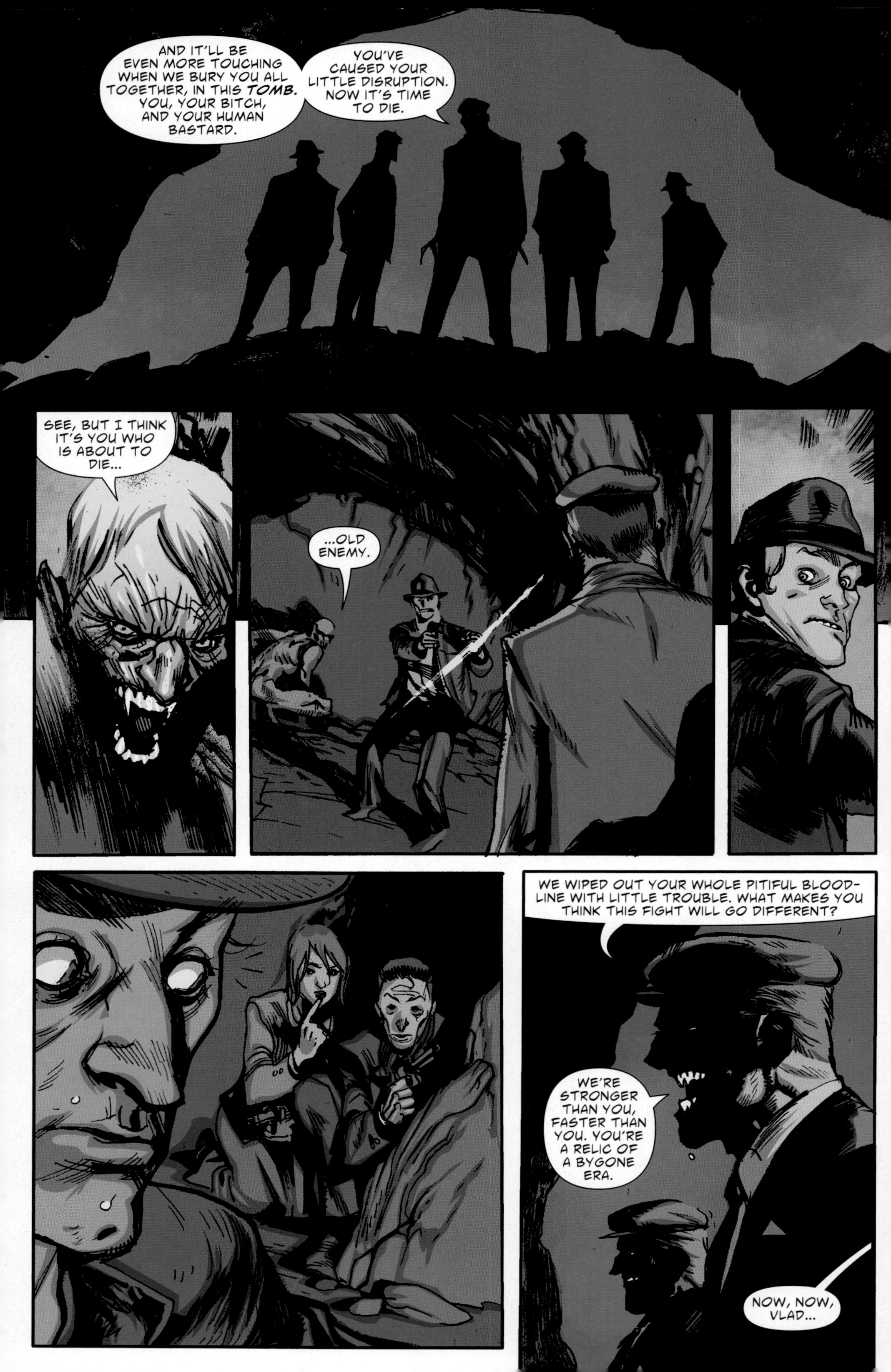
AND IT'LL BE EVEN MORE TOUCHING WHEN WE BURY YOU ALL TOGETHER, IN THIS TOMB. YOU, YOUR BITCH, AND YOUR HUMAN BASTARD.
YOU'VE CAUSED YOUR LITTLE DISRUPTION. NOW IT'S TIME TO DIE.
SEE, BUT I THINK IT'S YOU WHO IS ABOUT TO DIE...
...OLD ENEMY.
WE WIPED OUT YOUR WHOLE PITIFUL BLOOD-LINE WITH LITTLE TROUBLE. WHAT MAKES YOU THINK THIS FIGHT WILL GO DIFFERENT?
WE'RE STRONGER THAN YOU, FASTER THAN YOU. YOU'RE A RELIC OF A BYGONE ERA.
NOW, NOW, VLAD...

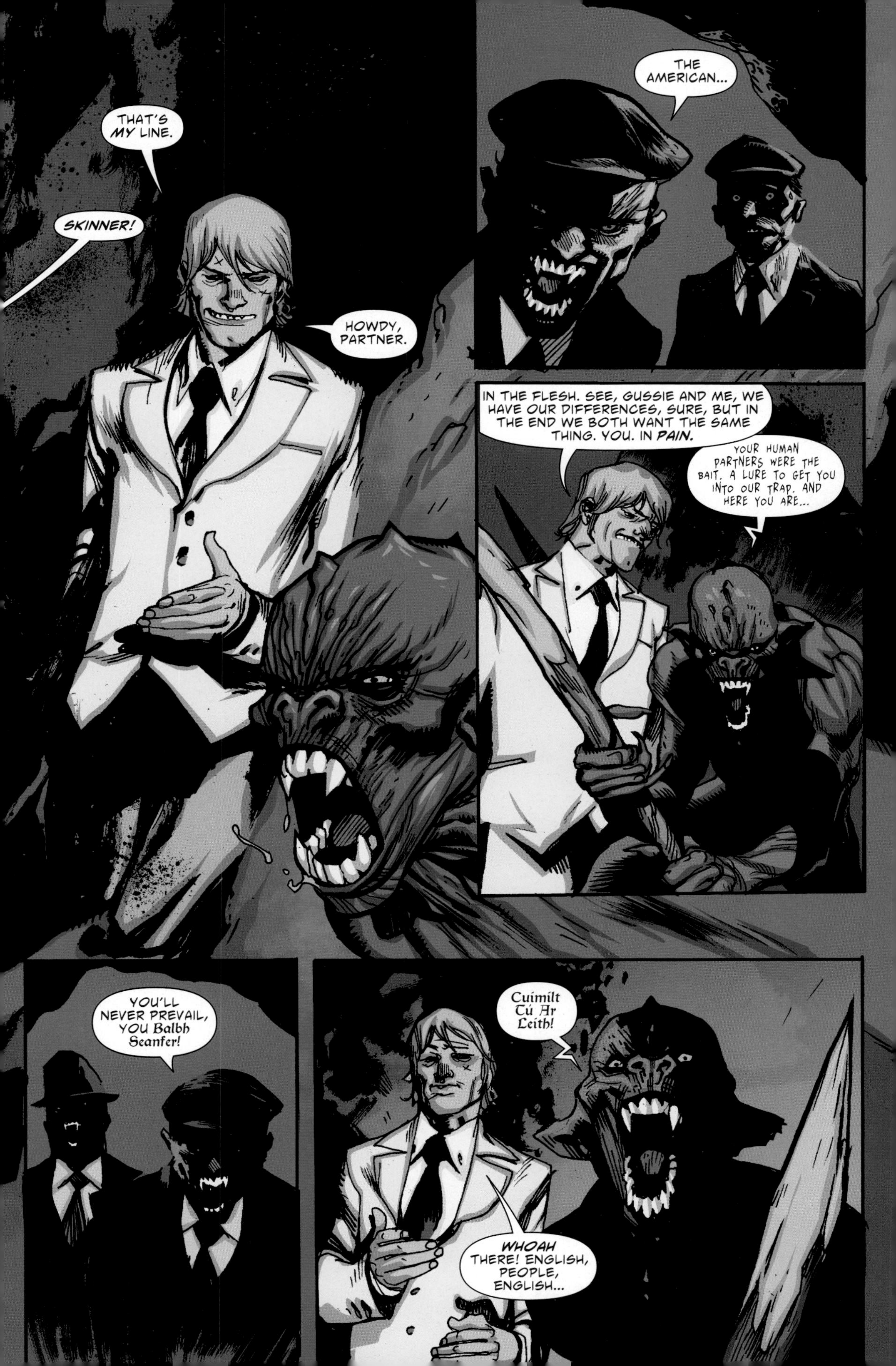
THAT'S MY LINE.
SKINNER!
HOWDY, PARTNER.
THE AMERICAN...
IN THE FLESH. SEE, GUSSIE AND ME, WE HAVE OUR DIFFERENCES, SURE, BUT IN THE END WE BOTH WANT THE SAME THING. YOU. IN PAIN.
YOUR HUMAN PARTNERS WERE THE BAIT. A LURE TO GET YOU INTO OUR TRAP. AND HERE YOU ARE...
YOU'LL NEVER PREVAIL, YOU Balbh Seanfer!
Cuimilt Tú Ar Leith!
WHOAH THERE! ENGLISH, PEOPLE, ENGLISH...

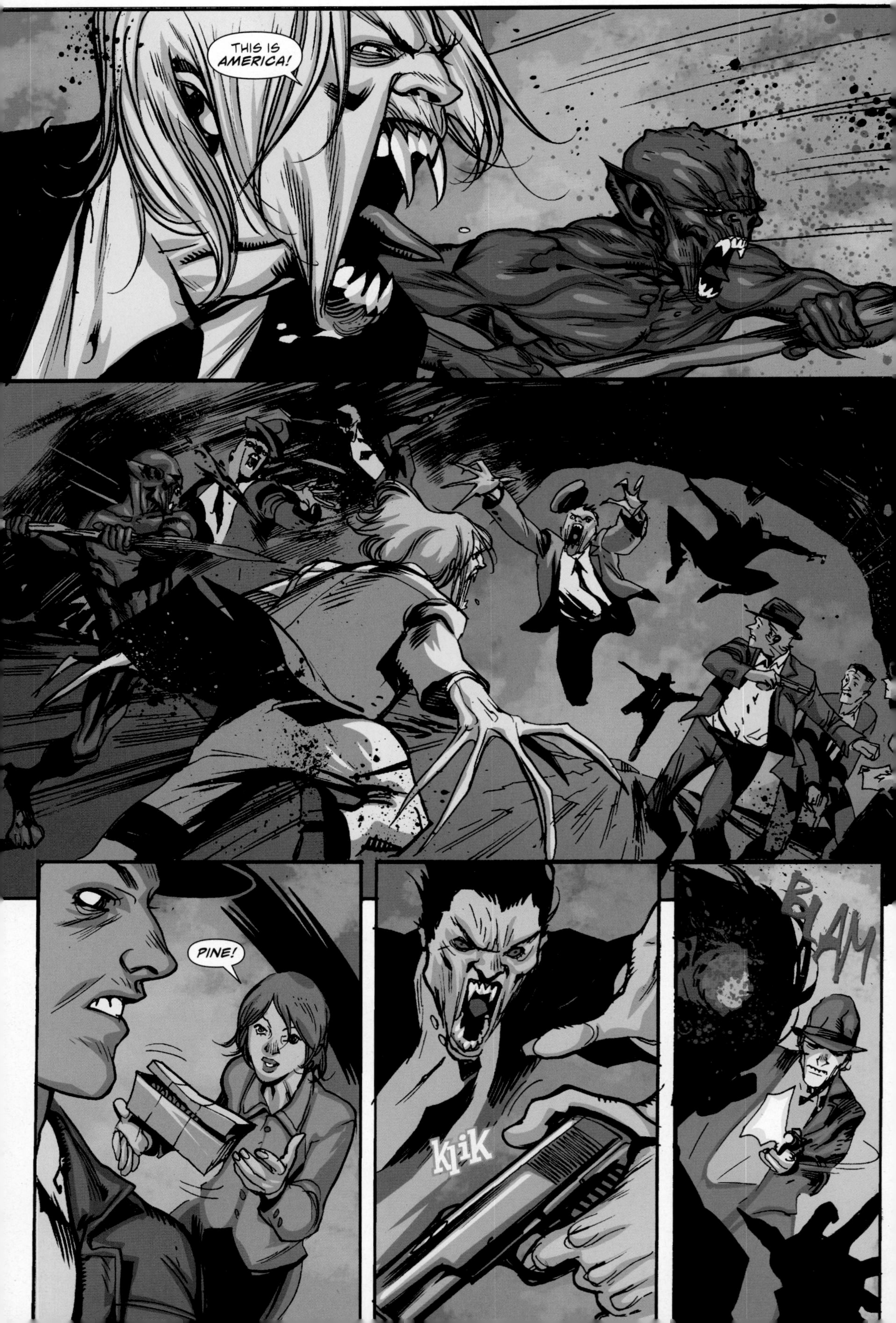
THIS IS AMERICA!
PINE!
KLIK
BLAM

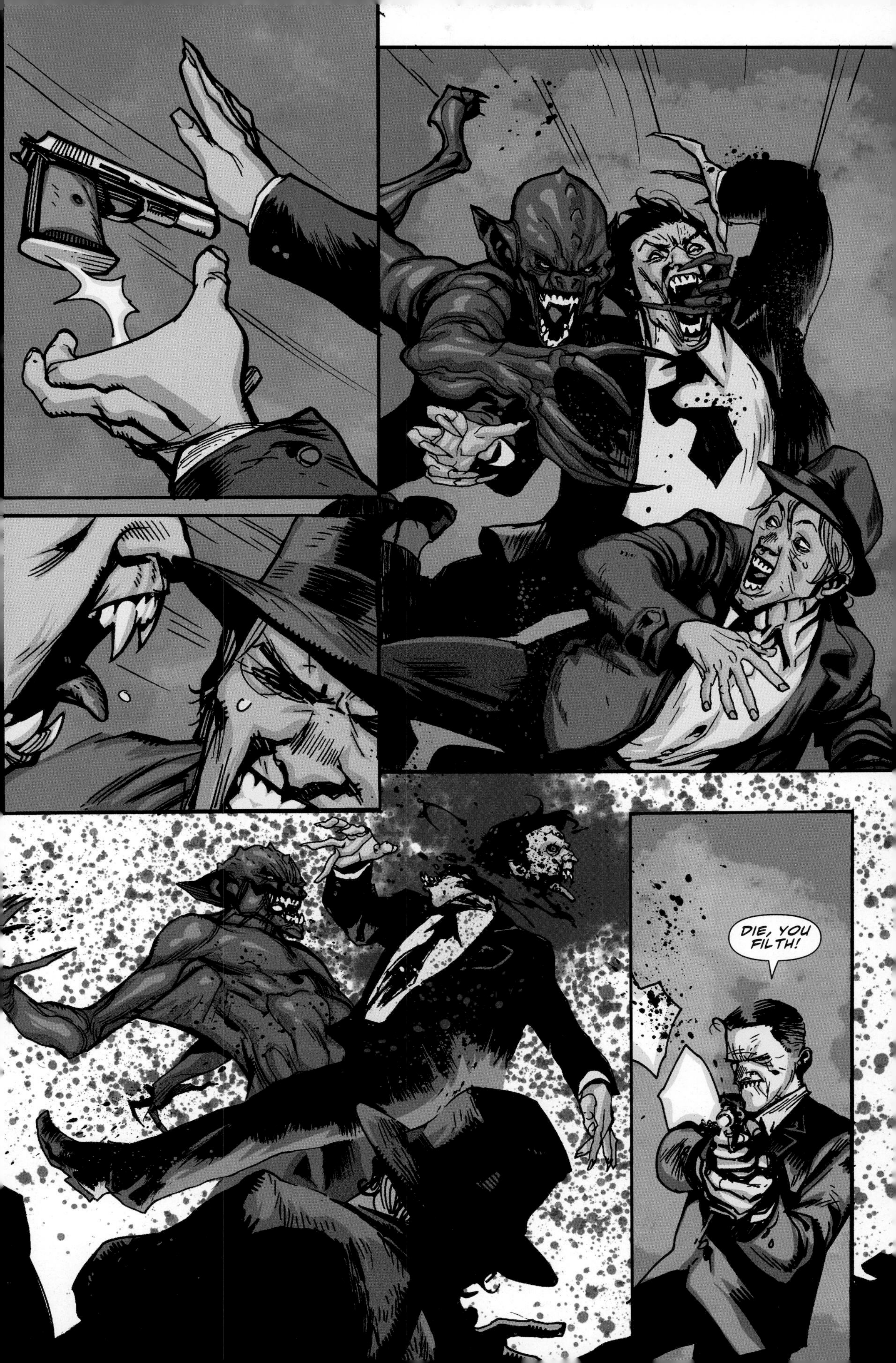
DIE, YOU FILTH!

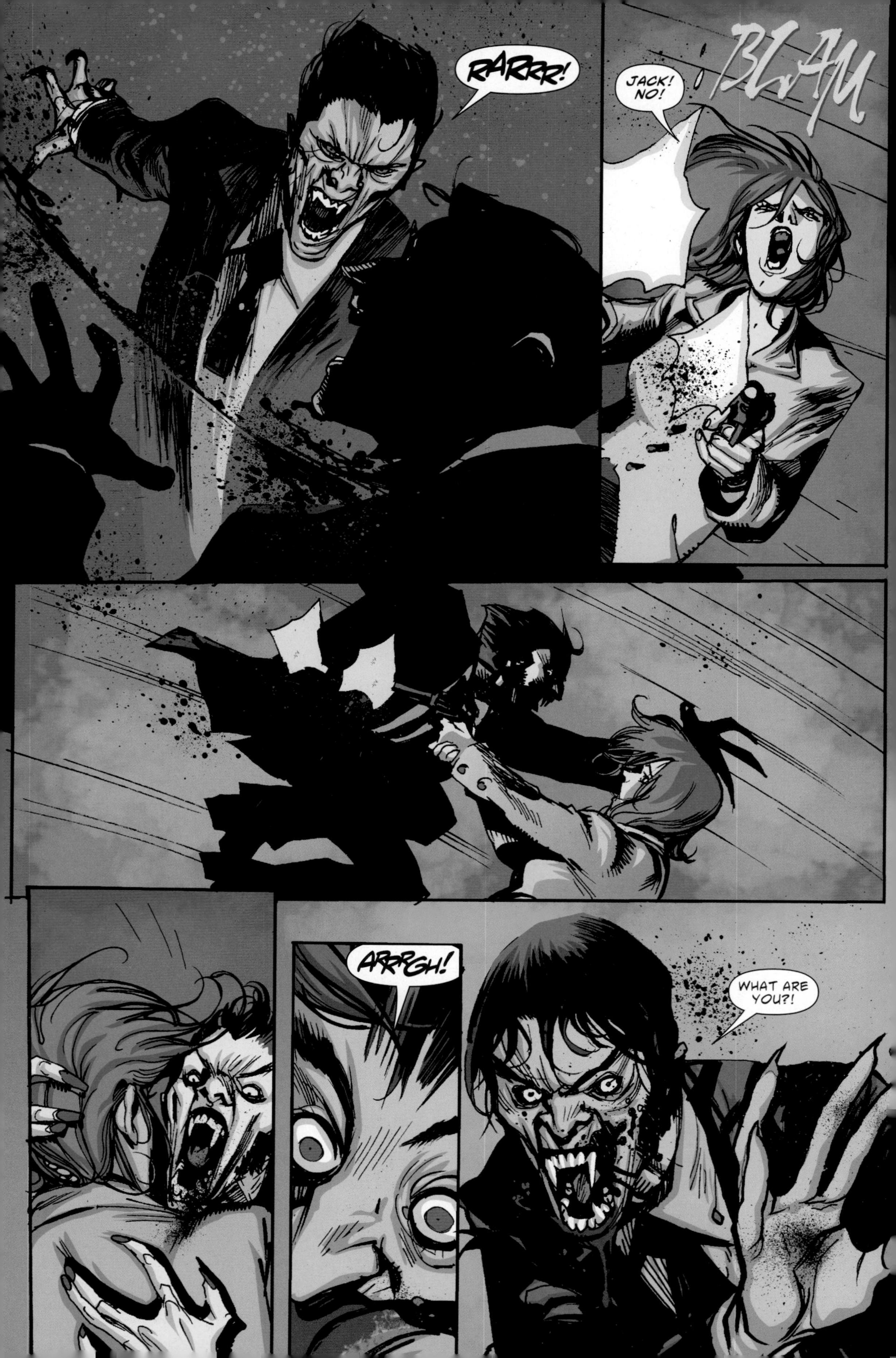
RARRR!
JACK! NO!
BLAM
ARRRGH!
WHAT ARE YOU?!

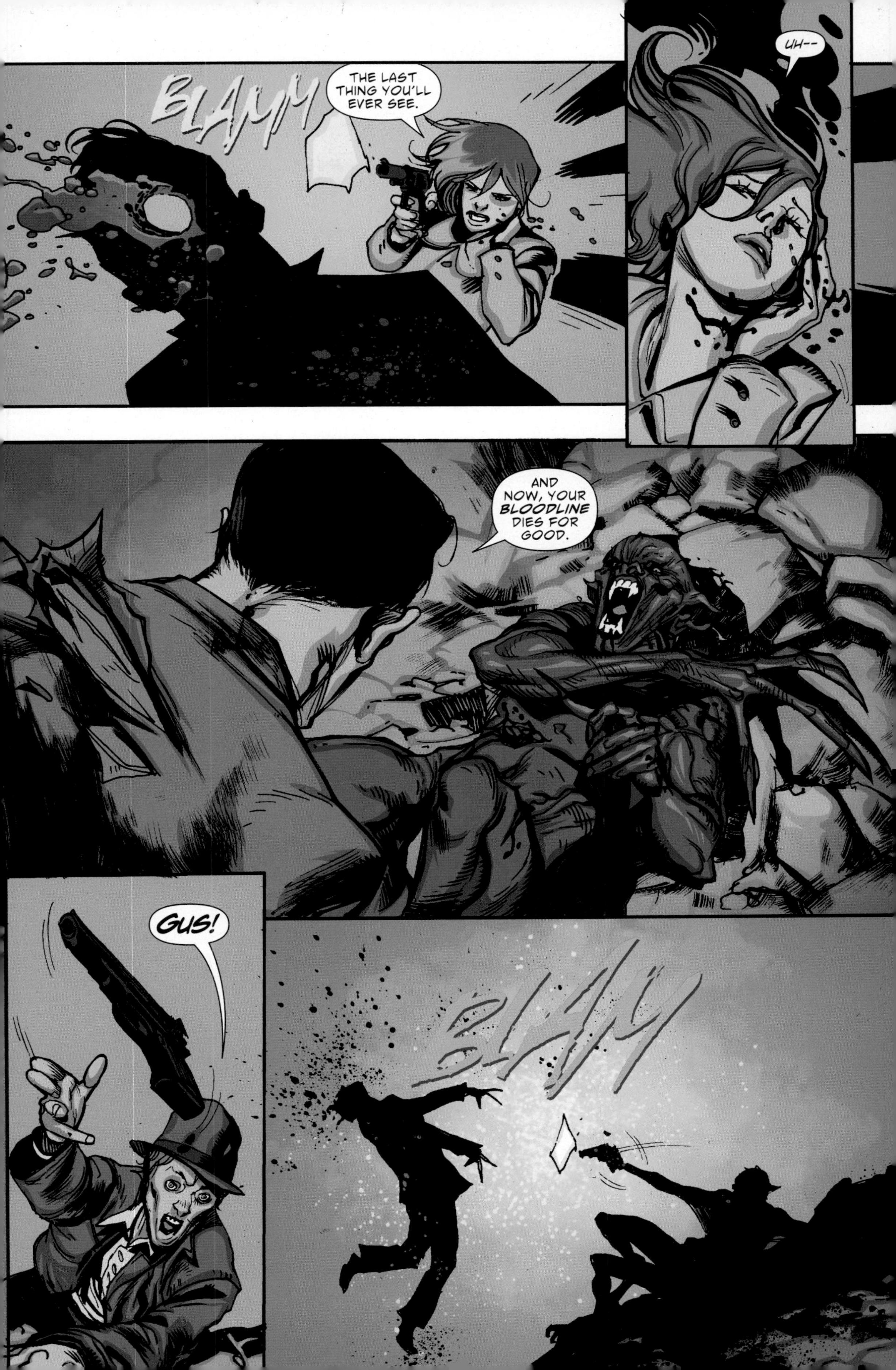
BLAMM
THE LAST THING YOU'LL EVER SEE.
UH--
AND NOW, YOUR BLOODLINE DIES FOR GOOD.
GUS!
BLAMM

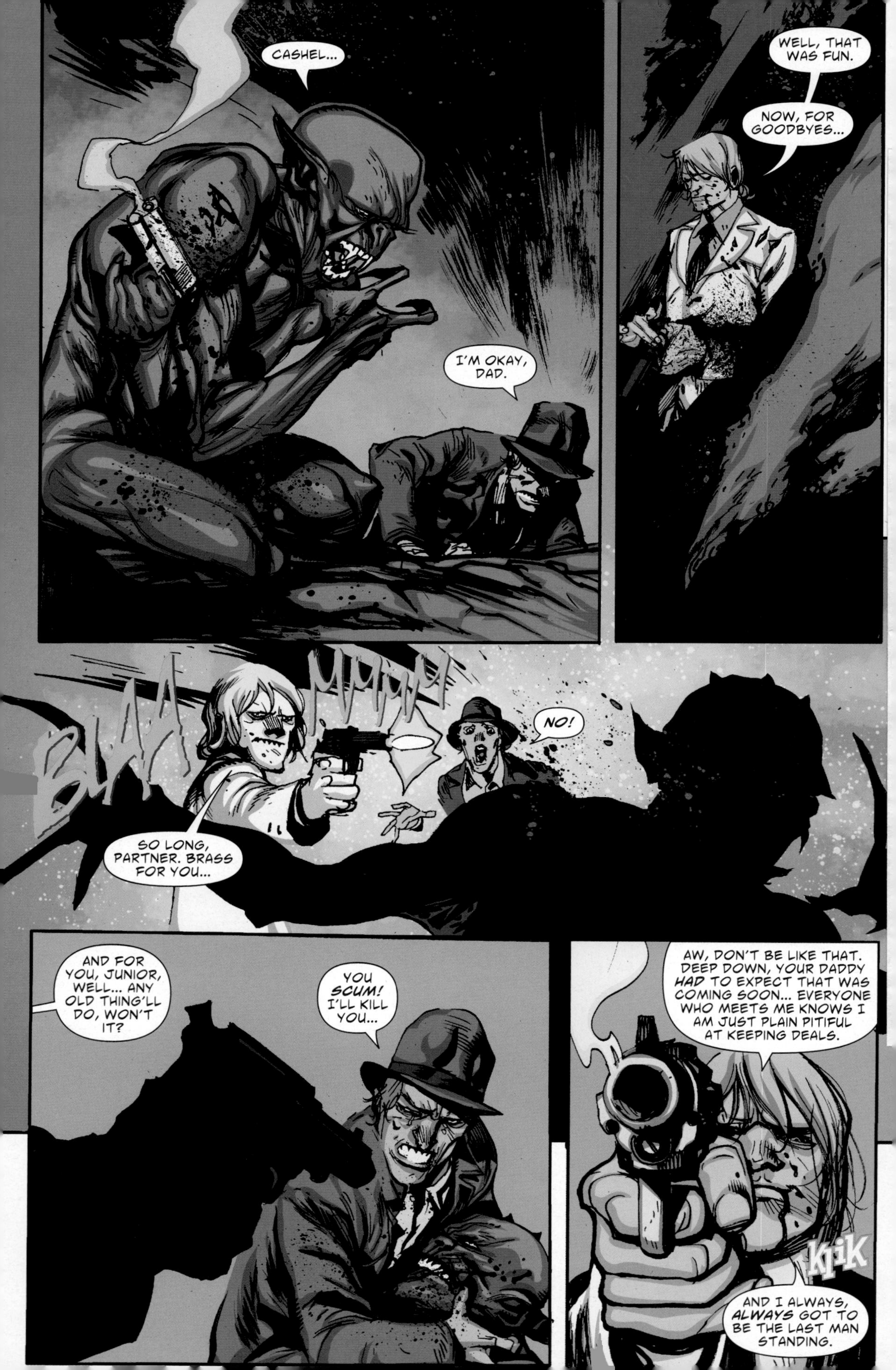
CASHEL...
I'M OKAY, DAD.
WELL, THAT WAS FUN.
NOW, FOR GOODBYES...
BLAMMMM
NO!
SO LONG, PARTNER. BRASS FOR YOU...
AND FOR YOU, JUNIOR, WELL... ANY OLD THING'LL DO, WON'T IT?
YOU SCUM! I'LL KILL YOU...
AW, DON'T BE LIKE THAT. DEEP DOWN, YOUR DADDY HAD TO EXPECT THAT WAS COMING SOON... EVERYONE WHO MEETS ME KNOWS I AM JUST PLAIN PITIFUL AT KEEPING DEALS.
KLIK
AND I ALWAYS, ALWAYS GOT TO BE THE LAST MAN STANDING.

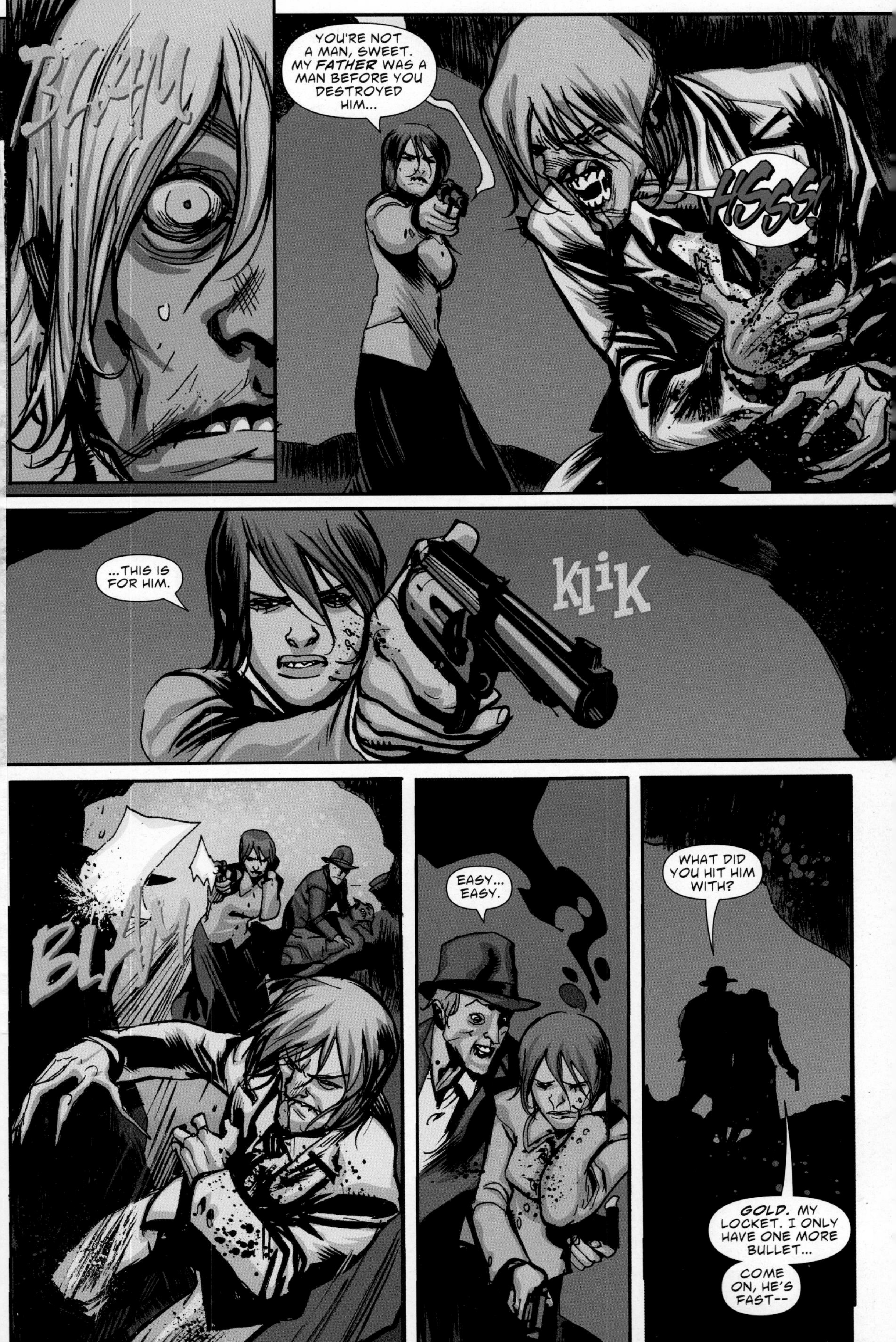
BLAM
YOU'RE NOT A MAN, SWEET. MY FATHER WAS A MAN BEFORE YOU DESTROYED HIM...
HSSS!
...THIS IS FOR HIM.
KLIK
BLAM
EASY... EASY.
WHAT DID YOU HIT HIM WITH?
GOLD. MY LOCKET. I ONLY HAVE ONE MORE BULLET...
COME ON, HE'S FAST--

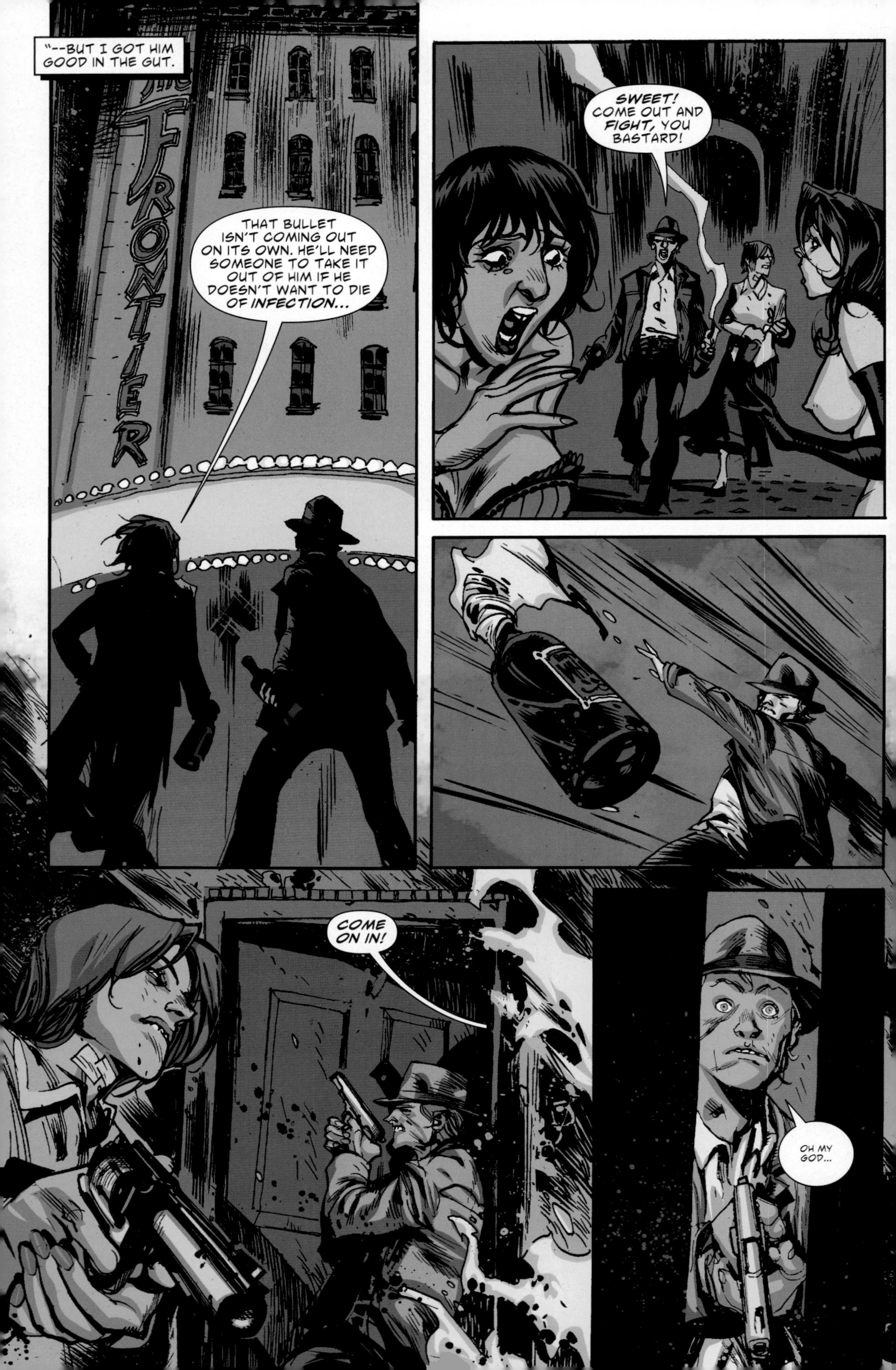
"--BUT I GOT HIM GOOD IN THE GUT.
THE FRONTIER
THAT BULLET ISN'T COMING OUT ON ITS OWN. HE'LL NEED SOMEONE TO TAKE IT OUT OF HIM IF HE DOESN'T WANT TO DIE OF INFECTION...
SWEET! COME OUT AND FIGHT, YOU BASTARD!
COME ON IN!
OH MY GOD...

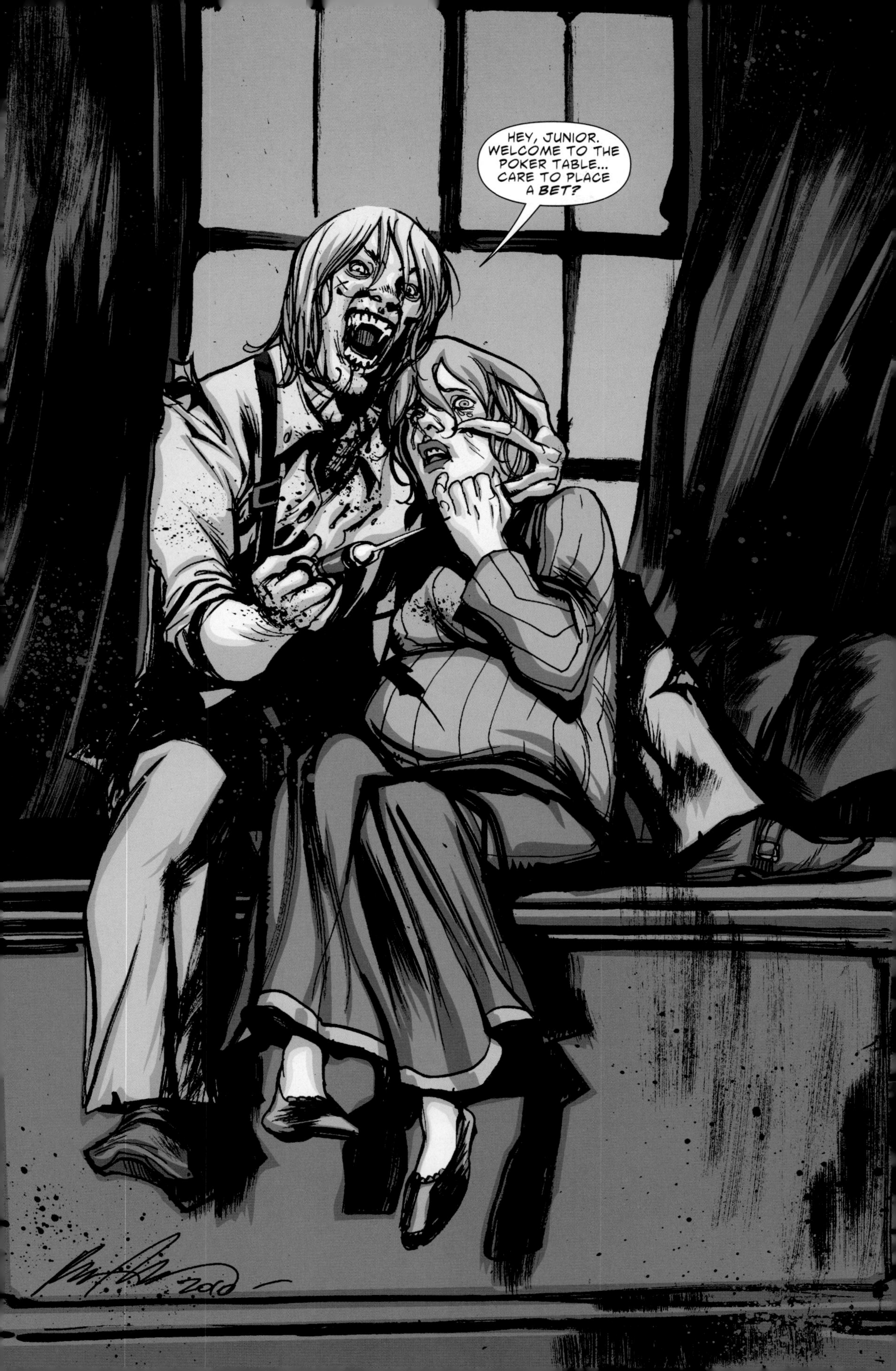
HEY, JUNIOR. WELCOME TO THE POKER TABLE... CARE TO PLACE A *BET?*

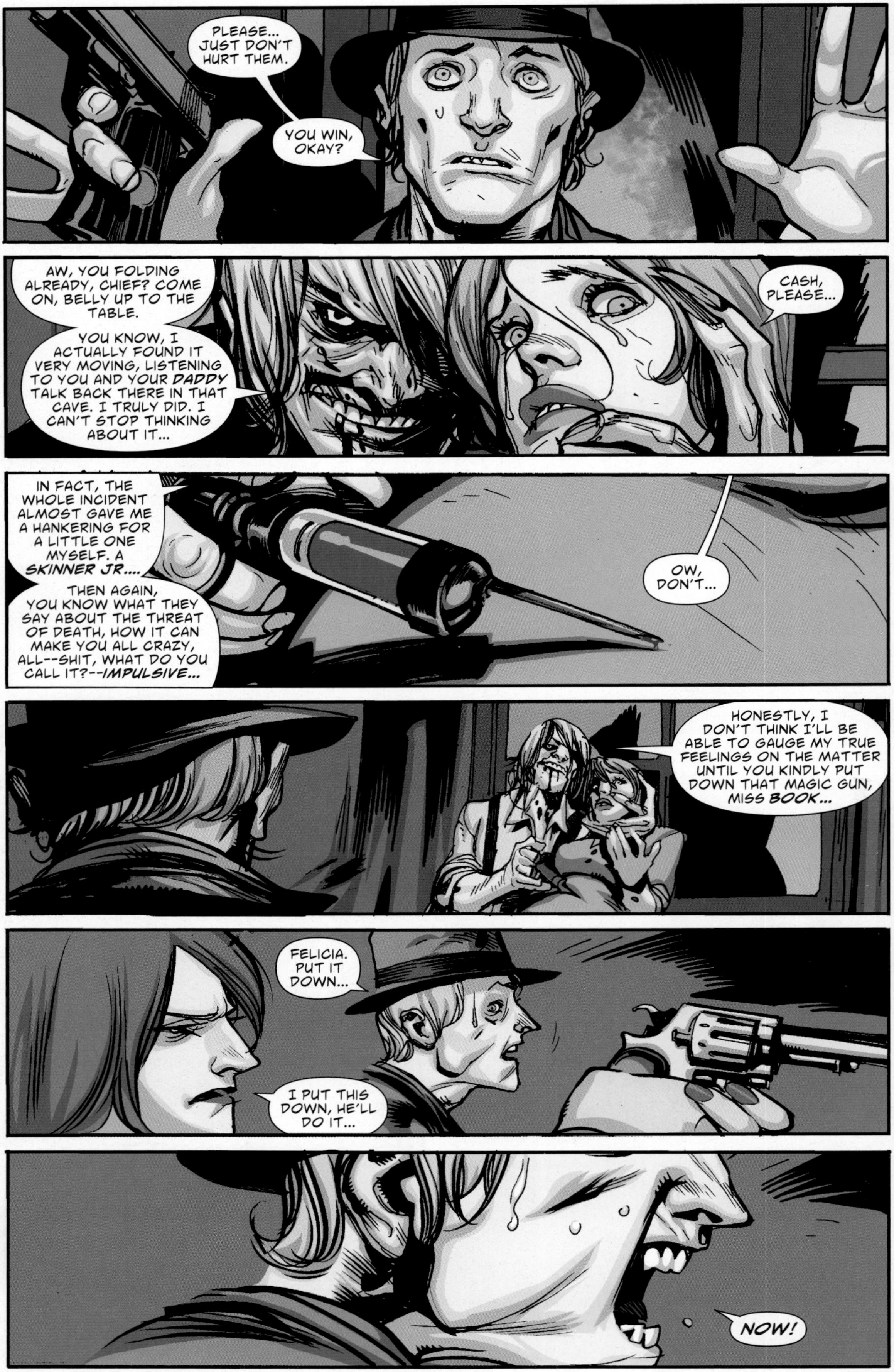
PLEASE... JUST DON'T HURT THEM.
YOU WIN, OKAY?
AW, YOU FOLDING ALREADY, CHIEF? COME ON, BELLY UP TO THE TABLE.
YOU KNOW, I ACTUALLY FOUND IT VERY MOVING, LISTENING TO YOU AND YOUR DADDY TALK BACK THERE IN THAT CAVE. I TRULY DID. I CAN'T STOP THINKING ABOUT IT...
CASH, PLEASE...
IN FACT, THE WHOLE INCIDENT ALMOST GAVE ME A HANKERING FOR A LITTLE ONE MYSELF. A SKINNER JR....
THEN AGAIN, YOU KNOW WHAT THEY SAY ABOUT THE THREAT OF DEATH, HOW IT CAN MAKE YOU ALL CRAZY, ALL--SHIT, WHAT DO YOU CALL IT?--IMPULSIVE...
OW, DON'T...
HONESTLY, I DON'T THINK I'LL BE ABLE TO GAUGE MY TRUE FEELINGS ON THE MATTER UNTIL YOU KINDLY PUT DOWN THAT MAGIC GUN, MISS BOOK...
FELICIA. PUT IT DOWN...
I PUT THIS DOWN, HE'LL DO IT...
NOW!

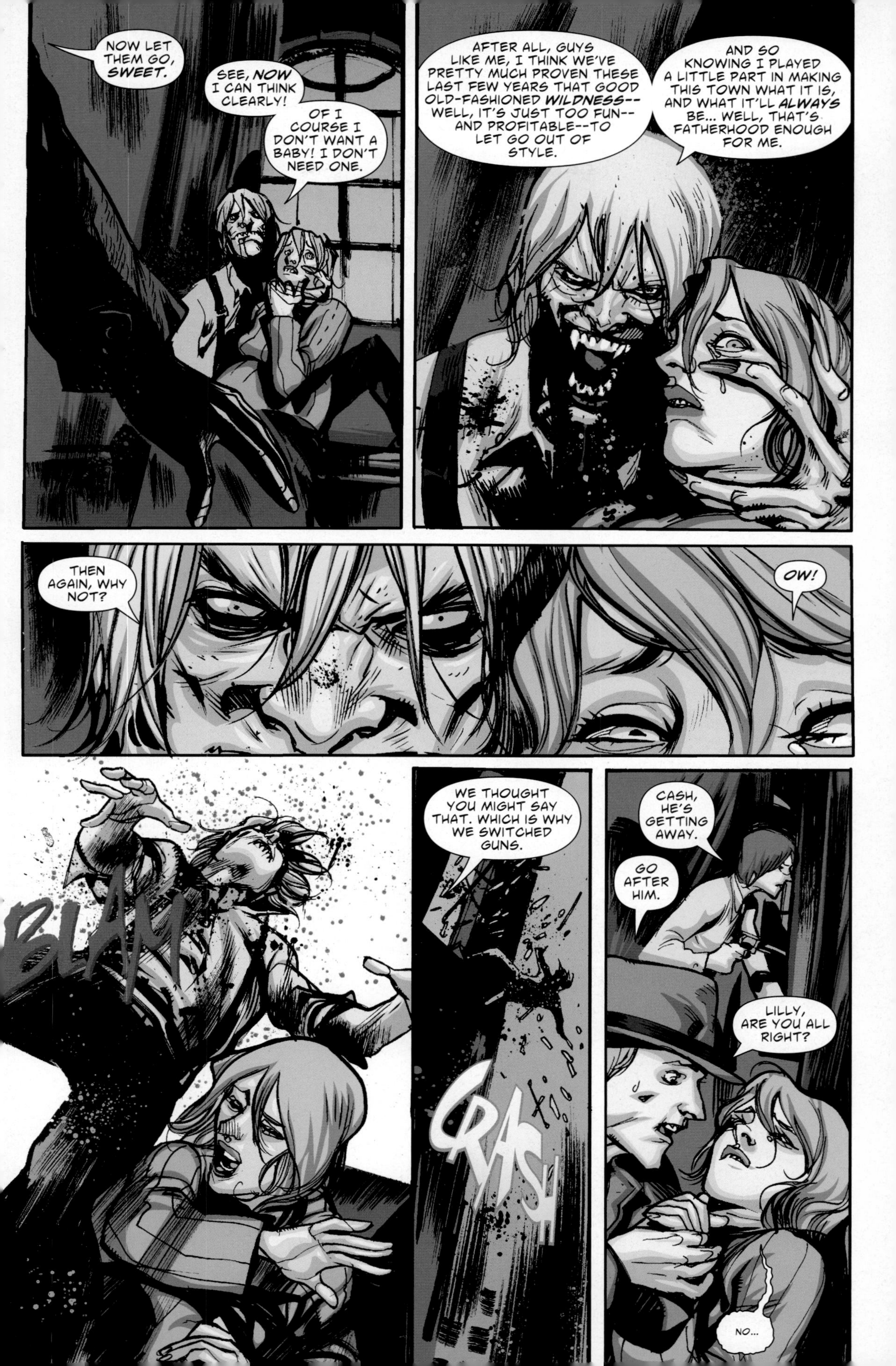
NOW LET THEM GO, SWEET.
SEE, NOW I CAN THINK CLEARLY!
OF COURSE I DON'T WANT A BABY! I DON'T NEED ONE.
AFTER ALL, GUYS LIKE ME, I THINK WE'VE PRETTY MUCH PROVEN THESE LAST FEW YEARS THAT GOOD OLD-FASHIONED WILDNESS--WELL, IT'S JUST TOO FUN--AND PROFITABLE--TO LET GO OUT OF STYLE.
AND SO KNOWING I PLAYED A LITTLE PART IN MAKING THIS TOWN WHAT IT IS, AND WHAT IT'LL ALWAYS BE... WELL, THAT'S FATHERHOOD ENOUGH FOR ME.
THEN AGAIN, WHY NOT?
OW!
BLAM
WE THOUGHT YOU MIGHT SAY THAT. WHICH IS WHY WE SWITCHED GUNS.
CRASH
CASH, HE'S GETTING AWAY.
GO AFTER HIM.
LILLY, ARE YOU ALL RIGHT?
NO...

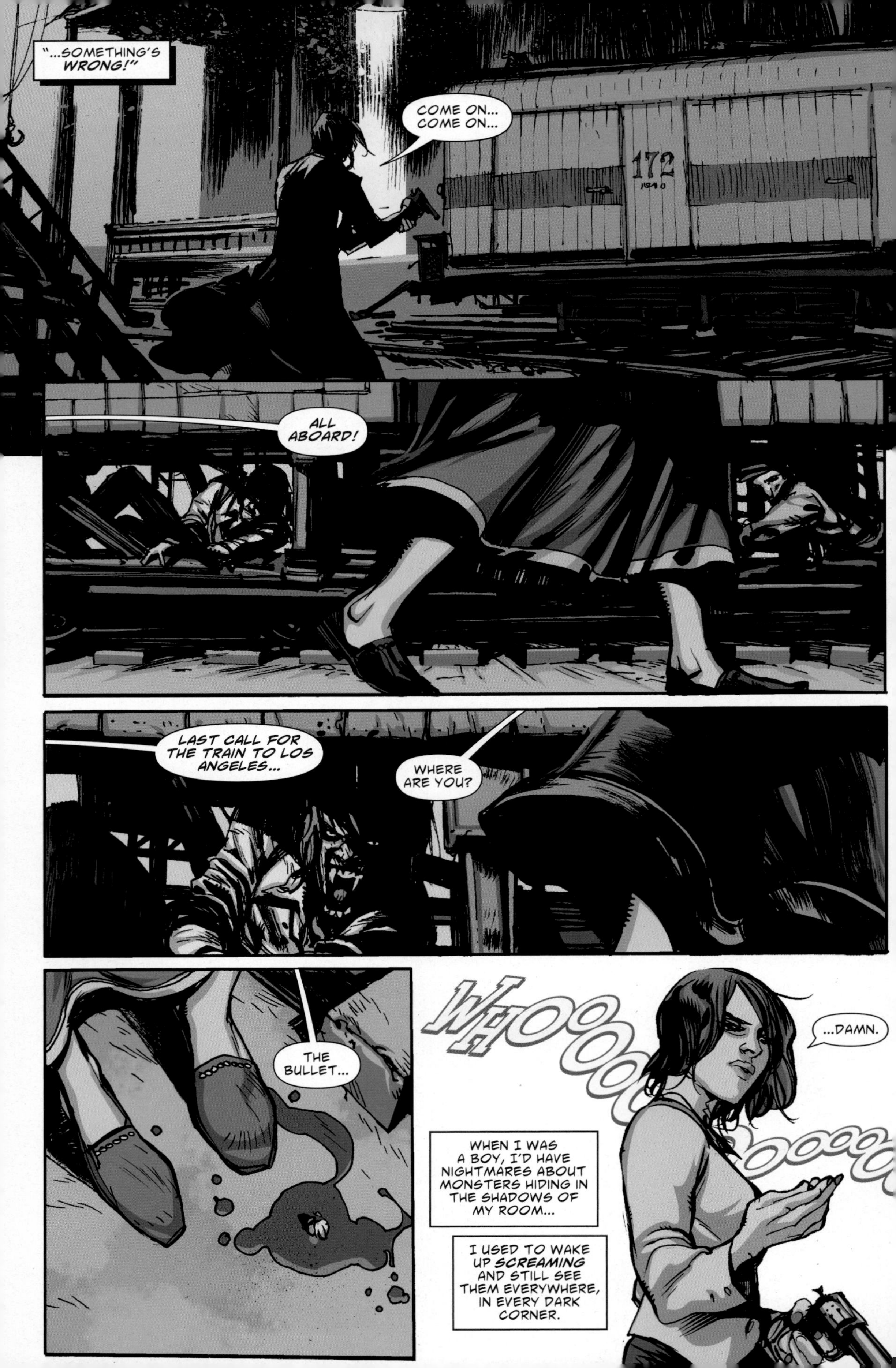
"...SOMETHING'S WRONG!"
COME ON... COME ON...
172
ALL ABOARD!
LAST CALL FOR THE TRAIN TO LOS ANGELES...
WHERE ARE YOU?
THE BULLET...
WHOOOOOOOOOO
...DAMN.
WHEN I WAS A BOY, I'D HAVE NIGHTMARES ABOUT MONSTERS HIDING IN THE SHADOWS OF MY ROOM...
I USED TO WAKE UP SCREAMING AND STILL SEE THEM EVERYWHERE, IN EVERY DARK CORNER.

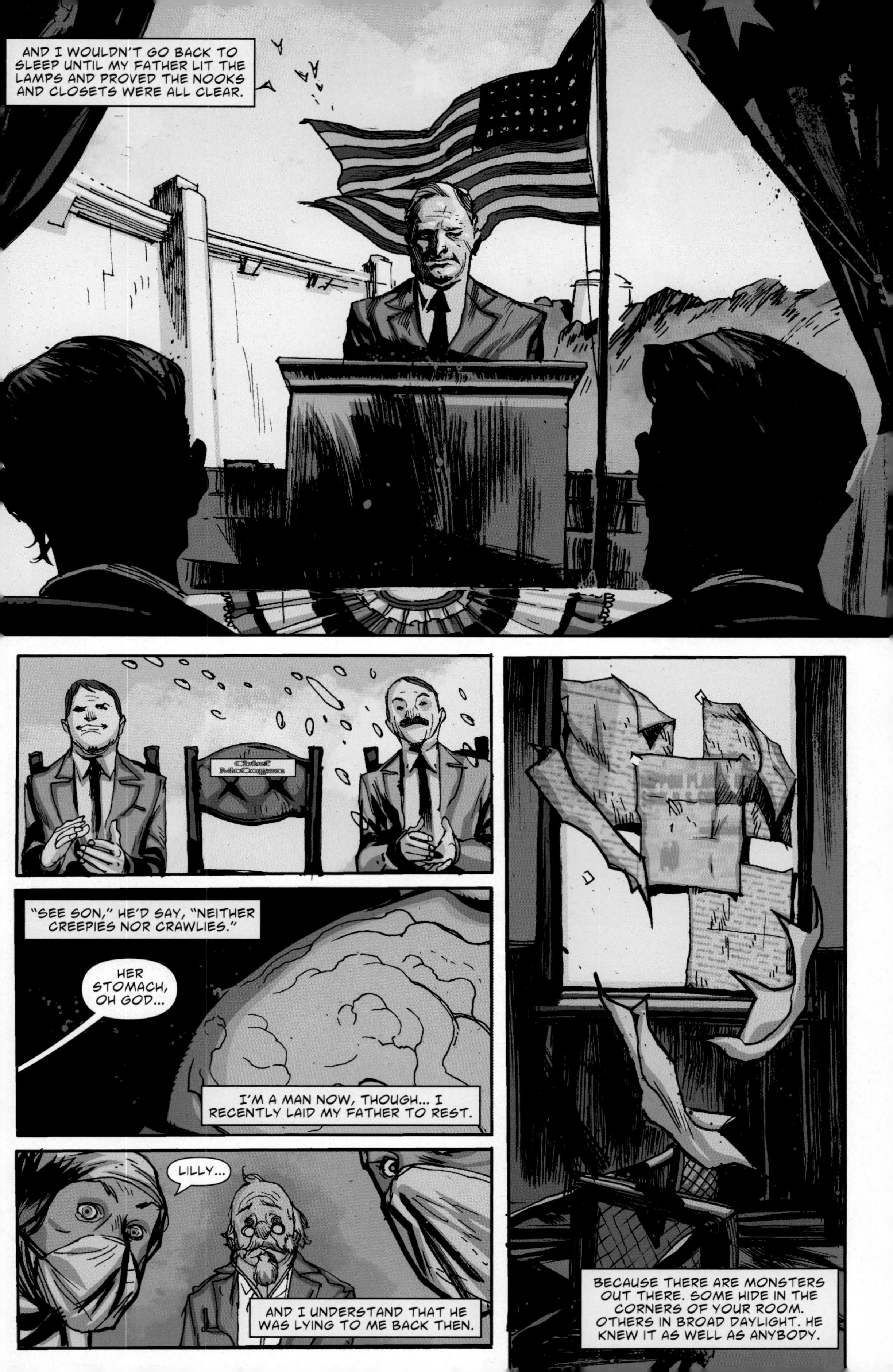
AND I WOULDN'T GO BACK TO SLEEP UNTIL MY FATHER LIT THE LAMPS AND PROVED THE NOOKS AND CLOSETS WERE ALL CLEAR.
Chief McCogan
"SEE SON," HE'D SAY, "NEITHER CREEPIES NOR CRAWLIES."
HER STOMACH, OH GOD...
I'M A MAN NOW, THOUGH... I RECENTLY LAID MY FATHER TO REST.
LILLY...
AND I UNDERSTAND THAT HE WAS LYING TO ME BACK THEN.
BECAUSE THERE ARE MONSTERS OUT THERE. SOME HIDE IN THE CORNERS OF YOUR ROOM. OTHERS IN BROAD DAYLIGHT. HE KNEW IT AS WELL AS ANYBODY.

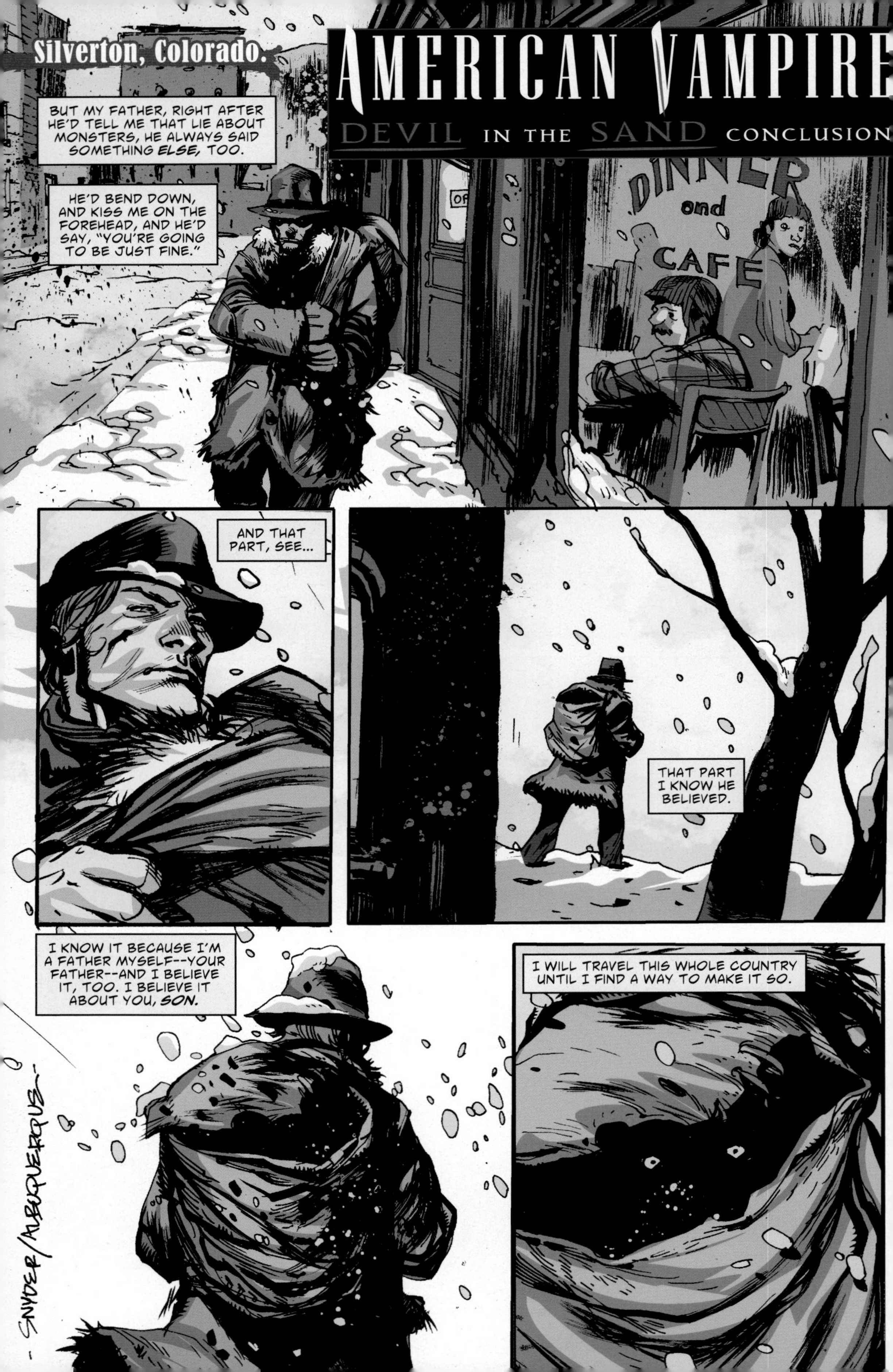
Silverton, Colorado.
AMERICAN VAMPIRE
DEVIL IN THE SAND CONCLUSION
BUT MY FATHER, RIGHT AFTER HE'D TELL ME THAT LIE ABOUT MONSTERS, HE ALWAYS SAID SOMETHING ELSE, TOO.
HE'D BEND DOWN, AND KISS ME ON THE FOREHEAD, AND HE'D SAY, "YOU'RE GOING TO BE JUST FINE."
DINNER and CAFE
AND THAT PART, SEE...
THAT PART I KNOW HE BELIEVED.
I KNOW IT BECAUSE I'M A FATHER MYSELF--YOUR FATHER--AND I BELIEVE IT, TOO. I BELIEVE IT ABOUT YOU, SON.
I WILL TRAVEL THIS WHOLE COUNTRY UNTIL I FIND A WAY TO MAKE IT SO.
SNYDER/ALBUQUERQUE

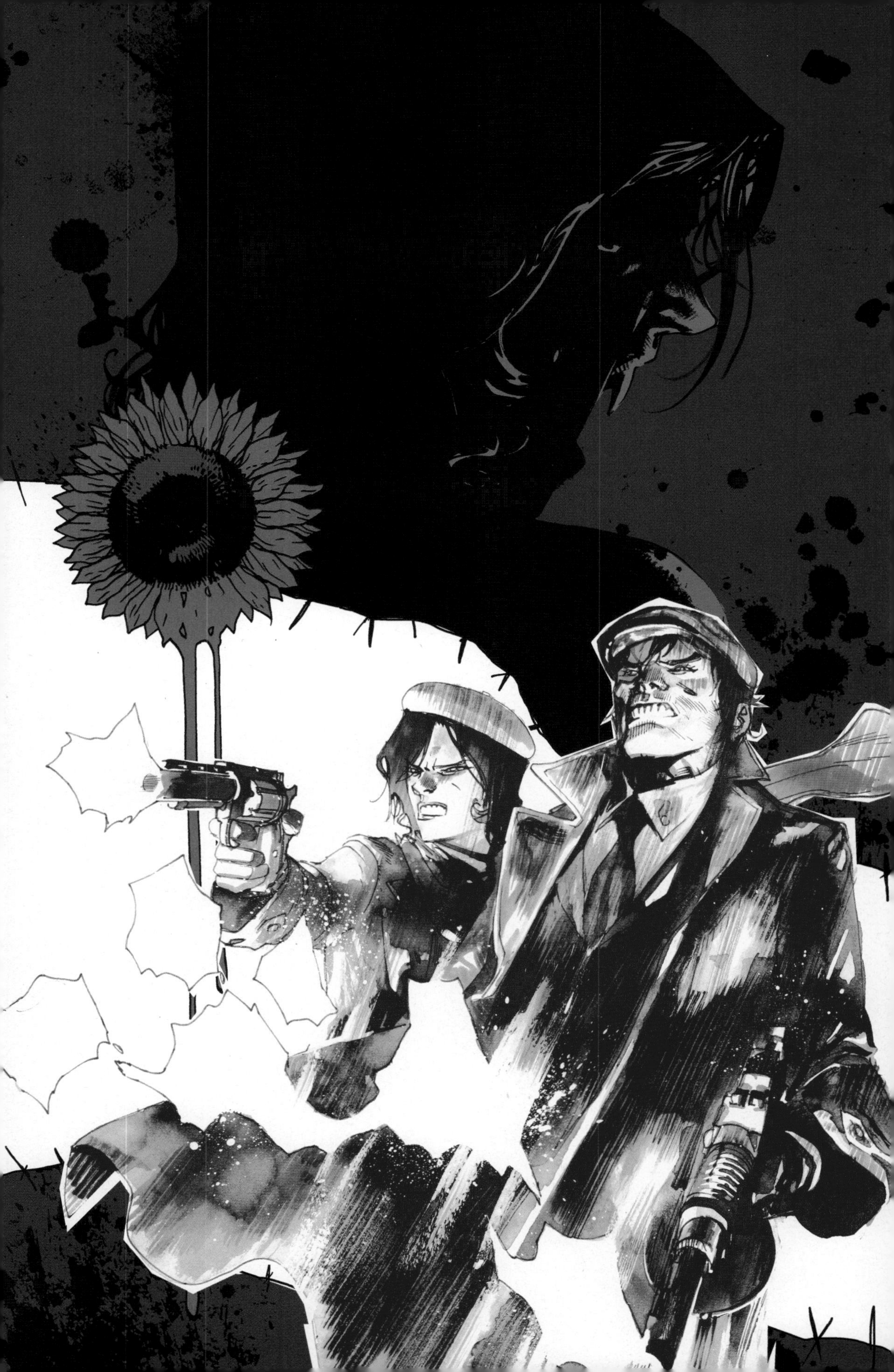

The Way Out
Part One

Mateus Santolouco
Artist

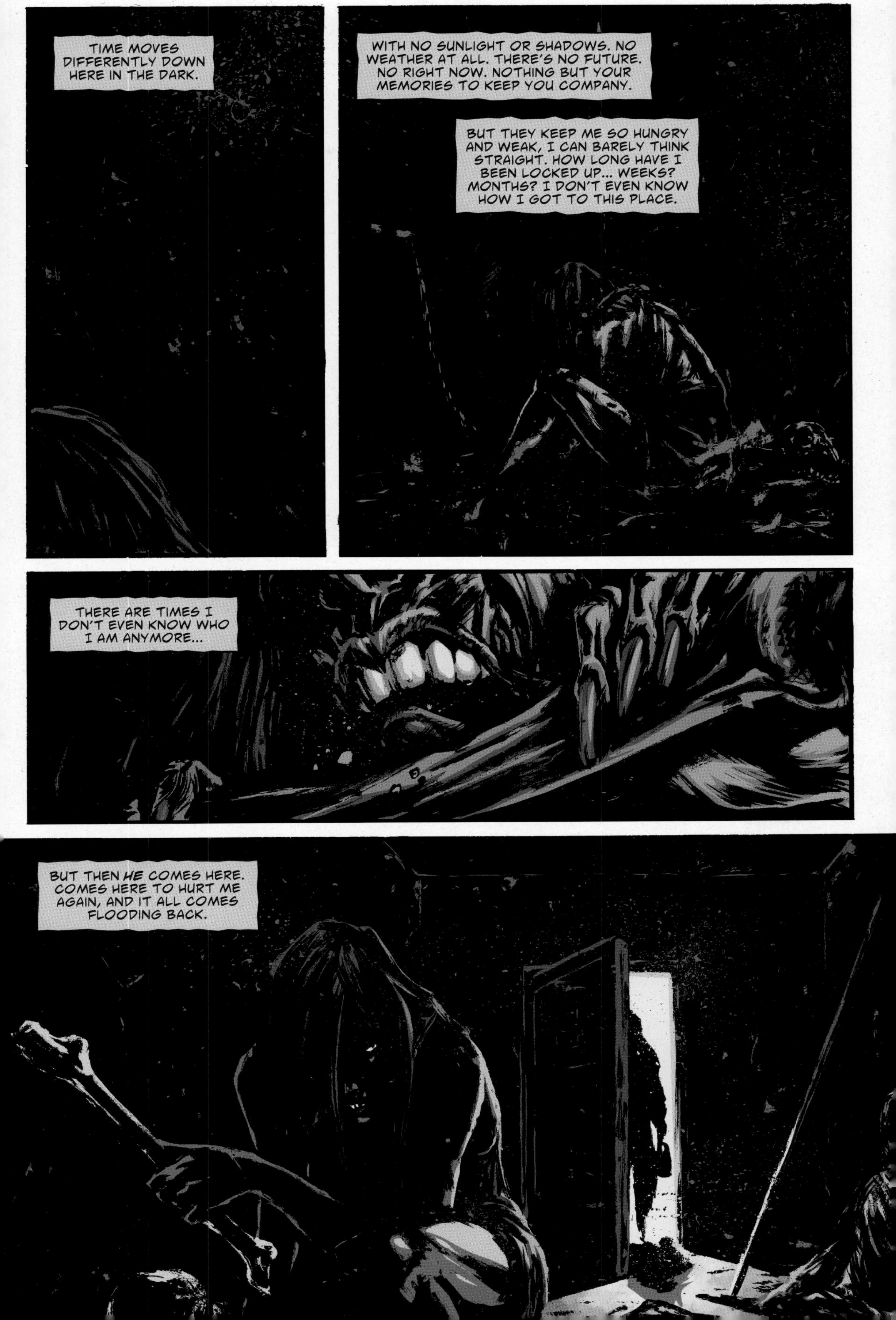
TIME MOVES DIFFERENTLY DOWN HERE IN THE DARK.
WITH NO SUNLIGHT OR SHADOWS. NO WEATHER AT ALL. THERE'S NO FUTURE. NO RIGHT NOW. NOTHING BUT YOUR MEMORIES TO KEEP YOU COMPANY.
BUT THEY KEEP ME SO HUNGRY AND WEAK, I CAN BARELY THINK STRAIGHT. HOW LONG HAVE I BEEN LOCKED UP... WEEKS? MONTHS? I DON'T EVEN KNOW HOW I GOT TO THIS PLACE.
THERE ARE TIMES I DON'T EVEN KNOW WHO I AM ANYMORE...
BUT THEN *HE* COMES HERE. COMES HERE TO HURT ME AGAIN, AND IT ALL COMES FLOODING BACK.

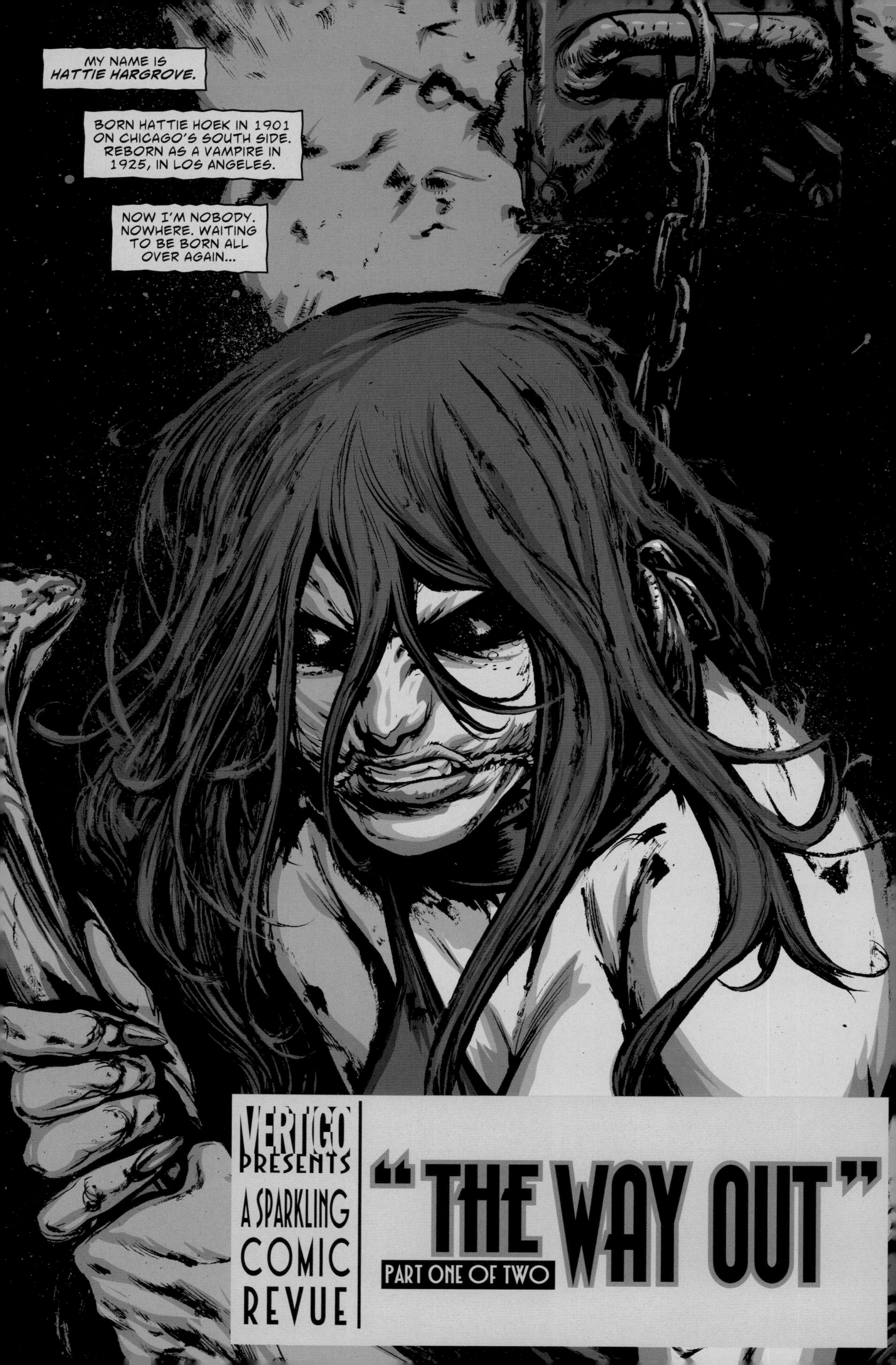
MY NAME IS HATTIE HARGROVE.
BORN HATTIE HOEK IN 1901 ON CHICAGO'S SOUTH SIDE. REBORN AS A VAMPIRE IN 1925, IN LOS ANGELES.
NOW I'M NOBODY. NOWHERE. WAITING TO BE BORN ALL OVER AGAIN...
VERTIGO PRESENTS A SPARKLING COMIC REVUE
"THE WAY OUT"
PART ONE OF TWO

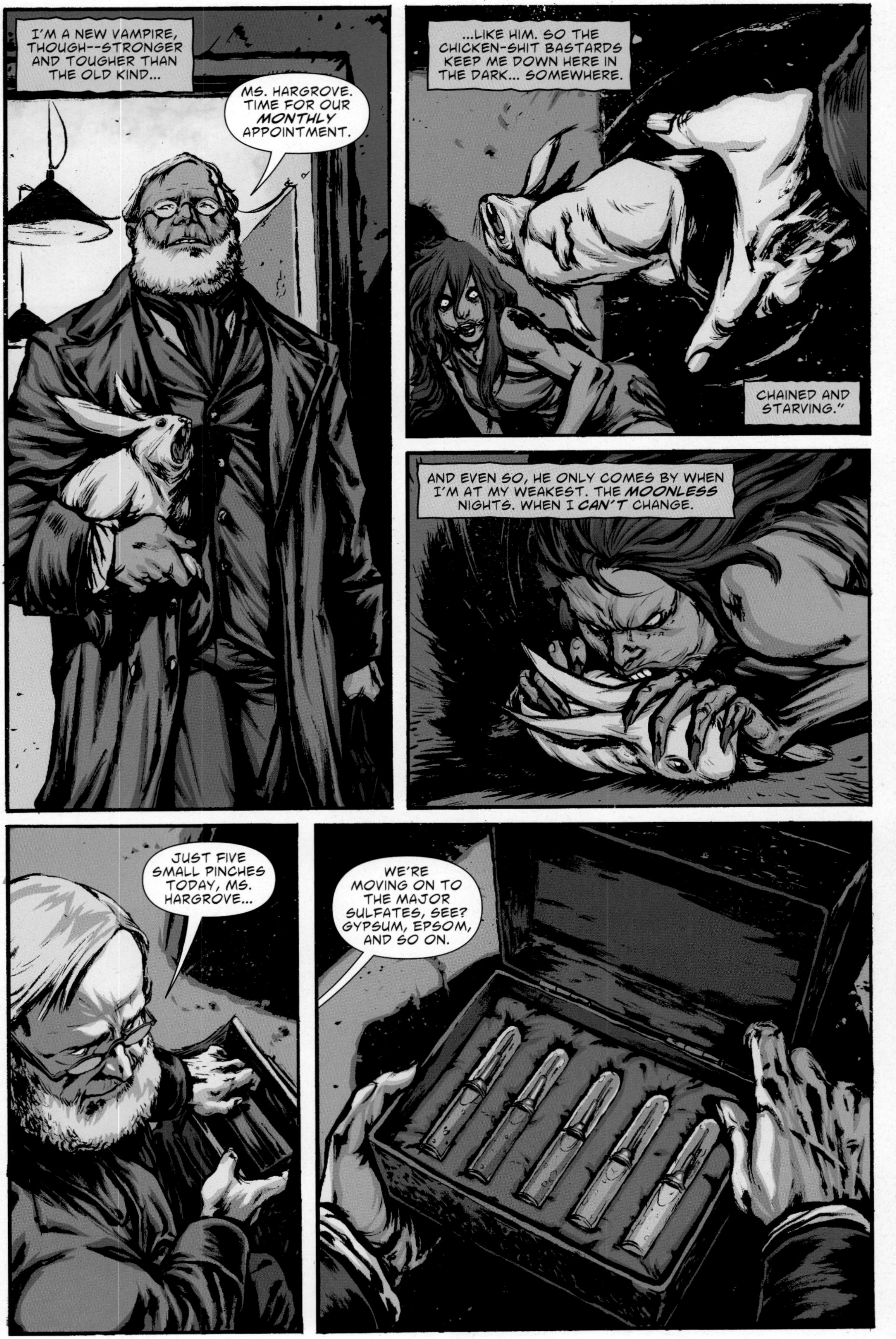
I'M A NEW VAMPIRE, THOUGH--STRONGER AND TOUGHER THAN THE OLD KIND...
MS. HARGROVE. TIME FOR OUR MONTHLY APPOINTMENT.
...LIKE HIM. SO THE CHICKEN-SHIT BASTARDS KEEP ME DOWN HERE IN THE DARK... SOMEWHERE.
CHAINED AND STARVING."
AND EVEN SO, HE ONLY COMES BY WHEN I'M AT MY WEAKEST. THE MOONLESS NIGHTS. WHEN I CAN'T CHANGE.
JUST FIVE SMALL PINCHES TODAY, MS. HARGROVE...
WE'RE MOVING ON TO THE MAJOR SULFATES, SEE? GYPSUM, EPSOM, AND SO ON.

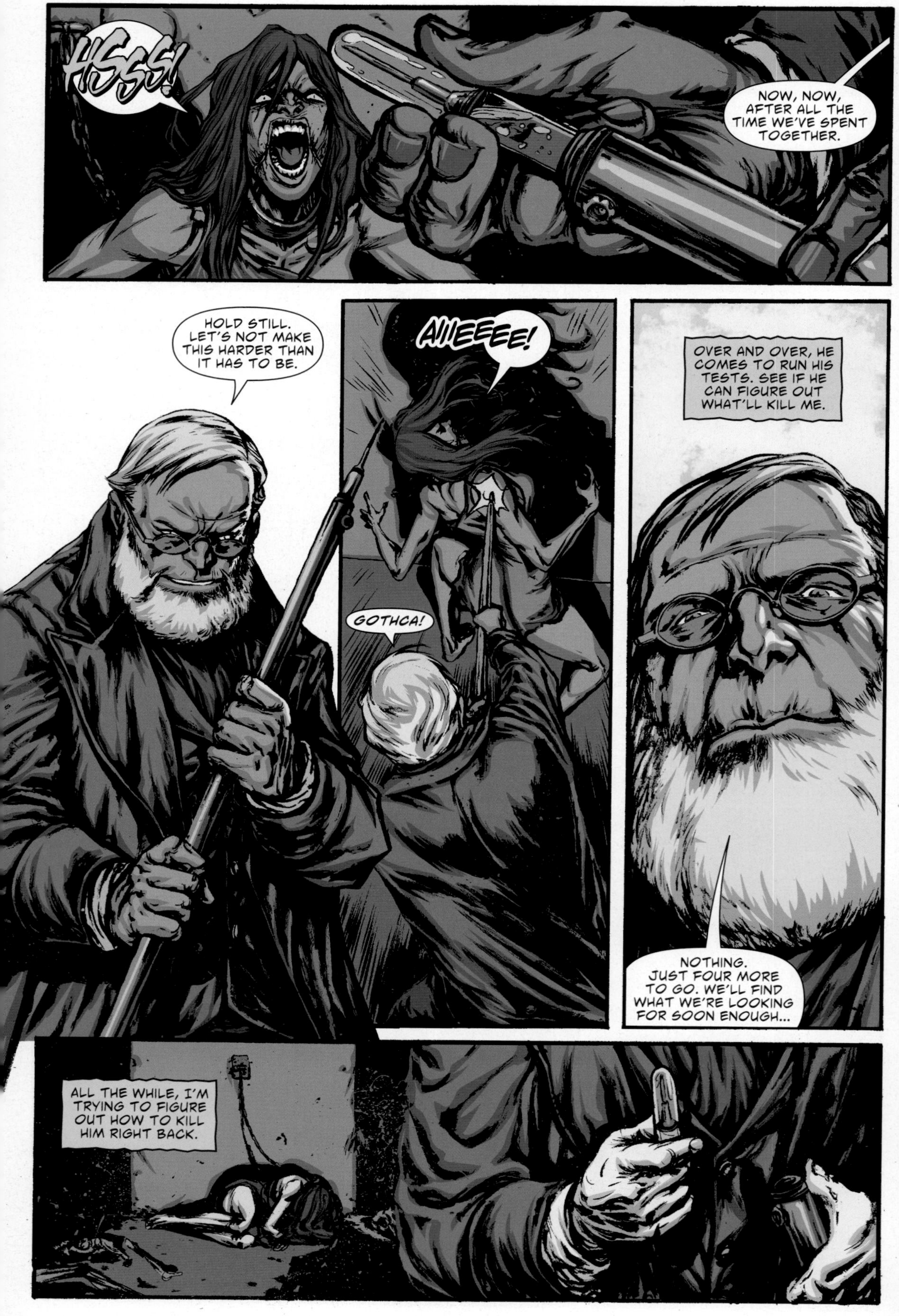
HSSS!
NOW, NOW, AFTER ALL THE TIME WE'VE SPENT TOGETHER.
HOLD STILL. LET'S NOT MAKE THIS HARDER THAN IT HAS TO BE.
AIIEEEEE!
GOTHCA!
OVER AND OVER, HE COMES TO RUN HIS TESTS. SEE IF HE CAN FIGURE OUT WHAT'LL KILL ME.
NOTHING. JUST FOUR MORE TO GO. WE'LL FIND WHAT WE'RE LOOKING FOR SOON ENOUGH...
ALL THE WHILE, I'M TRYING TO FIGURE OUT HOW TO KILL HIM RIGHT BACK.

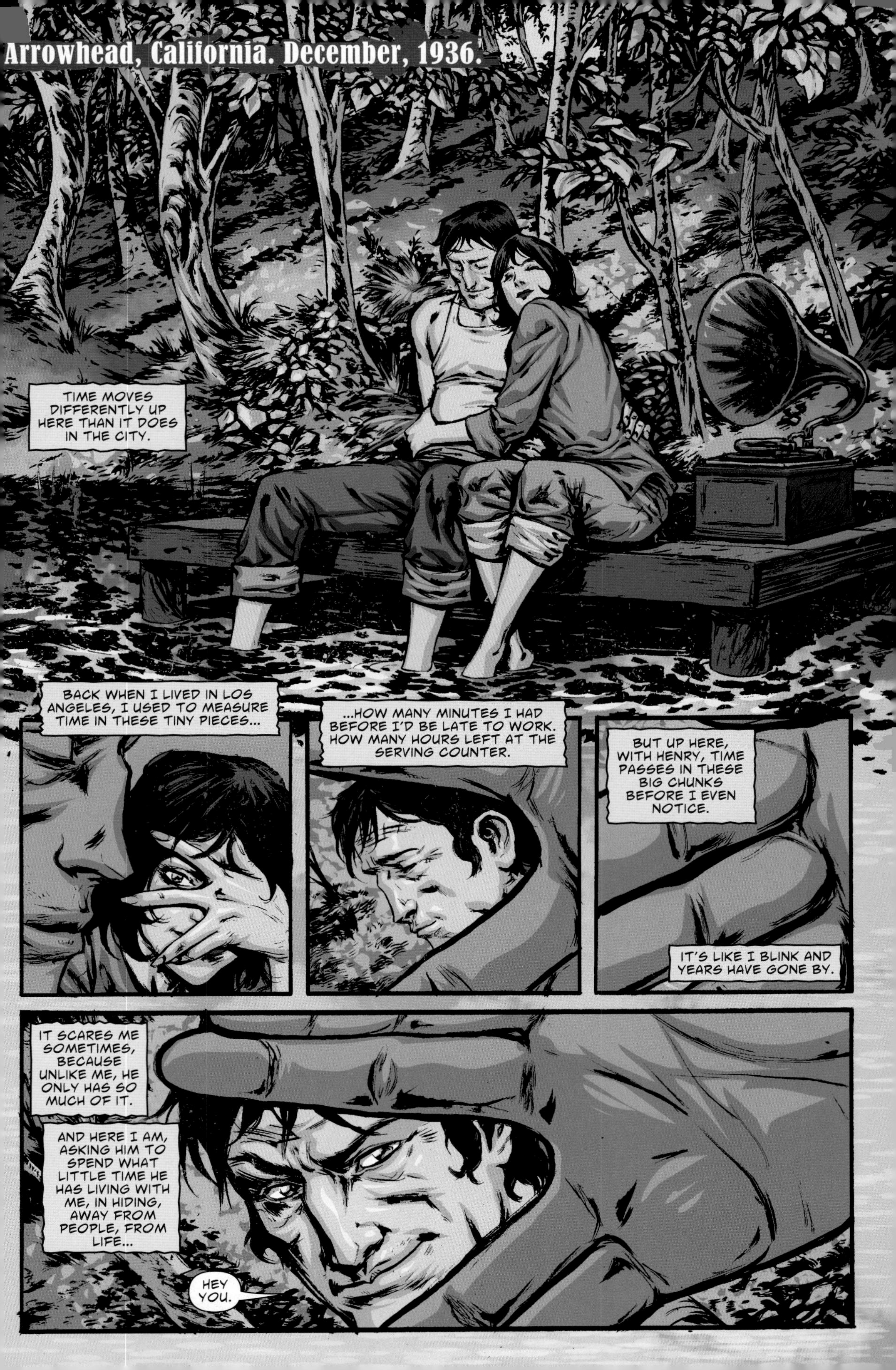
Arrowhead, California. December, 1936.
TIME MOVES DIFFERENTLY UP HERE THAN IT DOES IN THE CITY.
BACK WHEN I LIVED IN LOS ANGELES, I USED TO MEASURE TIME IN THESE TINY PIECES...
...HOW MANY MINUTES I HAD BEFORE I'D BE LATE TO WORK. HOW MANY HOURS LEFT AT THE SERVING COUNTER.
BUT UP HERE, WITH HENRY, TIME PASSES IN THESE BIG CHUNKS BEFORE I EVEN NOTICE.
IT'S LIKE I BLINK AND YEARS HAVE GONE BY.
IT SCARES ME SOMETIMES, BECAUSE UNLIKE ME, HE ONLY HAS SO MUCH OF IT.
AND HERE I AM, ASKING HIM TO SPEND WHAT LITTLE TIME HE HAS LIVING WITH ME, IN HIDING, AWAY FROM PEOPLE, FROM LIFE...
HEY YOU.

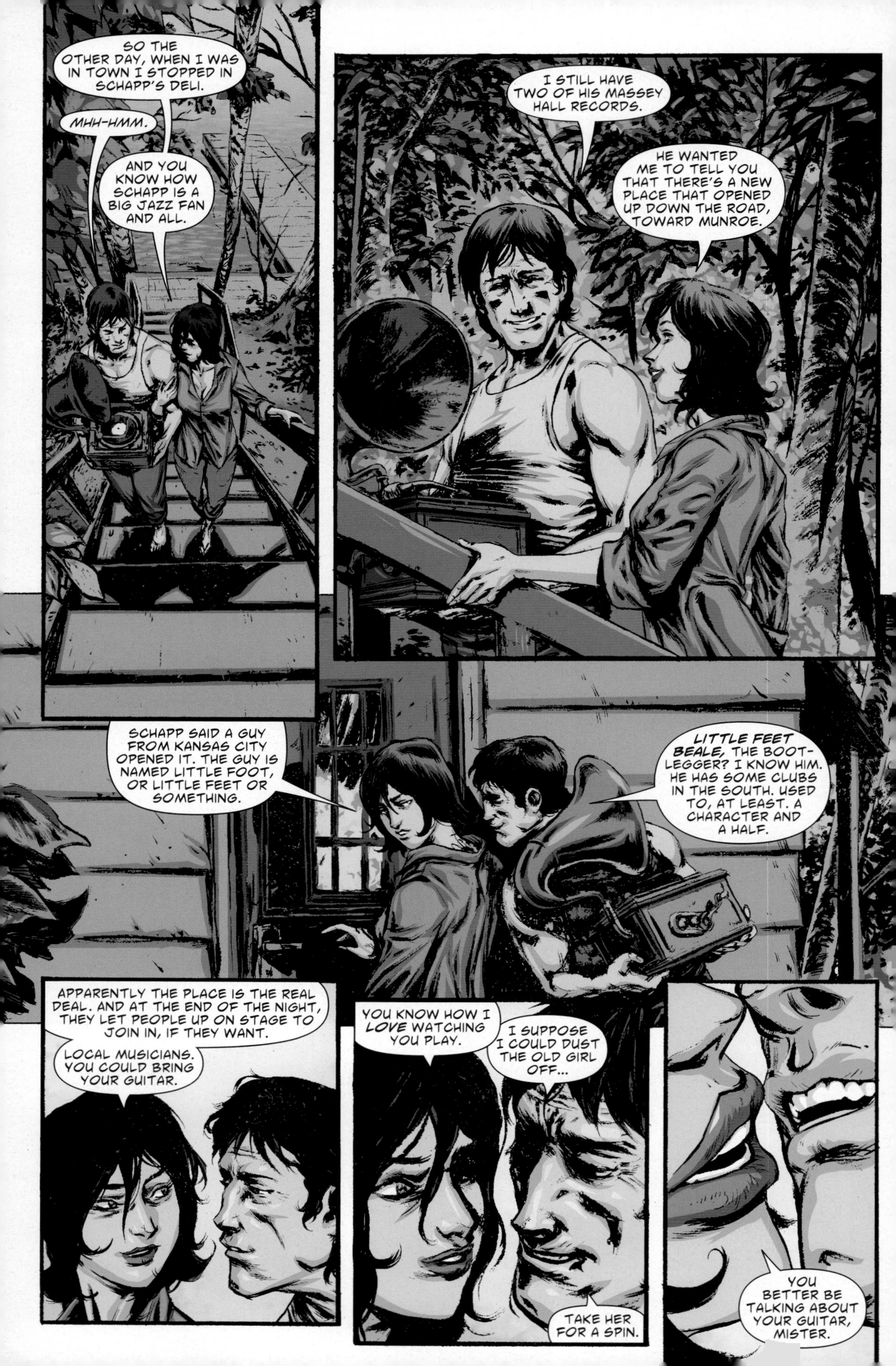
SO THE OTHER DAY, WHEN I WAS IN TOWN I STOPPED IN SCHAPP'S DELI.
MHH-HMM.
AND YOU KNOW HOW SCHAPP IS A BIG JAZZ FAN AND ALL.
I STILL HAVE TWO OF HIS MASSEY HALL RECORDS.
HE WANTED ME TO TELL YOU THAT THERE'S A NEW PLACE THAT OPENED UP DOWN THE ROAD, TOWARD MUNROE.
SCHAPP SAID A GUY FROM KANSAS CITY OPENED IT. THE GUY IS NAMED LITTLE FOOT, OR LITTLE FEET OR SOMETHING.
LITTLE FEET BEALE, THE BOOT-LEGGER? I KNOW HIM. HE HAS SOME CLUBS IN THE SOUTH. USED TO, AT LEAST. A CHARACTER AND A HALF.
APPARENTLY THE PLACE IS THE REAL DEAL. AND AT THE END OF THE NIGHT, THEY LET PEOPLE UP ON STAGE TO JOIN IN, IF THEY WANT.
LOCAL MUSICIANS. YOU COULD BRING YOUR GUITAR.
YOU KNOW HOW I LOVE WATCHING YOU PLAY.
I SUPPOSE I COULD DUST THE OLD GIRL OFF...
TAKE HER FOR A SPIN.
YOU BETTER BE TALKING ABOUT YOUR GUITAR, MISTER.

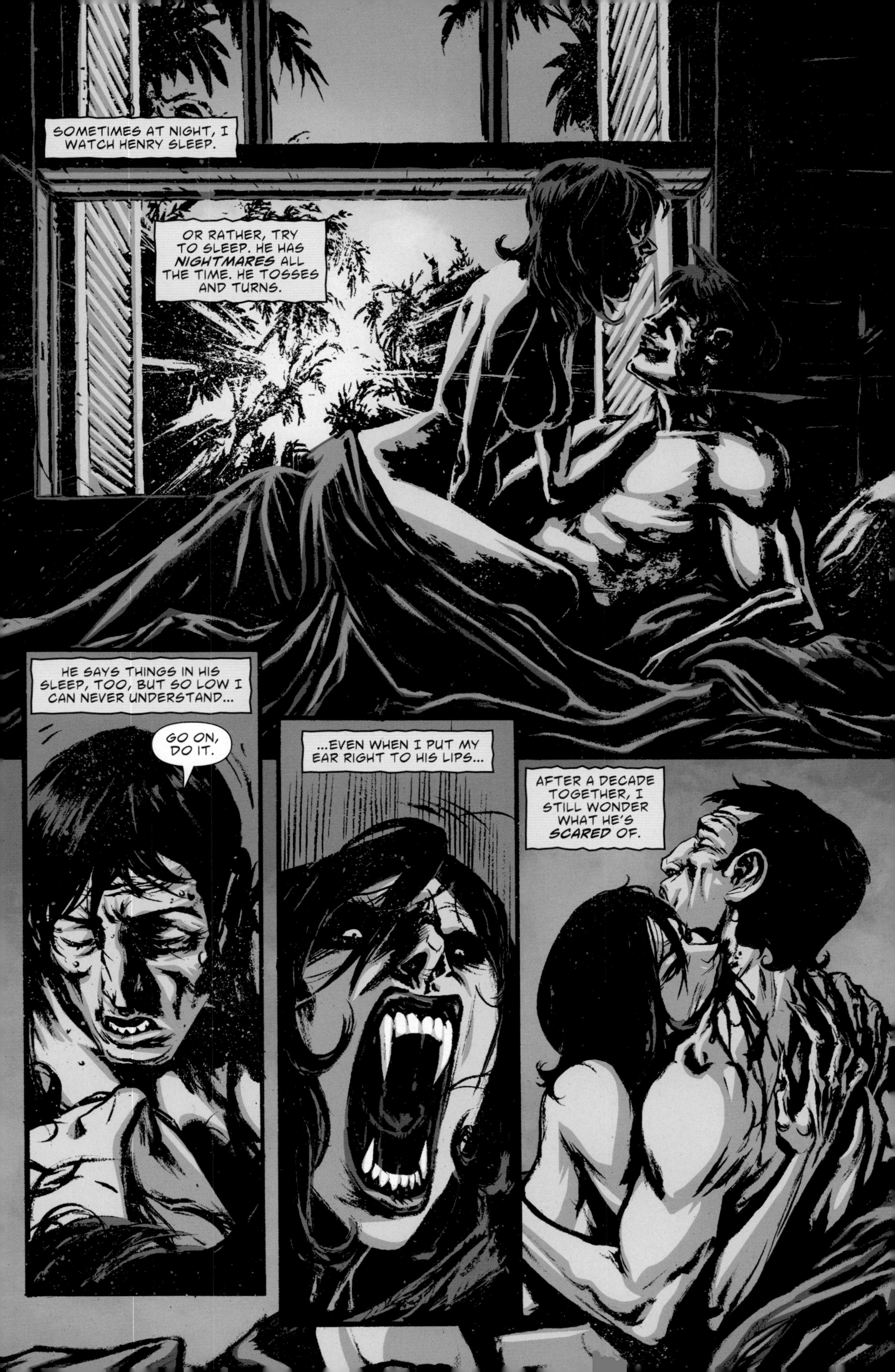
SOMETIMES AT NIGHT, I WATCH HENRY SLEEP.
OR RATHER, TRY TO SLEEP. HE HAS NIGHTMARES ALL THE TIME. HE TOSSES AND TURNS.
HE SAYS THINGS IN HIS SLEEP, TOO, BUT SO LOW I CAN NEVER UNDERSTAND...
GO ON, DO IT.
...EVEN WHEN I PUT MY EAR RIGHT TO HIS LIPS...
AFTER A DECADE TOGETHER, I STILL WONDER WHAT HE'S SCARED OF.

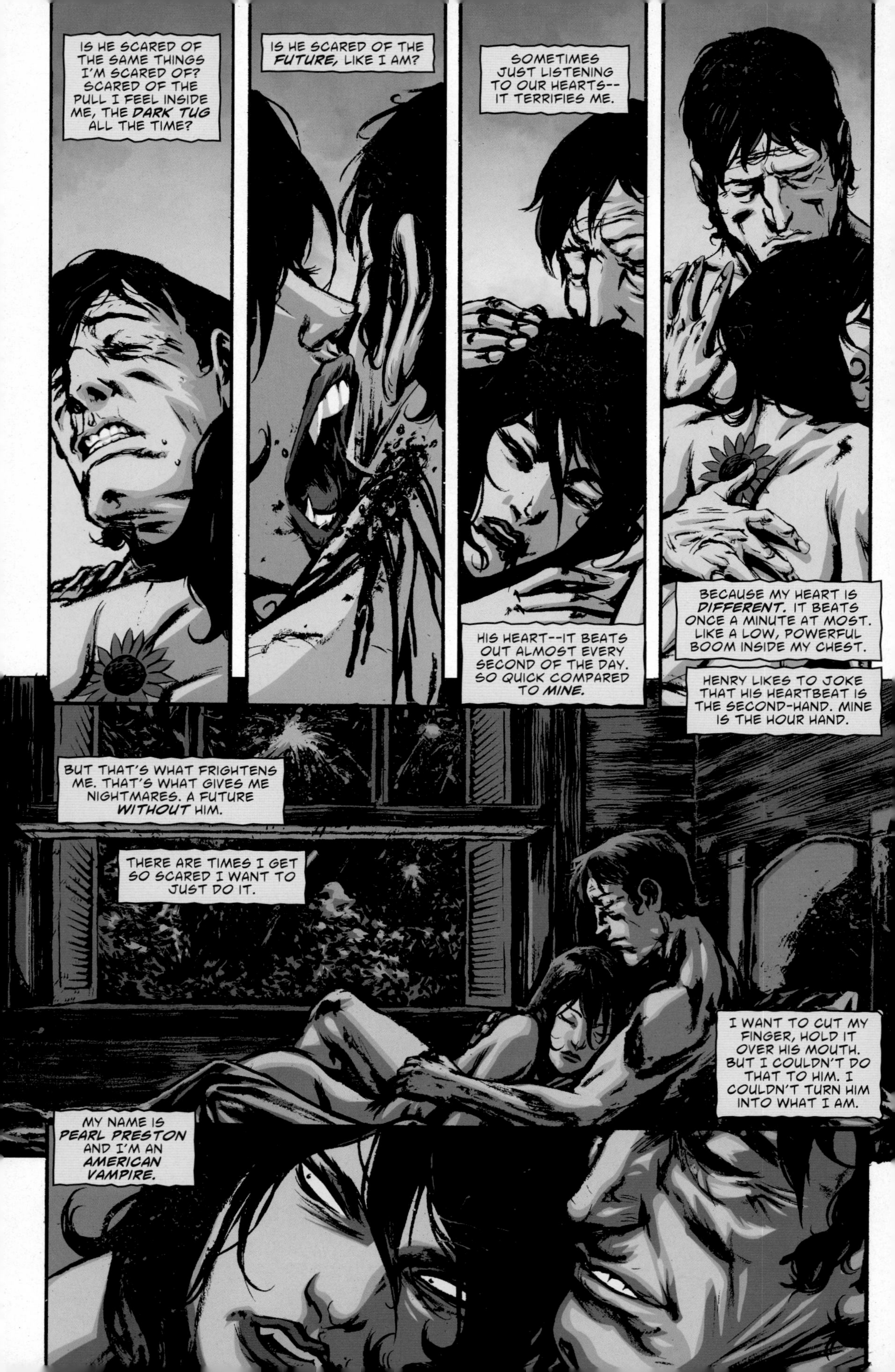
IS HE SCARED OF THE SAME THINGS I'M SCARED OF? SCARED OF THE PULL I FEEL INSIDE ME, THE DARK TUG ALL THE TIME?
IS HE SCARED OF THE FUTURE, LIKE I AM?
SOMETIMES JUST LISTENING TO OUR HEARTS-- IT TERRIFIES ME.
HIS HEART--IT BEATS OUT ALMOST EVERY SECOND OF THE DAY. SO QUICK COMPARED TO MINE.
BECAUSE MY HEART IS DIFFERENT. IT BEATS ONCE A MINUTE AT MOST. LIKE A LOW, POWERFUL BOOM INSIDE MY CHEST.
HENRY LIKES TO JOKE THAT HIS HEARTBEAT IS THE SECOND-HAND. MINE IS THE HOUR HAND.
BUT THAT'S WHAT FRIGHTENS ME. THAT'S WHAT GIVES ME NIGHTMARES. A FUTURE WITHOUT HIM.
THERE ARE TIMES I GET SO SCARED I WANT TO JUST DO IT.
I WANT TO CUT MY FINGER, HOLD IT OVER HIS MOUTH. BUT I COULDN'T DO THAT TO HIM. I COULDN'T TURN HIM INTO WHAT I AM.
MY NAME IS PEARL PRESTON AND I'M AN AMERICAN VAMPIRE.

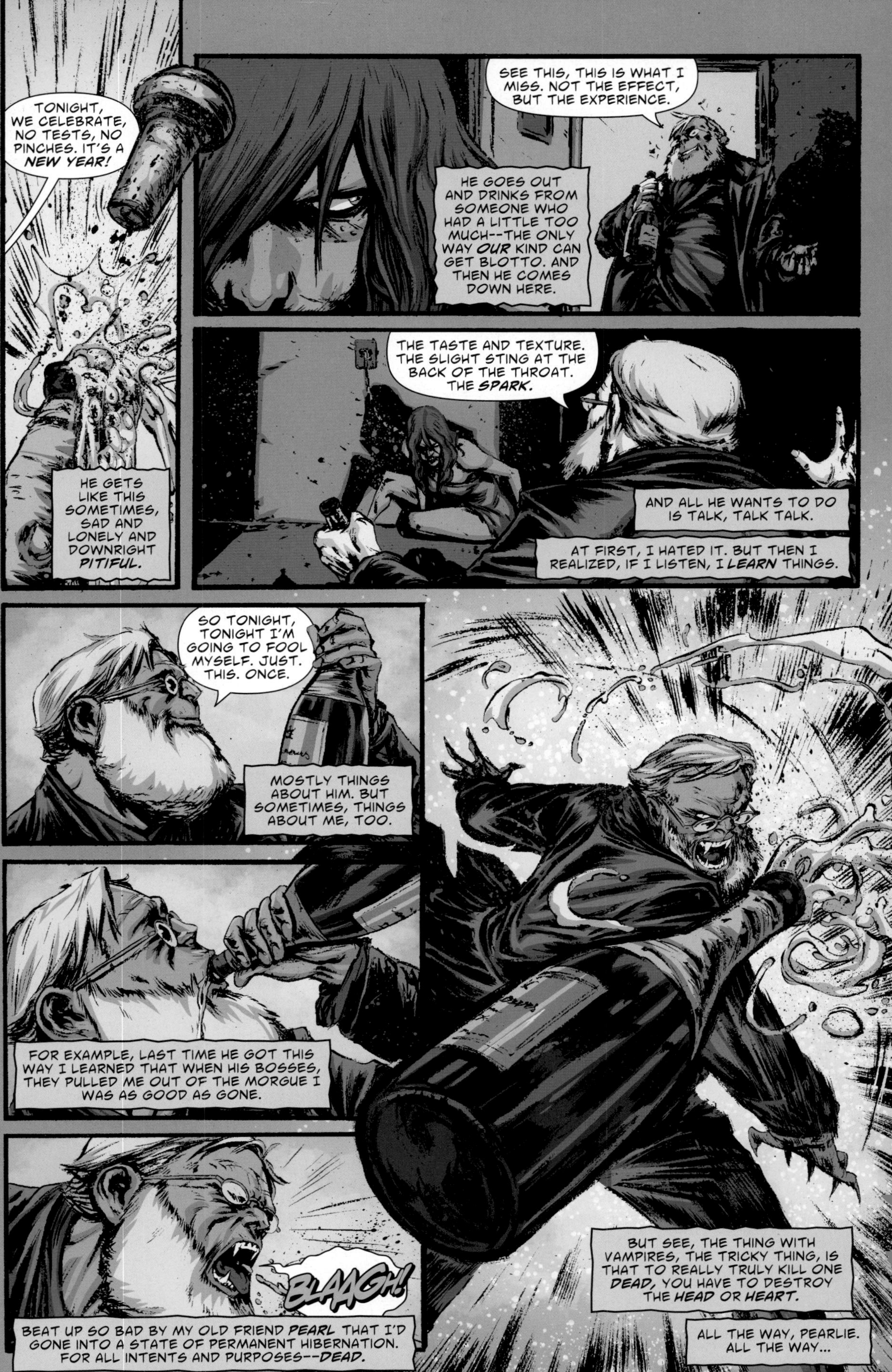
TONIGHT, WE CELEBRATE, NO TESTS, NO PINCHES. IT'S A NEW YEAR!
HE GETS LIKE THIS SOMETIMES, SAD AND LONELY AND DOWNRIGHT PITIFUL.
SEE THIS, THIS IS WHAT I MISS. NOT THE EFFECT, BUT THE EXPERIENCE.
HE GOES OUT AND DRINKS FROM SOMEONE WHO HAD A LITTLE TOO MUCH--THE ONLY WAY OUR KIND CAN GET BLOTTO. AND THEN HE COMES DOWN HERE.
THE TASTE AND TEXTURE. THE SLIGHT STING AT THE BACK OF THE THROAT. THE SPARK.
AND ALL HE WANTS TO DO IS TALK, TALK TALK.
AT FIRST, I HATED IT. BUT THEN I REALIZED, IF I LISTEN, I LEARN THINGS.
SO TONIGHT, TONIGHT I'M GOING TO FOOL MYSELF. JUST. THIS. ONCE.
MOSTLY THINGS ABOUT HIM. BUT SOMETIMES, THINGS ABOUT ME, TOO.
FOR EXAMPLE, LAST TIME HE GOT THIS WAY I LEARNED THAT WHEN HIS BOSSES, THEY PULLED ME OUT OF THE MORGUE I WAS AS GOOD AS GONE.
BLAAGH!
BEAT UP SO BAD BY MY OLD FRIEND PEARL THAT I'D GONE INTO A STATE OF PERMANENT HIBERNATION. FOR ALL INTENTS AND PURPOSES--DEAD.
BUT SEE, THE THING WITH VAMPIRES, THE TRICKY THING, IS THAT TO REALLY TRULY KILL ONE DEAD, YOU HAVE TO DESTROY THE HEAD OR HEART.
ALL THE WAY, PEARLIE. ALL THE WAY...

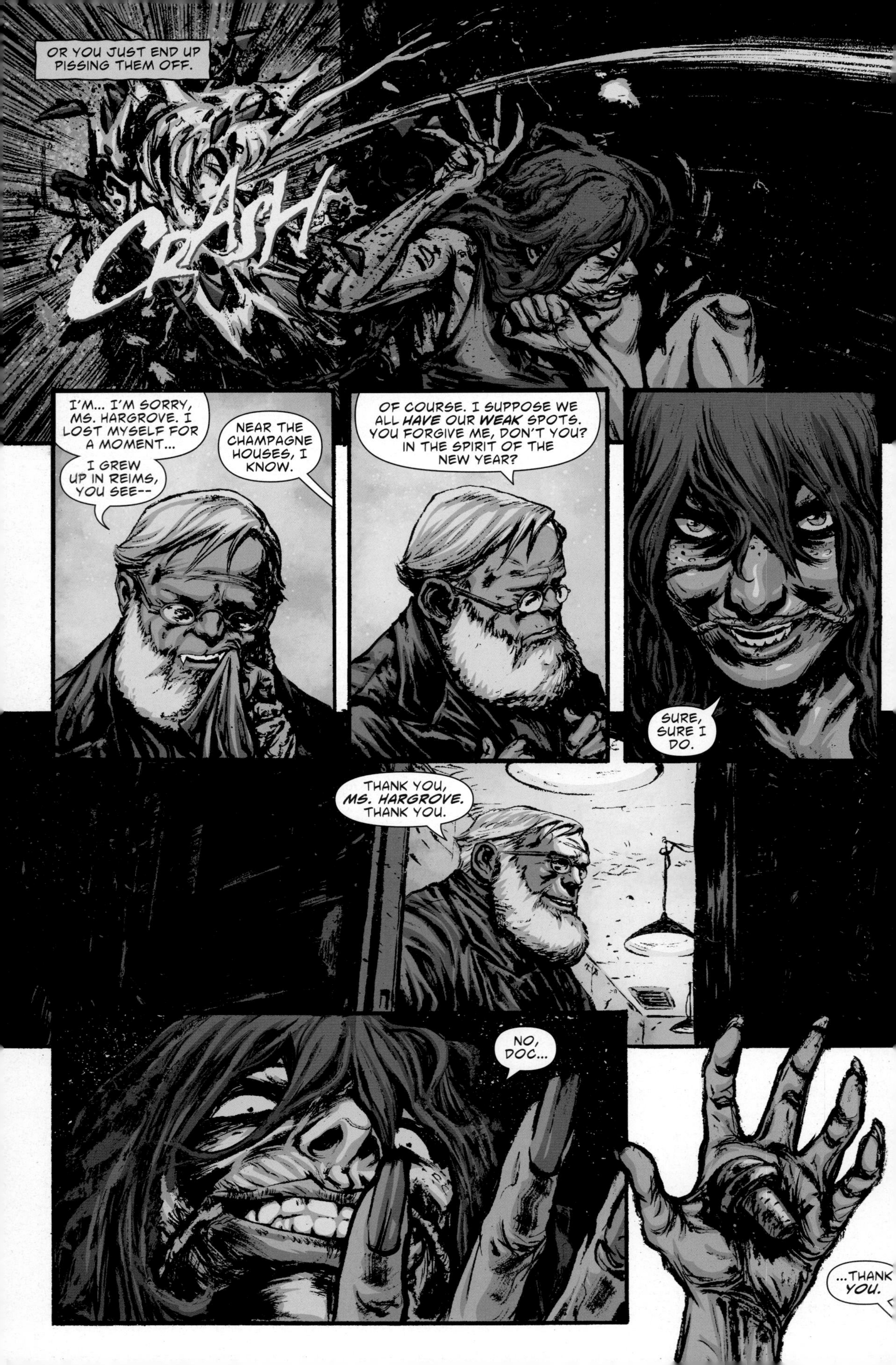
OR YOU JUST END UP PISSING THEM OFF.
CRASH
I'M... I'M SORRY, MS. HARGROVE. I LOST MYSELF FOR A MOMENT...
I GREW UP IN REIMS, YOU SEE--
NEAR THE CHAMPAGNE HOUSES, I KNOW.
OF COURSE. I SUPPOSE WE ALL HAVE OUR WEAK SPOTS. YOU FORGIVE ME, DON'T YOU? IN THE SPIRIT OF THE NEW YEAR?
SURE, SURE I DO.
THANK YOU, MS. HARGROVE. THANK YOU.
NO, DOC...
...THANK YOU.

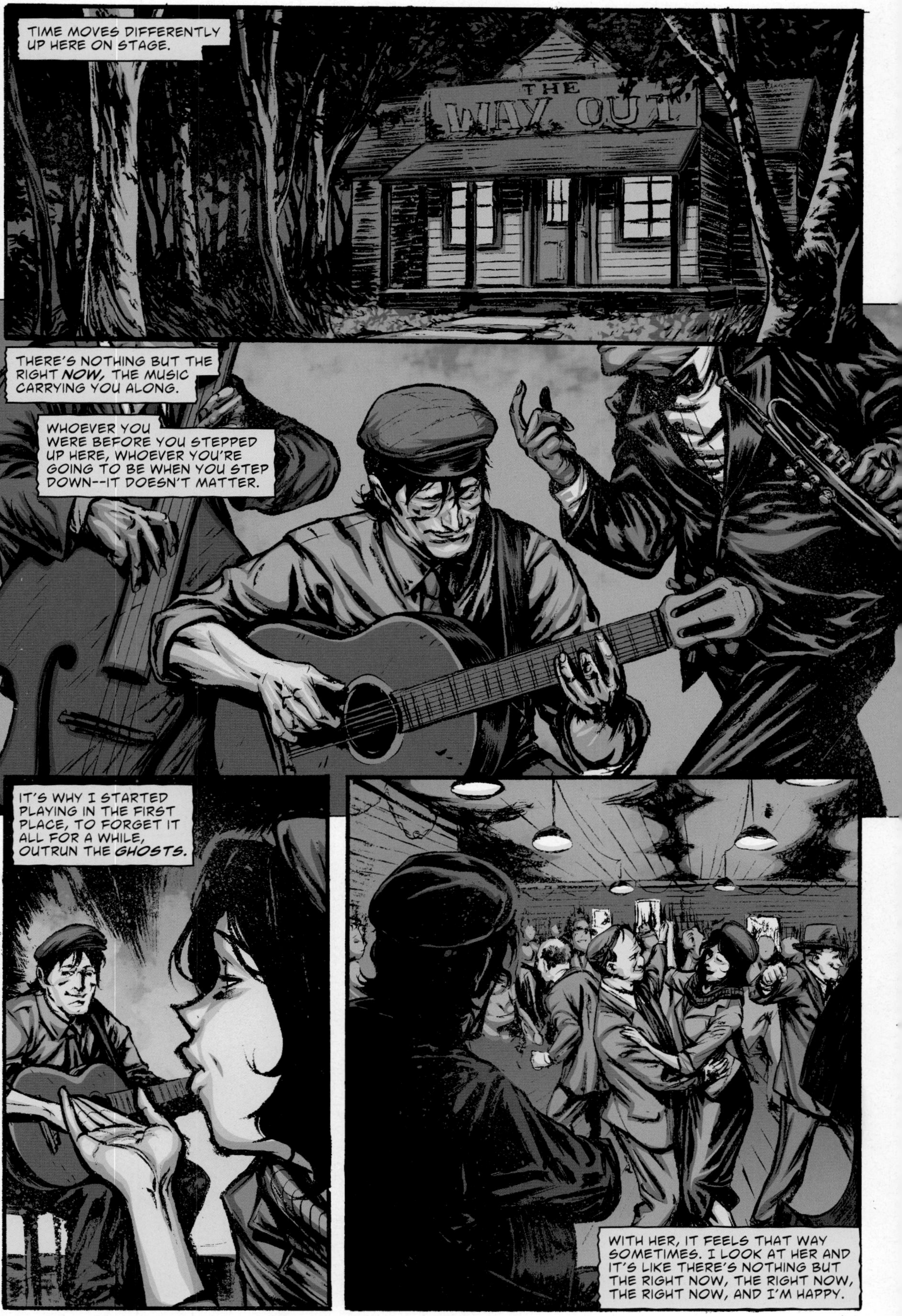

TIME MOVES DIFFERENTLY UP HERE ON STAGE.
THE WAY OUT
THERE'S NOTHING BUT THE RIGHT NOW, THE MUSIC CARRYING YOU ALONG.
WHOEVER YOU WERE BEFORE YOU STEPPED UP HERE, WHOEVER YOU'RE GOING TO BE WHEN YOU STEP DOWN--IT DOESN'T MATTER.
IT'S WHY I STARTED PLAYING IN THE FIRST PLACE, TO FORGET IT ALL FOR A WHILE, OUTRUN THE GHOSTS.
WITH HER, IT FEELS THAT WAY SOMETIMES. I LOOK AT HER AND IT'S LIKE THERE'S NOTHING BUT THE RIGHT NOW, THE RIGHT NOW, THE RIGHT NOW, AND I'M HAPPY.

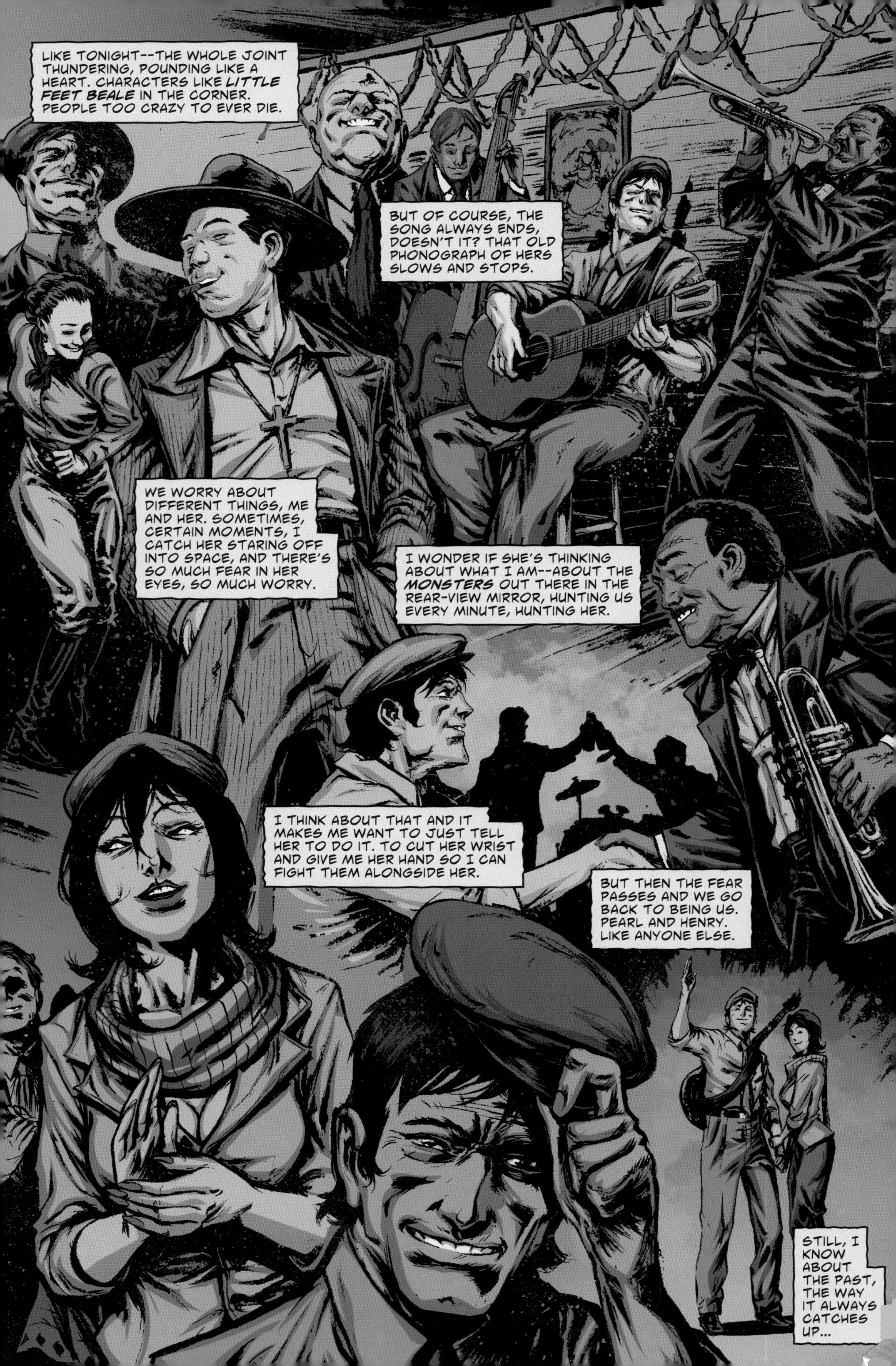
LIKE TONIGHT--THE WHOLE JOINT THUNDERING, POUNDING LIKE A HEART. CHARACTERS LIKE *LITTLE FEET BEALE* IN THE CORNER. PEOPLE TOO CRAZY TO EVER DIE.
BUT OF COURSE, THE SONG ALWAYS ENDS, DOESN'T IT? THAT OLD PHONOGRAPH OF HERS SLOWS AND STOPS.
WE WORRY ABOUT DIFFERENT THINGS, ME AND HER. SOMETIMES, CERTAIN MOMENTS, I CATCH HER STARING OFF INTO SPACE, AND THERE'S SO MUCH FEAR IN HER EYES, SO MUCH WORRY.
I WONDER IF SHE'S THINKING ABOUT WHAT I AM--ABOUT THE ***MONSTERS*** OUT THERE IN THE REAR-VIEW MIRROR, HUNTING US EVERY MINUTE, HUNTING HER.
I THINK ABOUT THAT AND IT MAKES ME WANT TO JUST TELL HER TO DO IT. TO CUT HER WRIST AND GIVE ME HER HAND SO I CAN FIGHT THEM ALONGSIDE HER.
BUT THEN THE FEAR PASSES AND WE GO BACK TO BEING US. PEARL AND HENRY. LIKE ANYONE ELSE.
STILL, I KNOW ABOUT THE PAST, THE WAY IT ALWAYS CATCHES UP...

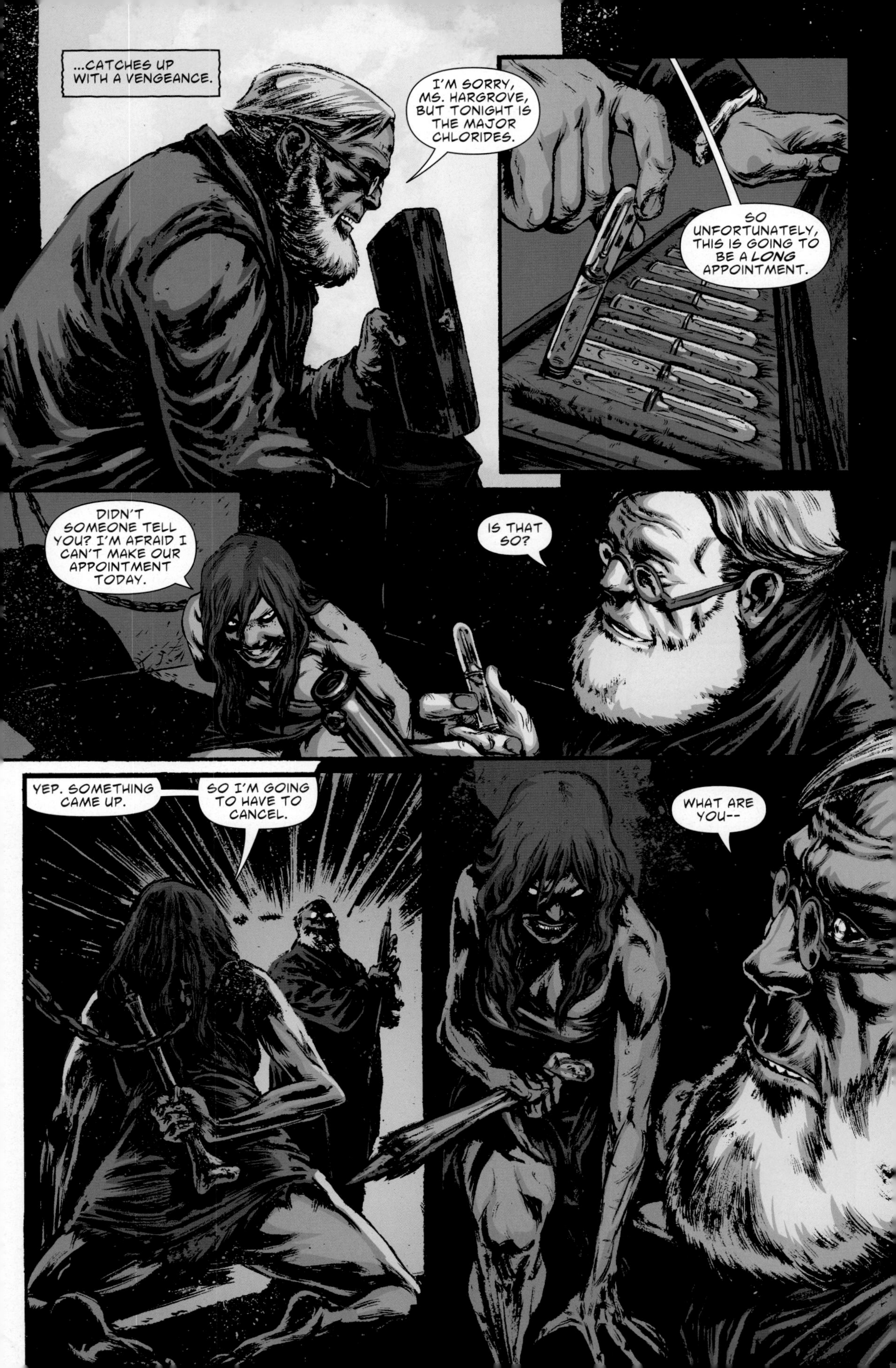
...CATCHES UP WITH A VENGEANCE.
I'M SORRY, MS. HARGROVE, BUT TONIGHT IS THE MAJOR CHLORIDES.
SO UNFORTUNATELY, THIS IS GOING TO BE A LONG APPOINTMENT.
DIDN'T SOMEONE TELL YOU? I'M AFRAID I CAN'T MAKE OUR APPOINTMENT TODAY.
IS THAT SO?
YEP. SOMETHING CAME UP.
SO I'M GOING TO HAVE TO CANCEL.
WHAT ARE YOU--

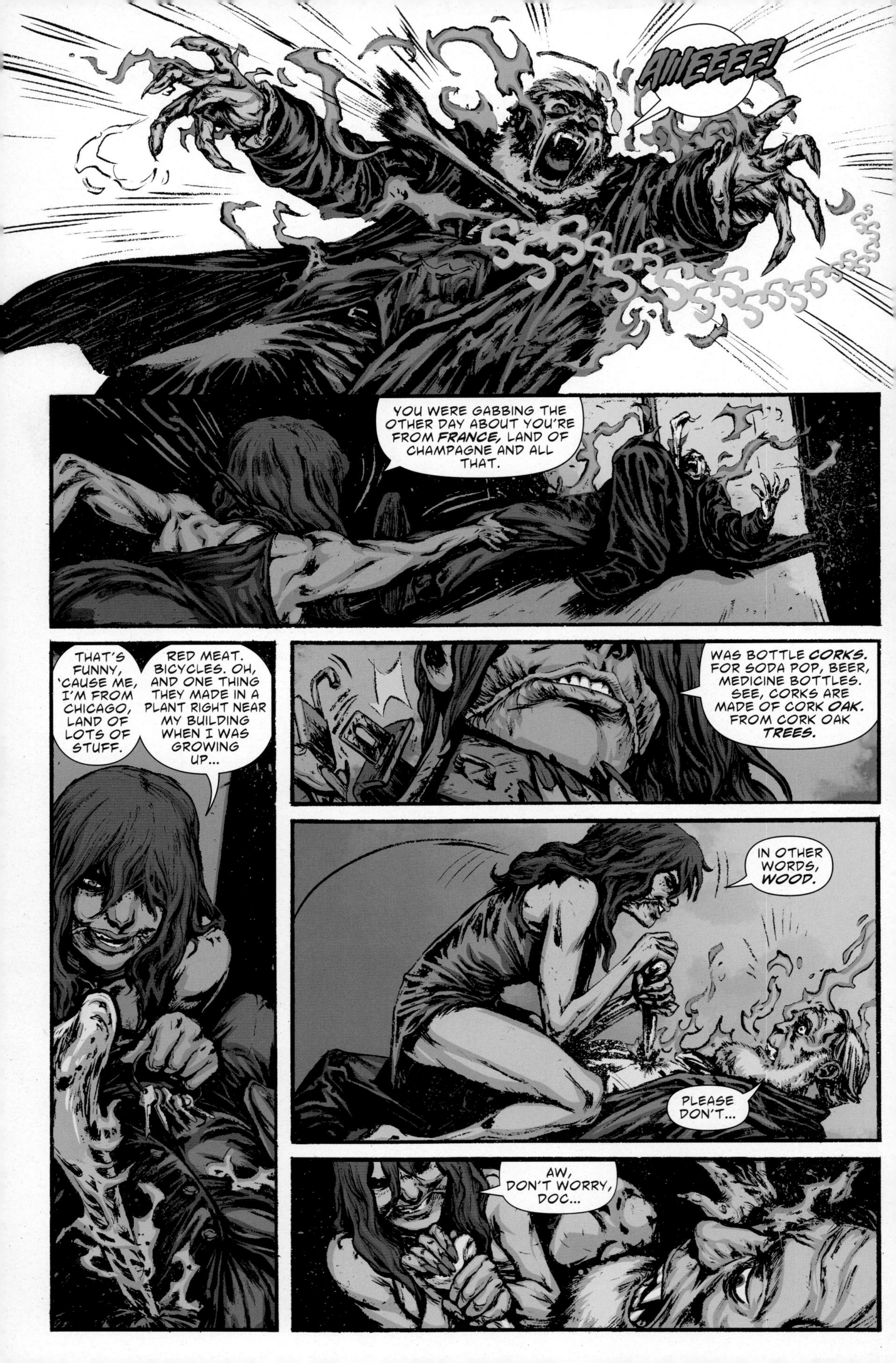
AIIIEEEE!
SSSSSSSSSS
YOU WERE GABBING THE OTHER DAY ABOUT YOU'RE FROM FRANCE, LAND OF CHAMPAGNE AND ALL THAT.
THAT'S FUNNY, 'CAUSE ME, I'M FROM CHICAGO, LAND OF LOTS OF STUFF.
RED MEAT. BICYCLES. OH, AND ONE THING THEY MADE IN A PLANT RIGHT NEAR MY BUILDING WHEN I WAS GROWING UP...
WAS BOTTLE CORKS. FOR SODA POP, BEER, MEDICINE BOTTLES. SEE, CORKS ARE MADE OF CORK OAK. FROM CORK OAK TREES.
IN OTHER WORDS, WOOD.
PLEASE DON'T...
AW, DON'T WORRY, DOC...

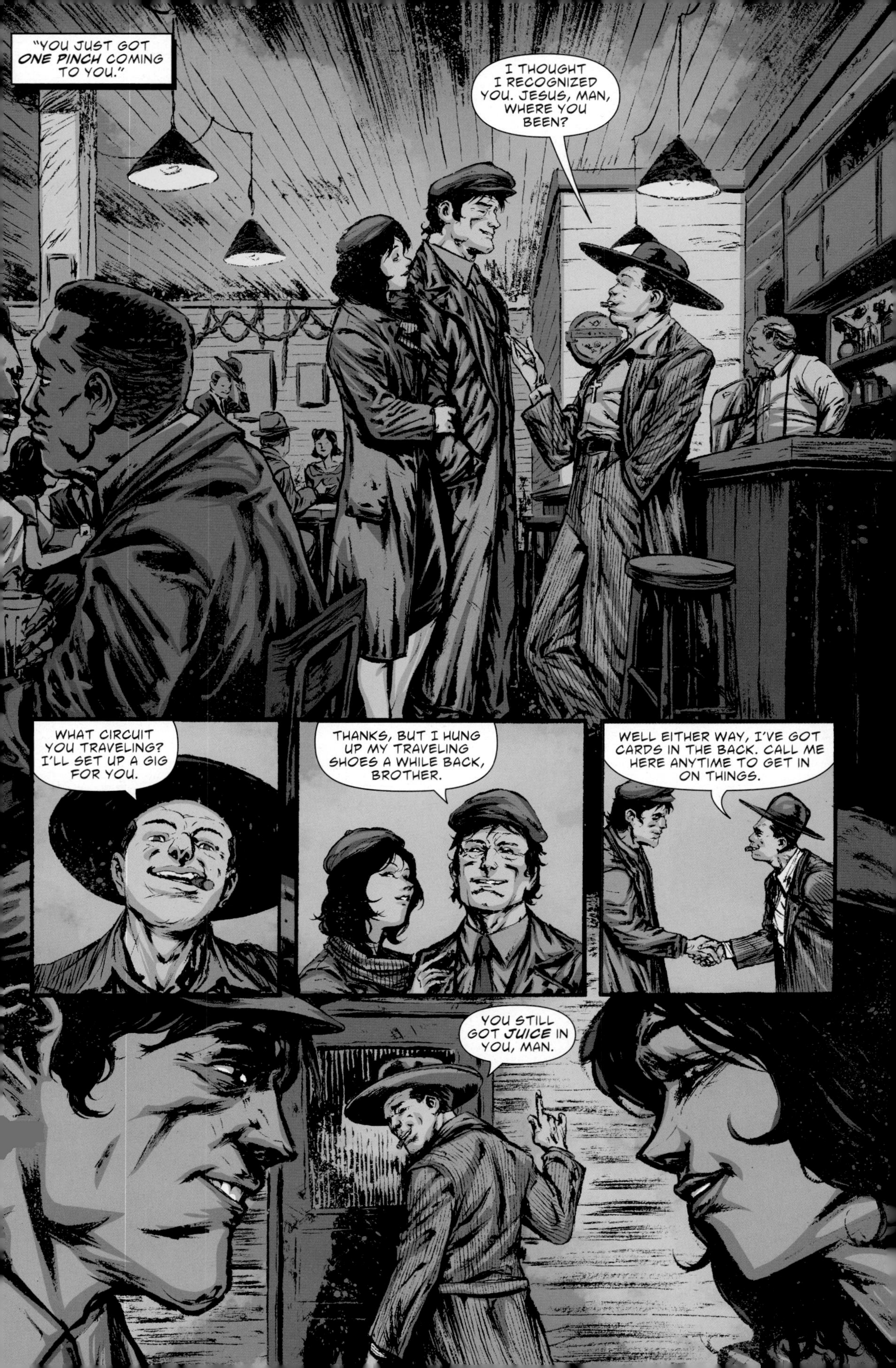
"YOU JUST GOT *ONE PINCH* COMING TO YOU."
I THOUGHT I RECOGNIZED YOU. JESUS, MAN, WHERE YOU BEEN?
WHAT CIRCUIT YOU TRAVELING? I'LL SET UP A GIG FOR YOU.
THANKS, BUT I HUNG UP MY TRAVELING SHOES A WHILE BACK, BROTHER.
WELL EITHER WAY, I'VE GOT CARDS IN THE BACK. CALL ME HERE ANYTIME TO GET IN ON THINGS.
YOU STILL GOT *JUICE* IN YOU, MAN.

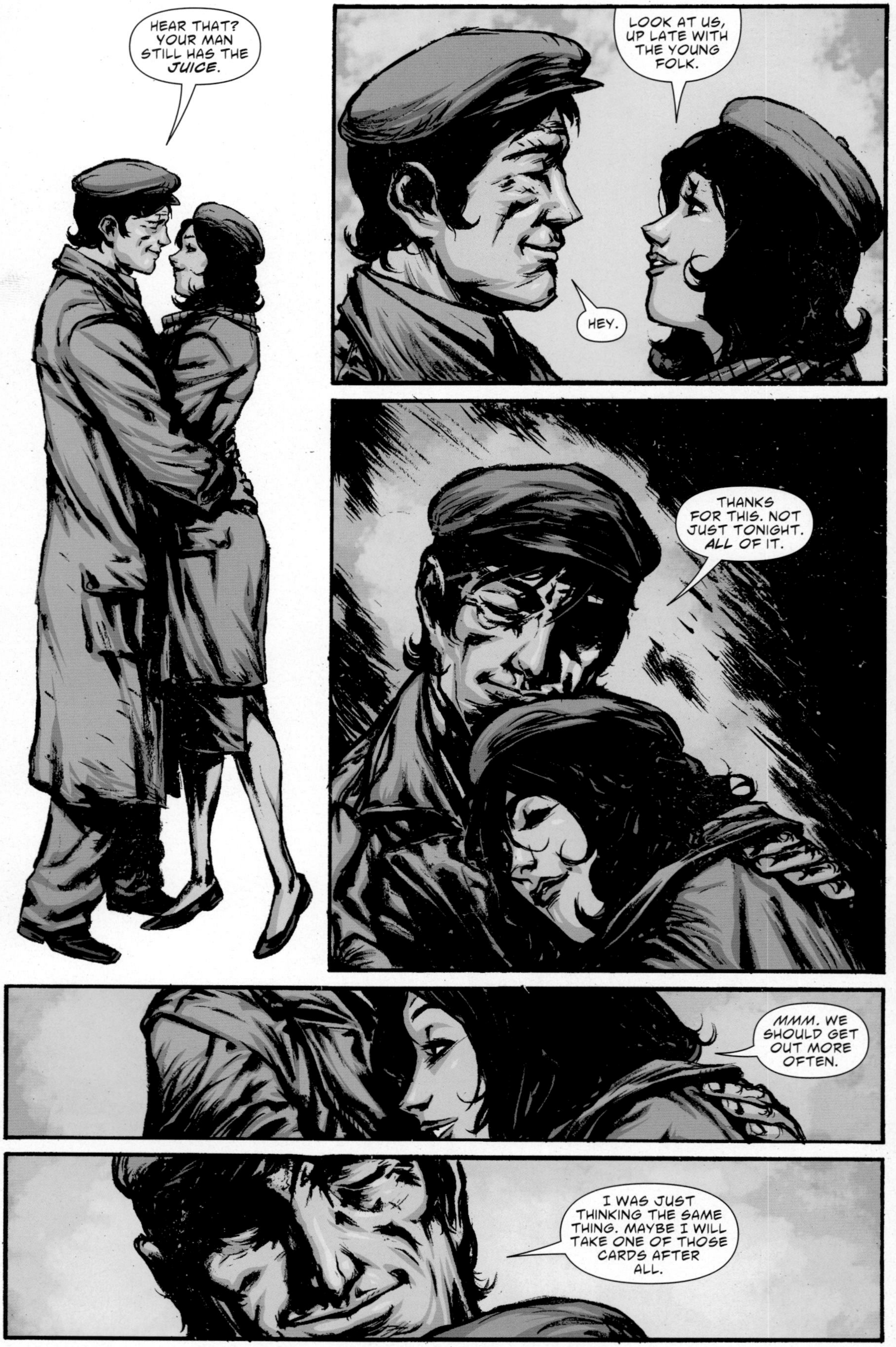
HEAR THAT? YOUR MAN STILL HAS THE *JUICE*.
LOOK AT US, UP LATE WITH THE YOUNG FOLK.
HEY.
THANKS FOR THIS. NOT JUST TONIGHT. *ALL* OF IT.
MMM. WE SHOULD GET OUT MORE OFTEN.
I WAS JUST THINKING THE SAME THING. MAYBE I WILL TAKE ONE OF THOSE CARDS AFTER ALL.

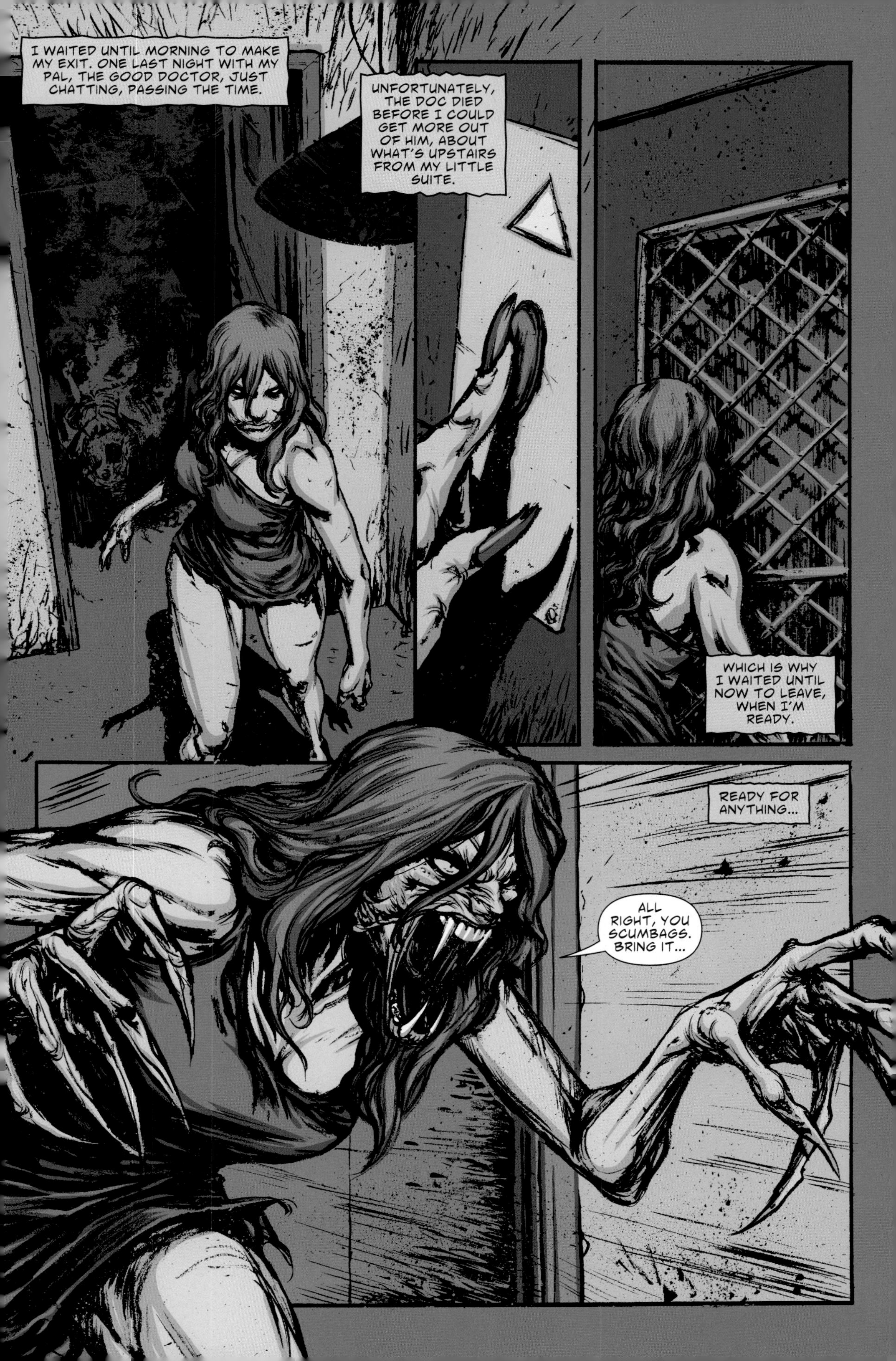

I WAITED UNTIL MORNING TO MAKE MY EXIT. ONE LAST NIGHT WITH MY PAL, THE GOOD DOCTOR, JUST CHATTING, PASSING THE TIME.
UNFORTUNATELY, THE DOC DIED BEFORE I COULD GET MORE OUT OF HIM, ABOUT WHAT'S UPSTAIRS FROM MY LITTLE SUITE.
WHICH IS WHY I WAITED UNTIL NOW TO LEAVE, WHEN I'M READY.
READY FOR ANYTHING...
ALL RIGHT, YOU SCUMBAGS. BRING IT...

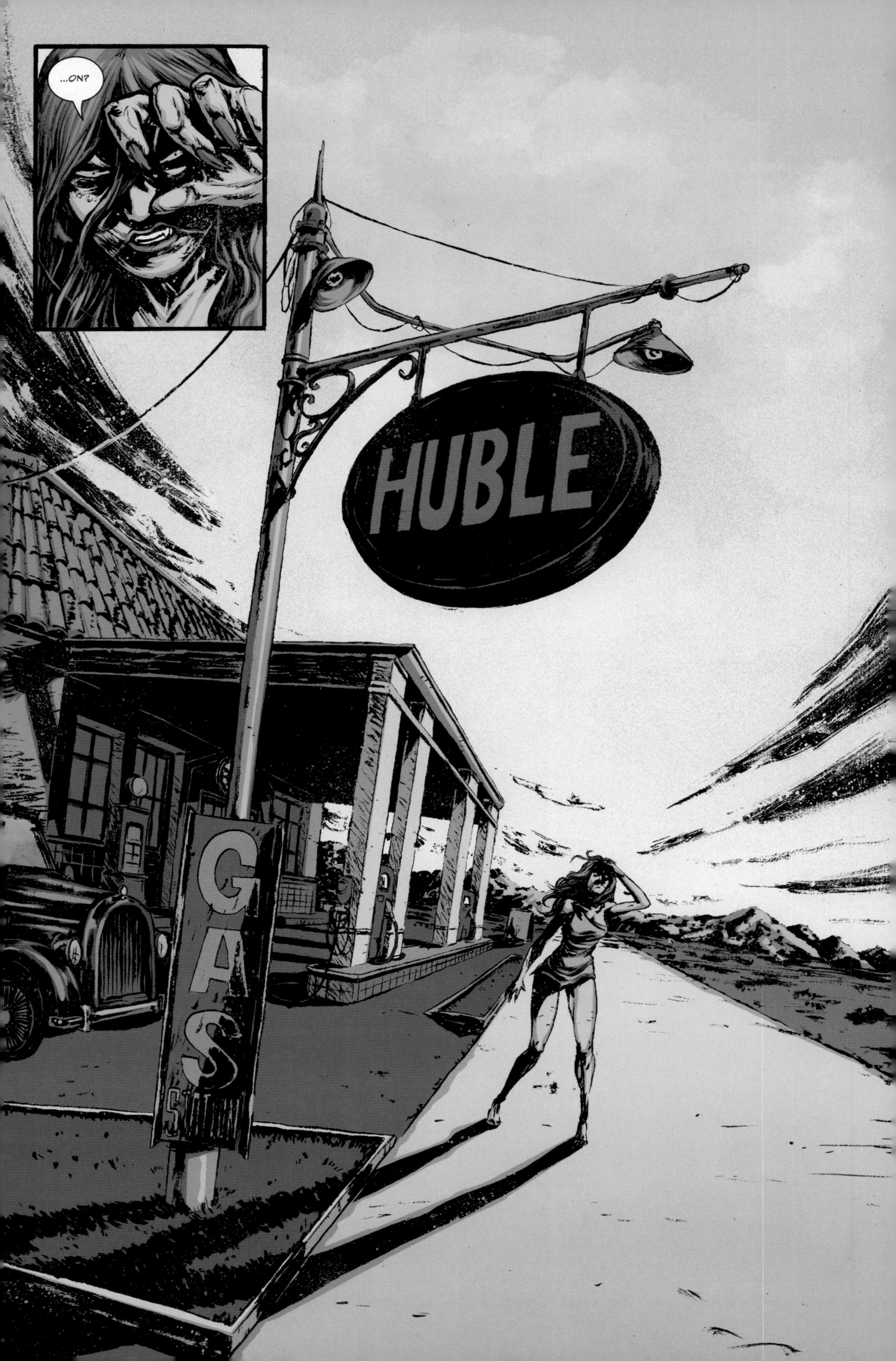
...ON?
HUBLE
GAS

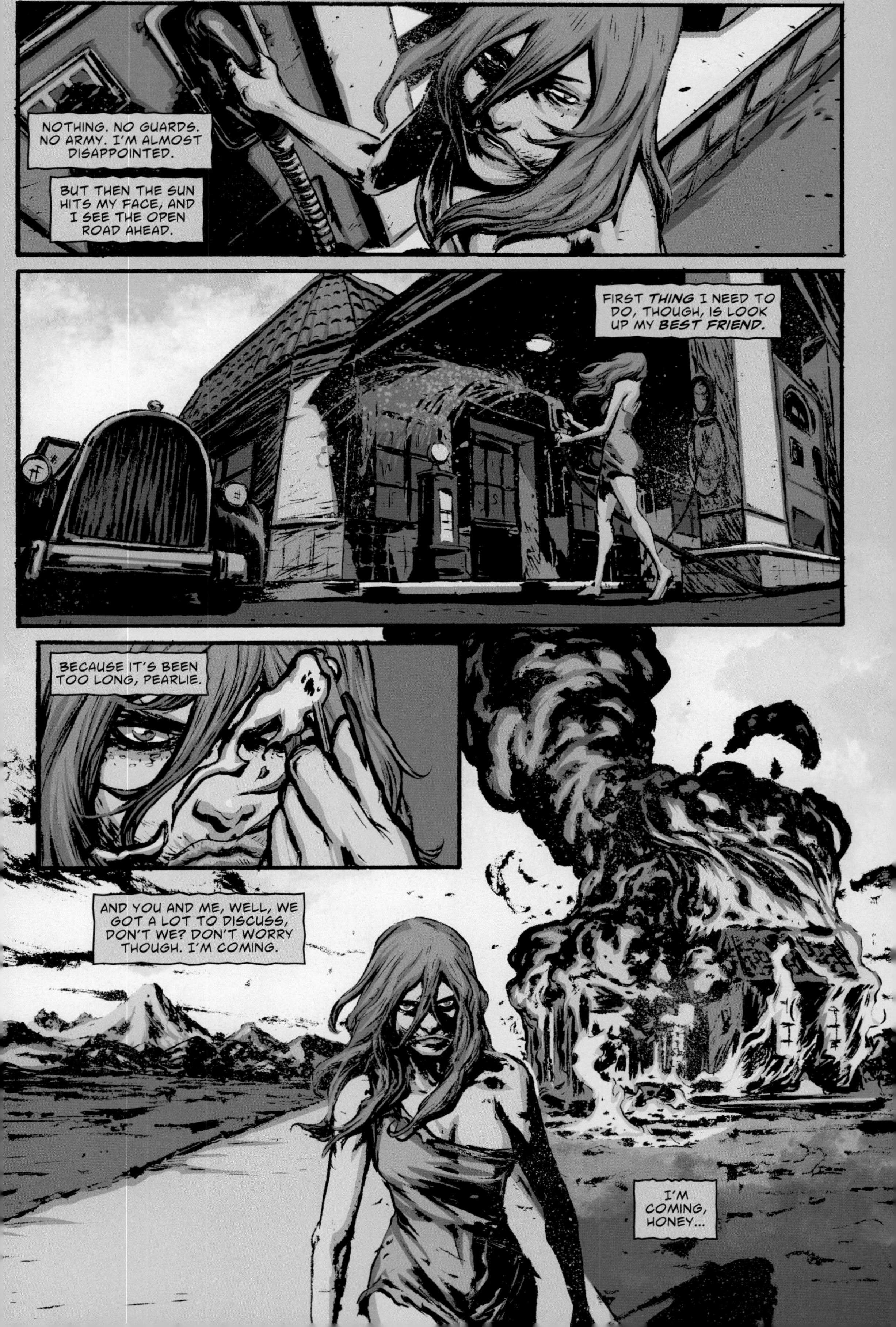
NOTHING. NO GUARDS. NO ARMY. I'M ALMOST DISAPPOINTED.
BUT THEN THE SUN HITS MY FACE, AND I SEE THE OPEN ROAD AHEAD.
FIRST *THING* I NEED TO DO, THOUGH, IS LOOK UP MY ***BEST FRIEND.***
BECAUSE IT'S BEEN TOO LONG, PEARLIE.
AND YOU AND ME, WELL, WE GOT A LOT TO DISCUSS, DON'T WE? DON'T WORRY THOUGH. I'M COMING.
I'M COMING, HONEY...

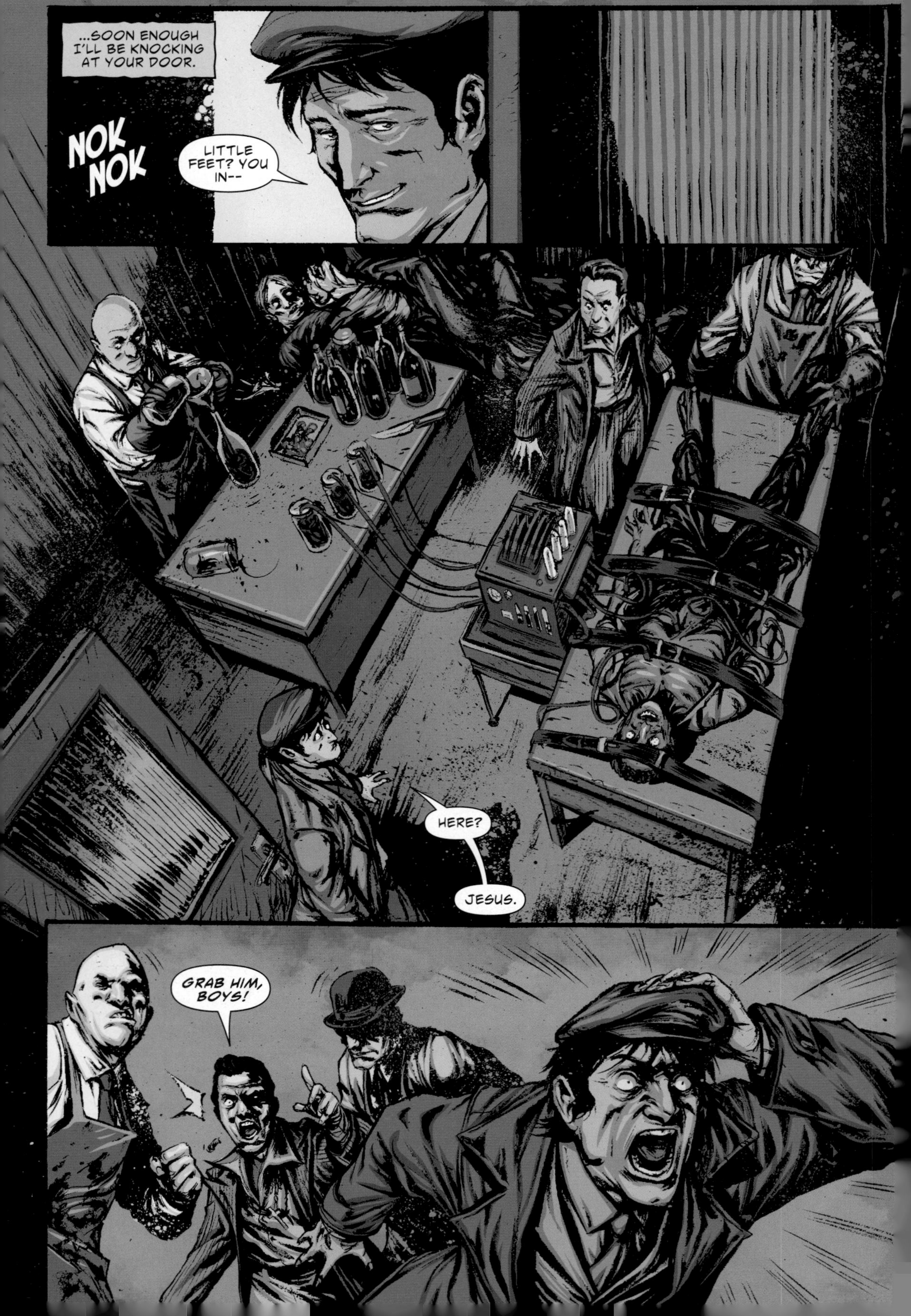
...SOON ENOUGH I'LL BE KNOCKING AT YOUR DOOR.
NOK NOK
LITTLE FEET? YOU IN--
HERE?
JESUS.
GRAB HIM, BOYS!

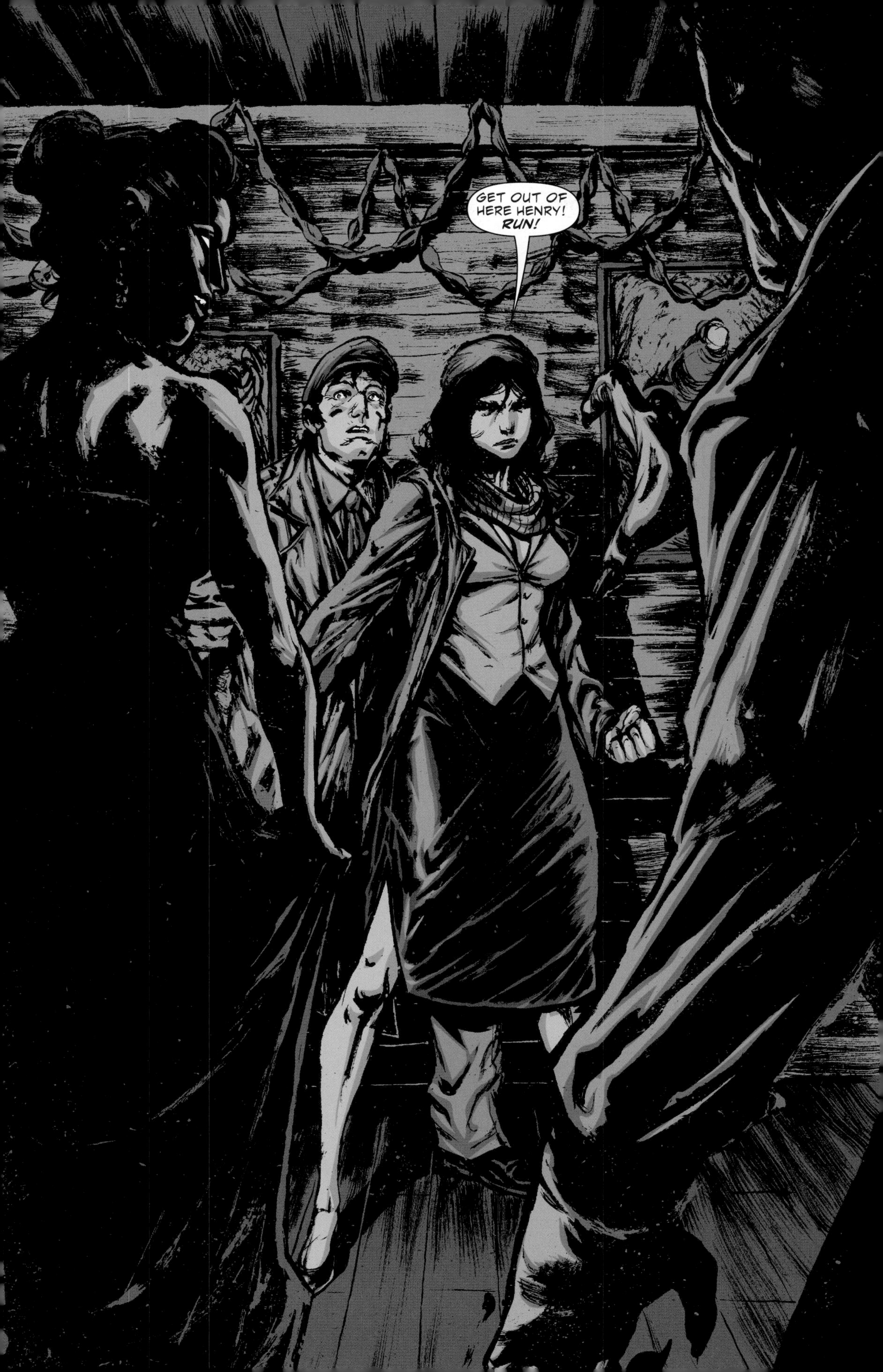
GET OUT OF HERE HENRY! RUN!

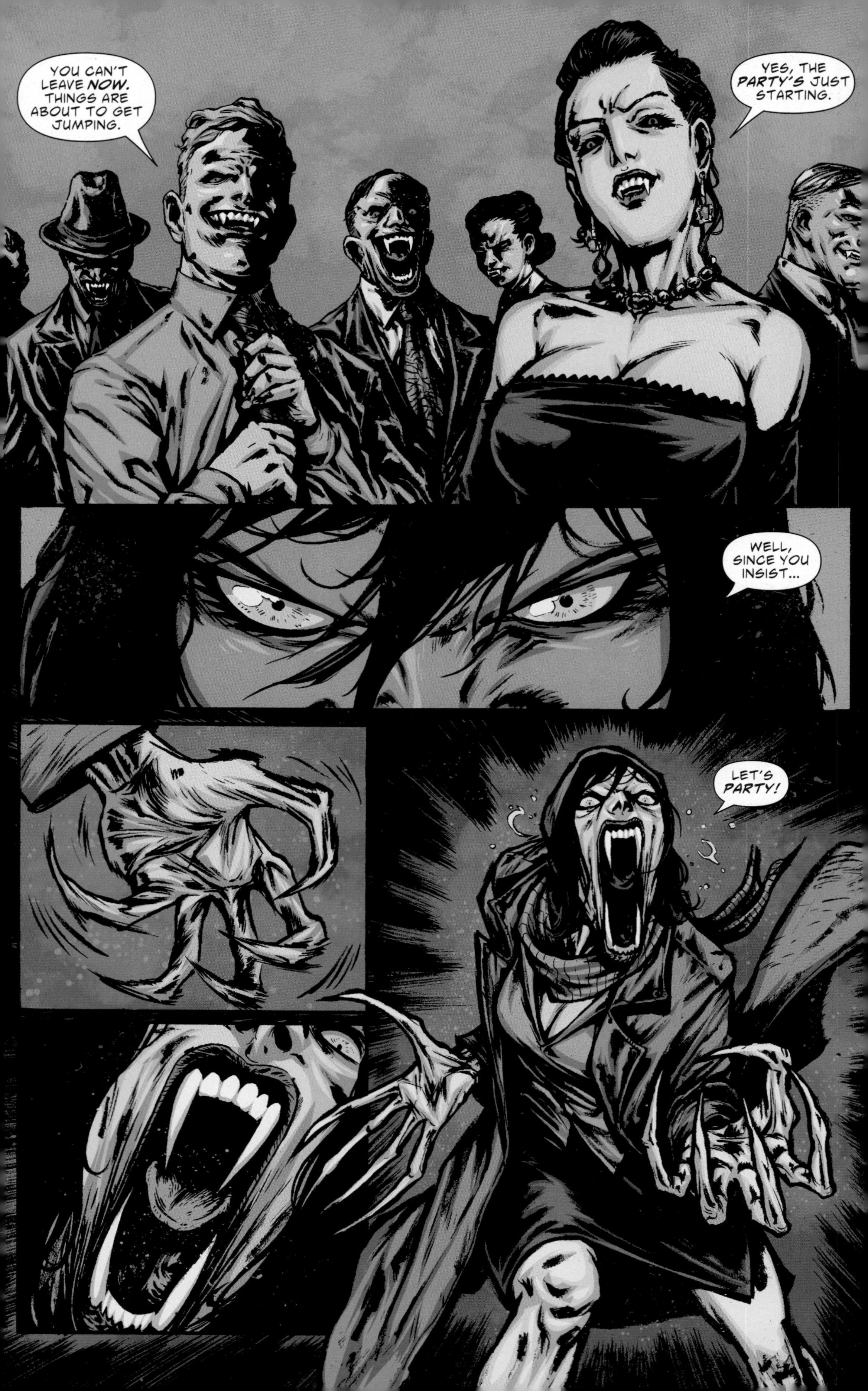
YOU CAN'T LEAVE NOW. THINGS ARE ABOUT TO GET JUMPING.
YES, THE PARTY'S JUST STARTING.
WELL, SINCE YOU INSIST...
LET'S PARTY!

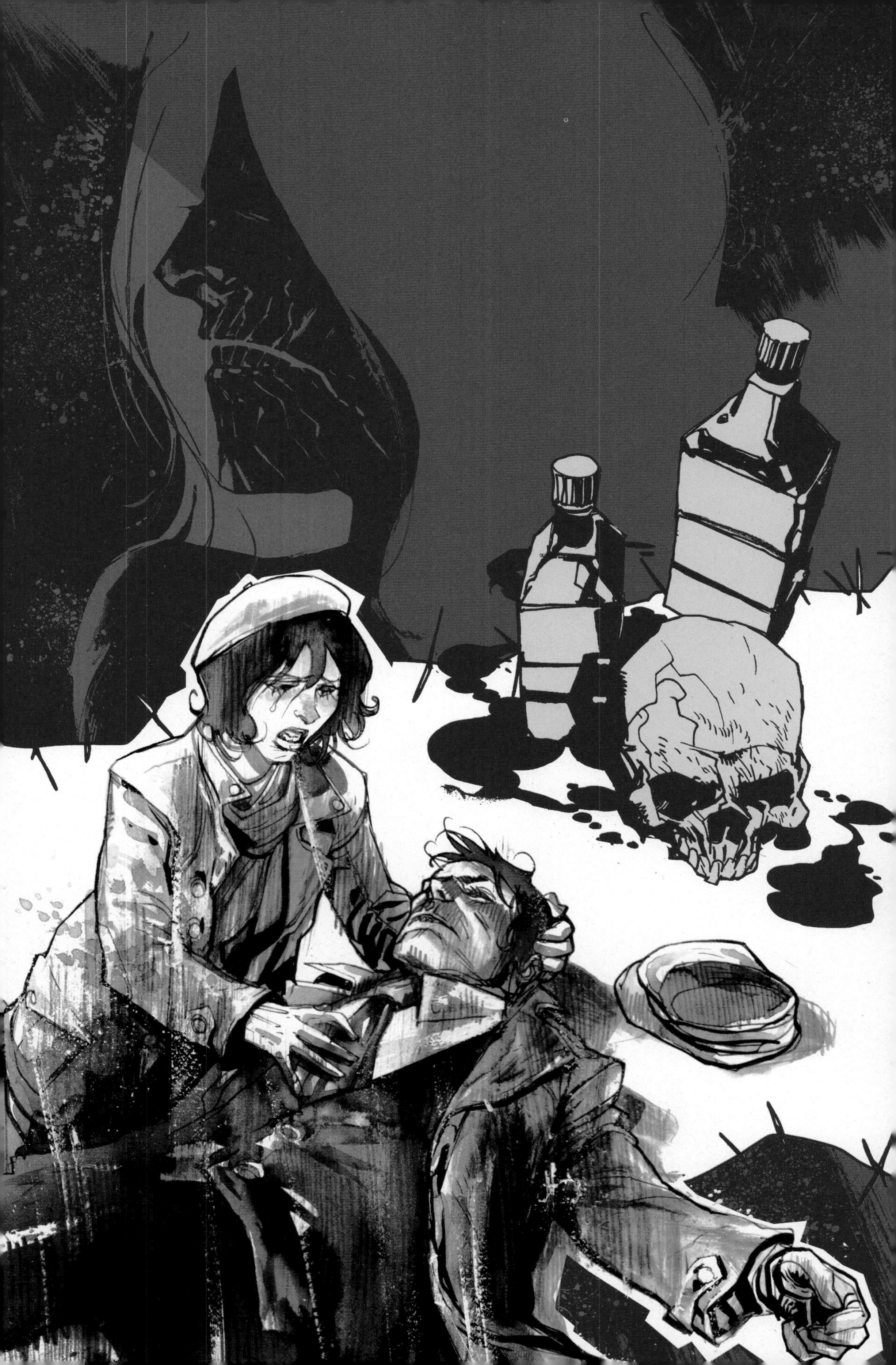

The Way Out

Part Two

Mateus Santolouco

Artist

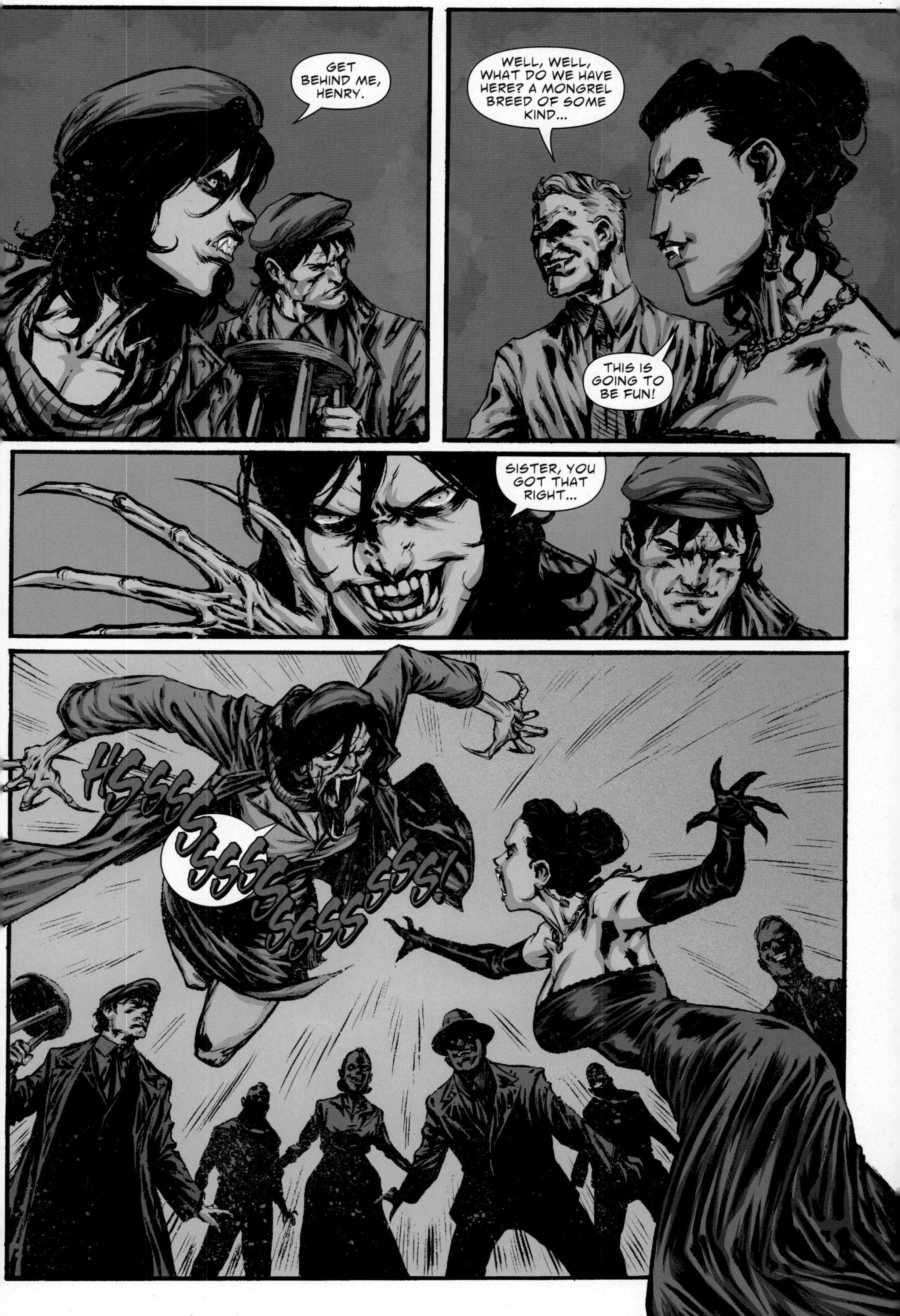
GET BEHIND ME, HENRY.
WELL, WELL, WHAT DO WE HAVE HERE? A MONGREL BREED OF SOME KIND...
THIS IS GOING TO BE FUN!
SISTER, YOU GOT THAT RIGHT...
HSSSSSSSSSSSSSSSSSSSS!

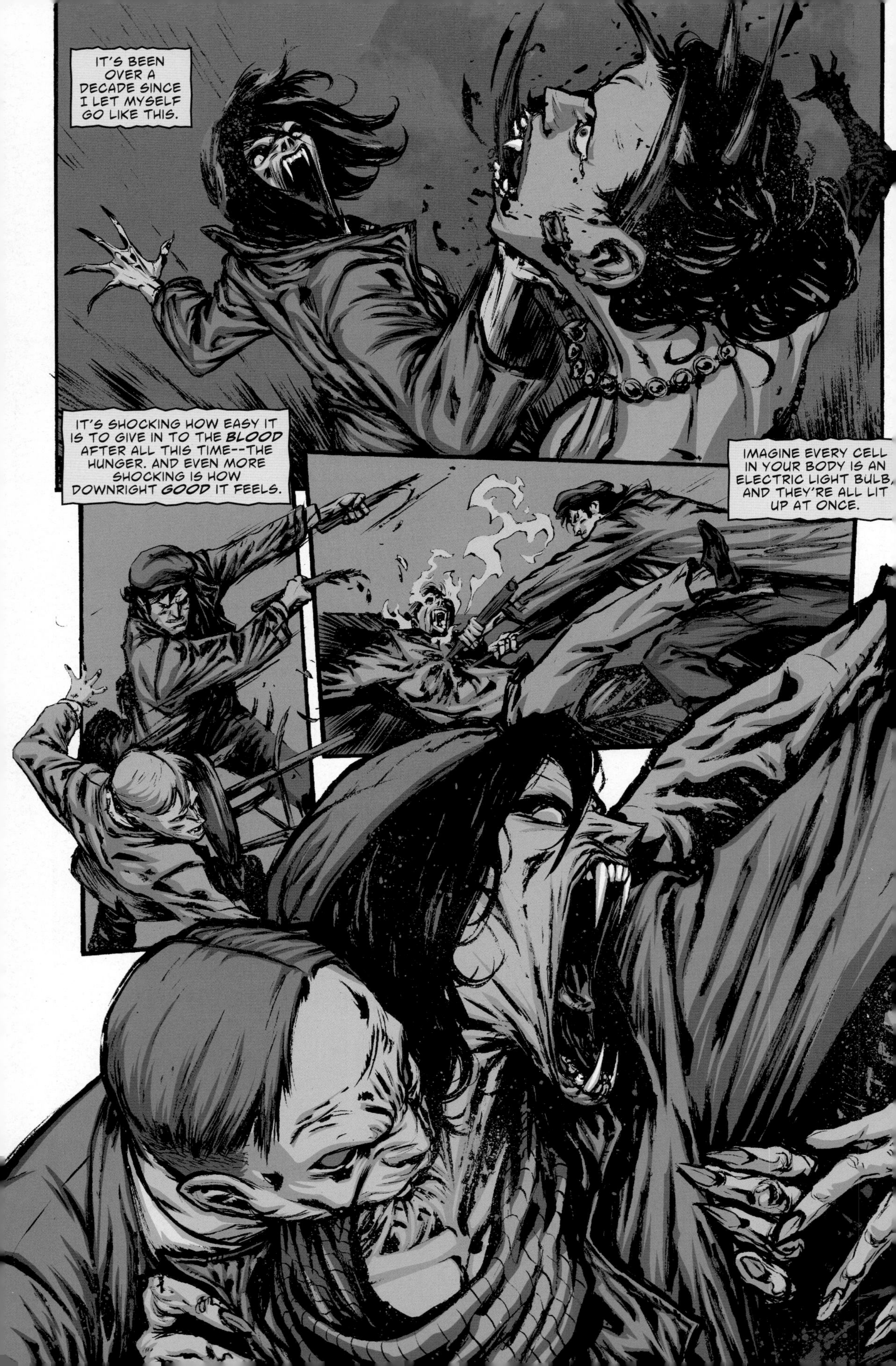
IT'S BEEN OVER A DECADE SINCE I LET MYSELF GO LIKE THIS.
IT'S SHOCKING HOW EASY IT IS TO GIVE IN TO THE *BLOOD* AFTER ALL THIS TIME--THE HUNGER. AND EVEN MORE SHOCKING IS HOW DOWNRIGHT *GOOD* IT FEELS.
IMAGINE EVERY CELL IN YOUR BODY IS AN ELECTRIC LIGHT BULB, AND THEY'RE ALL LIT UP AT ONCE.

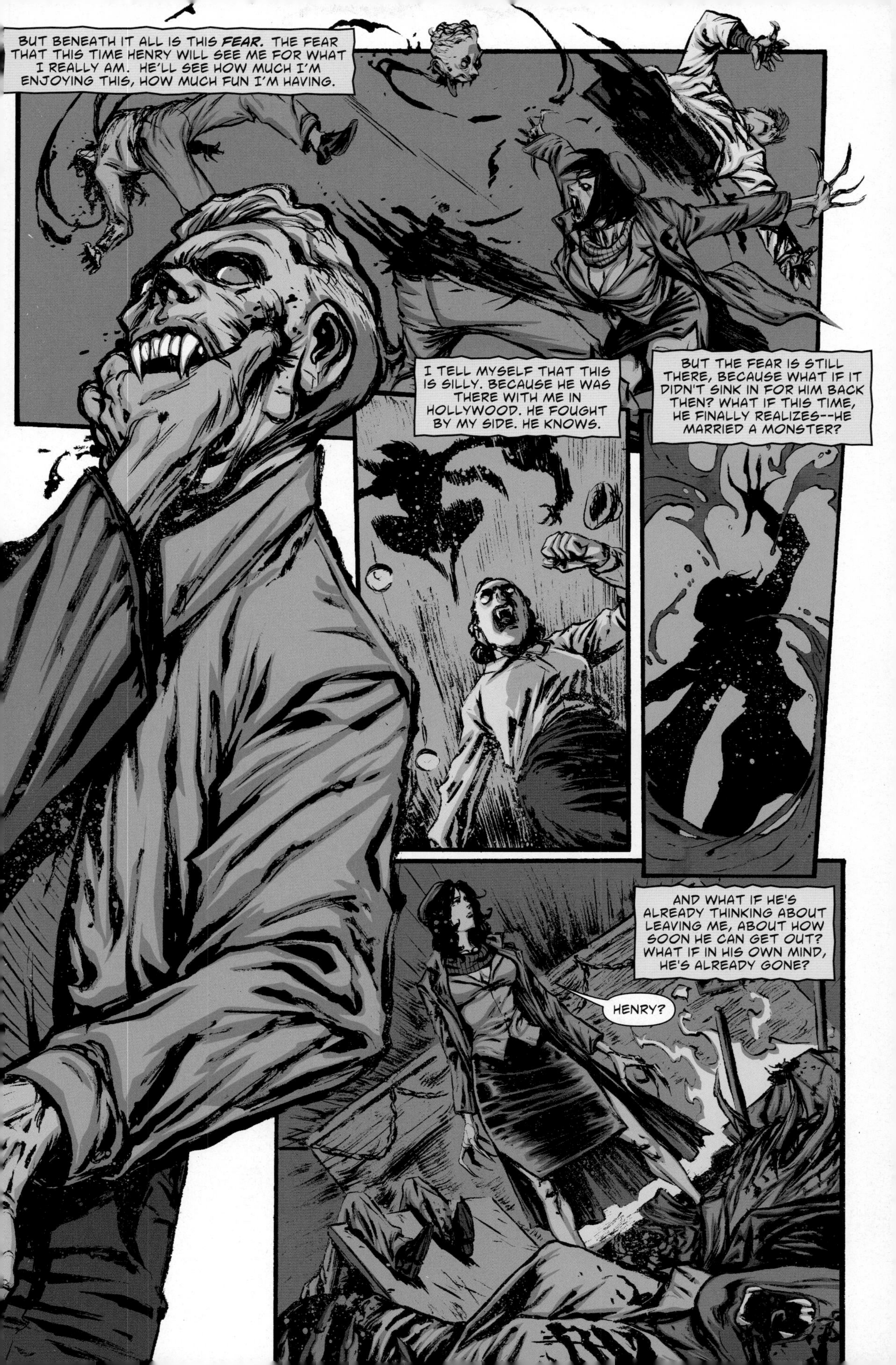
BUT BENEATH IT ALL IS THIS *FEAR.* THE FEAR THAT THIS TIME HENRY WILL SEE ME FOR WHAT I REALLY AM. HE'LL SEE HOW MUCH I'M ENJOYING THIS, HOW MUCH FUN I'M HAVING.
I TELL MYSELF THAT THIS IS SILLY. BECAUSE HE WAS THERE WITH ME IN HOLLYWOOD. HE FOUGHT BY MY SIDE. HE KNOWS.
BUT THE FEAR IS STILL THERE, BECAUSE WHAT IF IT DIDN'T SINK IN FOR HIM BACK THEN? WHAT IF THIS TIME, HE FINALLY REALIZES--HE MARRIED A MONSTER?
AND WHAT IF HE'S ALREADY THINKING ABOUT LEAVING ME, ABOUT HOW SOON HE CAN GET OUT? WHAT IF IN HIS OWN MIND, HE'S ALREADY GONE?
HENRY?

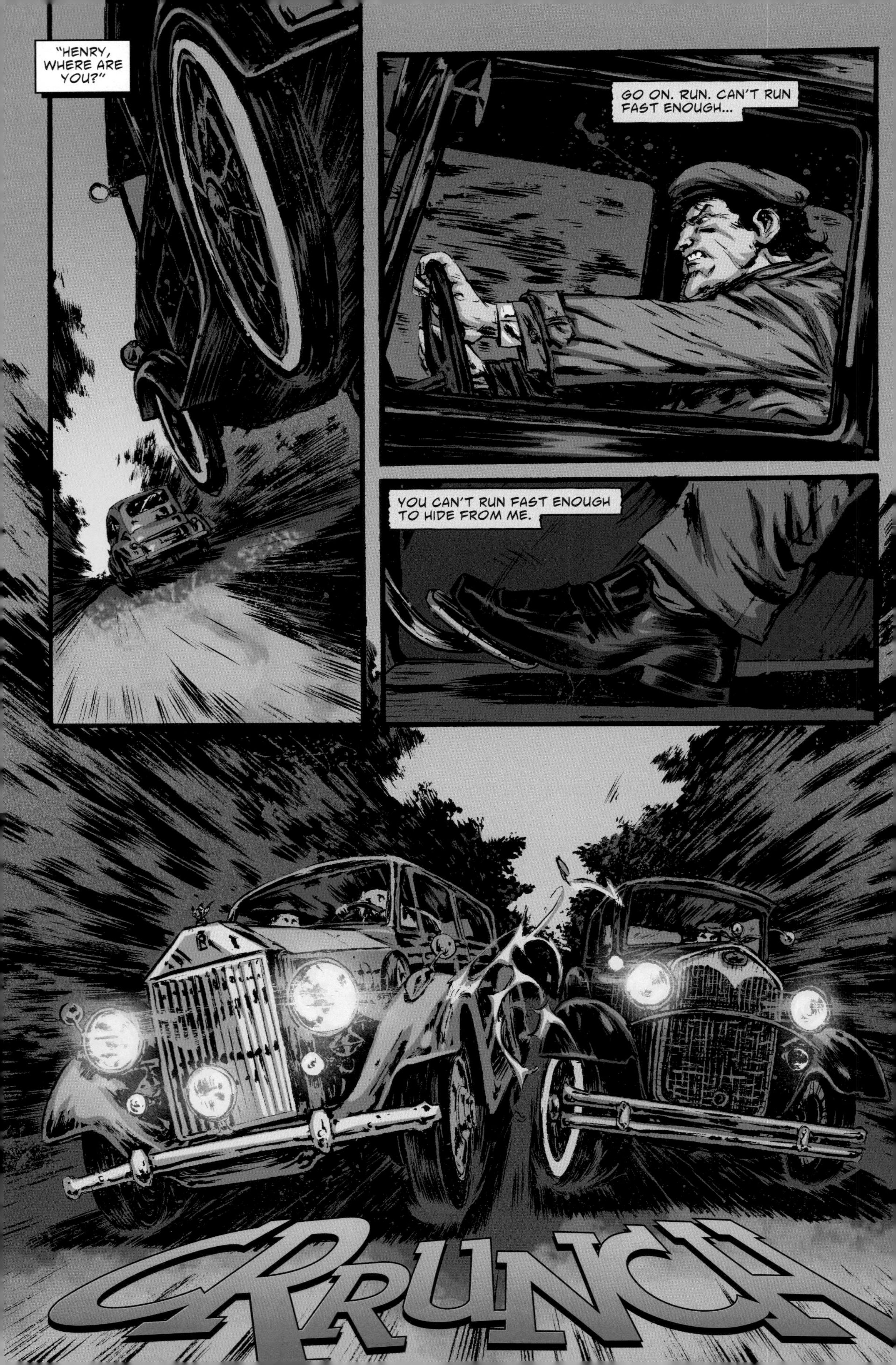
"HENRY, WHERE ARE YOU?"
GO ON. RUN. CAN'T RUN FAST ENOUGH...
YOU CAN'T RUN FAST ENOUGH TO HIDE FROM ME.
CRUNCH

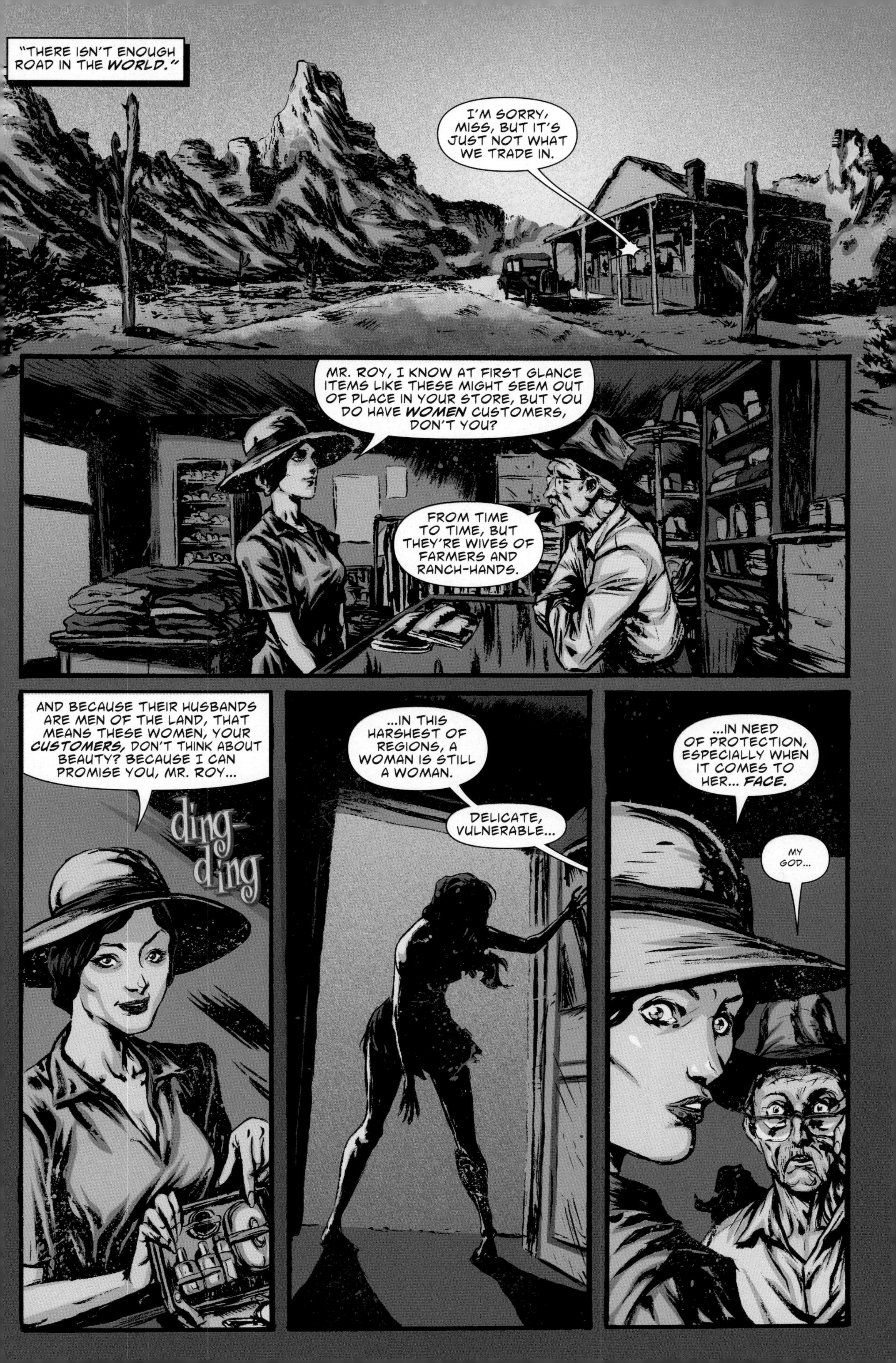
"THERE ISN'T ENOUGH ROAD IN THE WORLD."
I'M SORRY, MISS, BUT IT'S JUST NOT WHAT WE TRADE IN.
MR. ROY, I KNOW AT FIRST GLANCE ITEMS LIKE THESE MIGHT SEEM OUT OF PLACE IN YOUR STORE, BUT YOU DO HAVE WOMEN CUSTOMERS, DON'T YOU?
FROM TIME TO TIME, BUT THEY'RE WIVES OF FARMERS AND RANCH-HANDS.
AND BECAUSE THEIR HUSBANDS ARE MEN OF THE LAND, THAT MEANS THESE WOMEN, YOUR CUSTOMERS, DON'T THINK ABOUT BEAUTY? BECAUSE I CAN PROMISE YOU, MR. ROY...
ding-ding
...IN THIS HARSHEST OF REGIONS, A WOMAN IS STILL A WOMAN.
DELICATE, VULNERABLE...
...IN NEED OF PROTECTION, ESPECIALLY WHEN IT COMES TO HER... FACE.
MY GOD...

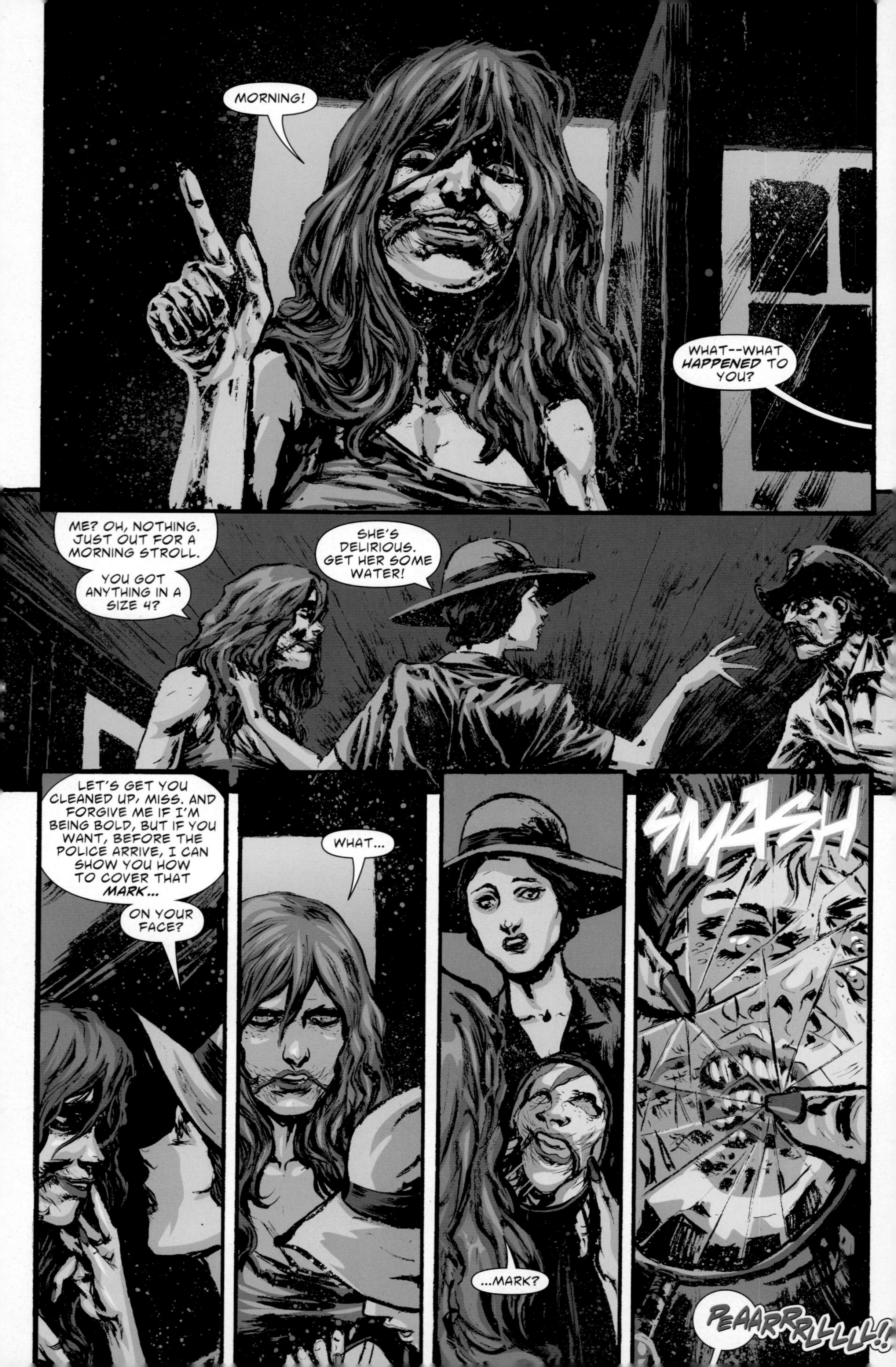
MORNING!
WHAT--WHAT HAPPENED TO YOU?
ME? OH, NOTHING. JUST OUT FOR A MORNING STROLL.
YOU GOT ANYTHING IN A SIZE 4?
SHE'S DELIRIOUS. GET HER SOME WATER!
LET'S GET YOU CLEANED UP, MISS. AND FORGIVE ME IF I'M BEING BOLD, BUT IF YOU WANT, BEFORE THE POLICE ARRIVE, I CAN SHOW YOU HOW TO COVER THAT MARK...
ON YOUR FACE?
WHAT...
...MARK?
SMASH
PEAARRRLLLLL!

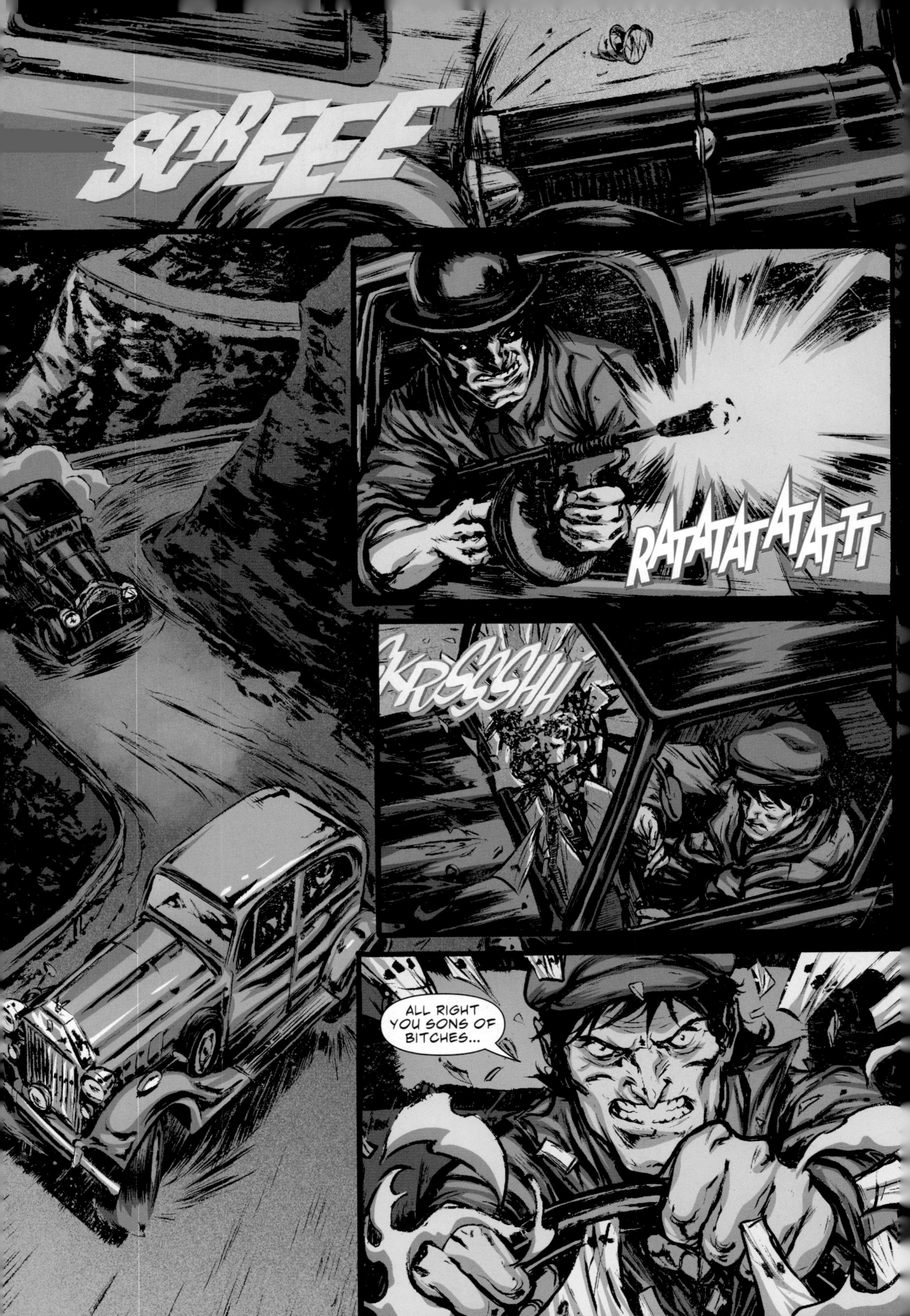
SCREEE
RATATATATATTT
KRSSSHH
ALL RIGHT YOU SONS OF BITCHES...

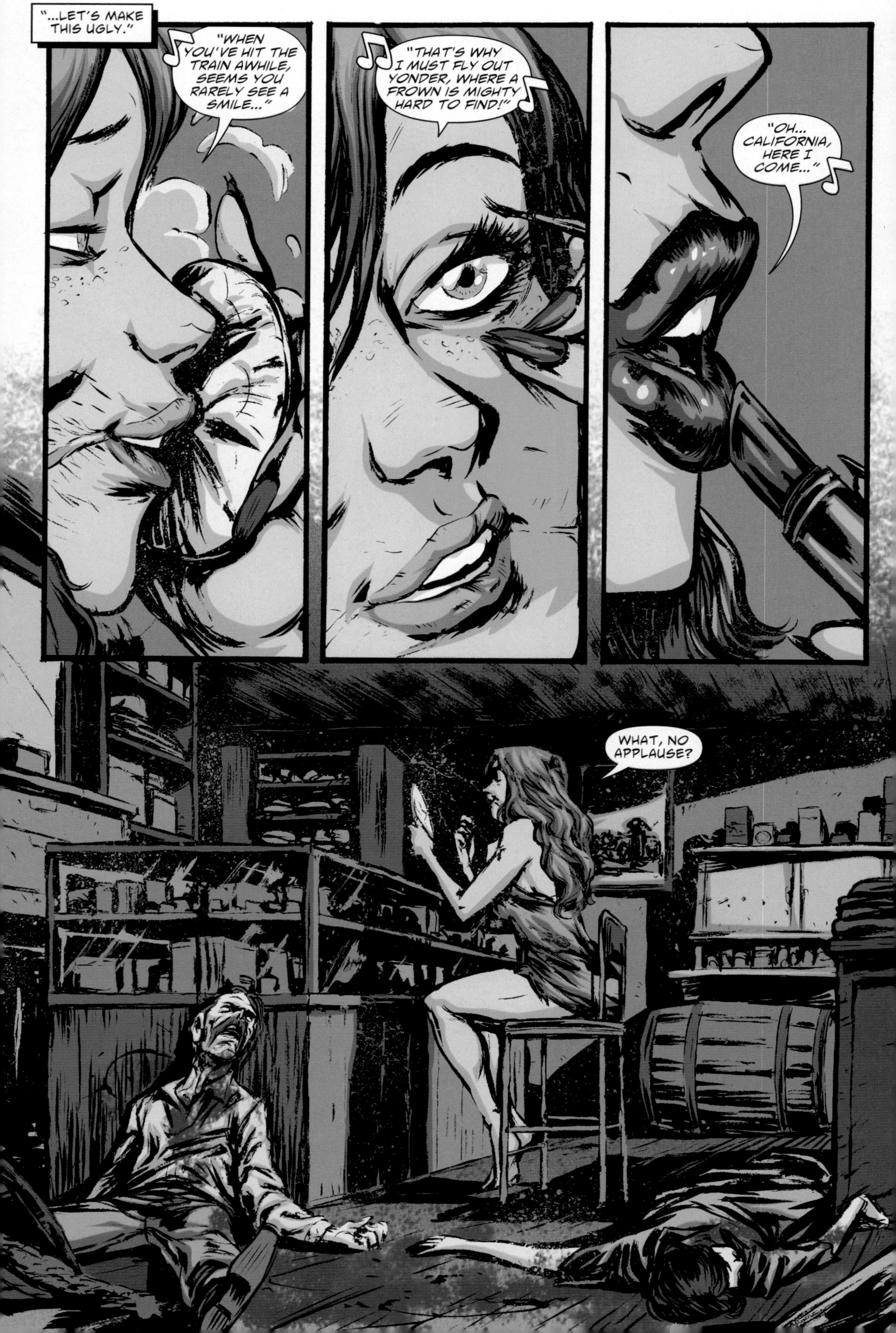
"...LET'S MAKE THIS UGLY."
"WHEN YOU'VE HIT THE TRAIN AWHILE, SEEMS YOU RARELY SEE A SMILE..."
"THAT'S WHY I MUST FLY OUT YONDER, WHERE A FROWN IS MIGHTY HARD TO FIND!"
"OH... CALIFORNIA, HERE I COME..."
WHAT, NO APPLAUSE?

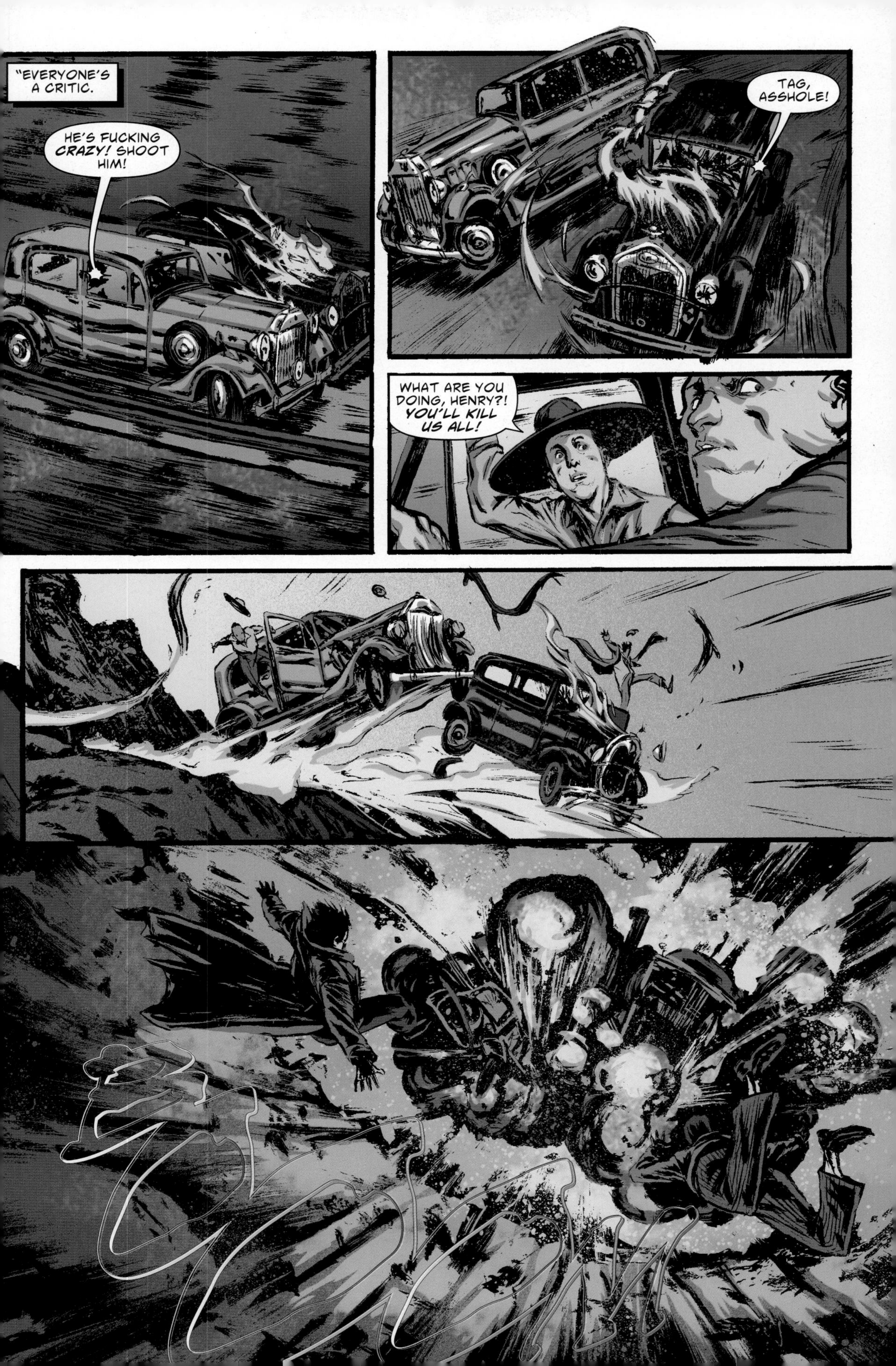
"EVERYONE'S A CRITIC.
HE'S FUCKING CRAZY! SHOOT HIM!
TAG, ASSHOLE!
WHAT ARE YOU DOING, HENRY?! YOU'LL KILL US ALL!

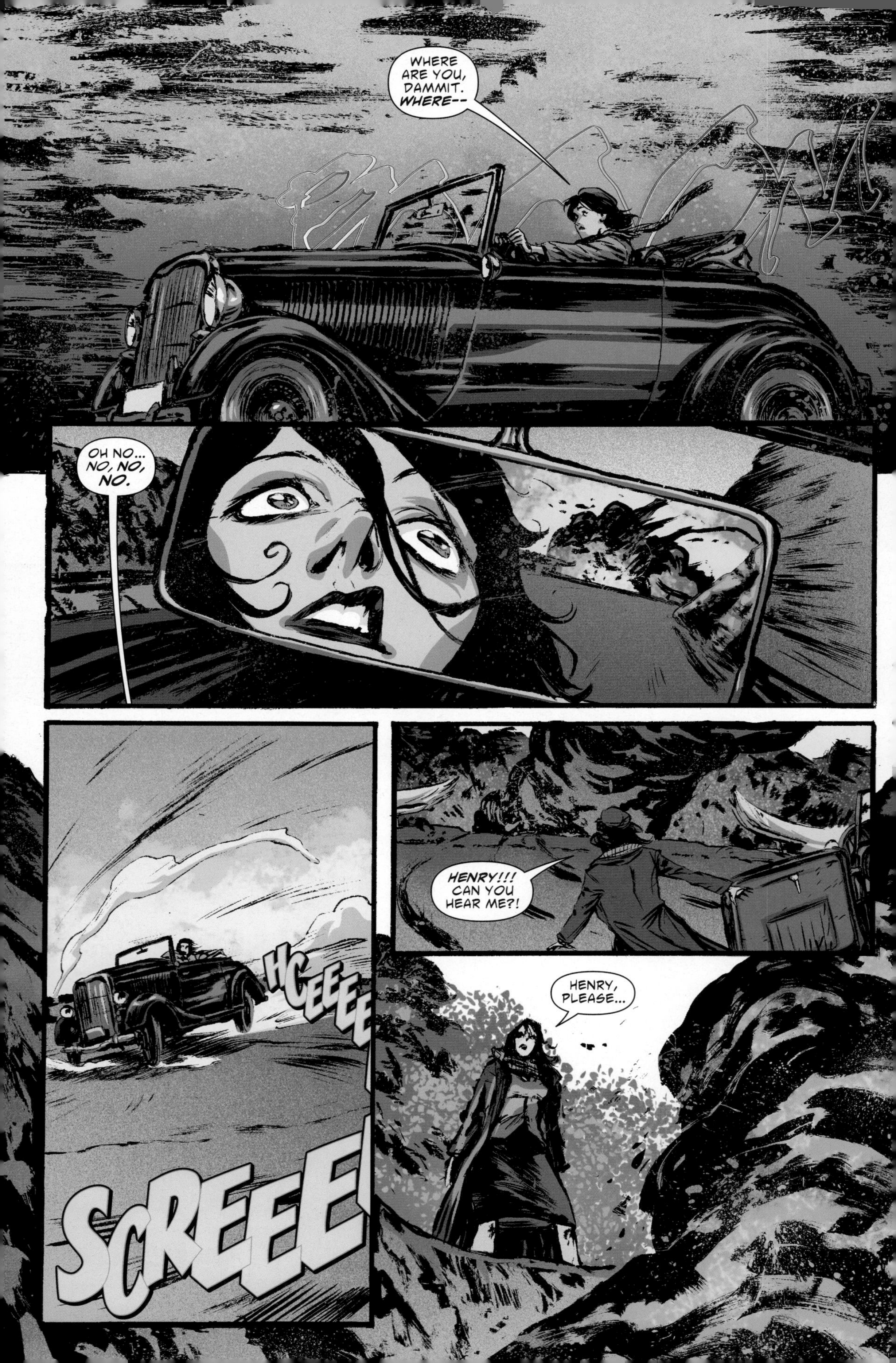

WHERE ARE YOU, DAMMIT. WHERE--
OH NO... NO, NO, NO.
HCEEEE
SCREEE
HENRY!!! CAN YOU HEAR ME?!
HENRY, PLEASE...

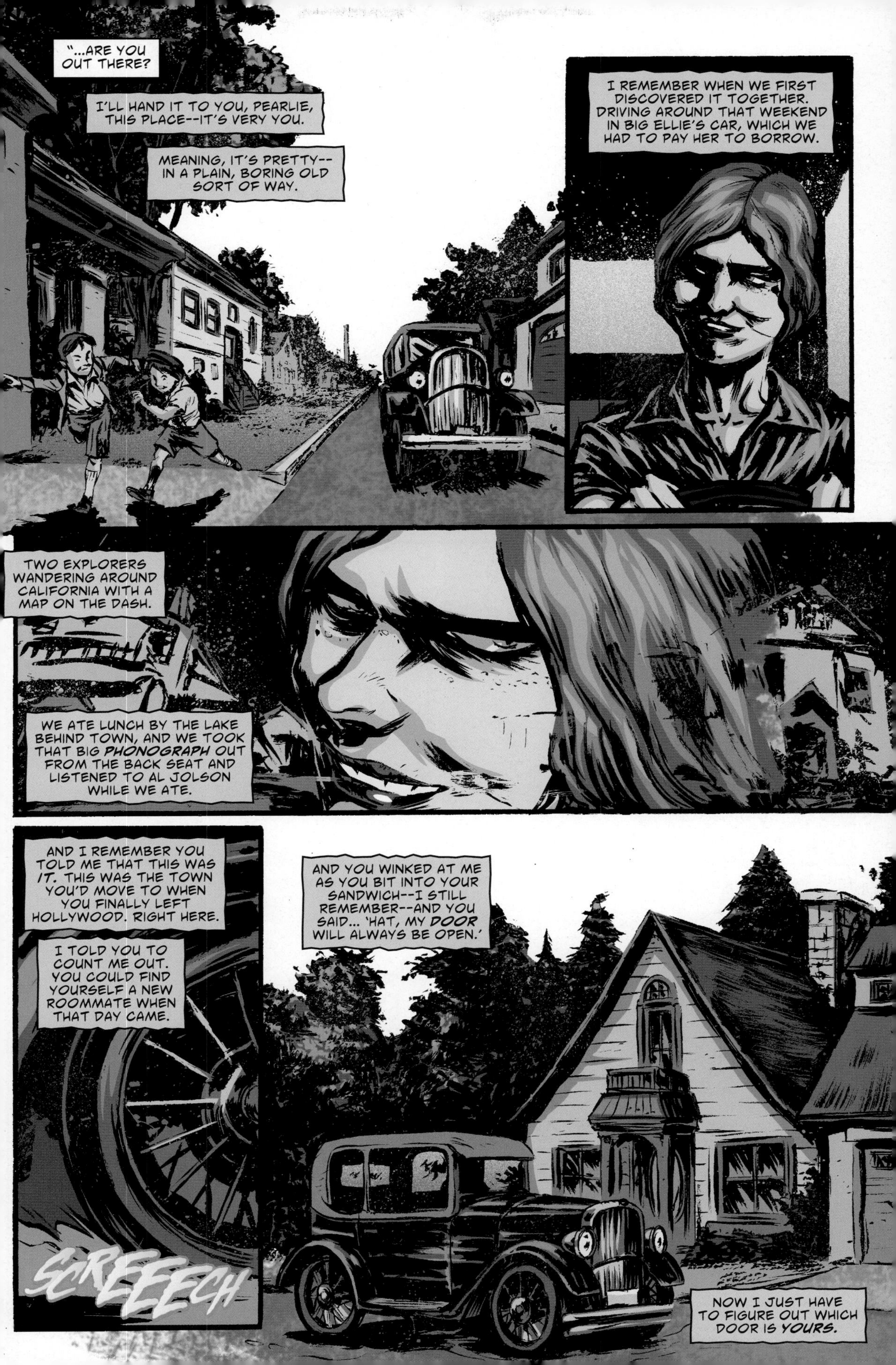
"...ARE YOU OUT THERE?
I'LL HAND IT TO YOU, PEARLIE, THIS PLACE--IT'S VERY YOU.
MEANING, IT'S PRETTY--IN A PLAIN, BORING OLD SORT OF WAY.
I REMEMBER WHEN WE FIRST DISCOVERED IT TOGETHER. DRIVING AROUND THAT WEEKEND IN BIG ELLIE'S CAR, WHICH WE HAD TO PAY HER TO BORROW.
TWO EXPLORERS WANDERING AROUND CALIFORNIA WITH A MAP ON THE DASH.
WE ATE LUNCH BY THE LAKE BEHIND TOWN, AND WE TOOK THAT BIG *PHONOGRAPH* OUT FROM THE BACK SEAT AND LISTENED TO AL JOLSON WHILE WE ATE.
AND I REMEMBER YOU TOLD ME THAT THIS WAS *IT*. THIS WAS THE TOWN YOU'D MOVE TO WHEN YOU FINALLY LEFT HOLLYWOOD. RIGHT HERE.
I TOLD YOU TO COUNT ME OUT. YOU COULD FIND YOURSELF A NEW ROOMMATE WHEN THAT DAY CAME.
AND YOU WINKED AT ME AS YOU BIT INTO YOUR SANDWICH--I STILL REMEMBER--AND YOU SAID... 'HAT, MY *DOOR* WILL ALWAYS BE OPEN.'
SCREEEECH
NOW I JUST HAVE TO FIGURE OUT WHICH DOOR IS *YOURS*.

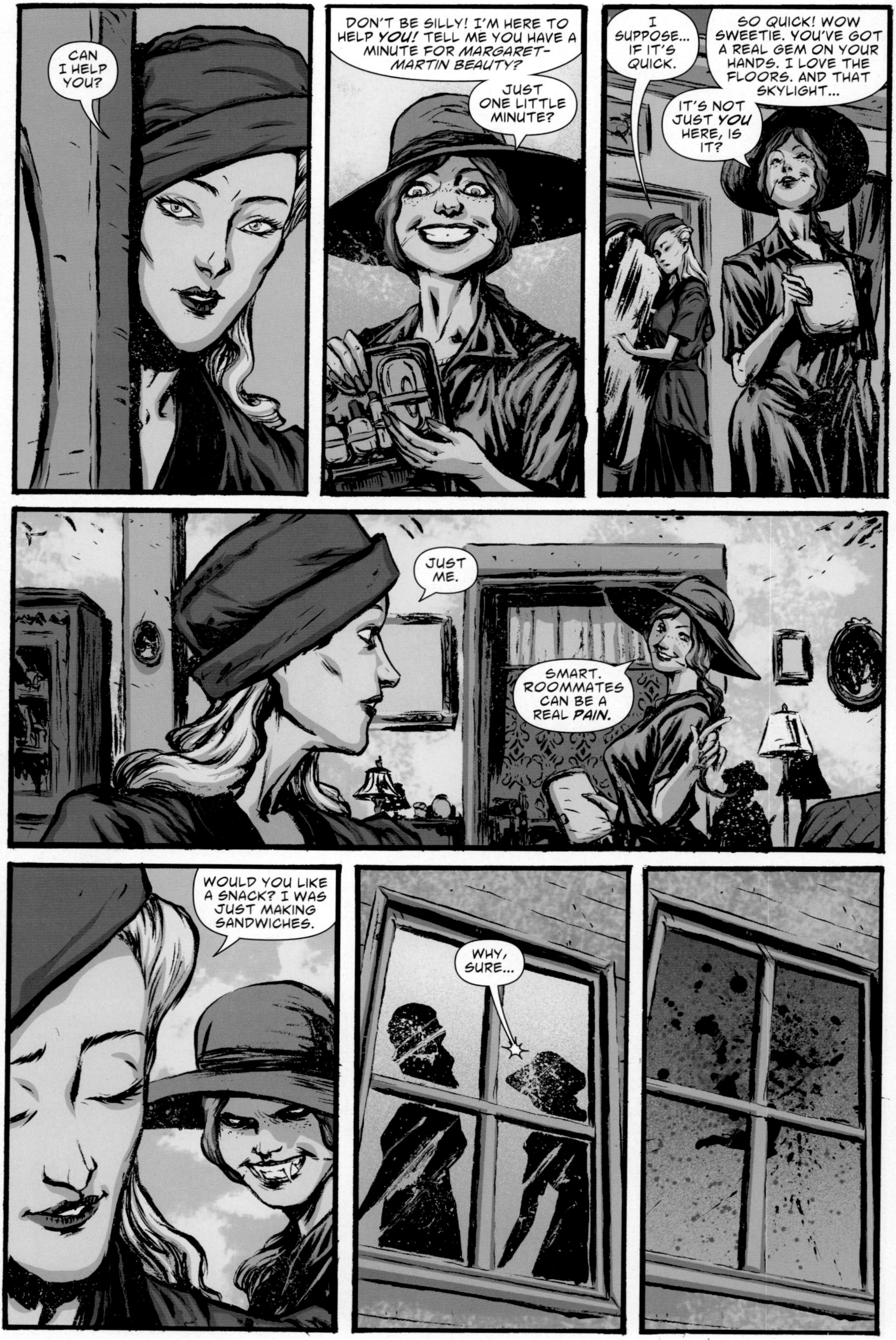
CAN I HELP YOU?
DON'T BE SILLY! I'M HERE TO HELP YOU! TELL ME YOU HAVE A MINUTE FOR MARGARET-MARTIN BEAUTY?
JUST ONE LITTLE MINUTE?
I SUPPOSE... IF IT'S QUICK.
SO QUICK! WOW SWEETIE. YOU'VE GOT A REAL GEM ON YOUR HANDS. I LOVE THE FLOORS. AND THAT SKYLIGHT...
IT'S NOT JUST YOU HERE, IS IT?
JUST ME.
SMART. ROOMMATES CAN BE A REAL PAIN.
WOULD YOU LIKE A SNACK? I WAS JUST MAKING SANDWICHES.
WHY, SURE...

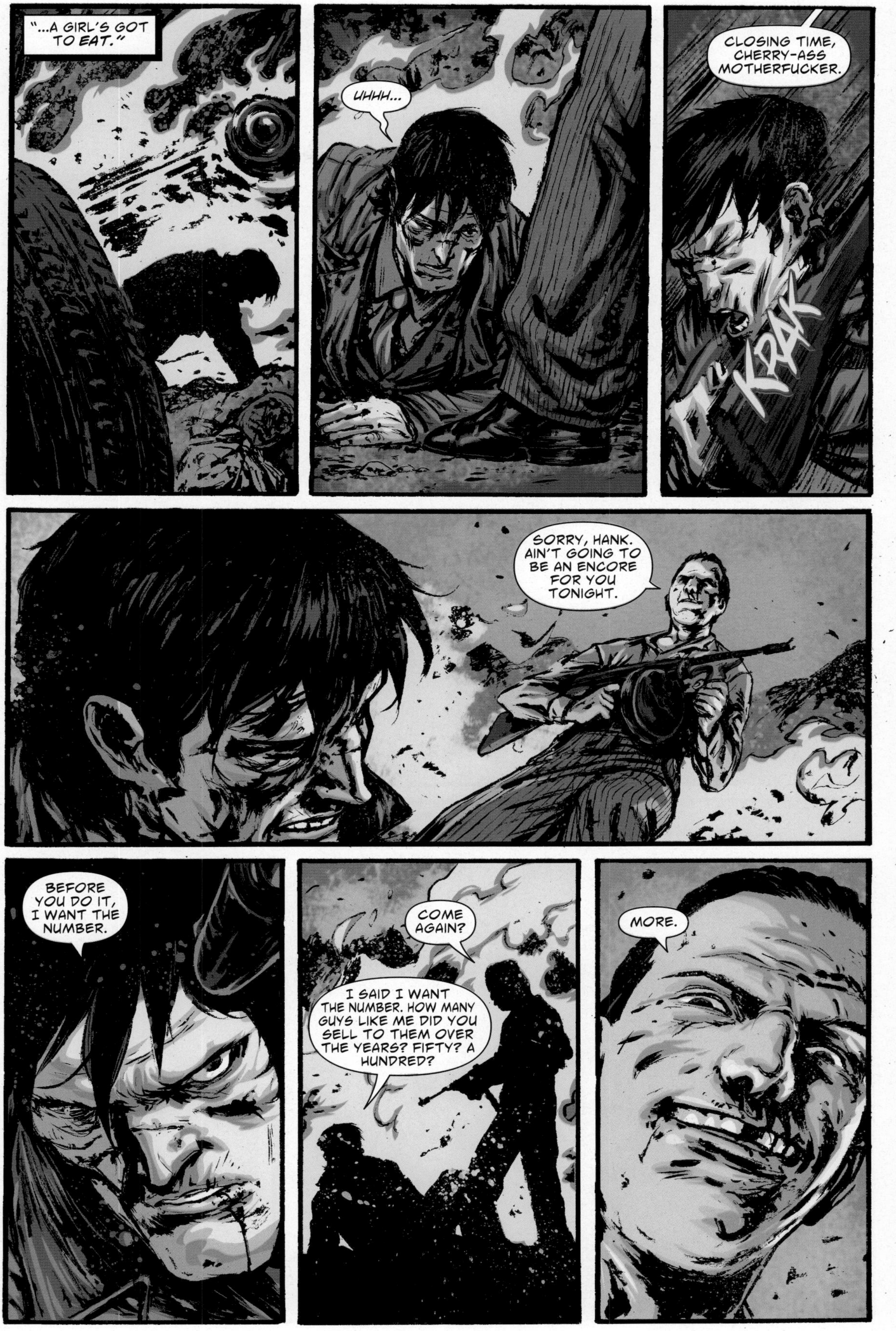
"...A GIRL'S GOT TO EAT."
UHHH...
CLOSING TIME, CHERRY-ASS MOTHERFUCKER.
KRAK
SORRY, HANK. AIN'T GOING TO BE AN ENCORE FOR YOU TONIGHT.
BEFORE YOU DO IT, I WANT THE NUMBER.
COME AGAIN?
I SAID I WANT THE NUMBER. HOW MANY GUYS LIKE ME DID YOU SELL TO THEM OVER THE YEARS? FIFTY? A HUNDRED?
MORE.

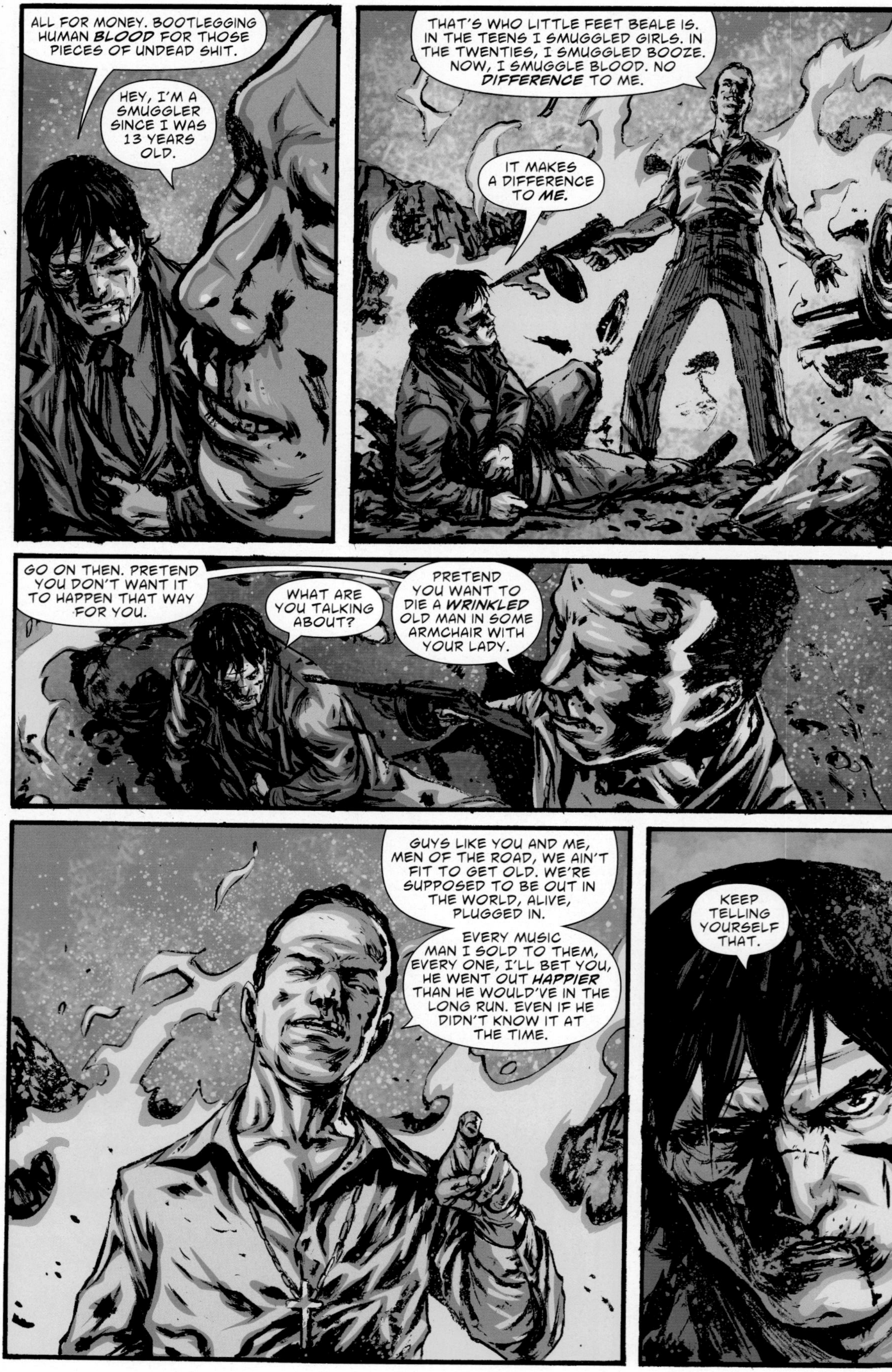
ALL FOR MONEY. BOOTLEGGING HUMAN BLOOD FOR THOSE PIECES OF UNDEAD SHIT.
HEY, I'M A SMUGGLER SINCE I WAS 13 YEARS OLD.
THAT'S WHO LITTLE FEET BEALE IS. IN THE TEENS I SMUGGLED GIRLS. IN THE TWENTIES, I SMUGGLED BOOZE. NOW, I SMUGGLE BLOOD. NO DIFFERENCE TO ME.
IT MAKES A DIFFERENCE TO ME.
GO ON THEN. PRETEND YOU DON'T WANT IT TO HAPPEN THAT WAY FOR YOU.
WHAT ARE YOU TALKING ABOUT?
PRETEND YOU WANT TO DIE A WRINKLED OLD MAN IN SOME ARMCHAIR WITH YOUR LADY.
GUYS LIKE YOU AND ME, MEN OF THE ROAD, WE AIN'T FIT TO GET OLD. WE'RE SUPPOSED TO BE OUT IN THE WORLD, ALIVE, PLUGGED IN.
EVERY MUSIC MAN I SOLD TO THEM, EVERY ONE, I'LL BET YOU, HE WENT OUT HAPPIER THAN HE WOULD'VE IN THE LONG RUN. EVEN IF HE DIDN'T KNOW IT AT THE TIME.
KEEP TELLING YOURSELF THAT.

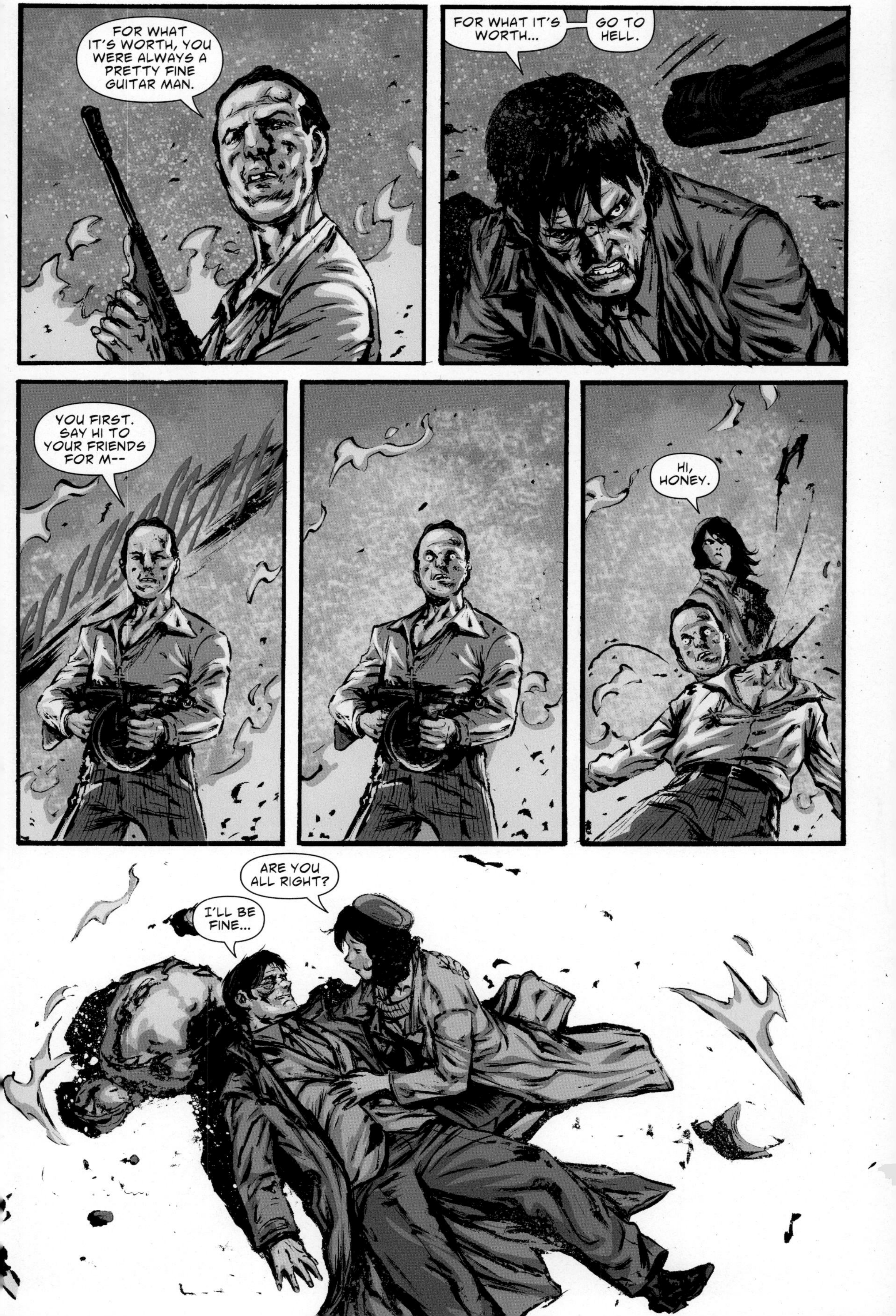
FOR WHAT IT'S WORTH, YOU WERE ALWAYS A PRETTY FINE GUITAR MAN.
FOR WHAT IT'S WORTH...
GO TO HELL.
YOU FIRST. SAY HI TO YOUR FRIENDS FOR M--
HI, HONEY.
ARE YOU ALL RIGHT?
I'LL BE FINE...

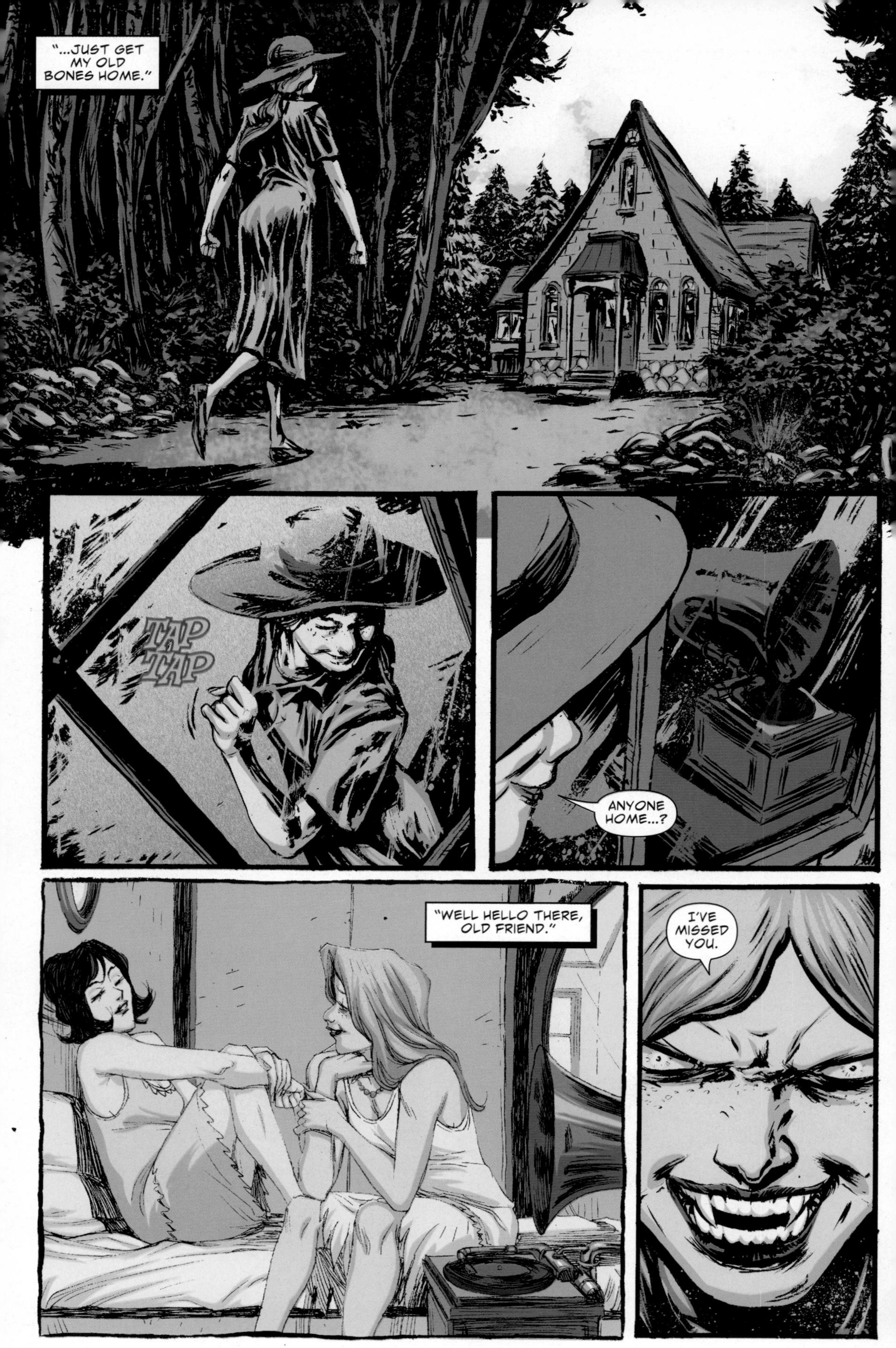
"...JUST GET MY OLD BONES HOME."
TAP TAP
ANYONE HOME...?
"WELL HELLO THERE, OLD FRIEND."
I'VE MISSED YOU.

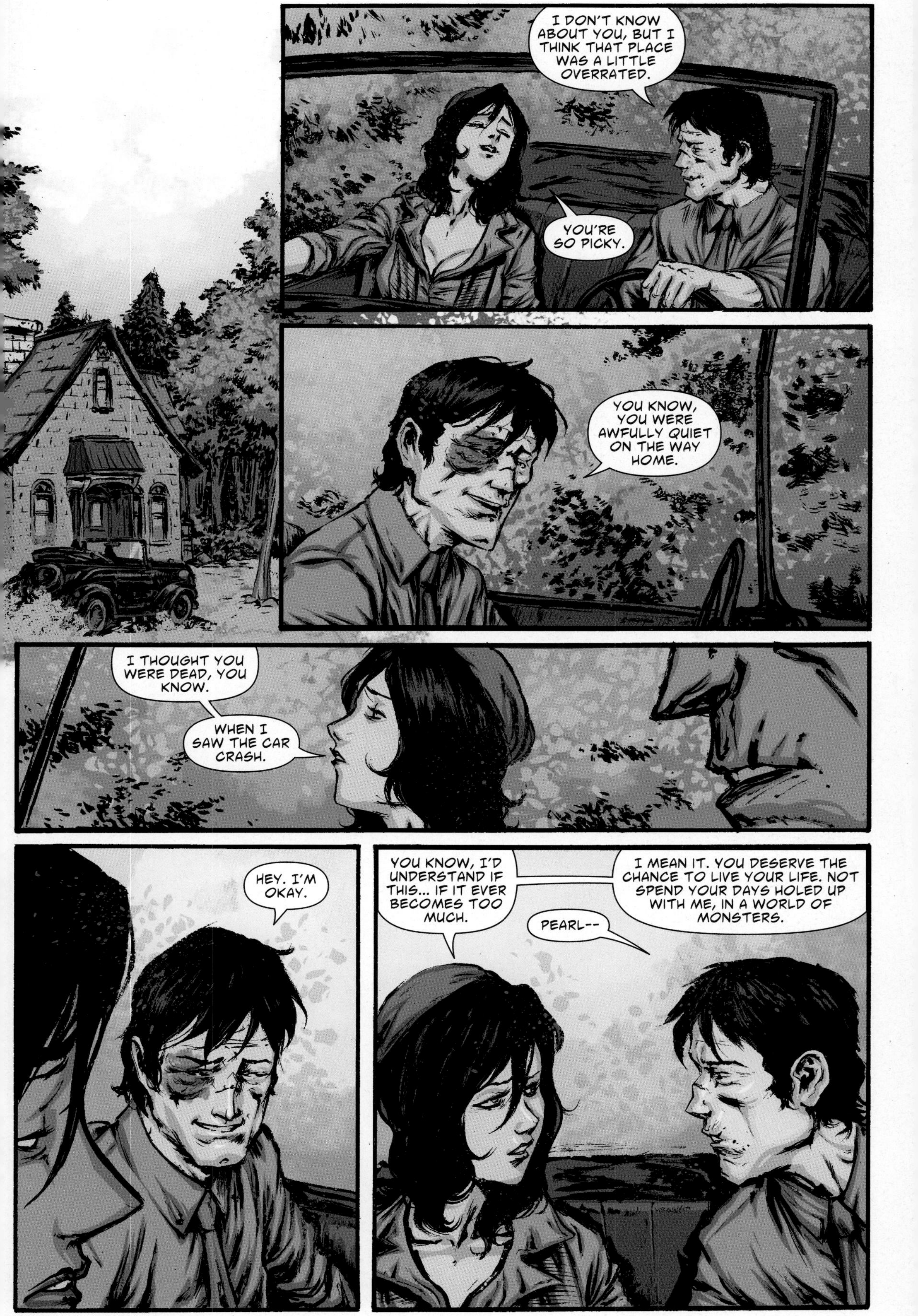

I DON'T KNOW ABOUT YOU, BUT I THINK THAT PLACE WAS A LITTLE OVERRATED.
YOU'RE SO PICKY.
YOU KNOW, YOU WERE AWFULLY QUIET ON THE WAY HOME.
I THOUGHT YOU WERE DEAD, YOU KNOW.
WHEN I SAW THE CAR CRASH.
HEY. I'M OKAY.
YOU KNOW, I'D UNDERSTAND IF THIS... IF IT EVER BECOMES TOO MUCH.
I MEAN IT. YOU DESERVE THE CHANCE TO LIVE YOUR LIFE. NOT SPEND YOUR DAYS HOLED UP WITH ME, IN A WORLD OF MONSTERS.
PEARL--

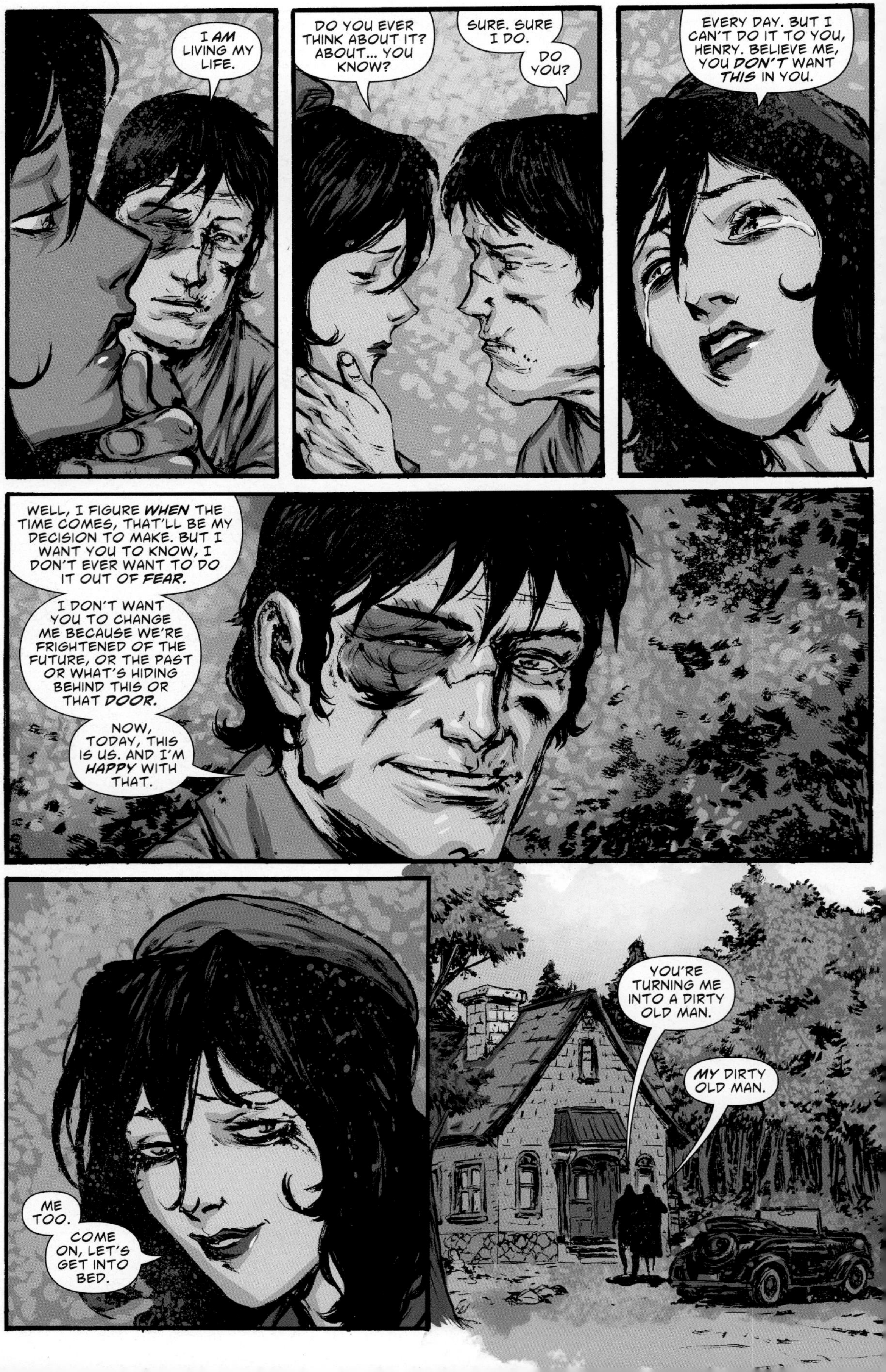
I AM LIVING MY LIFE.
DO YOU EVER THINK ABOUT IT? ABOUT... YOU KNOW?
SURE. SURE I DO.
DO YOU?
EVERY DAY. BUT I CAN'T DO IT TO YOU, HENRY. BELIEVE ME, YOU DON'T WANT THIS IN YOU.
WELL, I FIGURE WHEN THE TIME COMES, THAT'LL BE MY DECISION TO MAKE. BUT I WANT YOU TO KNOW, I DON'T EVER WANT TO DO IT OUT OF FEAR.
I DON'T WANT YOU TO CHANGE ME BECAUSE WE'RE FRIGHTENED OF THE FUTURE, OR THE PAST OR WHAT'S HIDING BEHIND THIS OR THAT DOOR.
NOW, TODAY, THIS IS US. AND I'M HAPPY WITH THAT.
ME TOO.
COME ON, LET'S GET INTO BED.
YOU'RE TURNING ME INTO A DIRTY OLD MAN.
MY DIRTY OLD MAN.

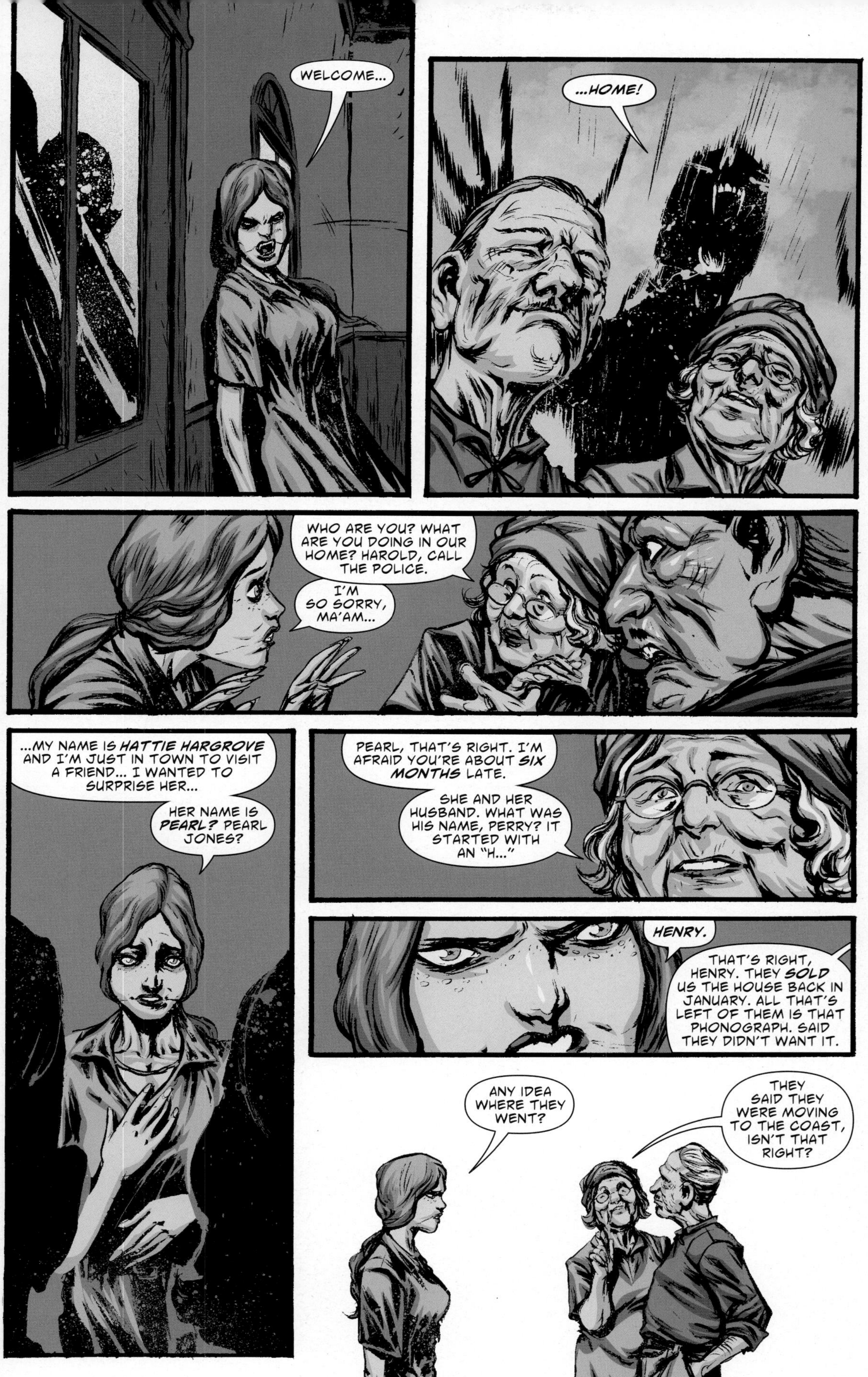
WELCOME...
...HOME!
WHO ARE YOU? WHAT ARE YOU DOING IN OUR HOME? HAROLD, CALL THE POLICE.
I'M SO SORRY, MA'AM...
...MY NAME IS HATTIE HARGROVE AND I'M JUST IN TOWN TO VISIT A FRIEND... I WANTED TO SURPRISE HER...
HER NAME IS PEARL? PEARL JONES?
PEARL, THAT'S RIGHT. I'M AFRAID YOU'RE ABOUT SIX MONTHS LATE.
SHE AND HER HUSBAND. WHAT WAS HIS NAME, PERRY? IT STARTED WITH AN "H..."
HENRY.
THAT'S RIGHT, HENRY. THEY SOLD US THE HOUSE BACK IN JANUARY. ALL THAT'S LEFT OF THEM IS THAT PHONOGRAPH. SAID THEY DIDN'T WANT IT.
ANY IDEA WHERE THEY WENT?
THEY SAID THEY WERE MOVING TO THE COAST, ISN'T THAT RIGHT?

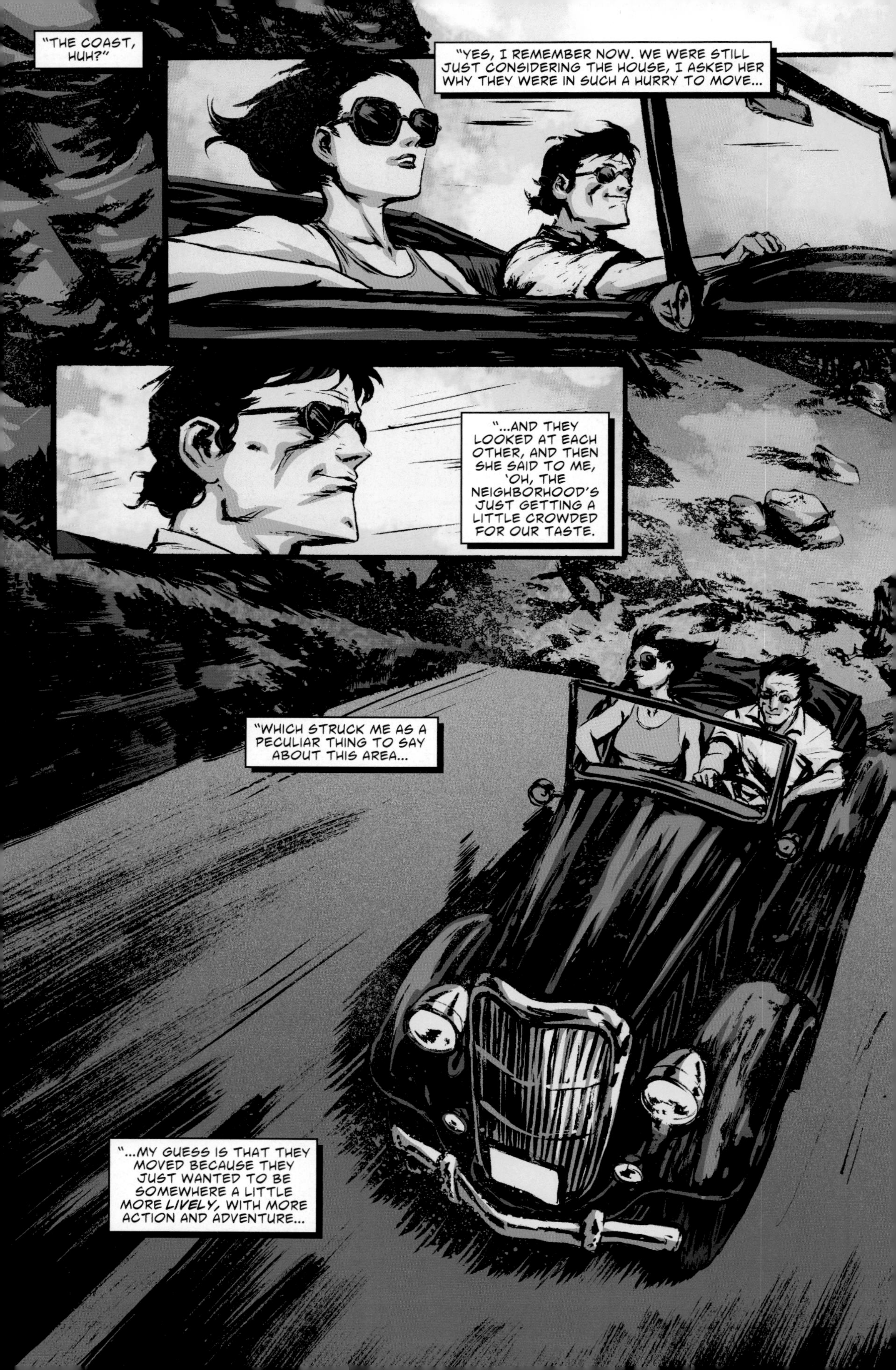
"THE COAST, HUH?"
"YES, I REMEMBER NOW. WE WERE STILL JUST CONSIDERING THE HOUSE, I ASKED HER WHY THEY WERE IN SUCH A HURRY TO MOVE...
"...AND THEY LOOKED AT EACH OTHER, AND THEN SHE SAID TO ME, 'OH, THE NEIGHBORHOOD'S JUST GETTING A LITTLE CROWDED FOR OUR TASTE.
"WHICH STRUCK ME AS A PECULIAR THING TO SAY ABOUT THIS AREA...
"...MY GUESS IS THAT THEY MOVED BECAUSE THEY JUST WANTED TO BE SOMEWHERE A LITTLE MORE *LIVELY*, WITH MORE ACTION AND ADVENTURE...

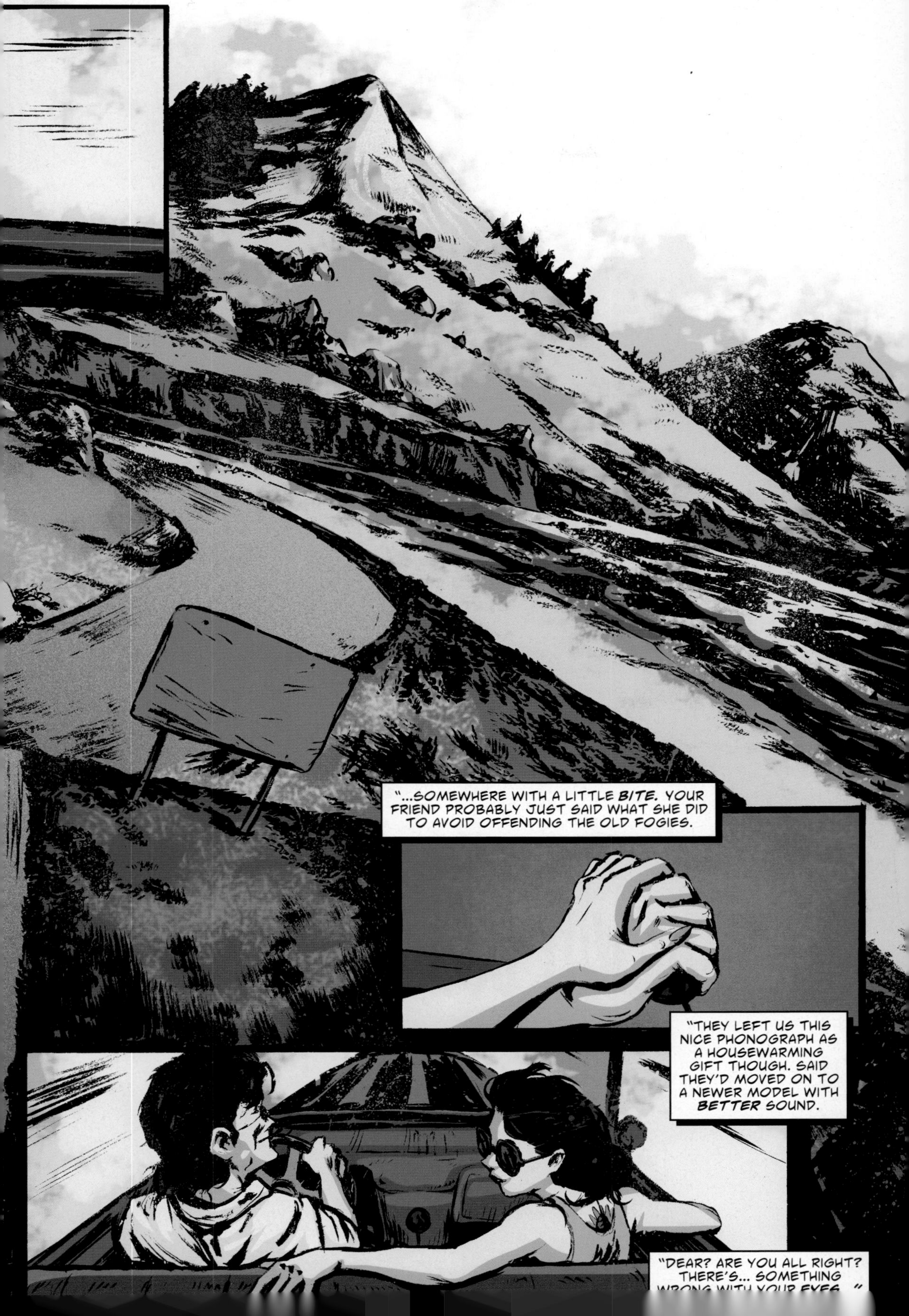
"...SOMEWHERE WITH A LITTLE *BITE*. YOUR FRIEND PROBABLY JUST SAID WHAT SHE DID TO AVOID OFFENDING THE OLD FOGIES.
"THEY LEFT US THIS NICE PHONOGRAPH AS A HOUSEWARMING GIFT THOUGH. SAID THEY'D MOVED ON TO A NEWER MODEL WITH *BETTER* SOUND.
"DEAR? ARE YOU ALL RIGHT? THERE'S... SOMETHING

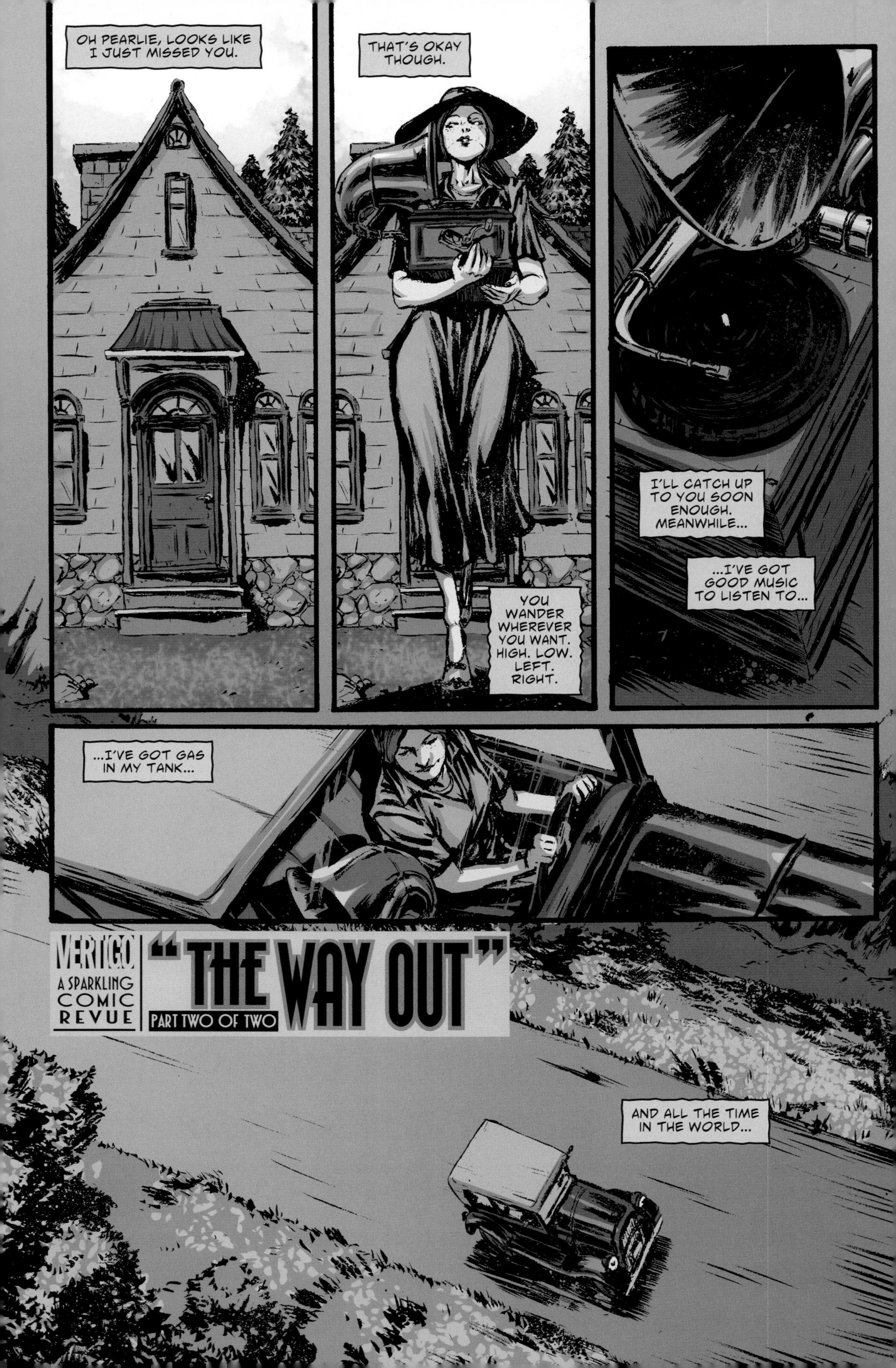
OH PEARLIE, LOOKS LIKE I JUST MISSED YOU.
THAT'S OKAY THOUGH.
YOU WANDER WHEREVER YOU WANT. HIGH. LOW. LEFT. RIGHT.
I'LL CATCH UP TO YOU SOON ENOUGH. MEANWHILE...
...I'VE GOT GOOD MUSIC TO LISTEN TO...
...I'VE GOT GAS IN MY TANK...
VERTIGO
A SPARKLING COMIC REVUE
"THE WAY OUT"
PART TWO OF TWO
AND ALL THE TIME IN THE WORLD...

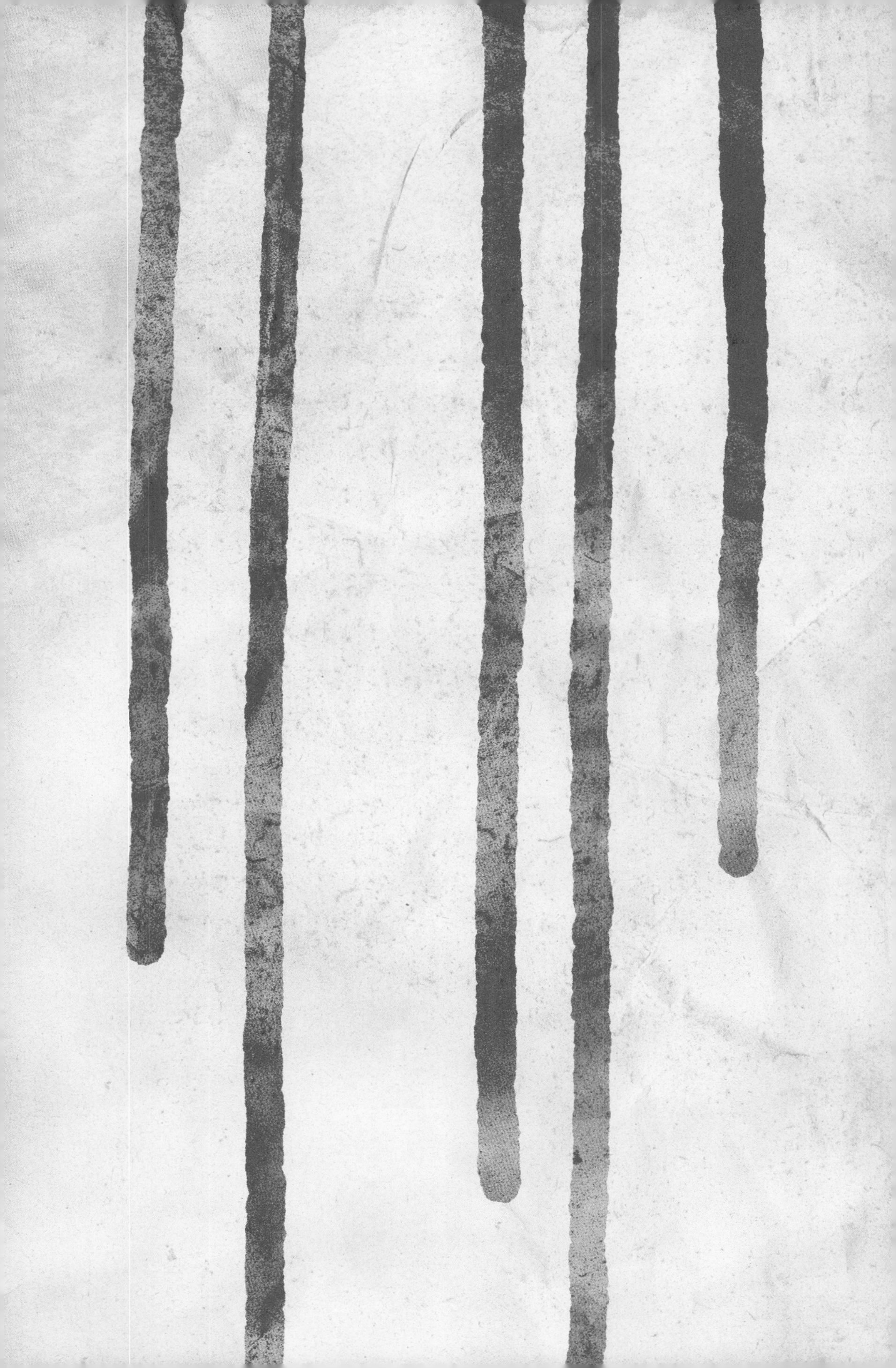

Variant to AMERICAN VAMPIRE #6 by Rafael Grampa

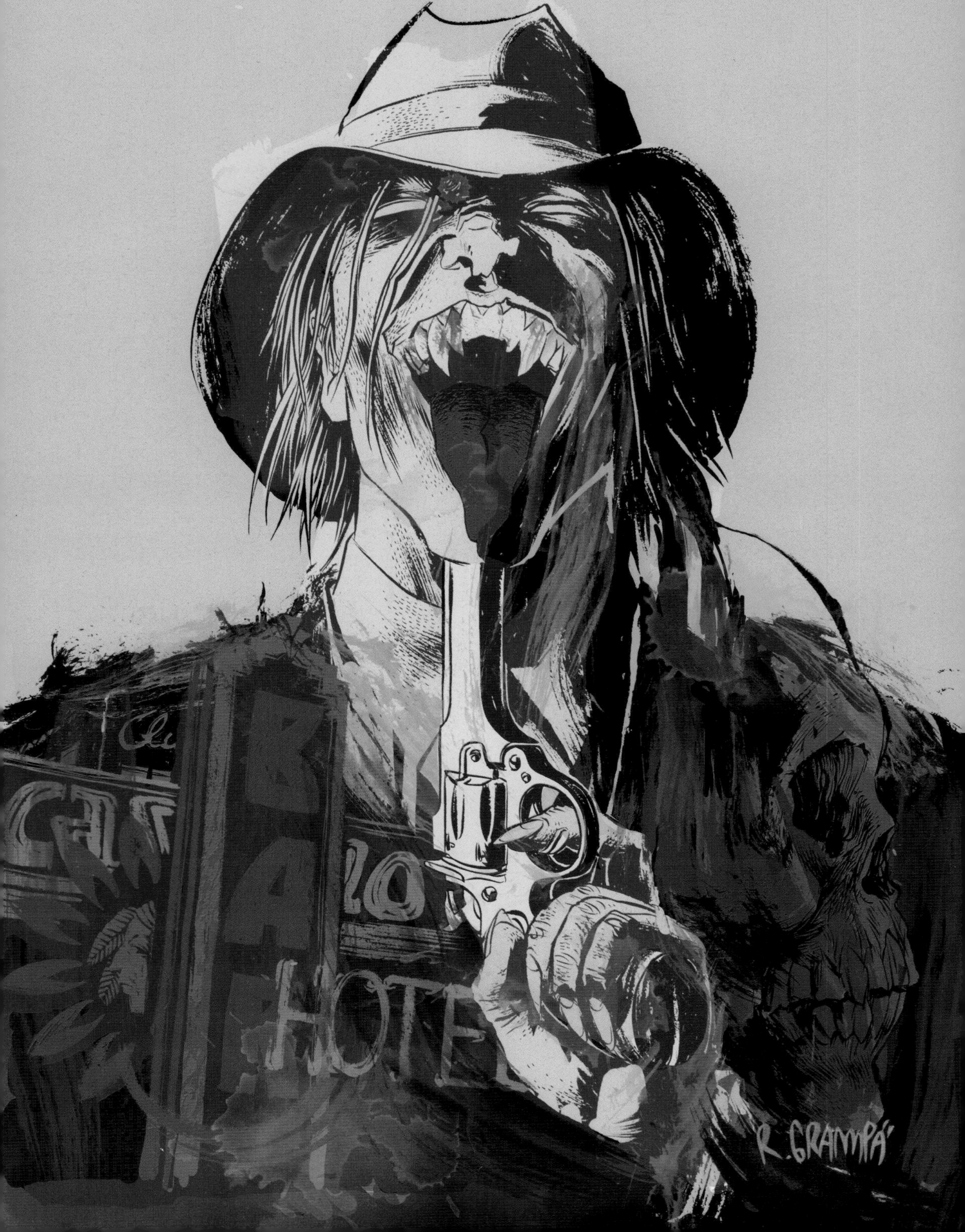
R.GRAMPA

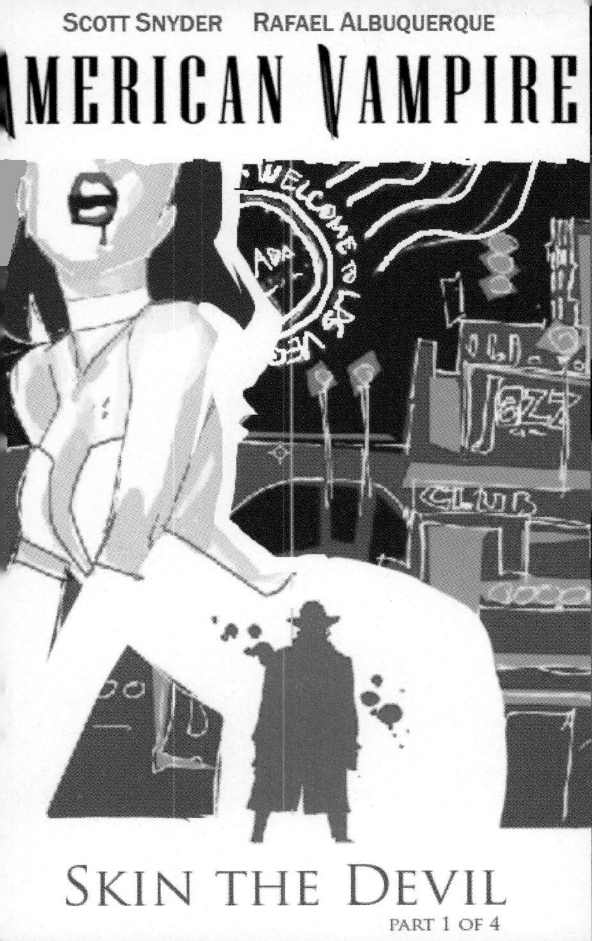
SCOTT SNYDER RAFAEL ALBUQUERQUE
AMERICAN VAMPIRE
WELCOME TO LAS VEGAS
JAZZ
CLUB
SKIN THE DEVIL
PART 1 OF 4

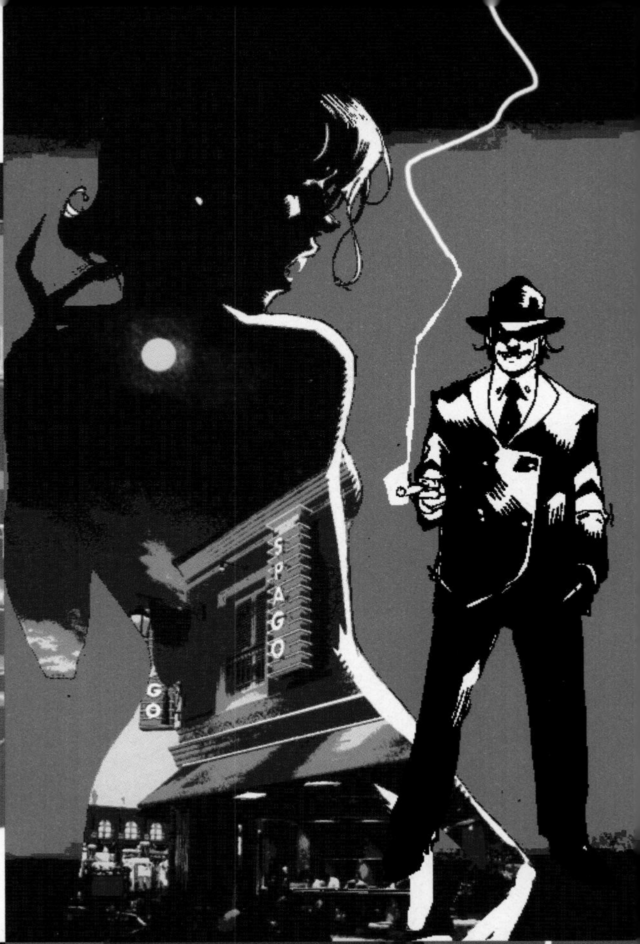
SPAGO

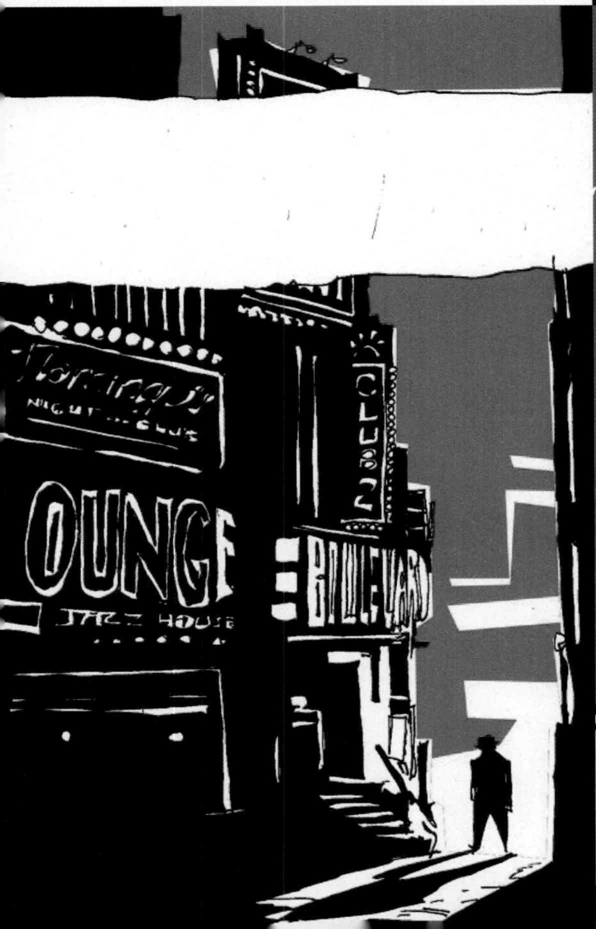
OUNGE

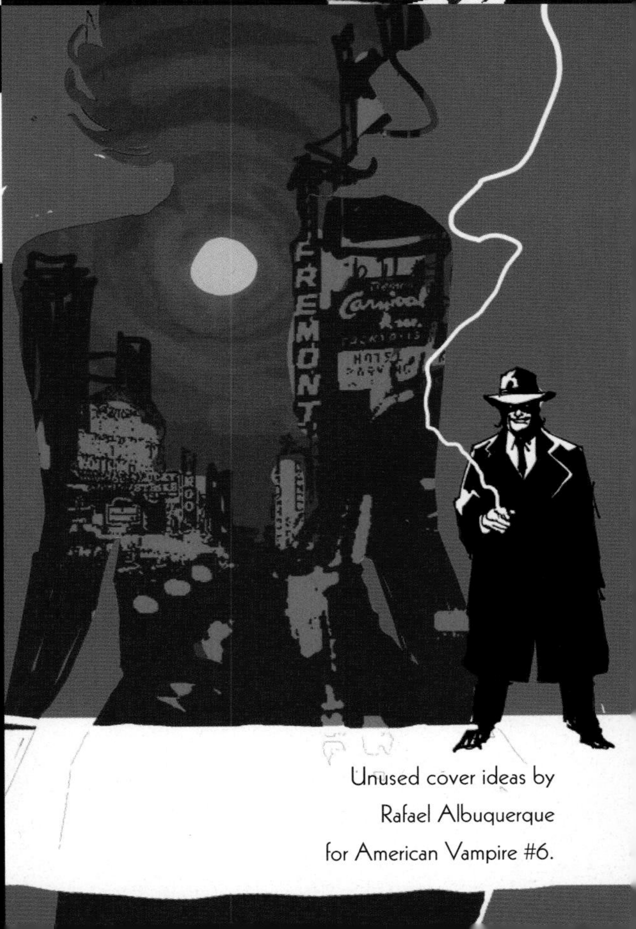
FREMONT

Unused cover ideas by
Rafael Albuquerque
for American Vampire #6.

Audition Sketches by Mateus Santolouco

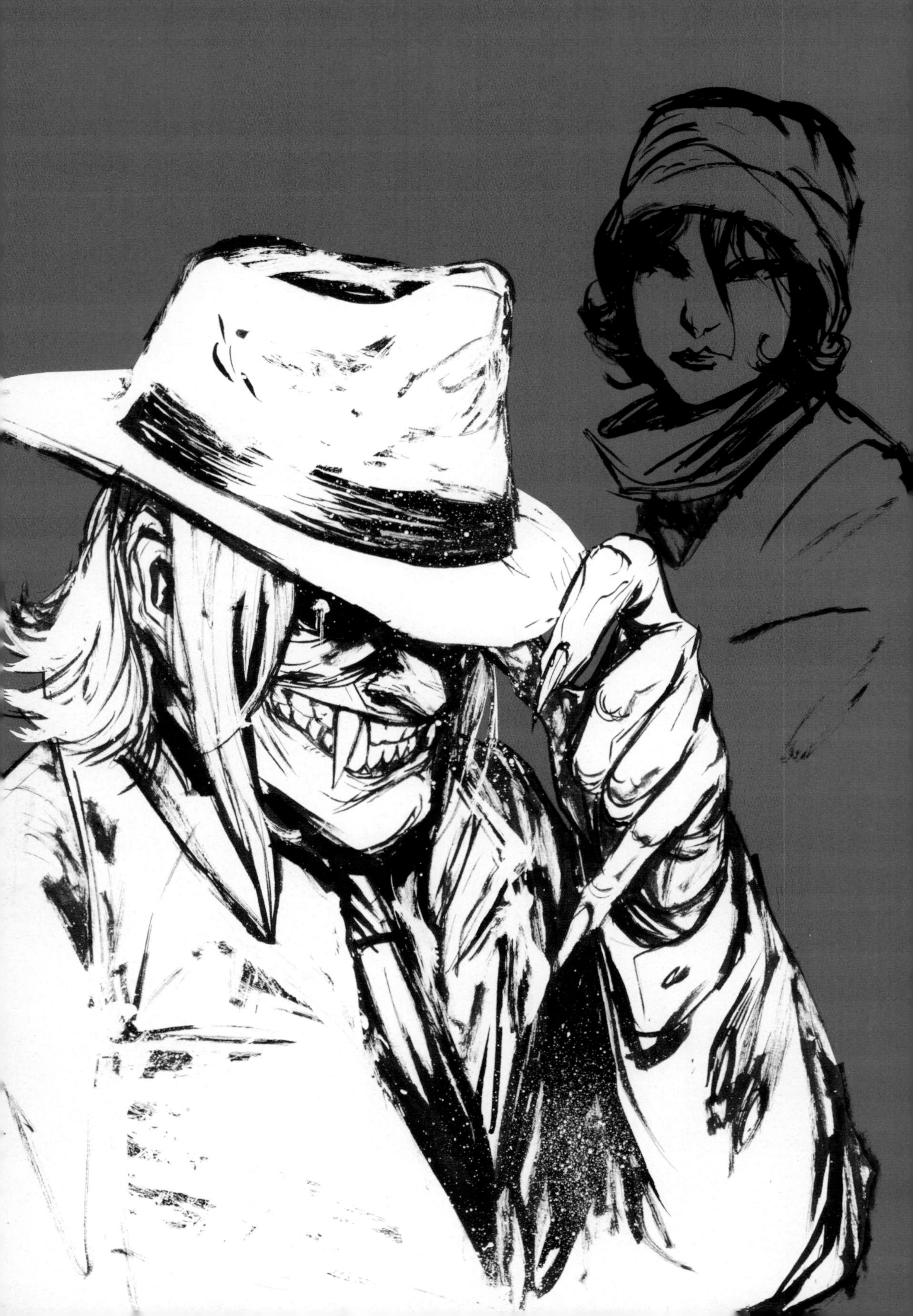

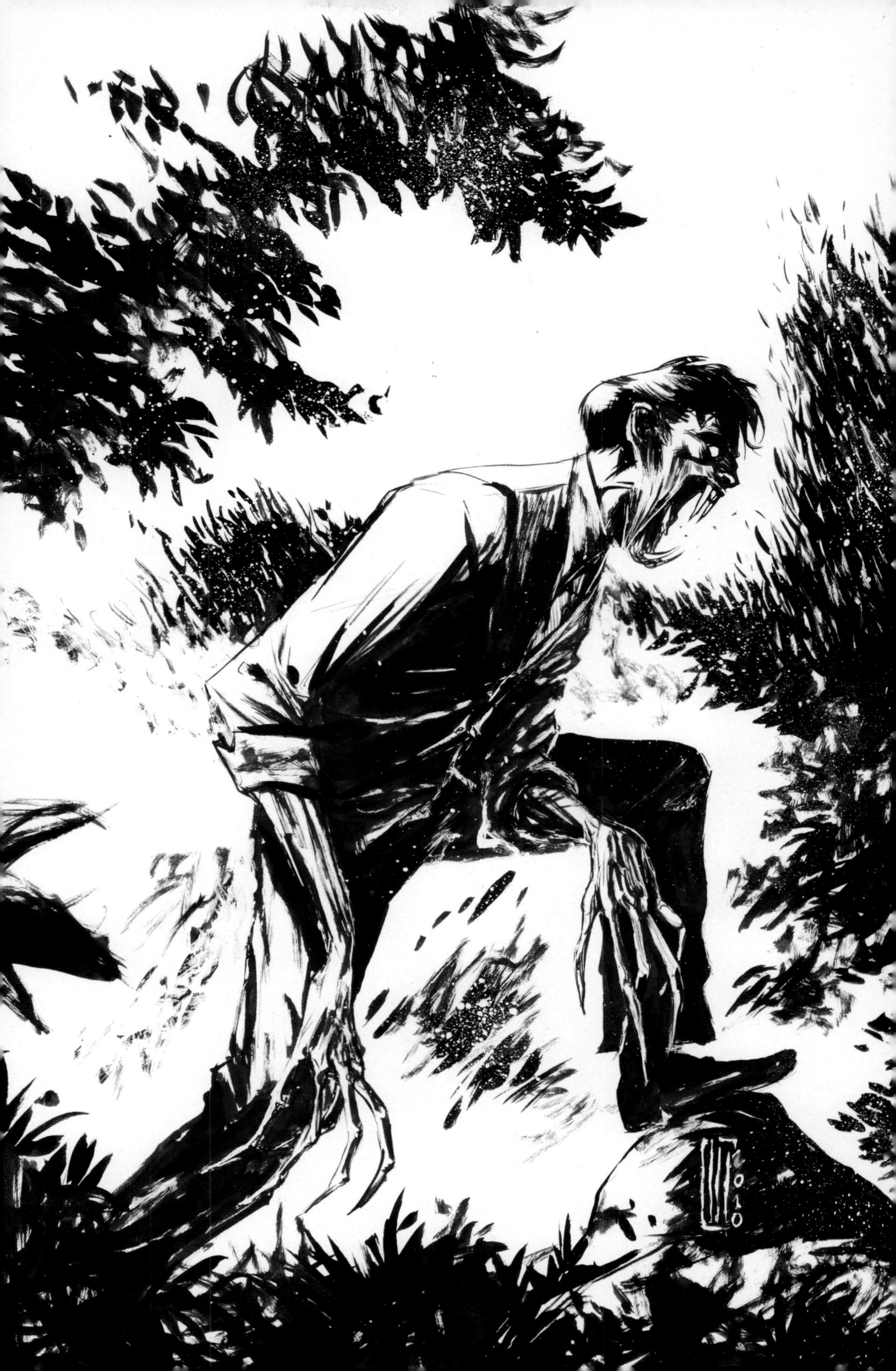

Character Designs by Rafael Albuquerque

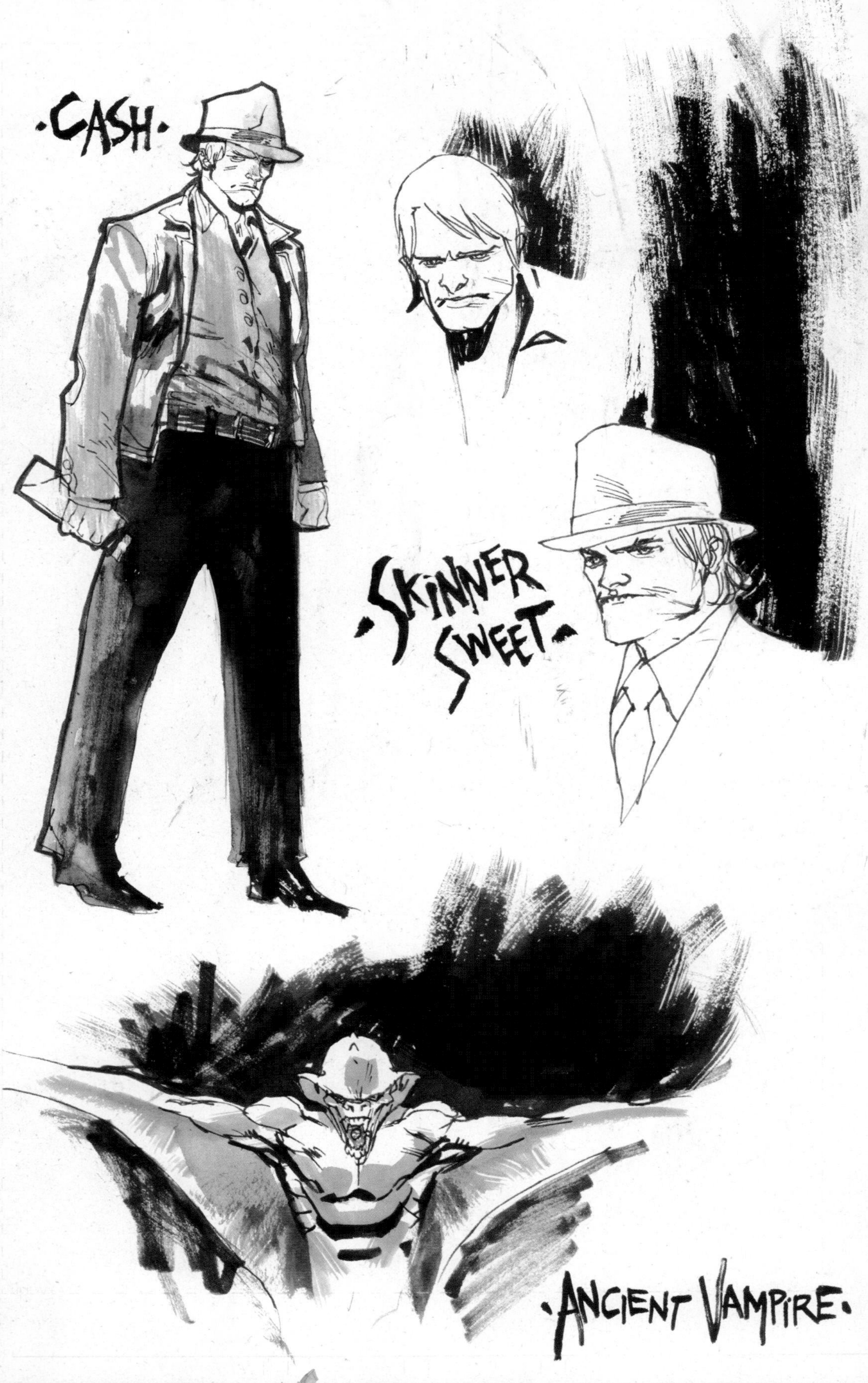

·CASH·
·SKINNER SWEET·
·ANCIENT VAMPIRE·

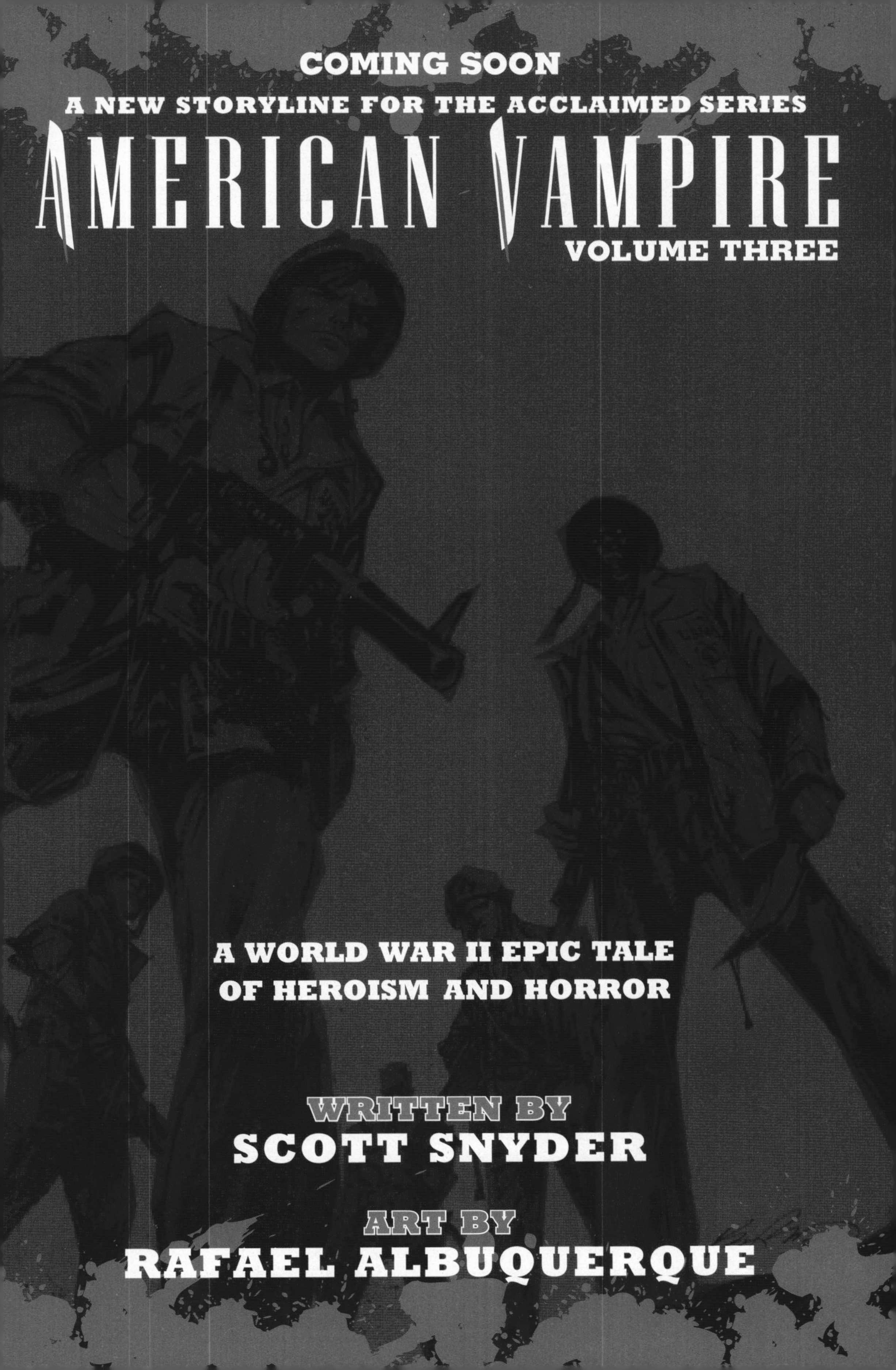
COMING SOON
A NEW STORYLINE FOR THE ACCLAIMED SERIES
AMERICAN VAMPIRE
VOLUME THREE
A WORLD WAR II EPIC TALE
OF HEROISM AND HORROR
WRITTEN BY
SCOTT SNYDER
ART BY
RAFAEL ALBUQUERQUE

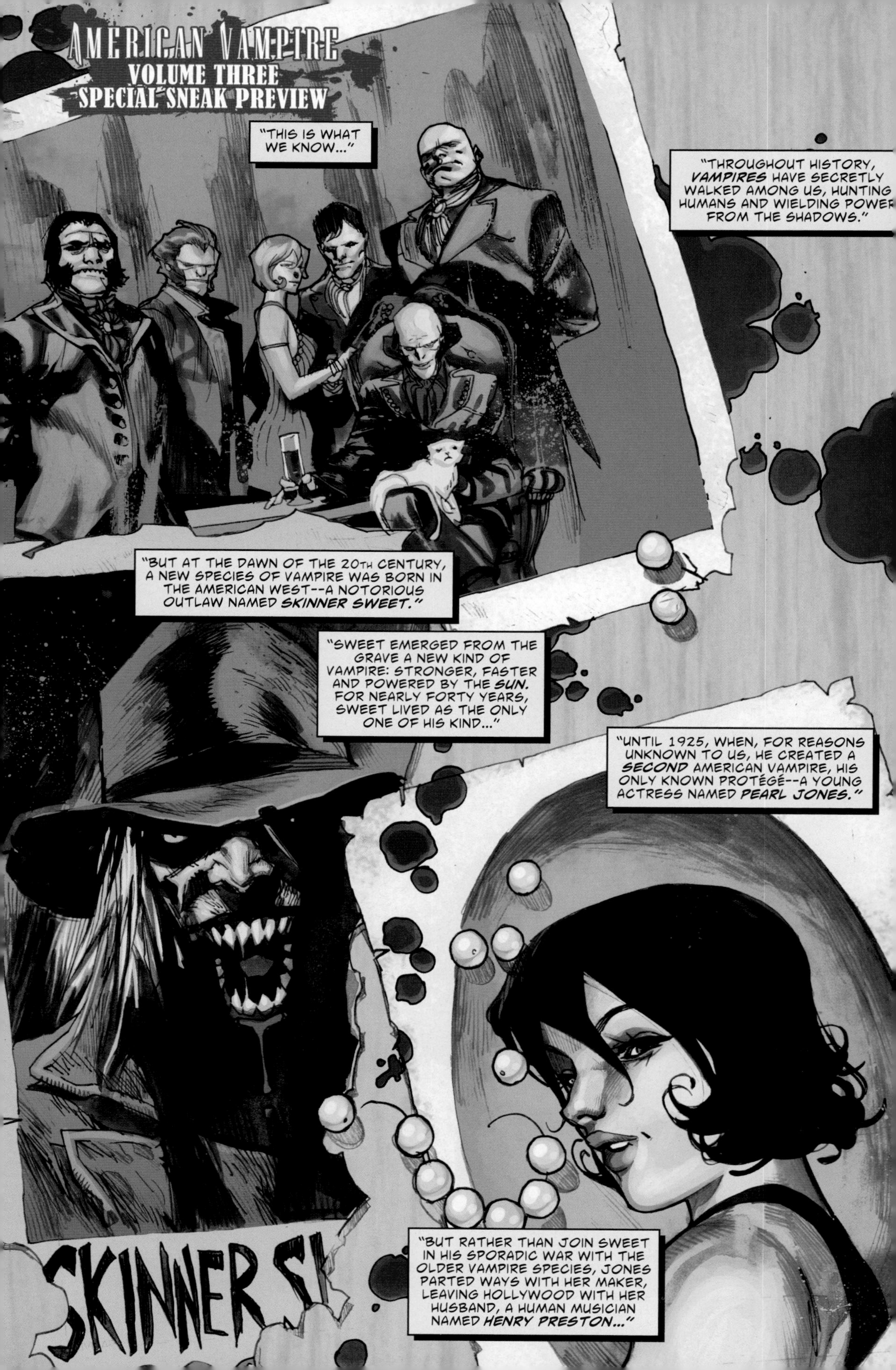
AMERICAN VAMPIRE
VOLUME THREE
SPECIAL SNEAK PREVIEW
"THIS IS WHAT WE KNOW..."
"THROUGHOUT HISTORY, VAMPIRES HAVE SECRETLY WALKED AMONG US, HUNTING HUMANS AND WIELDING POWER FROM THE SHADOWS."
"BUT AT THE DAWN OF THE 20TH CENTURY, A NEW SPECIES OF VAMPIRE WAS BORN IN THE AMERICAN WEST--A NOTORIOUS OUTLAW NAMED SKINNER SWEET."
"SWEET EMERGED FROM THE GRAVE A NEW KIND OF VAMPIRE: STRONGER, FASTER AND POWERED BY THE SUN. FOR NEARLY FORTY YEARS, SWEET LIVED AS THE ONLY ONE OF HIS KIND..."
"UNTIL 1925, WHEN, FOR REASONS UNKNOWN TO US, HE CREATED A SECOND AMERICAN VAMPIRE, HIS ONLY KNOWN PROTÉGÉ--A YOUNG ACTRESS NAMED PEARL JONES."
"BUT RATHER THAN JOIN SWEET IN HIS SPORADIC WAR WITH THE OLDER VAMPIRE SPECIES, JONES PARTED WAYS WITH HER MAKER, LEAVING HOLLYWOOD WITH HER HUSBAND, A HUMAN MUSICIAN NAMED HENRY PRESTON..."
SKINNER S

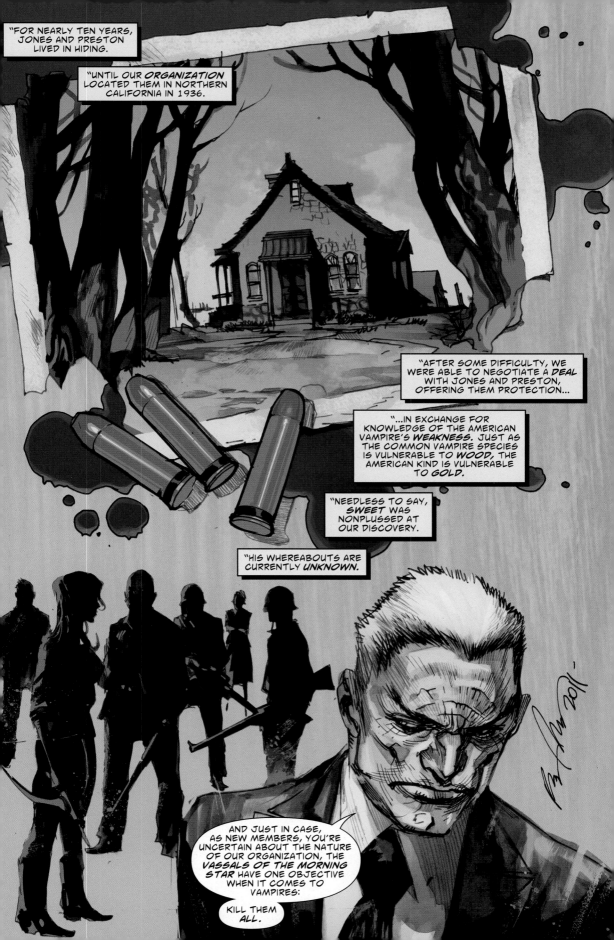

"FOR NEARLY TEN YEARS, JONES AND PRESTON LIVED IN HIDING.

"UNTIL OUR *ORGANIZATION* LOCATED THEM IN NORTHERN CALIFORNIA IN 1936.

"AFTER SOME DIFFICULTY, WE WERE ABLE TO NEGOTIATE A *DEAL* WITH JONES AND PRESTON, OFFERING THEM PROTECTION...

"...IN EXCHANGE FOR KNOWLEDGE OF THE AMERICAN VAMPIRE'S *WEAKNESS*. JUST AS THE COMMON VAMPIRE SPECIES IS VULNERABLE TO *WOOD*, THE AMERICAN KIND IS VULNERABLE TO *GOLD*.

"NEEDLESS TO SAY, *SWEET* WAS NONPLUSSED AT OUR DISCOVERY.

"HIS WHEREABOUTS ARE CURRENTLY *UNKNOWN*.

AND JUST IN CASE, AS NEW MEMBERS, YOU'RE UNCERTAIN ABOUT THE NATURE OF OUR ORGANIZATION, THE *VASSALS OF THE MORNING STAR* HAVE ONE OBJECTIVE WHEN IT COMES TO VAMPIRES:

KILL THEM *ALL*.

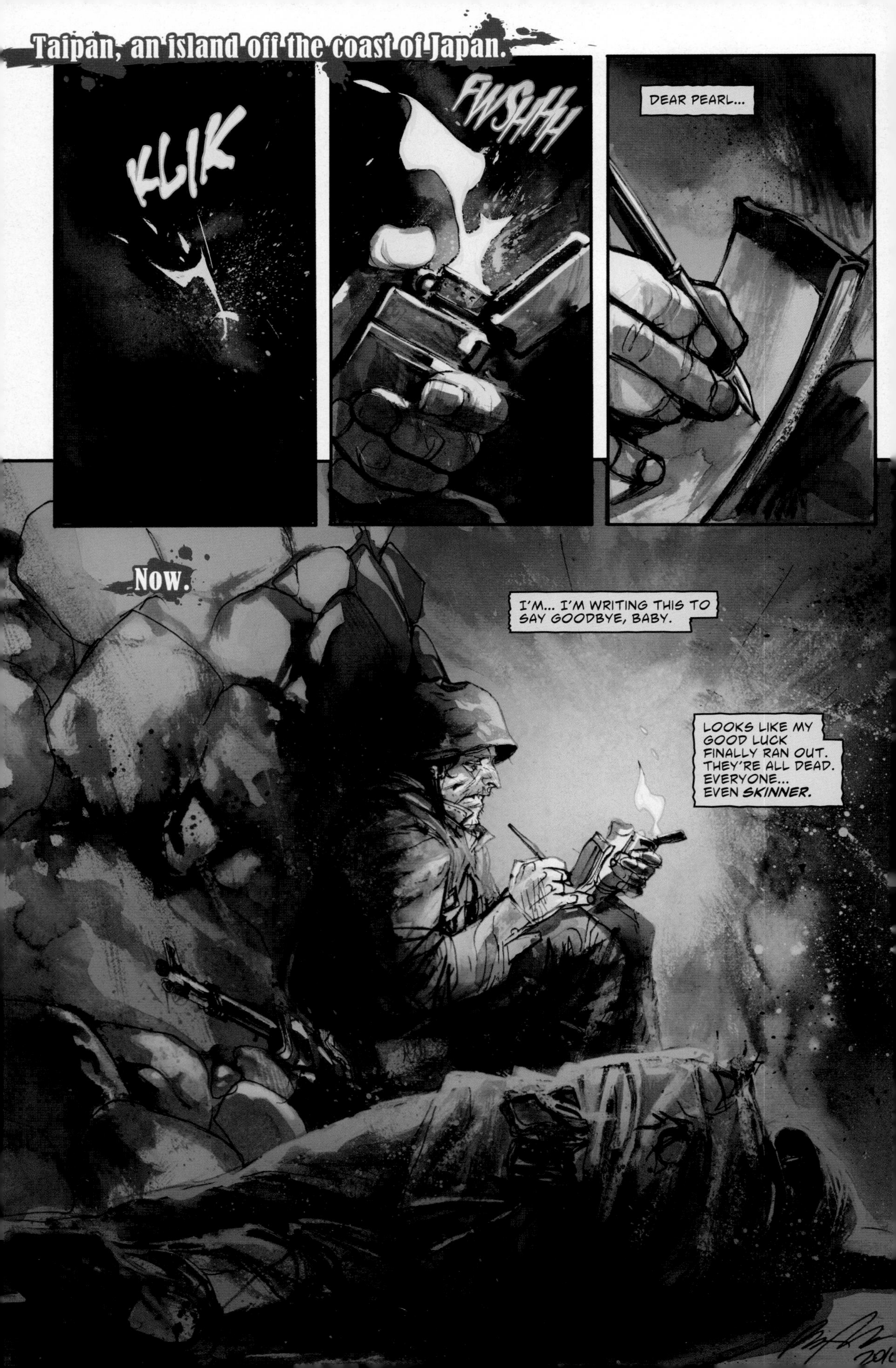
Taipan, an island off the coast of Japan.
KLIK
FWSHHH
DEAR PEARL...
Now.
I'M... I'M WRITING THIS TO SAY GOODBYE, BABY.
LOOKS LIKE MY GOOD LUCK FINALLY RAN OUT. THEY'RE ALL DEAD. EVERYONE... EVEN SKINNER.

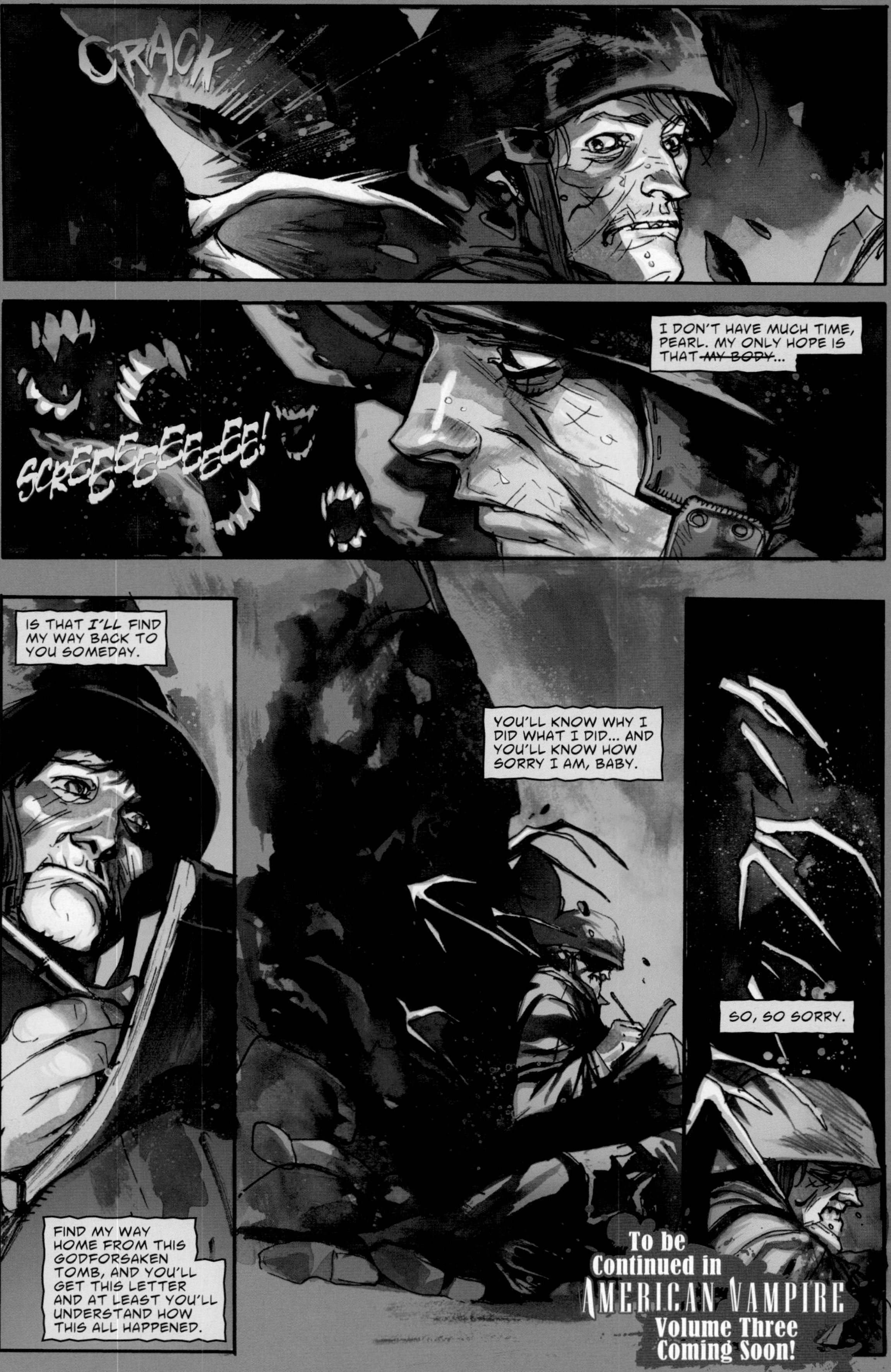
CRACK
SCREEEEEEEEEE!
I DON'T HAVE MUCH TIME, PEARL. MY ONLY HOPE IS THAT ~~MY BODY~~...
IS THAT I'LL FIND MY WAY BACK TO YOU SOMEDAY.
YOU'LL KNOW WHY I DID WHAT I DID... AND YOU'LL KNOW HOW SORRY I AM, BABY.
SO, SO SORRY.
FIND MY WAY HOME FROM THIS GODFORSAKEN TOMB, AND YOU'LL GET THIS LETTER AND AT LEAST YOU'LL UNDERSTAND HOW THIS ALL HAPPENED.
To be Continued in AMERICAN VAMPIRE Volume Three Coming Soon!

Scott Snyder has written comics for both Marvel and DC, and is the author of the story collection *Voodoo Heart* (The Dial Press). He teaches writing at Sarah Lawrence College, NYU and Columbia University. He lives on Long Island with his wife, Jeanie, and his son, Jack. He is a dedicated and un-ironic fan of Elvis Presley.

Rafael Albuquerque was born in Porto Alegre, south of Brazil, Rafael Albuquerque has been working in the American comic book industry since 2005. Best known from his work on the *Savage Brothers*, BLUE BEETLE and SUPERMAN/BATMAN, he has also published the creator-owned graphic novels *Crimeland* (2007) and *Mondo Urbano*, recently published in 2010.

Mateus Santolouco was born in the city of Porto Alegre, Brazil. He has worked on comics for Boom! Studios, Image Comics, Oni Press and Marvel Comics.